the PARIS REVIEW
Interviews, IV

*the*PARIS REVIEW

Interviews, IV

WITH AN INTRODUCTION BY
SALMAN RUSHDIE

PICADOR • NEW YORK

THE PARIS REVIEW INTERVIEWS, IV. Copyright © 2009 by The Paris Review. All rights
reserved. Printed in the United States of America. For information, address Picador,
175 Fifth Avenue, New York, N.Y. 10010.

See also pp. 477–78 for individual copyright information.

www.picadorusa.com

Picador® is a U.S. registered trademark and is used by St. Martin's Press under
license from Pan Books Limited.

For information on Picador Reading Group Guides, please contact Picador.
E-mail: readinggroupguides@picadorusa.com

The Library of Congress has catalogued the first volume as follows:

The Paris review interviews, I / with an introduction by Salman Rushdie.—3rd ed.
      p. cm.
      ISBN-13: 978-0-312-36175-4 (v. 1)
            1. Authors, American—20th century—Interviews.   2. Authors,
English—20th century—Interviews.   3. American literature—20th century—
History and criticism.   4. English literature—20th century—History and
criticism.   5. Authorship.   I. Rushdie, Salman 1947-   II. Paris review.
   PS225.P26   2006
   823'.9109—dc22
                                                          2006051097

ISBN 978-0-312-42744-3

First Edition: November 2009

10 9 8 7 6 5 4 3 2 1

Contents

Introduction

by Salman Rushdie

I once asked a maker of fine gold jewelry why she only worked in such an expensive material, and she replied that the point about gold was its malleability: you can do anything with gold, you can twist it and turn it and it will take whatever shape you want it to take. I thought then, and think now, that English is the gold of languages—that, unlike some other languages I could name, its syntactical freedom and its elasticity allow you to make of it what you will, and that this is why, as it has spread across the world, it has made so many successful local metamorphoses—into Irish English, West Indian English, Australian English, Indian English, and, of course, the many varieties of American English. I was happy to see that, in the *Paris Review* interview reprinted in this volume, Maya Angelou feels the same way, speaking of "how beautiful, how pliable the language is, how it will lend itself. If you pull it, it says, OK."

Foolishly, perhaps, I have long assumed that English possesses this quality to a greater degree than any other language, and so it is salutary to be reminded by David Grossman that other writers in other languages feel the same way. "Hebrew," Grossman says, "is a flexible language and it surrenders enthusiastically to all kinds of wordplay. You can talk in slang about the Bible and you can speak biblically about everyday life. You can invent words that people can easily understand, because almost every word has a root, and people know the derivation or can usually figure it out. It is a very sexy language. It is gigantic, heroic, and glorious, but at the same time it has large gaps that yearn to be filled by writers." Oh, OK, I find myself conceding, just a touch grumpily; OK, so maybe among languages there's more than one variety of gold.

This is one of the reasons why the *Paris Review* interviews are so terrific. They don't just entertain you, they make you think, and they even make you rethink what you think you know. Like many writers (and would-be writers, and readers, too) I've been a fan of the Art of Fiction series for as long as I can remember. I've pulled my old copies of the magazine off their shelf and have them beside me as I write, and I am reminded of the eagerness with which, in the spring of 1979, when I was hard at work on my second novel, *Midnight's Children*, I pored over John Gardner's interview in *The Paris Review* and thought that if this magazine were ever to say of anything I wrote that it represented "a new and exhilarating phase in the enterprise of modern writing," as the *Review*'s four-headed interviewer said of Gardner, then I would be able to die a happy man.

In the summer of 1981, which was a good time for me, the summer after the publication of *Midnight's Children*, the summer when I was writing the first draft of its successor, *Shame*, I was greatly inspired by Donald Barthelme in his *Paris Review* interview, in particular his comments about his use of fantastic effects. To give a woman golden buttocks in a story was "a way of allowing you to see buttocks." And: "If I didn't have roaches as big as ironing boards in the story I couldn't show Cortés and Montezuma holding hands, it would be merely sentimental. You look around for offsetting material, things that tell the reader that although X is happening, X is to be regarded in the light of Y." How very *useful* that was to me then and, indeed, how useful it still is!

The Art of Fiction interviews satisfy our—all right, *my*—deep and abiding inquisitiveness about the writing life. Like most writers, I am interested in other writers, both as a reader and as a nosey parker. I want to know their work but I also want to know where it came from, and how. Perhaps the only writer I can think of who denies feeling like this is V. S. Naipaul. I was once present at Hay-on-Wye's literary festival when Naipaul was being interviewed on stage by the American writer and editor Bill Buford. He replied to Buford's question about the writers he read with a majestic dismissal: "I'm not a reader, I'm a writer." Yet here he is in these pages, offering up one of his many published accounts of his own literary origins, and his writing process, too, presumably because he is willing to go along with the idea that; while he himself is uninterested in reading or learning about other writers, those other writers—and readers, too, of course—might be interested in learning about *him*. But then, as he tells us, there are many excellent reasons why we might wish to learn about him. "It is immensely hard to be the first to write about anything. It is always easy afterwards to copy," he says, speaking of *Miguel Street*, and of *In a Free State* he is happy to tell us that "it is very well made."

It is at moments like these that the Art of Fiction interviews are most revealing, showing us, perhaps, more of the author than even the author knows. The great P. G. Wodehouse's well-known sunniness of spirit acquires an almost shockingly innocent quality when he talks about his wartime broadcasts from Berlin—broadcasts that led many to denounce him as a traitor, and that, as he himself says, "altered his whole life," leading him to spend the rest of it in the United States and never go home again. It has always felt painful to me that this most English of English writers, creator of the fantasy England of Jeeves, Bertie Wooster, the Drones Club, Blandings Castle, and the imperishable pig the Empress of Blandings should have spent so long in exile. But Wodehouse sounds perfectly happy about the whole thing. Does he resent the way he was treated by the English? "Oh, no, no, no. Nothing of that sort. The whole thing seems to have blown over now." And how about his American exile? "I'd much sooner live here than in England, I think. I can't think of any place in England I prefer to this. I used to like London, but I don't think I'd like it now . . . I'm rather blessed in a way. I really don't worry about anything much. I can adjust myself to things pretty well." Oh, so that's all right, then.

In these pages Jack Kerouac comes over exactly as he should, at once vivid and muddy, full of Kerouacity. Here he is, explaining his own name: "Now, *kairn*. K (or C) A-I-R-N. What is a cairn? It's a heap of stones. Now *Cornwall*, cairn-wall. Now, right, *kern*, also K-E-R-N, means the same thing as *cairn*. Kern. Cairn. *Ouac* means 'language of.' So, *Kernouac* means the language of Cornwall. *Kerr*, which is like Deborah Kerr. *Ouack* means language of water. Because *Kerr*, *Carr*, etectera means water. And *cairn* means heap of stones. There is no language in a heap of stones. Kerouac. *Ker-* (water), *-ouac* (language of). And it's related to the old Irish name, Kerwick, which is a corruption. And it's a Cornish name, which in itself means cairnish. And according to Sherlock Holmes, it's all Persian." It's a sign of the skill with which these interviews are conducted and afterwards edited—a process in which the interviewees are closely involved— that the writers come out sounding so honestly and (for the most part) undefendedly like themselves.

And there's disagreement, too. William Styron accepts the influence of Faulkner, among others, and praises him, but with some reservations. "I'm all for the complexity of Faulkner, but not for the confusion . . . As for *The Sound and the Fury*, I think it succeeds in spite of itself. Faulkner often simply stays too damn intense for too long a time." Maya Angelou, though, is politely but firmly unimpressed by both Faulkner and Styron. She is asked, "What do you think of white writers who have written of the black experience—Faulkner's *The Sound and the Fury* or William Styron's *Confessions of Nat Turner*?" And she replies, "Well, sometimes I am disappointed—more often than not." Literature, we are reminded, is disputed territory.

Three of the writers collected in this volume are friends of mine: Auster, Grossman, Pamuk. But writers talk less to each other about their craft than perhaps they should, so even in these cases what the interviews have to tell me is revealing. Auster talks about "reading with [his] fingers," the act of retyping the whole book once it's finished, and how valuable he finds it—"it's amazing." He marvels at "how many errors your fingers will find that your eyes never noticed." Then there's Grossman's paean to Hebrew, which I've already quoted; and perhaps best of all are Pamuk's wonderful manuscript pages, so astonishingly illustrated by him.

Here, too, are John Ashbery being at once vague and sharp ("I have such an imprecise impression of what kind of a person I am," he says, but he also says, with some asperity, that he tries "to avoid the well-known cliché that you learn from your students"); Philip Roth being sufficient unto himself ("I don't ask writers about their work habits. I really don't care. Joyce Carol Oates says somewhere that when writers ask each other what time they start working and when they finish and how much time they take for lunch, they're actually trying to find out Is he as crazy as I am? I don't need that question answered"); Stephen Sondheim admitting that he uses the Clement Wood rhyming dictionary and *Roget's Thesaurus*; E. B. White on *Charlotte's Web* ("Anyone who writes down to children is simply wasting his time. You have to write up, not down"); Ezra Pound talking about Disney's "squirrel film" *Perri* and praising "the Confucian side of Disney" as "absolute genius"; Marilynne Robinson on how *Housekeeping* grew out of a "stack of metaphors"; Marianne Moore, interviewed on the day before the election of President Kennedy, but belonging to another age entirely; and Haruki Murakami, as much a writer of his moment as it is possible to be, admitting his fear of having lunch with Toni Morrison and Joyce Carol Oates.

If you aren't a writer, don't worry: this book won't teach you how to be one. If you are a writer, I suspect it will teach you a lot. Either way, it's a treasure chest, and a delight. Begin.

the PARIS
REVIEW
Interviews, IV

William Styron

The Art of Fiction

William Styron was interviewed in Paris, in early autumn, at Patrick's, a café on the boulevard du Montparnasse that has little to distinguish it from its neighbors—the Dome, the Rotonde, Le Chapelain—except a faintly better brand of coffee. Across the boulevard from the café and its sidewalk tables, a red poster portrays a skeletal family. They are behind bars, and the caption reads: TAKE YOUR VACATION IN HAPPY RUSSIA! The lower part of the poster has been ripped and scarred and plastered with stickers shouting: LES AMÉRICANS EN AMÉRIQUE! U.S. GO HOME! An adjoining poster advertises carbonated water: PERRIER! It sings: L'EAU QUI FAIT PSCHITT! The sun reflects strongly off their vivid colors, and Styron, shading his eyes, peers down into his coffee. He is a young man of good appearance, though not this afternoon; he is a little paler than is healthy in this quiet hour when the denizens of the quarter lie hiding, their weak night eyes insulted by the light.

—*George Plimpton, Peter Matthiessen, 1954*

INTERVIEWER

You were about to tell us when you started to write.

WILLIAM STYRON

What? Oh, yes. Write. I figure I must have been about thirteen. I wrote an imitation Conrad thing, "Typhoon and the Tor Bay" it was

1

Abruptly he was conscious of a dry, parched
thirst, and, ~~rising~~ to his feet, ~~then~~ put on a robe, and
hobbled out into the hallway toward the water-cooler.
There he saw Mannix, naked except for a towel
around his waist, making his slow and agonizing way
down the hall. He was hairy and enormous, and as
he inched his way toward the shower-room, clawing
at the wall for support, his face with its clenched lips
and taut, drawn-down mouth was one of tortured and
gigantic suffering. The swelling at his ankle was the
size of a grapefruit, an ugly blue, and this leg he
dragged behind him, a ~~dead~~ weight no longer
capable of motion.

Culver started to limp toward him, said, "Al—"
in an effort to help him along, but just then a
Negro maid, bespectacled, bandanna'd, came
scrounging along with a mop, stopped, seeing him,
ceased the singsong little tune she was humming,
too, and said, "Oh my, you poor man. What you
been doin'? Do it hurt?" Culver halted.

"Do it hurt?" she repeated, "Oh I bet it does.
Deed it does." Mannix looked up at her from the
short yards that separated them, blank, blinking.
Culver would remember this: the two of them
communicating across that chasm one unspoken
moment of sympathy and understanding before the
woman, ~~full blooded~~ said again, "Deed it does,"
and before, almost ~~at~~ precisely the same instant, the
towel slipped away slowly from Mannix's waist
and fell with a soft plop to the floor; Mannix
then, standing there, weaving dizzily and clutching
for support at the wall, a mass of scars and
naked as the day he emerged from his mother's
womb, save for the soap which he clutched
feebly in one hand. He seemed to have neither
the strength nor the ability to bend down and
retrieve the towel, and so he merely stood there
huge and naked in the slanting dusty light and
blinked and ~~wiped his~~ finally, a sour apologetic
smile. "Deed it does," he said.

THE END

Oh Deed
it does
Negro
"delish," — crowd

called, you know, a ship's hold swarming with crazy Chinks. I think I had some sharks in there, too. I gave it the full treatment.

INTERVIEWER

And how did you happen to start? That is, why did you want to write?

STYRON

I wish I knew. I wanted to express myself, I guess. But after "Typhoon and the Tor Bay" I didn't give writing another thought until I went to Duke University and landed in a creative writing course under William Blackburn. He was the one who got me started.

INTERVIEWER

What value does the creative-writing course have for young writers?

STYRON

It gives them a start, I suppose. But it can be an awful waste of time. Look at those people who go back year after year to summer writers' conferences. You get so you can pick them out a mile away. A writing course can only give you a start, and help a little. It can't teach writing. The professor should weed out the good from the bad, cull them like a farmer, and not encourage the ones who haven't got something. At one school I know in New York, which has a lot of writing courses, there are a couple of teachers who moon in the most disgusting way over the poorest, most talentless writers, giving false hope where there shouldn't be any hope at all. Regularly they put out dreary little anthologies, the quality of which would chill your blood. It's a ruinous business, a waste of paper and time, and such teachers should be abolished.

INTERVIEWER

The average teacher can't teach anything about technique or style?

STYRON

Well, he can teach you something in matters of technique. You know—don't tell a story from two points of view and that sort of thing. But I don't think even the most conscientious and astute teachers can teach anything about style. Style comes only after long, hard practice and writing.

INTERVIEWER

Do you enjoy writing?

STYRON

I certainly don't. I get a fine, warm feeling when I'm doing well, but that pleasure is pretty much negated by the pain of getting started each day. Let's face it, writing is hell.

INTERVIEWER

How many pages do you turn out each day?

STYRON

When I'm writing steadily—that is, when I'm involved in a project that I'm really interested in, one of those rare pieces that has a foreseeable end—I average two-and-a-half or three pages a day, longhand on yellow sheets. I spend about five hours at it, of which very little is spent actually writing. I try to get a feeling of what's going on in the story before I put it down on paper, but actually most of this breaking-in period is one long, fantastic daydream, in which I think about anything but the work at hand. I can't turn out slews of stuff each day. I wish I could. I seem to have some neurotic need to perfect each paragraph—each sentence, even—as I go along.

INTERVIEWER

And what time of the day do you find best for working?

STYRON

The afternoon. I like to stay up late at night and get drunk and sleep late. I wish I could break the habit but I can't. The afternoon is the only time I have left and I try to use it to the best advantage, with a hangover.

INTERVIEWER

Do you use a notebook?

STYRON

No, I don't feel the need for it. I've tried, but it does no good, since I've never used what I've written down. I think the use of a notebook depends upon the individual.

INTERVIEWER

Do you find you need seclusion?

STYRON

I find it's difficult to write in complete isolation. I think it would be hard for me on a South Sea island or in the Maine woods. I like company and entertainment, people around. The actual process of writing, though, demands complete, noiseless privacy, without even music; a baby howling two blocks away will drive me nuts.

INTERVIEWER

Does your emotional state have any bearing on your work?

STYRON

I guess like everybody I'm emotionally fouled up most of the time, but I find I do better when I'm relatively placid. It's hard to say, though. If writers had to wait until their precious psyches were completely serene there wouldn't be much writing done. Actually—though I don't take advantage of the fact as much as I should—I find that I'm simply the happiest, the placidest, when I'm writing, and so I suppose that that, for me, is the final answer. When I'm writing

I find it's the only time that I feel completely self-possessed, even when the writing itself is not going too well. It's fine therapy for people who are perpetually scared of nameless threats as I am most of the time—for jittery people. Besides, I've discovered that when I'm not writing I'm prone to developing certain nervous tics, and hypochondria. Writing alleviates those quite a bit. I think I resist change more than most people. I dislike traveling, like to stay settled. When I first came to Paris all I could think about was going home, home to the old James River. One of these days I expect to inherit a peanut farm. Go back home and farm them old peanuts and be real old Southern whiskey gentry.

INTERVIEWER

Your novel was linked to the Southern school of fiction. Do you think the critics were justified in doing this?

STYRON

No, frankly, I don't consider myself in the Southern school, whatever that is. *Lie Down in Darkness*, or most of it, was set in the South, but I don't care if I never write about the South again, really. Only certain things in the book are particularly Southern. I used leitmotifs—the negroes, for example—that run throughout the book, but I would like to believe that my people would have behaved the way they did anywhere. The girl, Peyton, for instance, didn't have to come from Virginia. She would have wound up jumping from a window no matter where she came from. Critics are always linking writers to "schools." If they couldn't link people to schools, they'd die. When what they condescendingly call "a genuinely fresh talent" arrives on the scene, the critics rarely try to point out what makes him fresh or genuine but concentrate instead on how he behaves in accordance with their preconceived notion of what school he belongs to.

INTERVIEWER

You don't find that it's true of most of the so-called Southern novels that the reactions of their characters are universal?

STYRON

Look, I don't mean to repudiate my Southern background completely, but I don't believe that the South alone produces "universal"
literature. That universal quality comes far more from a single writer's
mind and his individual spirit than from his background. Faulkner's a
writer of extraordinary stature more because of the great breadth of his
vision than because he happened to be born in Mississippi. All you have
to do is read one issue of the *Times Book Review* to see how much junk
comes out regularly from south of the Mason-Dixon line, along with the
good stuff. I have to admit, though, that the South has a definite literary
tradition, which is the reason it probably produces a better quality of
writing, proportionately. Perhaps it's just true that Faulkner, if he had
been born in, say, Pasadena, might very well still have had that universal
quality of mind, but instead of writing *Light in August* he would have
gone into television or written universal ads for Jantzen bathing suits.

INTERVIEWER

Well, why do you think this Southern tradition exists at all?

STYRON

Well, first, there's that old heritage of biblical rhetoric and storytelling. Then the South simply provides such wonderful material.
Take, for instance, the conflict between the ordered Protestant
tradition, the fundamentalism based on the Old Testament, and the
twentieth century—movies, cars, television. The poetic juxtaposi-
tions you find in this conflict—a crazy, colored preacher howling those
tremendously moving verses from Isaiah 40, while riding around in a
maroon Packard. It's wonderful stuff and comparatively new, too,
which is perhaps why the renaissance of Southern writing coincided
with these last few decades of the machine age. If Faulkner had written in the 1880s he would have been writing, no doubt, safely within
the tradition, but his novels would have been genteel novels, like
those of George Washington Cable or Thomas Nelson Page. In fact,
the modern South is such powerful material that the author runs the
danger of capturing the local color and feeling that's enough. He gets

so bemused by decaying mansions that he forgets to populate them with people. I'm beginning to feel that it's a good idea for writers who come from the South, at least some of them, to break away a little from all them magnolias.

INTERVIEWER

You refer a number of times to Faulkner. Even though you don't think of yourself as a "Southern" writer, would you say that he influenced you?

STYRON

I would certainly say so. I'd say I've been influenced as much, though, by Joyce and Flaubert. Old Joyce and Flaubert have influenced me stylistically, given me arrows, but then a lot of the contemporary works I've read have influenced me as a craftsman. Dos Passos, Scott Fitzgerald, both have been valuable in teaching me how to write the novel, but not many of these modern people have contributed much to my emotional climate. Joyce comes closest, but the strong influences are out of the past—the Bible, Marlowe, Blake, Shakespeare. As for Flaubert, *Madame Bovary* is one of the few novels that move me in every way—not only in its style, but in its total communicability, like the effect of good poetry. What I really mean is that a great book should leave you with many experiences, and slightly exhausted at the end. You live several lives while reading it. Its writer should, too. Without condescending, he should be conscious of himself as a reader, and while he's writing it he should be able to step outside of it from time to time and say to himself, Now if I were just reading this book, would I like this part here? I have the feeling that that's what Flaubert did—maybe too much, though, finally, in books like *Sentimental Education*.

INTERVIEWER

While we're skirting this question, do you think Faulkner's experiments with time in *The Sound and the Fury* are justified?

STYRON

Justified? Yes, I do.

INTERVIEWER

Successful, then?

STYRON

No, I don't think so. Faulkner doesn't give enough help to the reader. I'm all for the complexity of Faulkner, but not for the confusion. That goes for Joyce, too. All that fabulously beautiful poetry in the last part of *Finnegans Wake* is pretty much lost to the world simply because not many people are ever going to put up with the chaos that precedes it. As for *The Sound and the Fury*, I think it succeeds in spite of itself. Faulkner often simply stays too damn intense for too long a time. It ends up being great stuff, somehow, though, and the marvel is how it could be so wonderful being pitched for so long in that one high, prolonged, delirious key.

INTERVIEWER

Was the problem of time development acute in the writing of *Lie Down in Darkness*?

STYRON

Well, the book started with the man, Loftis, standing at the station with the hearse, waiting for the body of his daughter to arrive from up North. I wanted to give him density, but all the tragedy in his life had happened in the past. So the problem was to get into the past, and this man's tragedy, without breaking the story. It stumped me for a whole year. Then it finally occurred to me to use separate moments in time, four or five long dramatic scenes revolving around the daughter, Peyton, at different stages in her life. The business of the progression of time seems to me one of the most difficult problems a novelist has to cope with.

INTERVIEWER

Did you prefigure the novel? How much was planned when you started?

STYRON

Very little. I knew about Loftis and all his domestic troubles. I had the funeral. I had the girl in mind, and her suicide in Harlem. I thought I knew why, too. But that's all I had.

INTERVIEWER

Did you start with emphasis on character or story?

STYRON

Character, definitely. And by character I mean a person drawn full-round, not a caricature. E. M. Forster refers to "flat" and "round" characters. I try to make all of mine round. It takes an extrovert like Dickens to make flat characters come alive. But story as such has been neglected by today's introverted writers. Story and character should grow together; I think I'm lucky so far in that in practically everything I've tried to write these two elements have grown together. They must, to give an impression of life being lived, just because each man's life is a story, if you'll pardon the cliché. I used to spend a lot of time worrying over word order, trying to create beautiful passages. I still believe in the value of a handsome style. I appreciate the sensibility that can produce a nice turn of phrase, like Scott Fitzgerald. But I'm not interested any more in turning out something shimmering and impressionistic—Southern, if you will—full of word-pictures, damn Dixie baby talk, and that sort of thing. I guess I just get more and more interested in people. And story.

INTERVIEWER

Are your characters real-life or imaginary?

I don't know if that's answerable. I really think, frankly, though, that most of my characters come closer to being entirely imaginary than the other way round. Maybe that's because they all seem to end up, finally, closer to being like myself than like people I've actually observed. I sometimes feel that the characters I've created are not much more than sort of projected facets of myself, and I believe that a lot of fictional characters have been created that way.

How far removed must you be from your subject matter?

Pretty far. I don't think people can write immediately, and well, about an experience emotionally close to them. I have a feeling, for example, that I won't be able to write about all the time I've spent in Europe until I get back to America.

Do you feel yourself to be in competition with other writers?

No, I don't. "Some of my best friends are writers." In America there seems to be an idea that writing is one big cat-and-dog fight among the various practitioners of the craft. Got to hole up in the woods. Me, I'm a farmer, I don't know no writers. Hate writers. That sort of thing. I think that, just as in everything else, writers can be too cozy and cliquish and end up nervous and incestuous and scratching each other's backs. In London once, I was at a party where everything was so literary and famous and intimate that if the place had suddenly been blown up by dynamite it would have demolished the flower of British letters. But I think that writers in the U.S. could stand a bit more of the attitude that prevailed in France in the last century. Flaubert and Maupassant, Victor Hugo and Musset, they didn't suffer from knowing each other. Turgenev knew Gogol. Chekhov knew

Tolstoy and Andreiev, and Gorky knew all three. I think it was Henry James who said of Hawthorne that he might have been even better than he was if he had occasionally communicated a little bit more with others working at the same sort of thing. A lot of this philosophy of isolation in America is a dreary pose. I'm not advocating a Writers' Supper Club on Waverly Place, just for chums in the business, or a union, or anything like that, but I do think that writers in America might somehow benefit by the attitude that, What the hell, we're all in this together, instead of, All my pals are bartenders on Third Avenue. As a matter of fact, I do have a pal who's a bartender on Third Avenue, but he's a part-time writer on the side.

INTERVIEWER

In general, what do you think of critics, since they are a subject that must be close to a writer's heart?

STYRON

From the writer's point of view, critics should be ignored, although it's hard not to do what they suggest. I think it's unfortunate to have critics for friends. Suppose you write something that stinks, what are they going to say in a review? Say it stinks? So if they're honest, they do, and if you were friends you're still friends, but the knowledge of your lousy writing and their articulate admission of it will always be something between the two of you, like the knowledge between a man and his wife of some shady adultery. I know very few critics, but I usually read their reviews. Bad notices always give me a sense of humility, or perhaps humiliation, even when there's a tone of envy or sour grapes or even ignorance in them, but they don't help me much. When *Lie Down in Darkness* came out, my hometown paper scraped up the local literary figure to review the book, a guy who'd written something on hydraulics, I think, and he came to the conclusion that I was a decadent writer. Styron is a decadent writer, he said, because he writes a line like "the sea sucking at the shore," when for that depraved bit he should have substituted "the waves lapping at the shore." Probably his hydraulic background. No, I'm afraid I don't think much of critics for the most part, although I have to admit that some of them have so far treated me quite kindly. Look, there's only one person a writer should listen to, pay any attention to. It's not any damn critic. It's the reader. And that doesn't mean any compromise or sellout. The writer must criticize his own work as a reader. Every day I pick up the story or whatever it is I've been working on and read it through. If I enjoy it as a reader then I know I'm getting along all right.

INTERVIEWER

In your preface to the first issue of this magazine, you speak of there being signs in the air that this generation can and will produce literature to rank with that of any other generation. What are these signs? And do you consider yourself, perhaps, a spokesman for this new generation?

STYRON

What the hell is a spokesman, anyway? I hate the idea of spokesmen. Everybody, especially the young ones, in the writing game jockeying for position to give a name to a generation. I must confess that I was guilty of that in the preface, too. But don't you think it's tiresome, really, all these so-called spokesmen trumpeting around, elbowing one another out of the way to see who'll be the first to give a new and original name to twenty-five million people—the Beat Generation, or the Silent Generation, and God knows what-all? I think the damn generation should be let alone. And that goes for the eternal idea of competition—whether the team of new writers can beat the team of Dos Passos, Faulkner, Fitzgerald, and Hemingway. As I read in a review not long ago by some fellow reviewing an anthology of new writing—which had just that sort of proprietary essay in it and which compared the new writers with the ones of the twenties—the reviewer said, in effect, What the hell, there's plenty of *Lebensraum* and *Liebestraum* for everybody.

INTERVIEWER

But you did say, in the preface, just what we were speaking of—that this generation can and will—

STYRON

Yes, can and will produce literature equal to that of any other generation, especially that of the twenties. It was probably rash to say, but I don't see any reason to recant. For instance, I think those "signs in the air" are apparent from just three first novels, those being *From Here to Eternity*, *The Naked and the Dead*, and *Other Voices, Other Rooms*. It's true that a first novel is far from a fair standard with which to judge a writer's potential future output, but aren't those three novels far superior to the first novels of Dos Passos, Faulkner, and Fitzgerald? In fact I think one of those novels—*The Naked and the Dead*—is so good by itself that it can stand up respectably well with the mature work of any of those writers of the twenties. But there I go again, talking in competition with the older boys. Anyway, I think that a lot of the younger writers around today are stuffed with talent. A lot of them, it's true, are shameless and terrible self-promoters—mainly the members of what a friend of mine calls "the fairy axis"—but they'll drop by the wayside and don't count for much anyway. The others, including the ones I've mentioned, plus people like Salinger and Carson McCullers and Hortense Calisher—all those have done, and will go on doing, fine work, unless somebody drops an atom bomb on them, or they get locked up in jail by Velde and that highly cultured crowd.

INTERVIEWER

Speaking of atom bombs and Representative Velde, among other such contemporary items, do you think—as some people have been saying—that the young writer today works at a greater disadvantage than those of preceding—uh—generations?

STYRON

Hell no, I don't. Writers ever since writing began have had problems, and the main problem narrows down to just one word—life.
Certainly this might be an age of so-called faithlessness and despair
we live in, but the new writers haven't cornered any market on faithlessness and despair, any more than Dostoyevsky or Marlowe or
Sophocles did. Every age has its terrible aches and pains, its peculiar
new horrors, and every writer since the beginning of time, just like
other people, has been afflicted by what that same friend of mine calls
"the fleas of life"—you know, colds, hangovers, bills, sprained ankles,
and little nuisances of one sort or another. They are the constants of
life, at the core of life, along with nice little delights that come along
every now and then. Dostoyevsky had them and Marlowe had them
and we all have them, and they're a hell of a lot more invariable than
nuclear fission or the Revocation of the Edict of Nantes. So is Love
invariable, and Unrequited Love, and Death and Insult and Hilarity.
Mark Twain was as baffled and appalled by Darwin's theories as anyone else, and those theories seemed as monstrous to the Victorians as
atomic energy, but he still wrote about riverboats and old Hannibal,
Missouri. No, I don't think the writer today is any worse off than at
any other time. It's true that in Russia he might as well be dead and
that in Youngstown, Ohio, that famous police chief, whatever his
name is, has taken to inspecting and banning books. But in America
he can still write practically anything he pleases, so long as it isn't li-
belous or pornographic. Also in America he certainly doesn't have to
starve, and there are few writers so economically strapped that they
can't turn out work regularly. In fact, a couple of young writers—and
good writers—are damn near millionaires.

INTERVIEWER

Then you believe in success for a writer? Financial, that is, as well
as critical?

STYRON

I sure do. I certainly have sympathy for a writer who hasn't made enough to live comfortably—comfortably, I mean, not necessarily lavishly—because I've been colossally impoverished at times, but impoverished writers remind me of Somerset Maugham's remark about multilingual people. He admired them, he said, but did not find that their condition made them necessarily wise.

INTERVIEWER

But getting back to the original point, in *Lie Down in Darkness* didn't your heroine commit suicide on the day the atom bomb was dropped on Hiroshima? This seems to us to be a little bit more than fortuitous symbolism, and perhaps to indicate a sense of that inescapable and overpowering despair of our age, which you just denied was our peculiar lot.

STYRON

That was just gilding the lily. If I were writing the same thing now, I'd leave that out and have her jump on the Fourth of July. Really, I'm not trying to be rosy about things like the atom bomb and war and the failure of the Presbyterian Church. Those things are awful. All I'm trying to say is that those things don't alter one bit a writer's fundamental problems, which are Love, Requited and Unrequited, Insult, etcetera.

INTERVIEWER

Then you believe that young writers today have no cause to be morbid and depressing, which is a charge so often leveled at them by the critics?

STYRON

Certainly they do. They have a perfect right to be anything they honestly are, but I'd like to risk saying that a great deal of this morbidity and depression doesn't arise so much from political conditions, or the threat of war, or the atom bomb, as from the terrific increase of the

scientific knowledge that has come to us about the human self—
Freud, that is, abnormal psychology, and all the new psychiatric wisdom. My God, think of how morbid and depressing Dostoyevsky
would have been if he could have gotten hold of some of the juicy
work of Dr. Wilhelm Stekel, say *Sadism and Masochism*. What people
like John Webster and, say, Hieronymus Bosch, felt intuitively about
some of the keen horrors that lurk in the human mind, we now have
neatly cataloged and clinically described by Krafft-Ebing and the
Menningers and Karen Horny, and they're available to any fifteen
year old with a pass-card to the New York Public Library. I don't say
that this new knowledge is the cause of the so-called morbidity and
gloom, but I do think it has contributed to a new trend toward the
introspective in fiction. And when you get an eminent journal like
Time magazine complaining, as it often has, that to the young writers
of today life seems short on rewards, and that what they write is a
product of their own neuroses, in its silly way the magazine is merely
stating the status quo and obvious truth. The good writing of any age
has always been the product of someone's neurosis, and we'd have a
mighty dull literature if all the writers that came along were a bunch
of happy chuckleheads.

INTERVIEWER

To sort of round this out, we'd like to ask finally what might sound
like a rather obvious question. That is, what should be the purpose of
a young writer? Should he, for instance, be engagé, not concerned as
much with the story aspects of the novel as with the problems of the
contemporary world?

STYRON

It seems to me that only a great satirist can tackle the world's problems and articulate them. Most writers write simply out of some
strong interior need, and that, I think, is the answer. A great writer,
writing out of this need, will give substance to, and perhaps even explain, all the problems of the world without even knowing it, until a
scholar comes along one hundred years after he's dead and digs up

some symbols. The purpose of a young writer is to write, and he shouldn't drink too much. He shouldn't think that after he's written one book he's God Almighty and air all his immature opinions in pompous interviews. Let's have another cognac and go up to Le Chapelain.

Issue 5, 1954

Marianne Moore

The Art of Poetry

A merican poetry is a great literature, and it has come to its maturity only in the last seventy years; Walt Whitman and Emily Dickinson in the last century were rare examples of genius in a hostile environment. One decade gave America the major figures of our modern poetry: Wallace Stevens was born in 1879, and T. S. Eliot in 1888. To the ten years that these dates enclose belong H.D., Robinson Jeffers, John Crowe Ransom, William Carlos Williams, Ezra Pound, and Marianne Moore.

Marianne Moore began to publish during the First World War. She was printed and praised in Europe by the expatriates T. S. Eliot and Ezra Pound. In Chicago, Harriet Monroe's magazine *Poetry*, which provided the enduring showcase for the new poetry, published her, too. But she was mainly a poet of New York, part of the Greenwich Village group that created magazines called *Others* and *Broom*.

To visit Marianne Moore at her home in Brooklyn, you had to cross the Brooklyn Bridge, turn left at Myrtle Avenue, follow the elevated for a mile or two, and then turn right onto her street. It was pleasantly lined with a few trees, and Miss Moore's apartment was conveniently near a grocery store and the Presbyterian church that she attended.

The interview took place in November 1960, the day before the presidential election. The front door of Miss Moore's apartment opened onto a long narrow corridor. Rooms led off to the right, and at

RESCUE WITH YUL BRYNNER
(appointed by President Eisenhower, consultant
to the United Nations commission of Refugees,
1959-1960)

with Dances Galanta by Zoltán Kodály
favorites of Budapest Symphony Orchestra -
now refugee Symphonia Hungarica in Marl-
CBS; December 10, 1960

Head, down low over the guitar,
he barely seemed to hum; ending "all come home";
did not smile; came by air;
did not have to come.
        The guitar's an event.
        Guests of honor is old, doesn't dance; can't smile.
    "Have a home?" a boy asks. "Shall we live in a tent?"
        "In a house", Yul answers. His neat cloth hat
has nothing like the glitter that reflected on the face
of milkweed-seed brown dominating a palace-place
in those halls devoid of solace that are nothing like the place
where he is now. His deliberate pace
is a king's however. "You'll have plenty of space."

    "Recital"? 'concert is the word,-
in Marl Austria's Marl, by the Budapest Symphonia Symphony —
    displaced but not deterred;
listened to me - / with detachment then -
    detachedly then -
        like a frog or grasshopper that did not
        know it had missed the mower, a pigmy citizen;
        in any case, too slow a grower.
There were thirty million; there are thirteen still -
healthy to begin with, kept waiting till they're ill;
History judges. It certainly will
remember Winnipeg's incredible
conditions: "Ill; no sponsor; and no kind of skill."
Odd - a reporter with small guitar - a puzzle.
Mysterious Yul did not come to dazzle.

    Magic bird with multiple tongue -
five tongues - embarked on a crazy twelve-month tramp
or plod; he flew among
the damned, / found each camp
where hope had slowly died
and came to end that sort of death;
Instead did not feather himself, he
        "Two small fishes and five loaves of bread",
        Nourished seeds of dignity. All were fed.
He said, You may feel strange; not dressed the way they dress.
Nobody notices; you'll find some happiness,
No new "big fear"; no distress."
He can sing - twinned with an enchantress -
elephant-borne sequined-spangled dress -
    aloft by trunk, with star-tipped wand,
    truer to the beat than Symphonia Hungarica. Hungarica.

the end of the corridor was a large sitting room that overlooked the street. On top of a bookcase that ran the length of the corridor was a Nixon button.

Miss Moore and the interviewer sat in her sitting room, a microphone between them. Piles of books stood everywhere. On the walls hung a variety of paintings. One came from Mexico, a gift of Mabel Dodge. Others were examples of the heavy, tea-colored oils that Americans hung in the years before 1914. The furniture was old-fashioned and dark.

Miss Moore spoke with an accustomed scrupulosity, and with a humor that her readers will recognize. When she ended a sentence with a phrase that was particularly telling, or even tart, she glanced quickly at the interviewer to see if he was amused, and then snickered gently. Later Miss Moore took the interviewer to an admirable lunch at a nearby restaurant. She decided not to wear her Nixon button because it clashed with her coat and hat.

                                                        —*Donald Hall, 1960*

INTERVIEWER

Miss Moore, I understand that you were born in St. Louis only about ten months before T. S. Eliot. Did your families know each other?

MARIANNE MOORE

No, we did not know the Eliots. We lived in Kirkwood, Missouri, where my grandfather was pastor of the First Presbyterian Church. T. S. Eliot's grandfather—Dr. William Eliot—was a Unitarian. We left when I was about seven, my grandfather having died in 1894, February 20. My grandfather, like Dr. Eliot, had attended ministerial meetings in St. Louis. Also, at stated intervals, various ministers met for luncheon. After one of these luncheons my grandfather said, When Dr. William Eliot asks the blessing and says, "and this we ask in the name of our Lord Jesus Christ," he is Trinitarian enough for me. The Mary Institute, for girls, was endowed by him as a memorial to his daughter Mary, who had died.

INTERVIEWER

How old were you when you started to write poems?

MOORE

Well, let me see, in Bryn Mawr. I think I was eighteen when I entered Bryn Mawr. I was born in 1887, I entered college in 1906. Now, how old would I have been? Can you deduce my probable age?

INTERVIEWER

Eighteen or nineteen.

MOORE

I had no literary plans, but I was interested in the undergraduate monthly magazine, and to my surprise (I wrote one or two little things for it) the editors elected me to the board. It was my sophomore year—I am sure it was—and I stayed on, I believe. And then when I had left college I offered contributions (we weren't paid) to the *Lantern*, the alumnae magazine. But I didn't feel that my product was anything to shake the world.

INTERVIEWER

At what point did poetry become world-shaking for you?

MOORE

Never! I believe I was interested in painting then. At least I said so. I remember Mrs. Otis Skinner asking at commencement time, the year I was graduated, What would you like to be? A painter, I said. Well, I'm not surprised, Mrs. Skinner answered. I had something on that she liked, some kind of summer dress. She commended it—said, I'm not at all surprised.

I like stories. I like fiction. And—this sounds rather pathetic, bizarre as well—I think verse perhaps was for me the next best thing to it. Didn't I write something one time, "Part of a Poem, Part of a Novel, Part of a Play"? I think I was all too truthful. I could visualize scenes, and deplored the fact that Henry James had to do it unchallenged. Now, if I couldn't write fiction, I'd like to write plays. To me the theater is the most pleasant, in fact my favorite, form of recreation.

INTERVIEWER

Do you go often?

MOORE

No. Never. Unless someone invites me. Lillian Hellman invited me to *Toys in the Attic*, and I am very happy that she did. I would have had no notion of the vitality of the thing, I would have lost sight of her skill as a writer if I hadn't seen the play. I would like to go again. The accuracy of the vernacular! That's the kind of thing I am interested in, am always taking down little local expressions and accents. I think I should be in some philological operation or enterprise, am really much interested in dialect and intonations. I scarcely think of any that comes into my so-called poems at all.

INTERVIEWER

I wonder what Bryn Mawr meant for you as a poet. You write that most of your time there was spent in the biological laboratory. Did you like biology better than literature as a subject for study? Did the training possibly affect your poetry?

MOORE

I had hoped to make French and English my major studies, and took the required two-year English course—five hours a week—but was not able to elect a course until my junior year. I did not attain the requisite academic stand of eighty until that year. I then elected seventeenth-century imitative writing—Fuller, Hooker, Bacon, Bishop Andrewes, and others. Lectures in French were in French, and I had had no spoken French.

Did laboratory studies affect my poetry? I am sure they did. I found the biology courses—minor, major, and histology—exhilarating. I thought, in fact, of studying medicine. Precision, economy of statement,

logic employed to ends that are disinterested, drawing and identi-
fying, these at least have some bearing on the imagination, it seems
to me.

INTERVIEWER

Whom did you know in the literary world, before you came to New
York? Did you know Bryher and H.D.?

MOORE

It's very hard to get these things seriatim. I met Bryher in 1921 in
New York. H.D. was my classmate at Bryn Mawr. She was there, I
think, only two years. She was a nonresident and I did not realize that
she was interested in writing.

INTERVIEWER

Did you know Ezra Pound and William Carlos Williams through
her? Didn't she know them at the University of Pennsylvania?

MOORE

Yes. She did. I didn't meet them. I had met no writers until 1916,
when I visited New York, when a friend in Carlisle wanted me to ac-
company her.

INTERVIEWER

So you were isolated really from modern poetry until 1916?

MOORE

Yes.

INTERVIEWER

Was that your first trip to New York, when you went there for six
days and decided that you wanted to live there?

MOORE

Oh, no. Several times my mother had taken my brother and me
sightseeing and to shop on the way to Boston, or Maine, and to Washington and Florida. My senior year in college in 1909, I visited
Dr. Charles Spraguesmith's daughter, Hilda, at Christmastime in New
York. And Louis Anspacher lectured in a very ornamental way at
Cooper Union. There was plenty of music at Carnegie Hall, and I got
a sense of what was going on in New York.

INTERVIEWER

And what was going on made you want to come back?

MOORE

It probably did, when Miss Cowdrey in Carlisle invited me to
come with her for a week. It was the visit in 1916 that made me want
to live there. I don't know what put it into her head to do it, or why she
wasn't likely to have a better time without me. She was most skeptical
of my venturing forth to bohemian parties. But I was fearless about
that. In the first place, I didn't think anyone would try to harm me,
but if they did I felt impervious. It never occurred to me that chaper-
ones were important.

INTERVIEWER

Do you suppose that moving to New York, and the stimulation of
the writers whom you found there, led you to write more poems than
you would otherwise have written?

MOORE

I'm sure it did—seeing what others wrote, liking this or that. With
me it's always some fortuity that traps me. I certainly never intended
to write poetry. That never came into my head. And now, too, I think
each time I write that it may be the last time. Then I'm charmed by
something and seem to have to say something. Everything I have written is the result of reading or of interest in people, I'm sure of that. I
had no ambition to be a writer.

INTERVIEWER

Let me see. You taught at the Carlisle Indian School after Bryn Mawr. Then after you moved to New York in 1918 you taught at a private school and worked in a library. Did these occupations have anything to do with you as a writer?

MOORE

I think they hardened my muscles considerably, my mental approach to things. Working as a librarian was a big help, a tremendous help. Miss Leonard of the Hudson Park branch of the New York Public Library opposite our house came to see me one day. I wasn't in, and she asked my mother did she think I would care to be on the staff, work in the library, because I was so fond of books and liked to talk about them to people. My mother said no, she thought not—the shoemaker's children never have shoes. I probably would feel if I joined the staff that I'd have no time to read. When I came home she told me, and I said, Why, certainly. Ideal. I'll tell her. Only I couldn't work more than half a day. If I had worked all day and maybe evenings or overtime, like the mechanics, why, it would *not* have been ideal.

As a free service we were assigned books to review and I did like that. We didn't get paid but we had the chance to diagnose. I reveled in it. Somewhere I believe I have carbon copies of those "P-slip" summaries. They were the kind of things that brought the worst/best out. I was always wondering why they didn't honor me with an art book or medical book or even a history, or criticism. But no, it was fiction, silent-movie fiction.

INTERVIEWER

Did you travel at this time? Did you go to Europe at all?

MOORE

In 1911. My mother and I went to England for about two months, July and August probably. We went to Paris and we stayed on the Left Bank, in a pension in the rue Valette, where Calvin wrote his

Institutes, I believe. Not far from the Panthéon and the Luxembourg Gardens. I have been much interested in Sylvia Beach's book—reading about Ezra Pound and his Paris days. Where was I and what was I doing? I think, with the objective of an evening stroll—it was one of the hottest summers the world has ever known, 1911—we walked along to 12, rue de l'Odéon, to see Sylvia Beach's shop. It wouldn't occur to me to say, Here am I, I'm a writer, would you talk to me a while? I had no feeling at all like that. I wanted to observe things. And we went to every museum in Paris, I think, except two.

INTERVIEWER

Have you been back since?

MOORE

Not to Paris. Only to England in 1935 or 1936. I like England.

INTERVIEWER

You have mostly stayed put in Brooklyn, then, since you moved here in 1929?

MOORE

Except for four trips to the West: Los Angeles, San Francisco, Puget Sound, and British Columbia. My mother and I went through the canal previously, to San Francisco, and by rail to Seattle.

INTERVIEWER

Have you missed the Dodgers here since they went West?

MOORE

Very much, and I am told that they miss us.

INTERVIEWER

I am still interested in those early years in New York. William Carlos Williams, in his *Autobiography*, says that you were "a rafter holding up the superstructure of our uncompleted building," when he talks about the Greenwich Village group of writers. I guess these were people who contributed to *Others*.

MOORE

I never was a rafter holding up anyone! I have his *Autobiography* and took him to task for his misinformed statements about Robert McAlmon and Bryher. In my indignation I missed some things I ought to have seen.

INTERVIEWER

To what extent did the *Others* contributors form a group?

MOORE

We did foregather a little. Alfred Kreymborg was editor, and was married to Gertrude Lord at the time,* one of the loveliest persons you could ever meet. And they had a little apartment somewhere in the village. There was considerable unanimity about the group.

INTERVIEWER

Someone called Alfred Kreymborg your American discoverer. Do you suppose this is true?

MOORE

It could be said, perhaps. He did all he could to promote me. Miss Monroe and the Aldingtons had asked me simultaneously to contribute to *Poetry* and the *Egoist* in 1915. Alfred Kreymborg was not inhibited. I was a little different from the others. He thought I might pass as a novelty, I guess.

INTERVIEWER

What was your reaction when H.D. and Bryher brought out your first collection, which they called *Poems*, in 1921 without your knowledge? Why had you delayed to do it yourself?

* Moore was likely referring to Dorothy Bloom.

MOORE

To issue my slight product—conspicuously tentative—seemed to me premature. I disliked the term "poetry" for any but Chaucer's or Shakespeare's or Dante's. I do not now feel quite my original hostility to the word, since it is a convenient, almost unavoidable term for the thing (although hardly for me—my observations, experiments in rhythm, or exercises in composition). What I write, as I have said before, could only be called poetry because there is no other category in which to put it. For the chivalry of the undertaking—issuing my verse for me in 1921, certainly in format choicer than the content— I am intensely grateful. Again, in 1935, it seemed to me not very self-interested of Faber and Faber, and simultaneously of the Macmillan Company, to propose a *Selected Poems* for me. Desultory occasional magazine publications seemed to me sufficient, conspicuous enough.

INTERVIEWER

Had you been sending poems to magazines before the *Egoist* printed your first poem?

MOORE

I must have. I have a little curio, a little wee book about two by three inches, or two and a half by three inches, in which I systematically entered everything sent out, when I got it back, if they took it, and how much I got for it. That lasted about a year, I think. I can't care as much as all that. I don't know that I submitted anything that wasn't extorted from me.

I have at present three onerous tasks, and each interferes with the others, and I don't know how I am going to write anything. If I get a promising idea I set it down, and it stays there. I don't make myself do anything with it. I've had several things in *The New Yorker*. And I said to them, I might never write again, and not to expect me to. I never knew anyone who had a passion for words who had as much difficulty in saying things as I do and I very seldom say them in a manner I like. If I do it's because I don't know I'm trying.

I've written several things for *The New Yorker*—and I did want to write them.

INTERVIEWER

When did you last write a poem?

MOORE

It appeared in August. What was it about? Oh . . . Carnegie Hall. You see, anything that really rouses me . . .

INTERVIEWER

How does a poem start for you?

MOORE

A felicitous phrase springs to mind—a word or two, say—simultaneous usually with some thought or object of equal attraction: "Its leaps should be *set*/to the flageo*let*"; "Katydid-wing subdivided by *sun*/till the nettings are *legion*." I like light rhymes, inconspicuous rhymes, and unpompous conspicuous rhymes. Gilbert and Sullivan:

> Yet, when the danger's near,
> We manage to appear
> As insensible to fear
> As anybody here.

I have a passion for rhythm and accent, so blundered into versifying. Considering the stanza the unit, I came to hazard hyphens at the end of the line, but found that readers are distracted from the content by hyphens, so I try not to use them. My interest in La Fontaine originated entirely independent of content. I then fell prey to that surgical kind of courtesy of his:

> I fear that appearances are worshiped throughout France
> Whereas pre-eminence perchance
> Merely means a pushing person.

I like the unaccented syllable and accented near-rhyme:

By love and his blindness
Possibly a service was done,
Let lovers say. A lonely man has no criterion.

INTERVIEWER

What in your reading or your background led you to write the way
you do write? Was imagism a help to you?

MOORE

No. I wondered why anyone would adopt the term.

INTERVIEWER

The descriptiveness of your poems has nothing to do with them,
you think?

MOORE

No, I really don't. I was rather sorry to be a pariah, or at least that
I had no connection with anything. But I did feel gratitude to *Others*.

INTERVIEWER

Where do you think your style of writing came from? Was it a
gradual accumulation, out of your character? Or does it have literary
antecedents?

MOORE

Not so far as I know. Ezra Pound said, Someone has been reading
Laforgue, and French authors. Well, sad to say, I had not read any of
them until fairly recently. Retroactively I see that Francis Jammes's
titles and treatment are a good deal like my own. I seem almost a plagiarist.

INTERVIEWER

And the extensive use of quotations?

MOORE

I was just trying to be honorable and not to steal things. I've always felt that if a thing had been said in the best way, how can you say it better? If I wanted to say something and somebody had said it ideally, then I'd take it but give the person credit for it. That's all there is to it. If you are charmed by an author, I think it's a very strange and invalid imagination that doesn't long to share it. Somebody else should read it, don't you think?

INTERVIEWER

Did any prose stylists help you in finding your poetic style? Elizabeth Bishop mentions Poe's prose in connection with your writing, and you have always made people think of Henry James.

MOORE

Prose stylists, very much. Dr. Johnson on Richard Savage: "He was in two months illegitimated by the Parliament, and disowned by his mother, doomed to poverty and obscurity, and launched upon the ocean of life only that he might be swallowed by its quicksands, or dashed upon its rocks. . . . It was his peculiar happiness that he scarcely ever found a stranger whom he did not leave a friend; but it must likewise be added, that he had not often a friend long without obliging him to become a stranger." Or Edmund Burke on the colonies: "You can shear a wolf; but will he comply?" Or Sir Thomas Browne: "States are not governed by Ergotisms." He calls a bee "that industrious flie," and his home his "hive." His manner is a kind of erudition-proof sweetness. Or Sir Francis Bacon: "Civil War is like the heat of fever; a foreign war is like the heat of exercise." Or Cellini: "I had a dog, black as a mulberry . . . I was fuming with fury and swelling like an asp." Or Caesar's *Commentaries*, and Xenophon's *Cynegeticus*—the gusto and interest in every detail! In Henry James it is the essays and letters especially that affect me. In Ezra Pound, *The Spirit of Romance*, his definiteness, his indigenously unmistakable accent. Charles Norman says in his biography of Ezra Pound that he said to a poet, "Nothing, *nothing*, that you couldn't in some circum-

stance, under stress of some emotion, *actually say*." And Ezra said of
Shakespeare and Dante, "Here we are with the masters; of neither can
we say, 'He is the greater'; of each we must say, 'He is unexcelled.'"

INTERVIEWER

Do you have in your own work any favorites and unfavorites?

MOORE

Indeed, I do. I think the most difficult thing for me is to be satisfactorily lucid, yet have enough implication in it to suit myself. That's a
problem. And I don't approve of my "enigmas," or as somebody said,
"the not ungreen grass." I said to my mother one time, How did you
ever permit me to let this be printed? And she said, You didn't ask my
advice.

INTERVIEWER

One time I heard you give a reading, and I think you said that you
didn't like "In Distrust of Merits," which is one of your most popular
poems.

MOORE

I do like it. It is sincere but I wouldn't call it a poem. It's truthful—it
is testimony to the fact that war is intolerable, and unjust.

INTERVIEWER

How can you call it not a poem, on what basis?

MOORE

Haphazard—as form, what has it? It is just a protest—disjointed, ex-
clamatory. Emotion overpowered me. First this thought and then that.

INTERVIEWER

Your mother said that you hadn't asked her advice. Did you ever?
Do you go for criticism to your family or friends?

MOORE

Well, not friends, but my brother if I get a chance. When my mother said, You didn't ask my advice, it must have been years ago, because when I wrote "A Face," I had written something first about "the adder and the child with a bowl of porridge," and she said, It won't do. All right, I said, but I have to produce something. Cyril Connolly had asked me for something for *Horizon*. So I wrote "A Face." That is one of the few things I ever set down that didn't give me any trouble. She said, I like it. I remember that.

Then, much before that, I wrote "The Buffalo." I thought it would probably outrage a number of persons because it had to me a kind of pleasing jerky progress. I thought, Well, if it seems bad my brother will tell me, and if it has a point he'll detect it. And he said, with considerable gusto, It takes my fancy. I was happy as could be.

INTERVIEWER

Did you ever suppress anything because of family objections?

MOORE

Yes, "the adder and the child with a bowl of porridge." I never even wanted to improve it. You know, Mr. Saintsbury said that Andrew Lang wanted him to contribute something on Poe, and he did, and Lang returned it. Mr. Saintsbury said, Once a thing has been rejected, I would not offer it to the most different of editors. That shocked me. I have offered a thing, submitted it thirty-five times. Not simultaneously, of course.

INTERVIEWER

A poem?

MOORE

Yes. I am very tenacious.

INTERVIEWER

Do people ever ask you to write poems for them?

MOORE

Continually. Everything from on the death of a dog to a little item for an album.

INTERVIEWER

Do you ever write them?

MOORE

Oh, perhaps. Usually I quote something. Once when I was in the library we gave a party for Miss Leonard, and I wrote a line or two of doggerel about a bouquet of violets we gave her. It has no life or point. It was meant well but didn't amount to anything. Then in college, I had a sonnet as an assignment. The epitome of weakness.

INTERVIEWER

I'm interested in asking about the principles, and the methods, of your way of writing. What is the rationale behind syllabic verse? How does it differ from free verse, in which the line length is controlled visually but not arithmetically?

MOORE

It never occurred to me that what I wrote was something to define. I am governed by the pull of the sentence as the pull of a fabric is governed by gravity. I like the end-stopped line and dislike the reversed order of words. I like symmetry.

INTERVIEWER

How do you plan the shape of your stanzas? I am thinking of the poems, usually syllabic, which employ a repeated stanza form. Do you ever experiment with shapes before you write, by drawing lines on a page?

MOORE

Never, I never "plan" a stanza. Words cluster like chromosomes, determining the procedure. I may influence an arrangement or thin

it, then try to have successive stanzas identical with the first. Spontaneous initial originality—say, impetus—seems difficult to reproduce
consciously later. As Stravinsky said about pitch, "If I transpose it for
some reason, I am in danger of losing the freshness of first contact and
will have difficulty in recapturing its attractiveness."

No, I never "draw lines." I make a rhyme conspicuous, to me at a
glance, by underlining with red, blue, or other pencil—as many colors as I have rhymes to differentiate. However, if the phrases recur in
too incoherent an architecture—as print—I notice that the words as a
tune do not sound right. I may start a piece, find it obstructive, lack
a way out, and not complete the thing for a year, or years. I am thrifty.
I salvage anything promising and set it down in a small notebook.

INTERVIEWER

I wonder if the act of translating La Fontaine's *Fables* helped you as
a writer.

MOORE

Indeed it did. It was the best help I've ever had. I suffered frustration. I'm so naive, so docile, I tend to take anybody's word for anything the person says, even in matters of art. The publisher who had
commissioned the *Fables* died. I had no publisher. Well, I struggled
on for a time and it didn't go very well. I thought, I'd better ask if
they don't want to terminate the contract; then I could offer it elsewhere. I thought Macmillan, who took an interest in me, might like
it. *Might*. The editor in charge of translations said, Well, I studied
French at Cornell, took a degree in French, I love French, and . . .
well, I think you'd better put it away for a while. How long? I said.
About ten years. Besides, it will hurt your own work. You won't
write so well afterward. Oh, I said, that's one reason I was undertaking it; I thought it would train me and give me momentum. Much
dejected, I asked, What is wrong? Have I not a good ear? Are the
meanings not sound? Well, there are conflicts, the editor reiterated,
as it seemed to me, countless times. I don't know yet what they are or

were. I said, Don't write me an extenuating letter, please. Just send back the material in the envelope I put with it. I had submitted it in January and this was May. I had had a kind of uneasy hope that all would be well. Meanwhile I had volumes, hours, and years of work yet to do and might as well go on and do it, I had thought. The ultimatum was devastating.

At the same time Monroe Engel of the Viking Press wrote to me and said that he had supposed I had a commitment for my *Fables*, but if I hadn't would I let the Viking Press see them? I feel an everlasting gratitude to him.

However, I said, I can't offer you something which somebody else thinks isn't fit to print. I would have to have someone to stabilize it and guarantee that the meanings are sound.

Mr. Engel said, Who do you think could do that? Whom would you like?

I said, Harry Levin, because he had written a cogent, very shrewd review of Edna St. Vincent Millay's and George Dillon's translation of Baudelaire. I admired its finesse.

Mr. Engel said, I'll ask him. But you won't hear for a long time. He's very busy. And how much do you think we ought to offer him?

Well, I said, not less than ten dollars a book; there would be no incentive in undertaking the bother of it, if it weren't twenty.

He said, That would reduce your royalties too much on an advance.

I said, I don't want an advance, wouldn't even consider one.

And then Harry Levin said, quite soon, that he would be glad to do it as a refreshment against the chores of the term, but of course he would accept no remuneration. It was a very dubious refreshment, let me tell you. (He is precise, and not abusive, and did not "resign.")

INTERVIEWER

I've been asking you about your poems, which is of course what interests me most. But you were editor of *The Dial*, too, and I want to ask you a few things about that. You were editor from 1925 until it ended in 1929, I think. How did you first come to be associated with it?

MOORE

Let me see. I think I took the initiative. I sent the editors a couple of things and they sent them back. And Lola Ridge had a party—she had a large apartment on a ground floor somewhere—and John Reed and Marsden Hartley, who was very confident with the brush, and Scofield Thayer, editor of *The Dial*, were there. And much to my disgust, we were induced each to read something we had written. And Scofield Thayer said of my piece, Would you send that to us at *The Dial*?

I did send it, I said.

And he said, Well, send it again. That is how it began, I think. Then he said one time, I'd like you to meet my partner, Sibley Watson, and invited me to tea at 152 West Thirteenth Street. I was impressed. Dr. Watson is rare. He said nothing, but what he did say was striking and the significance would creep over you because it was unanticipated. And they asked me to join the staff at *The Dial*.

INTERVIEWER

I have just been looking at that magazine, the years when you edited it. It's an incredible magazine.

MOORE

The Dial? There were good things in it, weren't there?

INTERVIEWER

Yes. It combined George Saintsbury and Ezra Pound in the same issue. How do you account for it? What made it so good?

MOORE

Lack of fear, for one thing. We didn't care what other people said. I never knew a magazine that was so self-propulsive. Everybody liked what he was doing, and when we made grievous mistakes we were sorry but we laughed over them.

INTERVIEWER

Louise Bogan said that *The Dial* made clear "the obvious division
between American avant-garde and American conventional writing."
Do you think this kind of division continues or has continued? Was
this in any way a deliberate policy?

MOORE

I think that individuality was the great thing. We were not con-
forming to anything. We certainly didn't have a policy, except I remember hearing the word *intensity* very often. A thing must have
intensity. That seemed to be the criterion.

As George Grosz said, at that last meeting he attended at the National Institute, "How did I come to be an artist? Endless curiosity,
observation, research—and a great amount of joy in the thing." It was
a matter of taking a liking to things. Things that were in accordance
with your taste. I think that was it. And we didn't care how unhomo-
geneous they might seem. Didn't Aristotle say that it is the mark of a
poet to see resemblances between apparently incongruous things?

INTERVIEWER

Do you think there is anything in the change of literary life in
America that would make *The Dial* different if it existed today under
the same editors? Were there any special conditions in the twenties
that made the literary life of America different?

MOORE

I think it is always about the same.

INTERVIEWER

I wonder, if it had survived into the thirties, if it might have made
that rather dry literary decade a little better.

MOORE

I think so. Because we weren't in captivity to anything.

INTERVIEWER

Was it just finances that made it stop?

MOORE

No, it wasn't the depression. Conditions changed. Scofield Thayer had a nervous breakdown, and he didn't come to meetings. Dr. Watson was interested in photography—was studying medicine, is a doctor of medicine, and lived in Rochester. I was alone. I didn't know that Rochester was about a night's journey away, and I would say to Dr. Watson, Couldn't you come in for a make-up meeting, or send us these manuscripts and say what you think of them? I may, as usual, have exaggerated my enslavement and my preoccupation with tasks—writing letters and reading manuscripts. Originally I had said I would come if I didn't have to write letters and didn't have to see contributors. And presently I was doing both. I think it was largely chivalry—the decision to discontinue the magazine—because I didn't have time for work of my own.

INTERVIEWER

I wonder how you worked as an editor. Hart Crane complains, in one of his letters, that you rearranged "The Wine Menagerie" and changed the title. Do you feel that you were justified? Did you ask for revisions from many poets?

MOORE

No. We had an inflexible rule: do not ask changes of so much as a comma. Accept it or reject it. But in that instance I felt that in compassion I should disregard the rule. Hart Crane complains of me? Well, I complain of him. He liked *The Dial* and we liked him—friends, and with certain tastes in common. He was in dire need of money. It seemed careless not to so much as ask if he might like to make some changes ("like" in quotations). His gratitude was ardent and later his repudiation of it commensurate—he perhaps being in both instances under a disability with which I was not familiar. (Penalizing us for compassion?

I say "us," and should say "me.") Really I am not used to having people in that bemused state. He was so anxious to have us take that thing, and so delighted. Well, if you would modify it a little, I said, we would like it better. I never attended "their" wild parties, as Lachaise once said. It was lawless of me to suggest changes. I disobeyed.

INTERVIEWER

Have you had editors suggest changes to you? Changes in your own poems, I mean?

MOORE

No, but my ardor to be helped being sincere, I sometimes induce assistance: the *Times*, the *Herald Tribune*, *The New Yorker*, have a number of times had to patch and piece me out. If you have a genius of an editor, you are blessed: e.g., T. S. Eliot and Ezra Pound, Harry Levin and others, Irita Van Doren and Miss Belle Rosenbaum.

Have I found "help" helpful? I certainly have—and in three instances when I was at *The Dial*, I hazarded suggestions the results of which were, to me, drama. Excoriated by Herman George Scheffauer for offering to suggest a verbal change or two in his translation of Thomas Mann's *Disorder and Early Sorrow*, I must have posted the suggestions before I was able to withdraw them. In any case, his joyous subsequent retraction of abuse, and his pleasure in the narrative, were not unwelcome. Gilbert Seldes strongly commended me for excisions proposed by me in his "Jonathan Edwards" (for *The Dial*); and I have not ceased to marvel at the overrating by Mark Van Doren of editorial conscience on my reverting (after an interval) to keeping some final lines I had wished he would omit. (Verse! but not a sonnet.)

We should try to judge the work of others by the most that it is, and our own, if not by the least that it is, take the least into consideration. I feel that I would not be worth a button if not grateful to be preserved from myself, and informed if what I have written is not to the point. I think we should feel free, like La Fontaine's captious critic, to say, if asked, Your phrases are too long, and the content is not good. Break up the type and put it in the font. As Kenneth Burke says in *Counter-Statement*: "[Great] artists feel as opportunity what others feel as a menace. This ability does not, I believe, derive from exceptional strength, it probably arises purely from professional interest the artist may take in his difficulties."

Lew Sarett says, in the *Poetry Society Bulletin*, we ask of a poet: Does this mean something? Does the poet say what he has to say and in his own manner? Does it stir the reader?

Shouldn't we replace vanity with honesty, as Robert Frost recommends? Annoyances abound. We should not find them lethal—a baffled printer's emendations for instance (my "elephant with frog-colored skin" instead of "fog-colored skin," and "the power of the invisible is the invisible," instead of "the power of the visible is the invisible") sounding like a parody on my meticulousness, a "glasshopper" instead of a "grasshopper."

INTERVIEWER

Editing *The Dial* must have acquainted you with the writers of the day whom you did not know already. Had you known Hart Crane earlier?

MOORE

Yes, I did. You remember *Broom*? Toward the beginning of that magazine, in 1921, Lola Ridge was very hospitable, and she invited to a party—previous to my work on *The Dial*—Kay Boyle and her husband, a French soldier, and Hart Crane, Elinor Wylie and some others. I took a great liking to Hart Crane. We talked about French bindings, and he was diffident and modest and seemed to have so much intuition, such a feel for things, for books—really a bibliophile—that I took special interest in him. And Dr. Watson and Scofield Thayer liked him—felt that he was one of our talents, that he couldn't fit himself into an IBM position to find a livelihood; that we ought to, whenever we could, take anything he sent us.

I know a cousin of his, Joe Nowak, who is rather proud of him. He lives here in Brooklyn, and is* at the Dry Dock Savings Bank and used to work in antiques. Joe was very convinced of Hart's sincerity and his innate love of all that I have specified. Anyhow, *The Bridge* is a grand theme. Here and there I think he could have firmed it up. A writer is unfair to himself when he is unable to be hard on himself.

INTERVIEWER

Did Crane have anything to do with *Others*?

MOORE

Others antedated *Broom*. *Others* was Alfred Kreymborg and Skipwith Cannéll, Wallace Stevens, William Carlos Williams. Wallace Stevens—odd. I nearly met him a dozen times before I did meet him in 1943 at Mount Holyoke, at the college's *Entretiens de Pontigny* of which Professor Gustave Cohen was chairman. Wallace Stevens was Henry Church's favorite American poet. Mr. Church had published him and some others, and me, in *Mesures*, in Paris. Raymond Queneau translated us.

During the French program at Mount Holyoke one afternoon Wallace Stevens had a discourse, the one about Goethe dancing on a packet boat in black wool stockings. My mother and I were there, and I gave a reading with commentary. Henry Church had an astoundingly beautiful Panama hat—a sort of porkpie with a wide brim, a little like Bernard Berenson's hats. I have never seen as fine a weave, and he had a pepper-and-salt shawl which he draped about himself. This lecture was on the lawn.

Wallace Stevens was extremely friendly. We should have had a tape recorder on that occasion, for at lunch they seated us all at a kind of refectory table and a girl kept asking him questions such as, Mr. Stevens, have you read the *Four Quartets*? Of course, he said, but I can't read much of Eliot or I wouldn't have any individuality of my own.

* *Was*; killed; his car run into by a reckless driver in April 1961.—M. M.

INTERVIEWER

Do you read new poetry now? Do you try to keep up?

MOORE

I am always seeing it—am sent some every day. Some good. But it does interfere with my work. I can't get much done. Yet I would be a monster if I tossed everything away without looking at it. I write more notes, letters, cards in an hour than is sane.

Although everyone is penalized by being quoted inexactly, I wonder if there is anybody alive whose remarks are so often paraphrased as mine—printed as verbatim. It is really martyrdom. In his book *Ezra Pound*, Charles Norman was very scrupulous. He got several things exactly right. The first time I met Ezra Pound, when he came here to see my mother and me, I said that Henry Eliot seemed to me more nearly the artist than anyone I had ever met. "Now, now," said Ezra. "Be careful." Maybe that isn't exact, but he quotes it just the way I said it.

INTERVIEWER

Do you mean Henry Ware Eliot, T. S. Eliot's brother?

MOORE

Yes. After the Henry Eliots moved from Chicago to New York to—is it Sixty-eighth Street? It's the street on which Hunter College is—to an apartment there, they invited me to dinner, I should think at T. S. Eliot's suggestion, and I took to them immediately. I felt as if I'd known them a great while. It was some time before I felt that way about T. S. Eliot.

About inaccuracies—when I went to see Ezra Pound at St. Elizabeths, about the third time I went, the official who escorted me to the grounds said, Good of you to come to see him, and I said, Good? You have no idea how much he has done for me, and others. This pertains to an early rather than final visit.

I was not in the habit of asking experts or anybody else to help me with things that I was doing, unless it was a librarian or someone whose business it was to help applicants, or a teacher. But I was desperate when Macmillan declined my *Fables*. I had worked about four years on them and sent Ezra Pound several—although I hesitated. I didn't like to bother him. He had enough trouble without that, but finally I said, Would you have time to tell me if the rhythms grate on you? Is my ear not good?

INTERVIEWER

He replied?

MOORE

Yes, he said, The least touch of merit upsets these blighters.

INTERVIEWER

When you first read Pound in 1916, did you recognize him as one of the great ones?

MOORE

Surely did. *The Spirit of Romance*. I don't think anybody could read that book and feel that a flounderer was writing.

INTERVIEWER

What about the early poems?

MOORE

Yes. They seemed a little didactic, but I liked them.

INTERVIEWER

I wanted to ask you a few questions about poetry in general. Somewhere you have said that originality is a by-product of sincerity. You often use moral terms in your criticism. Is the necessary morality specifically literary, a moral use of words, or is it larger? In what way must a man be good if he is to write good poems?

MOORE

If emotion is strong enough, the words are unambiguous. Someone asked Robert Frost (is that right?) if he was selective. He said, Call it passionate preference. Must a man be good to write good poems? The villains in Shakespeare are not illiterate, are they? But rectitude has a ring that is implicative, I would say. And with no integrity, a man is not likely to write the kind of book I read.

INTERVIEWER

Eliot, in his introduction to your *Selected Poems*, talks about your function as poet relative to the living language, as he calls it. Do you agree that this is a function of a poet? How does the poetry have the effect on the living language? What's the mechanics of it?

MOORE

You accept certain modes of saying a thing. Or strongly repudiate things. You do something of your own, you modify, invent a variant or revive a root meaning. Any doubt about that?

INTERVIEWER

I want to ask you a question about your correspondence with the Ford Motor Company, those letters that were printed in *The New Yorker*. They were looking for a name for the car they eventually called the Edsel, and they asked you to think of a name that would make people admire the car—

MOORE

Elegance and grace, they said it would have—

INTERVIEWER

". . . some visceral feeling of elegance, fleetness, advanced features and design. A name, in short, that flashes a dramatically desirable picture in people's minds."

MOORE

Really?

INTERVIEWER

That's what they said, in their first letter to you. I was thinking about this in connection with my question about language. Do you remember Pound's talk about expression and meaning? He says that when expression and meaning are far apart, the culture is in a bad way. I was wondering if this request doesn't ask you to remove expression a bit further from meaning.

MOORE

No, I don't think so. At least, to exposit the irresistibleness of the car. I got deep in motors and turbines and recessed wheels. No. That seemed to me a very worthy pursuit. I was more interested in the mechanics. I am interested in mechanisms, mechanics in general. And I enjoyed the assignment, for all that it was abortive. Dr. Pick at Marquette University procured a young demonstrator of the Edsel to call for me in a black one, to convey me to the auditorium. Nothing was wrong with that Edsel! I thought it was a very handsome car. It came out the wrong year.

INTERVIEWER

Another thing: in your criticism you make frequent analogies between the poet and the scientist. Do you think this analogy is helpful to the modern poet? Most people would consider the comparison a paradox, and assume that the poet and the scientist are opposed.

MOORE

Do the poet and scientist not work analogously? Both are willing to waste effort. To be hard on himself is one of the main strengths of each. Each is attentive to clues, each must narrow the choice, must strive for precision. As George Grosz says, "In art there is no place for gossip and but a small place for the satirist." The objective is fertile procedure. Is it not? Jacob Bronowski says in the *Saturday Evening Post* that science is not a mere collection of discoveries, but that science is the process of discovering. In any case it's not established once and for all—it's evolving.

INTERVIEWER

One last question. I was intrigued when you wrote that "America has in Wallace Stevens at least one artist whom professionalism will not demolish." What sort of literary professionalism did you have in mind? And do you find this a feature of America still?

MOORE

Yes. I think that writers sometimes lose verve and pugnacity, and he never would say "frame of reference" or "I wouldn't know." A question I am often asked is: What work can I find that will enable me to spend my whole time writing? Charles Ives, the composer, says, "You cannot set art off in a corner and hope for it to have vitality, reality, and substance. The fabric weaves itself whole. My work in music helped my business and my work in business helped my music." I am like Charles Ives. I guess Lawrence Durrell and Henry Miller would not agree with me.

INTERVIEWER

But how does professionalism make a writer lose his verve and pugnacity?

MOORE

Money may have something to do with it, and being regarded as a pundit. Wallace Stevens was really very much annoyed at being cataloged, categorized, and compelled to be scientific about what he was doing—to give satisfaction, to answer the teachers. He wouldn't do that. I think the same of William Carlos Williams. I think he wouldn't make so much of the great American language if he were plausible and tractable. That's the beauty of it—he is willing to be reckless. If you can't be that, what's the point of the whole thing?

Ezra Pound

The Art of Poetry

Since his return to Italy, Ezra Pound has spent most of his time in the Tirol, staying at Castle Brunnenburg with his wife, his daughter Mary, his son-in-law Prince Boris de Rachewiltz, and his grandchildren. However, the mountains in this resort country near Merano are cold in the winter, and Mr. Pound likes the sun. The interviewer was about to leave England for Merano, at the end of February, when a telegram stopped him at the door: "Merano icebound. Come to Rome."

Pound was alone in Rome, occupying a room in the apartment of an old friend named Ugo Dadone. It was the beginning of March and exceptionally warm. The windows and shutters of Pound's corner room swung open to the noises of the Via Angelo Poliziano. The interviewer sat in a large chair while Pound shifted restlessly from another chair to a sofa and back to the chair. Pound's impression on the room consisted of two suitcases and three books: the Faber *Cantos*, a Confucius, and Robinson's edition of Chaucer, which he was reading again.

In the social hours of the evening—dinner at Crispi's, a tour among the scenes of his past, ice cream at a café—Pound walked with the swaggering vigor of a young man. With his great hat, his sturdy stick, his tossed yellow scarf, and his coat, which he trailed like a cape, he was the lion of the Latin Quarter again. Then his talent for mimicry came forward, and laughter shook his gray beard.

NOTE TO BASE CENSOR

The Cantos contain nothing in the nature of cypher or

intended obscurity . The present Cantos do , naturally ,contain
a number of allusions and " recalls " to matter in the
earlier 71 cantos already published , and many of these
cannot be made clear to readers unacquainted with the
earlier parts of the poem.

There is also an extreme condensation in the quotations , for
example
             " Mine eyes have " (given as mi-hine eyes hev
refers to the Battle Hymn of the Republic as heard from the
loud speaker . There is not time or place in the narrative to
give the further remarks on X seeing the glory of the lord.

In like manner citations from Homer or XXXXXXXXX Sophokles
or Confucius are brief ,and serve to remind the ready reader
that we were not born yesterday.
                                  The Chinese ideograms are mainly
    translated , or commented in the english text. At any rate
they contain nothing seditious .

    The form of the poem and main progress is conditioned by
its own inner shape , but the life of the D.T.C. passing
OUTSIDE the scheme cannot but impinge ,or break into the
main flow. The proper names given are mostly those of men
on sick call seen passing my tent. A very brief allusion to
further study in names ,that is , I am interested to note that
the prevalence of early american names ,either of whites
of the old tradition (most of the early presidents for example)
or of descendents of slaves who took the names of their
masters . Interesting in contrast to the relative scarcity of
melting-pot names.

Typescript of an explanatory note from Ezra Pound to the censor at the
detention camp north of Pisa where Pound was held in 1945. The officer, in
censoring Pound's correspondence (which included the manuscripts of verse
on its way to the publisher), suspected that the Pisan Cantos were in fact
coded messages. Pound is writing to explain this is not the case.

During the daytime hours of the interview, which took three days, he spoke carefully, and the questions sometimes tired him out. In the morning when the interviewer returned, Mr. Pound was eager to revise the failures of the day before.

—*Donald Hall, 1962*

INTERVIEWER

You are nearly through *The Cantos* now, and this sets me to wondering about their beginning. In 1916 you wrote a letter in which you talked about trying to write a version of Andreas Divus in *Seafarer* rhythms. This sounds like a reference to Canto 1. Did you begin *The Cantos* in 1916?

EZRA POUND

I began *The Cantos* about 1904, I suppose. I had various schemes, starting in 1904 or 1905. The problem was to get a form—something elastic enough to take the necessary material. It had to be a form that wouldn't exclude something merely because it didn't fit. In the first sketches, a draft of the present first Canto was the third.

Obviously you haven't got a nice little road map such as the Middle Ages possessed of Heaven. Only a musical form would take the material, and the Confucian universe as I see it is a universe of interacting strains and tensions.

INTERVIEWER

Had your interest in Confucius begun in 1904?

POUND

No, the first thing was this: you had six centuries that hadn't been packaged. It was a question of dealing with material that wasn't in the *Divina Commedia*. Hugo did a *Légende des Siècles* that wasn't an evaluative affair but just bits of history strung together. The problem was to build up a circle of reference—taking the modern mind to be the medieval mind with wash after wash of classical culture poured over it since the Renaissance. That was the psyche, if you like. One had to deal with one's own subject.

INTERVIEWER

It must be thirty or thirty-five years since you have written any poetry outside *The Cantos*, except for the Alfred Venison poems. Why is this?

POUND

I got to the point where, apart from an occasional lighter impulse, what I had to say fitted the general scheme. There has been a good deal of work thrown away because one is attracted to a historic character and then finds that he doesn't function within my form, doesn't embody a value needed. I have tried to make *The Cantos* historic (vid. G. Giovannini, re: relation history to tragedy. Two articles ten years apart in some philological periodical, not source material but relevant) but not fiction. The material one wants to fit in doesn't always work. If the stone isn't hard enough to maintain the form, it has to go out.

INTERVIEWER

When you write a Canto now, how do you plan it? Do you follow a special course of reading for each one?

POUND

One isn't necessarily reading. One is working on the life vouchsafed, I should think. I don't know about method. The *what* is so much more important than how.

INTERVIEWER

Yet when you were a young man, your interest in poetry concentrated on form. Your professionalism and your devotion to technique became proverbial. In the last thirty years, you have traded your interest in form for an interest in content. Was the change on principle?

POUND

I think I've covered that. Technique is the test of sincerity. If a thing isn't worth getting the technique to say, it is of inferior value. All that must be regarded as exercise. Richter in his *Treatise on Harmony*, you see, says, "These are the principles of harmony and counterpoint; they have nothing whatever to do with composition, which is quite a separate activity." The statement, which somebody made, that you couldn't write Provençal canzoni forms in English, is false. The question of whether it was advisable or not was another matter. When there wasn't the criterion of natural language without inversion, those forms were natural, and they realized them with music. In English the music is of a limited nature. You've got Chaucer's French perfection, you've got Shakespeare's Italian perfection, you've got Campion and Lawes. I don't think I got around to this kind of form until I got to the choruses in the *Trachiniae*. I don't know that I got to anything at all, really, but I thought it was an extension of the gamut. It may be a delusion. One was always interested in the implication of change of pitch in the union of *motz et son*, of the word and melody.

INTERVIEWER

Does writing *The Cantos*, now, exhaust all of your technical interest, or does the writing of translations, like the *Trachiniae* you just mentioned, satisfy you by giving you more finger work?

POUND

One sees a job to be done and goes at it. The *Trachiniae* came from reading the Fenollosa Noh plays for the new edition, and from wanting to see what would happen to a Greek play, given that same medium and the hope of its being performed by the Minorou company. The sight of Cathay in Greek, looking like poetry, stimulated crosscurrents.

INTERVIEWER

Do you think that free verse is particularly an American form? I imagine that William Carlos Williams probably does, and thinks of the iambic as English.

POUND

I like Eliot's sentence: "No verse is *libre* for the man who wants to do a good job." I think the best free verse comes from an attempt to get back to quantitative meter.

I suppose it may be *un-English* without being specifically *American*. I remember Cocteau playing drums in a jazz band as if it were a very difficult mathematical problem.

I'll tell you a thing that I think is an American form, and that is the Jamesian parenthesis. You realize that the person you are talking to hasn't got the different steps, and you go back over them. In fact the Jamesian parenthesis has immensely increased now. That, I think, is something that is definitely American. The struggle that one has when one meets another man who has had a lot of experience is to find the point where the two experiences touch, so that he really knows what you are talking about.

INTERVIEWER

Your work includes a great range of experience, as well as of form. What do you think is the greatest quality a poet can have? Is it formal, or is it a quality of thinking?

POUND

I don't know that you can put the needed qualities in hierarchic order, but he must have a continuous curiosity, which of course does not make him a writer, but if he hasn't got that he will wither. And the question of doing anything about it depends on a persistent energy. A man like Agassiz is never bored, never tired. The transit from the reception of stimuli to the recording, to the correlation—that is what takes the whole energy of a lifetime.

INTERVIEWER

Do you think that the modern world has changed the ways in which poetry can be written?

POUND

There is a lot of competition that never was there before. Take the serious side of Disney, the Confucian side of Disney. It's in having taken an ethos, as he does in *Perri*, that squirrel film, where you have the values of courage and tenderness asserted in a way that everybody can understand. You have got an absolute genius there. You have got a greater correlation of nature than you have had since the time of Alexander the Great. Alexander gave orders to the fishermen that if they found out anything about fish that was interesting, a specific thing, they were to tell Aristotle. And with that correlation you got ichthyology to the scientific point where it stayed for two thousand years. And now one has got with the camera an enormous correlation of particulars. That capacity for making contact is a tremendous challenge to literature. It throws up the question of what needs to be done and what is superfluous.

INTERVIEWER

Maybe it's an opportunity, too. When you were a young man in particular, and even through *The Cantos*, you changed your poetic style again and again. You have never been content to stick anywhere. Were you consciously looking to extend your style? Does the artist *need* to keep moving?

POUND

I think the artist *has* to keep moving. You are trying to render life in a way that won't bore people, and you are trying to put down what you see.

INTERVIEWER

I wonder what you think of contemporary movements. I haven't seen remarks of yours about poets more recent than Cummings, except for Bunting and Zukofsky. Other things have occupied you, I suppose.

One can't read everything. I was trying to find out a number of historic facts, and you can't see out of the back of your head. I do not think there is any record of a man being able to criticize the people who come after him. It is a sheer question of the amount of reading one man can do.

I don't know whether it is his own or whether it is a gem that he collected, but at any rate one of the things Frost said in London in 19—whenever it was—1912, was this: "Summary of prayer: 'Oh God, pay attention to *me*.'" And that is the approach of younger writers— not to divinity exactly!—and in general one has to limit one's reading to younger poets who are recommended by at least one other younger poet, as a sponsor. Of course a routine of that kind could lead to conspiracy, but at any rate . . .

As far as criticizing younger people, one has not the time to make a comparative estimate. People one is learning from, one does measure one against the other. I see a stirring now, but . . . For general conditions there is undoubtedly a liveliness. And Cal [Robert] Lowell is very good.

You have given advice to the young all your life. Do you have anything special to say to them now?

To improve their curiosity and not to fake. But that is not enough. The mere registering of bellyache and the mere dumping of the ash can is not enough. In fact the University of Pennsylvania student *Punchbowl* used to have as its motto, "Any damn fool can be spontaneous."

You once wrote that you had four useful hints from living literary predecessors, who were Thomas Hardy, William Butler Yeats, Ford Madox Ford, and Robert Bridges. What were these hints?

POUND

Bridges's was the simplest. Bridges's was a warning against homophones. Hardy's was the degree to which he would concentrate on the subject matter, not on the manner. Ford's in general was the *freshness* of language. And Yeats you say was the fourth? Well, Yeats by 1908 had written simple lyrics in which there were no departures from the natural order of words.

INTERVIEWER

You were secretary to Yeats in 1913 and 1914. What sort of things did you do for him?

POUND

Mostly reading aloud. Doughty's *Dawn in Britain*, and so on. And wrangling, you see. The Irish like contradiction. He tried to learn fencing at forty-five, which was amusing. He would thrash around with the foils like a whale. He sometimes gave the impression of being even a worse idiot than I am.

INTERVIEWER

There is an academic controversy about your influence on Yeats. Did you work over his poetry with him? Did you cut any of his poems in the way you cut *The Waste Land*?

POUND

I don't think I can remember anything like that. I am sure I objected to particular expressions. Once out at Rapallo I tried for God's sake to prevent him from printing a thing. I told him it was rubbish. All he did was print it with a preface saying that I *said* it was rubbish.

I remember when Tagore had taken to doodling on the edge of his proofs, and they told him it was art. There was a show of it in Paris. "Is this art?" Nobody was very keen on these doodlings, but of course so many people lied to him.

As far as the change in Yeats goes, I think that Ford Madox Ford might have some credit. Yeats never would have taken advice from Ford, but I think that Fordie helped him, via me, in trying to get toward a natural way of writing.

INTERVIEWER

Did anyone ever help you with your work as extensively as you have helped others? I mean by criticism or cutting.

POUND

Apart from Fordie, rolling on the floor undecorously and holding his head in his hands, and groaning on one occasion, I don't think anybody helped me through my manuscripts. Ford's stuff appeared too loose then, but he led the fight against tertiary archaisms.

INTERVIEWER

You have been closely associated with visual artists—Gaudier-Brzeska and Wyndham Lewis in the vorticist movement, and later Picabia, Picasso, and Brancusi. Has this had anything to do with you as a writer?

POUND

I don't believe so. One looked at paintings in galleries and one might have found out something. "The Game of Chess" poem shows the effect of modern abstract art, but vorticism from my angle was a renewal of the sense of construction. Color went dead and Manet and the impressionists revived it. Then what I would call the sense of form was blurred, and vorticism, as distinct from cubism, was an attempt to revive the sense of form—the form you had in Piero della Francesca's *De Prospectiva pingendi*, his treatise on the proportions and composition. I got started on the idea of comparative forms before I left America. A fellow named Poole did a book on composition. I did have *some* things in my head when I got to London, and I *had* heard of Catullus before I heard about modern French poetry. There's a bit of biography that might be rectified.

INTERVIEWER

I have wondered about your literary activities in America before you came to Europe. When did you first come over, by the way?

POUND

In 1898. At the age of twelve. With my great-aunt.

INTERVIEWER

Were you reading French poetry then?

POUND

No, I suppose I was reading Gray's "Elegy in a Country Church-yard" or something. No, I wasn't reading French poetry. I was starting Latin next year.

INTERVIEWER

You entered college at fifteen, I believe?

POUND

I did it to get out of drill at Military Academy.

INTERVIEWER

How did you get started being a poet?

POUND

My grandfather on one side used to correspond with the local bank president in verse. My grandmother on the other side and her brothers used verse back and forth in their letters. It was taken for granted that anyone could write it.

INTERVIEWER

Did you learn anything in your university studies which helped you as a poet? I think you were a student for seven or eight years.

POUND

Only six. Well, six years and four months. I was writing all the time, especially as a graduate student. I started in freshman year studying Layamon's *Brut* and Latin. I got into college on my Latin; it was the only reason they *did* take me in. I did have the idea, at fifteen, of making a general survey. Of course whether I was or wasn't a poet was a matter for the gods to decide, but at least it was up to me to find out what had been done.

INTERVIEWER

You taught for four months only, as I remember. But you know that now the poets in America are mostly teachers. Do you have any ideas on the connection of teaching in the university with writing poetry?

POUND

It is the economic factor. A man's got to get in his rent somehow.

INTERVIEWER

How did you manage all the years in Europe?

POUND

Oh, God. A miracle of God. My income gained from October 1914 to October 1915 was £42.10.0. That figure is clearly engraved on my memory . . .

I was never too good a hand at writing for the magazines. I once did a satirical article for *Vogue*, I think it was. On a painter whom I did not admire. They thought I had got just the right tone and then Verhaeren died and they asked me to do a note on Verhaeren. And I went down and said, You want a nice bright snappy obituary notice of the gloomiest man in Europe.

What, gloomy cuss, was he?

Yes, I said. He wrote about peasants.

Peasants or pheasants?

Peasants.

Oh, I don't think we ought to touch it.

That is the way I crippled my earning capacity by not knowing enough to keep quiet.

I read somewhere—I think you wrote it—that you once tried to write a novel. Did that get anywhere?

It got, fortunately, into the fireplace at Langham Place. I think there were two attempts, before I had any idea whatever of what a novel ought to be.

Did they have anything to do with "Hugh Selwyn Mauberley"?

These were long before "Mauberley." "Mauberley" was later, but it *was* the definite attempt to get the novel cut down to the size of verse. It really is "Contacts and Life." Wadsworth seemed to think "Propertius" difficult because it was about Rome, so one applied the same thing to the contemporary outside.

You said it was Ford who helped you toward a natural language, didn't you? Let's get back to London again.

One was hunting for a simple and natural language, and Ford was ten years older, and accelerated the process toward it. It was a continual discussion of that sort of thing. Ford knew the best of the people who were there before him, you see, and he had nobody to play with until Wyndham and I and my generation came along. He was definitely in opposition to the dialect, let us say, of Lionel Johnson and Oxford.

INTERVIEWER

You were for two or three decades at least in contact with all of the leading writers in English of the day and a lot of the painters, sculptors, and musicians. Of all these people, who were the most stimulating to you as an artist?

POUND

I saw most of Ford and Gaudier, I suppose. I should think that the people that I have written about were the most important to me. There isn't much revision to make there.

I may have limited my work, and limited the interest in it, by concentrating on the particular intelligence of particular people, instead of looking at the complete character and personality of my friends. Wyndham Lewis always claimed that I never *saw* people because I never noticed how wicked they were, what SOBs they were. I wasn't the least interested in the vices of my friends, but in their intelligence.

INTERVIEWER

Was James a kind of a standard for you in London?

POUND

When he died one felt there was no one to ask about anything. Up to then one felt someone knew. After I was sixty-five I had great difficulty in realizing that I was older than James had been when I met him.

INTERVIEWER

Did you know Remy de Gourmont personally? You've mentioned him frequently.

POUND

Only by letter. There was one letter, which Jean de Gourmont also considered important, where he said, "Franchement d'écrire ce qu'on pense, seul plaisir d'un écrivain."

INTERVIEWER

It is amazing that you could come to Europe and quickly associate yourself with the best living writers. Had you been aware of any of the poets writing in America before you left? Was Robinson anything to you?

POUND

Aiken tried to sell me Robinson and I didn't fall. This was in London, too. I then dragged it out of him that there was a guy at Harvard doing funny stuff. Mr. Eliot turned up a year or so later.

No, I should say that about 1900, you had Carman and Hovey, Carwine and Vance Cheney. The impression then was that the American stuff wasn't *quite* as good as the English at any point. And you had Mosher's pirated editions of the English stuff. No, I went to London because I thought Yeats knew more about poetry than anybody else. I made my life in London by going to see Ford in the afternoons and Yeats in the evenings. By mentioning one to the other one could always start a discussion. That was the exercise. I went to study with Yeats and found that Ford disagreed with him. So then I kept on disagreeing with *them* for twenty years.

INTERVIEWER

In 1942 you wrote that you and Eliot disagreed by calling each other Protestants. I wonder when you and Eliot diverged.

POUND

Oh, Eliot and I started diverging from the beginning. The fun of an intellectual friendship is that you diverge on something or other and agree on a few points. Eliot, having had the Christian patience of tolerance all his life and so forth, and working very hard, must have found me very trying. We started disagreeing about a number of things from the time we met. We also agreed on a few things and I suppose both of us must have been right about something or other.

INTERVIEWER

Well, was there a point at which poetically and intellectually you felt further apart than you had been?

POUND

There's the whole problem of the relation of Christianity to Confucianism, and there's the whole problem of the different brands of Christianity. There is the struggle for orthodoxy—Eliot for the Church, me gunning round for particular theologians. In one sense Eliot's curiosity would appear to have been focused on a smaller number of problems. Even that is too much to say. The actual outlook of the experimental generation was all a question of the private ethos.

INTERVIEWER

Do you think that as poets you felt a divergence on technical grounds, unrelated to your subject matter?

POUND

I should think the divergence was first a difference in subject matter. He has undoubtedly got a natural language. In the language in the plays, he seems to me to have made a very great contribution. And in being able to make contact with an extant milieu, and an extant state of comprehension.

INTERVIEWER

That reminds me of the two operas—*Villon* and *Cavalcanti*—that you wrote. How did you come to compose music?

POUND

One wanted the word *and* the tune. One wanted great poetry *sung*, and the technique of the English opera libretto was not satisfactory. One wanted, with the quality of the texts of Villon and of Cavalcanti, to get something more extended than the single lyric. That's all.

INTERVIEWER

I suppose your interest in words to be sung was especially stimulated by your study of Provence. Do you feel that the discovery of Provençal poetry was your greatest breakthrough? Or perhaps the Fenollosa manuscripts?

POUND

The Provençal began with a very early interest, so that it wasn't really a discovery. And the Fenollosa was a windfall and one struggled against one's ignorance. One had the inside knowledge of Fenollosa's notes and the ignorance of a five-year-old child.

INTERVIEWER

How did Mrs. Fenollosa happen to hit upon you?

POUND

Well, I met her at Sarojini Naidu's and she said that Fenollosa had been in opposition to all the profs and academes, and she had seen some of my stuff and said I was the only person who could finish up these notes as Ernest would have wanted them done. Fenollosa saw what needed to be done but he didn't have time to finish it.

INTERVIEWER

Let me change the subject now, and ask you some questions which are more biographical than literary. I have read that you were born in Hailey, Idaho, in 1885. I suppose it must have been pretty rough out there then?

POUND

I left at the age of eighteen months and I don't remember the roughness.

INTERVIEWER

You did not grow up in Hailey?

POUND

I did not grow up in Hailey.

INTERVIEWER

What was your family doing there when you were born?

POUND

Dad opened the Government Land Office out there. I grew up near Philadelphia. The suburbs of Philadelphia.

INTERVIEWER

The wild Indian from the West then was not . . . ?

POUND

The wild Indian from the West is apocryphal, and the assistant assayer of the mint was not one of the most noted bandits of the frontier.

INTERVIEWER

I believe it's true that your grandfather built a railroad. What was the story of that?

POUND

Well, he got the railroad into Chippewa Falls, and they ganged up on him and would not let him buy any rails. That's in *The Cantos*. He went up to the north of New York State and found some rails on an abandoned road up there, bought them and had them shipped out, and then used his credit with the lumberjacks to get the road going to Chippewa Falls. What one learns in the home one learns in a way one doesn't learn in school.

INTERVIEWER

Does your particular interest in coinage start from your father's work at the mint?

POUND

You can go on for a long time on that. The government offices were more informal then, though I don't know that any other kids got in and visited. Now the visitors are taken through glass tunnels and see things from a distance, but you could then be taken around in the smelting room and see the gold piled up in the safe. You were offered a large bag of gold and told you could have it if you could take it away with you. You couldn't lift it.

When the Democrats finally came back in, they recounted all the silver dollars, four million dollars in silver. All the bags had rotted in these enormous vaults, and they were heaving it into the counting machines with shovels bigger than coal shovels. This spectacle of coin being shoveled around like it was litter—these fellows naked to the waist shoveling it around in the gas flares—things like that strike your imagination.

Then there's the whole technique of making metallic money. First, the testing of the silver is much more tricky than testing gold. Gold is simple. It is weighed, then refined and weighed again. You can tell the grade of the ore by the relative weights. But the test for silver is a cloudy solution; the accuracy of the eye in measuring the thickness of the cloud is an aesthetic perception, like the critical sense. I like the idea of the *fineness* of the metal, and it moves by analogy to the habit of testing verbal manifestations. At that time, you see, gold bricks and specimens of iron pyrites mistaken for gold were brought up to Dad's office. You heard the talk about the last guy who brought a gold brick and it turned out to be fool's gold.

INTERVIEWER

I know you consider monetary reform the key to good government. I wonder by what process you moved from aesthetic problems toward governmental ones. Did the Great War, which slaughtered so many of your friends, do the moving?

POUND

The Great War came as a surprise, and certainly to see the English—these people who had never done anything—get hold of themselves, fight it, was immensely impressive. But as soon as it was over they went dead, and then one spent the next twenty years trying to prevent the Second War. I can't say exactly where my study of government started. I think the *New Age* office helped me to see the war not as a separate event but as part of a system, one war after another.

INTERVIEWER

One point of connection between literature and politics which you make in your writing interests me particularly. In the *ABC of Reading* you say that good writers are those who keep the language efficient, and that this is their function. You disassociate this function from party. Can a man of the wrong party use language efficiently?

POUND

Yes. That's the whole trouble! A gun is just as good, no matter who shoots it.

INTERVIEWER

Can an instrument which is orderly be used to create disorder? Suppose good language is used to forward bad government? Doesn't bad government make bad language?

POUND

Yes, but bad language is bound to make in addition bad government, whereas good language is *not* bound to make bad government. That again is clear Confucius: if the orders aren't clear they can't be carried out. Lloyd George's laws were such a mess, the lawyers never knew what they meant. And Talleyrand proclaimed that they changed the meaning of words between one conference and another. The means of communication breaks down, and that of course is what we are suffering now. We are enduring the drive to work on the subconscious without appealing to the reason. They repeat a trade name with the music a few times, and then repeat the music without it so that the music will give you the name. I think of the *assault*. We suffer from the use of language to conceal thought and to withhold all vital and direct answers. There is the definite use of propaganda, forensic language, merely to conceal and mislead.

INTERVIEWER

Where do ignorance and innocence end and the chicanery begin?

POUND

There is natural ignorance and there is artificial ignorance. I should say at the present moment the artificial ignorance is about eighty-five percent.

INTERVIEWER

What kind of action can you hope to take?

POUND

The only chance for victory over the brainwash is the right of every man to have his ideas judged one at a time. You never get clarity as long as you have these package words, as long as a word is used by twenty-five people in twenty-five different ways. That seems to me to be the first fight, if there is going to be any intellect left.

It is doubtful whether the individual soul is going to be allowed to survive at all. Now you get a Buddhist movement with everything *except* Confucius taken into it. An Indian Circe of negation and dissolution.

We are up against so many mysteries. There is the problem of benevolence, the point at which benevolence has ceased to be operative. Eliot says that they spend their time trying to imagine systems so perfect that nobody will have to be good. A lot of questions asked in that essay of Eliot's cannot be dodged, like the question of whether there need be any change from the Dantesque scale of values or the Chaucerian scale of values. If so, how much? People who have lost reverence have lost a great deal. That was where I split with Tiffany Thayer. All these large words fall into clichés.

There is the mystery of the scattering, the fact that the people who presumably understand each other are geographically scattered. A man who fits in his milieu as Frost does, he is to be considered a happy man.

Oh, the luck of a man like Mavrocordato, who is in touch with other scholars, so that there is somewhere where he can verify a point! Now for certain points where I want verification there is a fellow named Dazzi in Venice that I write to and he comes up with an answer, as it might be about the forged Donation of Constantine. But the advantages which were supposed to inhere in the university—where there are other people to *contrôl* opinion or to *contrôl* the data*—were very great. It is crippling not to have had them. Of course I have been trying over a ten-year period to get any member of an American faculty to mention any other member of his same faculty, in his own department or outside it, whose intelligence he respects or with whom he will discuss serious matters. In one case the gentleman regretted that someone else had *left* the faculty.

I have been unable to get straight answers out of people on what appeared to me to be vital questions. That may have been due to my violence or the obscurity with which I framed the questions. Often, I think, so-called obscurity is not obscurity in the language but in the other person's not being able to make out *why* you are saying a thing. For instance the attack on *Endymion* was complicated because Gifford and company couldn't see why the deuce Keats was doing it.

Another struggle has been the struggle to keep the value of a local and particular character, of a particular culture in this awful mael-

---

* Pound indicates that he is using the French *contrôler*, "to verify, check information, a fact."

strom, this awful avalanche toward uniformity. The whole fight is for the conservation of the individual soul. The enemy is the suppression of history; against us is the bewildering propaganda and brainwash, luxury and violence. Sixty years ago, poetry was the poor man's art: a man off on the edge of the wilderness, or Frémont, going off with a Greek text in his pocket. A man who wanted the best could have it on a lonely farm. Then there was the cinema, and now television.

INTERVIEWER

The political action of yours that everybody remembers are your broadcasts from Italy during the war. When you gave these talks, were you conscious of breaking the American law?

POUND

No, I was completely surprised. You see, I had that promise. I was given the freedom of the microphone twice a week. "He will not be asked to say anything contrary to his conscience or contrary to his duty as an American citizen." I thought that covered it.

INTERVIEWER

Doesn't the law of treason talk about "giving aid and comfort to the enemy," and isn't the enemy the country with whom we are at war?

POUND

I thought I was fighting for a constitutional point. I mean to say, I may have been completely nuts, but I certainly *felt* that it wasn't committing treason.

Wodehouse went on the air and the British asked him not to. Nobody asked me not to. There was no announcement until the collapse that the people who had spoken on the radio would be prosecuted.

Having worked for years to prevent war, and seeing the folly of Italy and America being at war—! I certainly wasn't telling the troops to revolt. I thought I was fighting an internal question of constitutional government. And if any man, any individual man, can say he has had a bad deal from me because of race, creed, or color, let him come out and state it with particulars. The *Guide to Kulchur* was dedicated to Basil Bunting and Louis Zukofsky, a Quaker and a Jew.

I don't know whether you think the Russians ought to be in Berlin or not. I don't know whether I was doing any good or not, whether I was doing any harm. Oh, I was probably offside. But the ruling in Boston was that there is no treason without treasonable intention.

What I was right about was the conservation of individual rights. If, when the executive or any other branch exceeds its legitimate powers, no one protests, you will lose all your liberties. My method of opposing tyranny was wrong over a thirty-year period; it had nothing to do with the Second World War in particular. If the individual, or heretic, gets hold of some essential truth, or sees some error in the system being practiced, he commits so many marginal errors himself that he is worn out before he can establish his point.

The world in twenty years has piled up hysteria—anxiety over a third war, bureaucratic tyranny, and hysteria from paper forms. The immense and undeniable loss of freedoms, as they were in 1900, is undeniable. We have seen the acceleration in efficiency of the tyrannizing factors. It's enough to keep a man worried. Wars are made to make debt. I suppose there's a possible out in space satellites and other ways of making debt.

INTERVIEWER

When you were arrested by the Americans, did you then expect to be convicted? To be hanged?

POUND

At first I puzzled over having missed a cog somewhere. I expected to turn myself in and to be asked about what I learned. I did and I wasn't. I know that I checked myself, on several occasions during the broadcasts, on reflecting that it was not up to me to do certain things, or to take service with a foreign country. Oh, it was paranoia to think one could argue against the usurpations, against the folks who got the war started to get America into it. Yet I hate the idea of obedience to something which is wrong.

Then later I was driven into the courtyard at Chiavari. They had been shooting them, and I thought I was finished then and there. Then finally a guy came in and said he was damned if he would hand me over to the Americans unless I wanted to be handed over to them.

INTERVIEWER

In 1942, when the war started for America, I understand you tried to leave Italy and come back to the United States. What were the circumstances of the refusal?

POUND

Those circumstances were by hearsay. I am a bit hazy in my head about a considerable period, and I think that . . . I know that I had a chance to get as far as Lisbon, and be cooped up there for the rest of the war.

INTERVIEWER

Why did you want to get back to the States at that time?

POUND

I wanted to get back during the election, before the election.

INTERVIEWER

The election was in 1940, wasn't it?

POUND

That would be 1940. I don't honestly remember what happened. My parents were too old to travel. They would have had to stay there in Rapallo. Dad retired there on his pension.

INTERVIEWER

During those years in the war in Italy did you write poetry? The *Pisan Cantos* were written when you were interned. What did you write during those years?

POUND

Arguments, arguments, and arguments. Oh, I did some of the Confucius translation.

INTERVIEWER

How was it that you began to write poetry again only after you were interned? You didn't write any Cantos at all during the war, did you?

POUND

Let's see—the Adams stuff came out just before the war shut off. No. There was *Oro e Lavoro*. I was writing economic stuff in Italian.

INTERVIEWER

Since your internment, you've published three collections of Cantos—*Thrones* just recently. You must be near the end. Can you say what you are going to do in the remaining Cantos?

POUND

It is difficult to write a paradiso when all the superficial indications are that you ought to write an apocalypse. It is obviously much easier to find inhabitants for an inferno or even a purgatorio. I am trying to collect the record of the top flights of the mind. I might have done better to put Agassiz on top instead of Confucius.

INTERVIEWER

Are you more or less stuck?

POUND

Okay, I am stuck. The question is, am I dead, as Messrs. A, B, C, might wish? In case I conk out, this is provisionally what I have to do: I must clarify obscurities; I must make clearer definite ideas or dissociations. I must find a verbal formula to combat the rise of brutality—the principle of order versus the split atom. There was a man in the bughouse, by the way, who insisted that the atom had never been split.

An epic is a poem containing history. The modern mind contains heteroclite elements. The past epos has succeeded when all or a great many of the answers were assumed, at least between author and audience, or a great mass of audience. The attempt in an experimental age is therefore rash. Do you know the story:

> What are you drawing, Johnny?
> God.
> But nobody knows what He looks like.
> They will when I get through!
> That confidence is no longer obtainable.

There *are* epic subjects. The struggle for individual rights is an epic subject, consecutive from jury trial in Athens, to Anselm versus William Rufus, to the murder of Becket and to Coke and through John Adams.

Then the struggle appears to come up against a block. The nature of sovereignty is epic matter, though it may be a bit obscured by circumstance. Some of this *can* be traced, pointed; obviously it has to be condensed to get into the form. The nature of the individual, the heteroclite contents of contemporary consciousness. It's the fight for light versus subconsciousness; it demands obscurities and penumbras. A lot of contemporary writing avoids inconvenient areas of the subject.

I am writing to resist the view that Europe and civilization are going to Hell. If I am being "crucified for an idea"—that is, the coherent idea around which my muddles accumulated—it is probably the idea that European culture ought to survive, that the best qualities of it ought to survive along with whatever other cultures, in whatever universality. Against the propaganda of terror and the propaganda of luxury, have you a nice simple answer? One has worked on certain materials trying to establish bases and axes of reference. In writing so as to be understood, there is always the problem of rectification without giving up what is correct. There is the struggle not to sign on the dotted line for the opposition.

INTERVIEWER

Do the separate sections of *The Cantos*, now—the last three sections have appeared under separate names—mean that you are attacking particular problems in particular sections?

POUND

No. *Rock Drill* was intended to imply the necessary resistance in getting a certain main thesis across—hammering. I was not following the three divisions of the *Divine Comedy* exactly. One can't follow the Dantesque cosmos in an age of experiment. But I have made the division between people dominated by emotion, people struggling upwards, and those who have some part of the divine vision. The thrones in Dante's *Paradiso* are for the spirits of the people who have been responsible for good government. The thrones in *The Cantos* are an attempt to move out from egoism and to establish some definition of an order possible or at any rate conceivable on earth. One is held up by the low percentage of reason which seems to operate in human affairs. *Thrones* concerns the states of mind of people responsible for something more than their personal conduct.

INTERVIEWER

Now that you come near the end, have you made any plans for revising *The Cantos*, after you've finished?

POUND

I don't know. There's need of elaboration, of clarification, but I don't know that a comprehensive revision is in order. There is no doubt that the writing is too obscure as it stands, but I hope that the order of ascension in the *Paradiso* will be toward a greater limpidity. Of course there ought to be a corrected edition because of errors that have crept in.

INTERVIEWER

Let me change the subject again, if I may. In all those years in St. Elizabeths, did you get a sense of contemporary America from your visitors?

POUND

The trouble with visitors is that you don't get enough of the opposition. I suffer from the cumulative isolation of not having had enough contact—fifteen years living more with ideas than with persons.

INTERVIEWER

Do you have any plans for going back to the States? Do you want to?

POUND

I undoubtedly want to. But whether it is nostalgia for an America that isn't there any more or not I don't know. This is a difference between an abstract Adams–Jefferson, Adams–Jackson America, and whatever is really going on. I undoubtedly have moments when I should like very much to live in America. There are these concrete difficulties against the general desire. Richmond is a beautiful city, but you can't live in it unless you drive an automobile. I'd like at least to spend a month or two a year in the U.S.

INTERVIEWER

You said the other day that as you grew older you felt more American all the time. How does this work?

POUND

It works. Exotics were necessary as an attempt at a foundation. One is transplanted and grows, and one is pulled up and taken back to what one has been transplanted from and it is no longer there. The contacts aren't there and I suppose one reverts to one's organic nature and finds it merciful. Have you ever read Andy White's memoirs? He's the fellow who founded Cornell University. That was the period of euphoria, when everybody thought that all the good things in America were going to function, before the decline, about 1900. White covers a period of history that goes back to Buchanan on one side. He alternated between being ambassador to Russia and head of Cornell.

INTERVIEWER

Your return to Italy has been a disappointment, then?

POUND

Undoubtedly. Europe was a shock. The shock of no longer feeling oneself in the center of something is probably part of it. Then there is the incomprehension, Europe's incomprehension, of organic America. There are so many things which I, as an American, cannot say to a European with any hope of being understood. Somebody said that I am the last American living the tragedy of Europe.

NOTE: Mr. Pound's health made it impossible for him to finish proofreading this interview. The text is complete, but may contain details which Mr. Pound would have changed under happier circumstances.

Issue 28, 1962

Jack Kerouac

The Art of Fiction

T he Kerouacs have no telephone. Ted Berrigan had contacted
Jack Kerouac some months earlier and had persuaded him to do
the interview. When he felt the time had come for their meeting to take
place Berrigan simply showed up at the Kerouacs' house. Two friends,
the poets Aram Saroyan and Duncan McNaughton, accompanied
him. Kerouac answered the door, and Berrigan quickly told him his
name and the visit's purpose. Kerouac welcomed the poets, but before
he could show them in, his wife, a very determined woman, seized
him from behind and told the group to leave at once.

"Jack and I began talking simultaneously, saying '*Paris Review*!,'
'Interview!,' etcetera," Berrigan recalls, "while Duncan and Aram began to slink back toward the car. All seemed lost, but I kept talking in
what I hoped was a civilized, reasonable, calming, and friendly tone
of voice, and soon Mrs. Kerouac agreed to let us in for twenty minutes, on the condition that there be no drinking.

"Once inside, as it became evident that we actually were in pursuit of
a serious purpose, Mrs. Kerouac became more friendly, and we were
able to commence the interview. It seems that people still show up constantly at the Kerouacs' looking for the author of *On the Road* and stay
for days, drinking all the liquor and diverting Jack from his serious occupations. As the evening progressed the atmosphere changed considerably, and Mrs. Kerouac, Stella, proved a gracious and charming
hostess.

Denver to... Denver + everybody / then on to the West Coast to get / a ship and make enough money / to support myself in my aunt's / house while I finished school.

II

In the month of July, 1947, having saved about fifty dollars from old veteran benefits I got ready to go to ~~the West Coast~~ ~~Remi Boncoeur had~~ ~~San Francisco saying I should~~ ~~come out there and ship out with him on an around-the-world liner. He~~ ~~swore he could get me in the engine room. I wrote back and said I'd be~~ ~~satisfied with any old freighter so long as I could take a few long Pa-~~ ~~cific trips and come back with enough money to support myself in my~~ ~~aunt's house while I finished school. He said he had a shack in Eldino~~ ~~and I would have all the time in the world to study there while we went~~ ~~through the rigmarole of getting the ship. He was living with a girl~~ ~~called LeeAnne, he said she was a marvelous cook and everything would~~ ~~jump. Remi was an old high school friend, a Frenchman brought up in~~ ~~Paris but born in New Jersey and a really mad guy---I never knew how~~ ~~and so mad at this time.~~ ... In innocence of how much I'd get involved on *I had big day dreams of joy over roadmaps and letters.* the road. My aunt was all in accord with my trip to the West, she said it would do me good, I'd been working so hard all winter and staying in too much; she even didn't ~~tsk-tsk~~ when I told her I'd hitch hike ⊙ ~~~~ . All she wanted was for me to come back in one piece. So leaving my books on top of the desk, and folding back my comfortable home sheets for the last time one morning, I left with my canvas bag in which a few fundamental things were packed, left a note to my aunt, who was at work, and took off for the ~~~~ *West Coast and China* ~~~~ with fifty dollars in my pocket.

What a hangup! ~~I got into this~~ ~~on wheels~~ As I look back on it, it's in-credible that I could have been so ~~simply~~ *Here I was* dumb. I'd been poring over maps of the United States ~~in Paterson~~ for months, even reading books about the pioneers and savoring names like Platte and Cimarron ~~~~ and on the roadmap was one long red line called Route 6 that led from the tip of Cape Cod clear to Ely, Nevada, *where it* dipped down to Los Angeles. "I'll just stay on route six all the way to Ely," I said to myself and confidently started. To get to route six I had to go up to Bear Mountain New York. Filled with dreams of what I'd do in Chicago, in Denver, and then finally in San Fran across the be-swelled bushy night to the west, I took the 7th avenue subway to the end of the line, ~~~~

A manuscript page from *On the Road* by Jack Kerouac.

"The most amazing thing about Jack Kerouac is his magic voice, which sounds exactly like his works. It is capable of the most astounding and disconcerting changes in no time flat. It dictates everything, including this interview.

"After the interview, Kerouac, who had been sitting throughout the interview in a President Kennedy–type rocker, moved over to a big poppa chair and said, 'So you boys are poets, hey? Well, let's hear some of your poetry.' We stayed for about an hour longer, and Aram and I read some of our things. Finally, he gave each of us a signed broadside of a recent poem of his, and we left."

—*Ted Berrigan, 1968*

INTERVIEWER

Could we put the footstool over here to put this on?

STELLA

Yes.

JACK KEROUAC

God, you're so inadequate there, Berrigan.

INTERVIEWER

Well, I'm no tape-recorder man, Jack. I'm just a big talker, like you. OK, we're off.

KEROUAC

OK? [*Whistles.*] OK?

INTERVIEWER

Actually I'd like to start . . . The first book I ever read by you, oddly enough, since most people first read *On the Road* . . . the first one I read was *The Town and the City* . . .

KEROUAC

Gee!

INTERVIEWER

I checked it out of the library . . .

KEROUAC

Gee! Did you read *Doctor Sax*? *Tristessa*?

INTERVIEWER

You better believe it. I even read *Rimbaud*. I have a copy of *Visions of Cody* that Ron Padgett bought in Tulsa, Oklahoma.

KEROUAC

Screw Ron Padgett! You know why? He started a little magazine called *White Dove Review*—in Kansas City, was it? Tulsa? Oklahoma . . . yes. He wrote, "Start our magazine off by sending us a great big poem." So I sent him "The Thrashing Doves." And then I sent him another one and he rejected the second one because his magazine was already started. That's to show you how punks try to make their way by scratching down on a man's back. Aw, he's no poet. You know who's a great poet? I know who the great poets are.

INTERVIEWER

Who?

KEROUAC

Let's see, is it . . . William Bissett of Vancouver. An Indian boy. Bill Bissett, or Bissonnette.

SAROYAN

Let's talk about Jack Kerouac.

KEROUAC

He's not better than Bill Bissett, but he's very original.

INTERVIEWER

Why don't we begin with editors. How do you . . .

KEROUAC

OK. All my editors since Malcolm Cowley have had instructions
to leave my prose exactly as I wrote it. In the days of Malcolm Cowley, with *On the Road* and *The Dharma Bums*, I had no power to
stand by my style for better or for worse. When Malcolm Cowley
made endless revisions and inserted thousands of needless commas
like, say, "Cheyenne, Wyoming" (why not just say "Cheyenne Wyoming" and let it go at that, for instance). Why, I spent five hundred
dollars making the complete restitution of the *Bums* manuscript and
got a bill from Viking Press called "Revisions." Ha ho ho. And so
you asked about how do I work with an editor . . . well nowadays I
am just grateful to him for his assistance in proofreading the manuscript and in discovering logical errors, such as dates, names of
places. For instance, in my last book I wrote "Firth of Forth," then
looked it up on the suggestion of my editor and found that I'd really
sailed off the Firth of Clyde. Things like that. Or I spelled Aleister
Crowley "Alisteir," or he discovered little mistakes about the yard-
age in football games and so forth. By not revising what you've already written you simply give the reader the actual workings of your
mind during the writing itself—you confess your thoughts about
events in your own unchangeable way . . . Well, look, did you ever
hear a guy telling a long wild tale to a bunch of men in a bar and all
are listening and smiling, did you ever hear that guy stop to revise
himself, go back to a previous sentence to improve it, to defray its
rhythmic thought impact? . . . If he pauses to blow his nose, isn't
he planning his next sentence? And when he lets that next sentence
loose, isn't it once and for all the way he wanted to say it? Doesn't he
depart from the thought of that sentence and, as Shakespeare says,
"forever holds his tongue" on the subject, since he's passed over it

like a part of a river that flows over a rock once and for all and never returns and can never flow any other way in time? Incidentally, as for my bug against periods, that was for the prose in *October in the Railroad Earth*—very experimental, intended to clack along all the way like a steam engine pulling a one-hundred-car freight with a talky caboose at the end. That was my way at the time and it still can be done if the thinking during the swift writing is confessional and pure and all excited with the life of it. And be sure of this, I spent my entire youth writing slowly with revisions and endless rehashing speculation and deleting and got so I was writing one sentence a day and the sentence had no feeling. Goddamn it, feeling is what I like in art, not craftiness and the hiding of feelings.

INTERVIEWER

What encouraged you to use the "spontaneous" style of *On the Road*?

KEROUAC

I got the idea for the spontaneous style of *On the Road* from seeing how good old Neal Cassady wrote his letters to me—all first person, fast, mad, confessional, completely serious, all detailed—with real names in his case, however, being letters. I remembered also Goethe's admonition—well, Goethe's prophecy—that the future literature of the West would be confessional in nature. Also Dostoyevsky prophesied as much and might have started in on that if he'd lived long enough to do his projected masterwork, *The Life of a Great Sinner*. Cassady also began his early youthful writing with attempts at slow, painstaking, and all-that-crap craft business, but got sick of it like I did, seeing it wasn't getting out his guts and heart the way it *felt* coming out. But I got the flash from his style. It's a cruel lie for those West Coast punks to say that I got the idea of *On the Road* from him. All his letters to me were about his younger days before I met him, a child with his father, etcetera, and about his later teenage experiences. The letter he sent me is erroneously reported to be a thirteen-thousand-word letter . . . no, the thirteen-thousand-word piece was his novel

The First Third, which he kept in his possession. The letter, the main letter I mean, was forty thousand words long, mind you, a whole short novel. It was the greatest piece of writing I ever saw, better'n anybody in America, or at least enough to make Melville, Twain, Dreiser, Wolfe, I dunno who, spin in their graves. Allen Ginsberg asked me to lend him this vast letter so he could read it. He read it, then loaned it to a guy called Gerd Stern who lived on a houseboat in Sausalito, California, in 1955, and this fellow lost the letter: overboard I presume. Neal and I called it, for convenience, the Joan Anderson Letter . . . all about a Christmas weekend in the pool halls, hotel rooms, and jails of Denver, with hilarious events throughout and tragic, too, even a drawing of a window, with measurements to make the reader understand, all that. Now listen: this letter would have been printed under Neal's copyright, if we could find it, but as you know, it was my property as a letter to me, so Allen shouldn't have been so careless with it, nor the guy on the houseboat. If we can unearth this entire forty-thousand-word letter Neal shall be justified. We also did so much fast talking between the two of us, on tape recorders, way back in 1952, and listened to them so much, we both got the secret of LINGO in telling a tale and figured that was the only way to express the speed and tension and ecstatic tomfoolery of the age . . . Is that enough?

How do you think this style has changed since *On the Road*?

What style? Oh, the style of *On the Road*. Well as I say, Cowley riddled the original style of the manuscript there, without my power to complain, and since then my books are all published as written, as I say, and the style has varied from the highly experimental speed-writing of *Railroad Earth* to the ingrown-toenail-packed mystical style of *Tristessa*, the *Notes from Underground* (by Dostoyevsky) confessional madness of *The Subterraneans*, the perfection of the three as one in *Big Sur*, I'd say, which tells a plain tale in a smooth buttery

literate run, to *Satori in Paris*, which is really the first book I wrote
with drink at my side (cognac and malt liquor) . . . and not to over-
look *Book of Dreams*, the style of a person half-awake from sleep and
ripping it out in pencil by the bed . . . yes, pencil . . . what a job!
Bleary eyes, insane mind bemused and mystified by sleep, details
that pop out even as you write them you don't know what they mean,
till you wake up, have coffee, look at it, and see the logic of dreams in
dream language itself, see? . . . And finally I decided in my tired
middle age to slow down and did *Vanity of Duluoz* in a more moderate
style so that, having been so esoteric all these years, some earlier
readers would come back and see what ten years had done to my life
and thinking . . . which is after all the only thing I've got to offer, the
true story of what I saw and how I saw it.

INTERVIEWER

You dictated sections of *Visions of Cody*. Have you used this
method since?

KEROUAC

I didn't dictate sections of *Visions of Cody*. I typed up a segment
of taped conversation with Neal Cassady, or Cody, talking about his
early adventures in LA. It's four chapters. I haven't used this method
since; it really doesn't come out right, well, with Neal and with myself, when all written down and with all the *ahs* and the *ohs* and the
ahums and the fearful fact that the damn thing is turning and you're
forced not to waste electricity or tape . . . Then again, I don't know,
I might have to resort to that eventually; I'm getting tired and going
blind. This question stumps me. At any rate, everybody's doing it,
I hear, but I'm still scribbling. McLuhan says we're getting more oral
so I guess we'll all learn to talk into the machine better and better.

INTERVIEWER

What is that state of "Yeatsian semi-trance" which provides the
ideal atmosphere for spontaneous writing?

KEROUAC

Well, there it is, how can you be in a trance with your mouth yapping away . . . writing at least is a silent meditation even though you're going a hundred miles an hour. Remember that scene in *La Dolce Vita* where the old priest is mad because a mob of maniacs has shown up to see the tree where the kids saw the Virgin Mary? He says, "Visions are not available in all this frenetic foolishness and yelling and pushing; visions are only obtainable in silence and meditation." Thar. Yup.

INTERVIEWER

You have said that haiku is not written spontaneously but is reworked and revised. Is this true of all your poetry? Why must the method for writing poetry differ from that of prose?

KEROUAC

No, first—haiku is *best* reworked and revised. I know, I tried. It has to be completely economical—no foliage and flowers and language rhythm—it has to be a simple little picture in three little lines. At least that's the way the old masters did it, spending months on three little lines and coming up, say, with:

In the abandoned boat,
The hail
Bounces about.

That's Shiki. But as for my regular English verse, I knocked it off fast like the prose, using, get this, the size of the notebook page for the form and length of the poem, just as a musician has to get out, a jazz musician, his statement within a certain number of bars, within one chorus, which spills over into the next, but he has to stop where the chorus page *stops*. And finally, too, in poetry you can be completely free to say anything you want, you don't have to tell a story, you can use secret puns, that's why I always say, when writing prose, "No time for poetry now, get your plain tale." [*Drinks are served.*]

How do you write haiku?

Haiku? You want to hear haiku? You see you got to compress into three short lines a great big story. First you start with a haiku situation—so you see a leaf, as I told her the other night, falling on the back of a sparrow during a great big October wind storm. A big leaf falls on the back of a little sparrow. How you going to compress that into three lines? Now in Japanese you got to compress it into seventeen syllables. We don't have to do that in American—or English—because we don't have the same syllabic bullshit that your Japanese language has. So you say: "Little sparrow"—you don't have to say *little*—everybody knows a sparrow is little because they fall so you say:

Sparrow
with big leaf on its back—
windstorm

No good, don't work, I reject it.

A little sparrow
when an autumn leaf suddenly sticks to its back
from the wind.

Hah, that does it. No, it's a little bit too long. See? It's already a little bit too long, Berrigan, you know what I mean?

Seems like there's an extra word or something, like *when*. How about leaving out *when*? Say:

A sparrow
an autumn leaf suddenly sticks to its back—
from the wind!

KEROUAC

Hey, that's all right. I think *when* was the extra word. You got the right idea there, O'Hara! "A sparrow, an autumn leaf suddenly"—we don't have to say *suddenly* do we?

A sparrow
an autumn leaf sticks to its back—
from the wind!

[*Kerouac writes final version into a spiral notebook.*]

INTERVIEWER

Suddenly is absolutely the kind of word we don't need there. When you publish that will you give me a footnote saying you asked me a couple of questions?

KEROUAC

[*writes*] Berrigan noticed. Right?

INTERVIEWER

Do you write poetry very much? Do you write other poetry besides haiku?

KEROUAC

It's hard to write haiku. I write long silly Indian poems. You want to hear my long silly Indian poem?

INTERVIEWER

What kind of Indian?

KEROUAC

Iroquois. As you know from looking at me. [*Reads from notebook.*]

On the lawn on the way to the store
forty-four years old for the neighbors to hear
hey, looka, Ma I hurt myself. Especially
with that squirt.

What's that mean?

INTERVIEWER

Say it again.

KEROUAC

Hey, looka, Ma, I hurt myself, while on the way to the store I hurt
myself I fell on the lawn I yell to my mother hey looka, Ma, I hurt myself. I add, especially with that squirt.

INTERVIEWER

You fell over a sprinkler?

KEROUAC

No, my father's squirt into my Ma.

INTERVIEWER

From that distance?

KEROUAC

Oh, I quit. No, I know you wouldn't get that one. I had to explain
it. [Opens notebook again and reads.]

Goy means joy.

INTERVIEWER

Send that one to Ginsberg.

KEROUAC
[Reads.]

Happy people so called are hypocrites—it means
the happiness wavelength can't work without
necessary deceit, without certain scheming and lies and
hiding. Hypocrisy and deceit, no Indians. No smiling.

INTERVIEWER
No Indians?

KEROUAC
The reason you really have a hidden hostility towards me, Berrigan, is because of the French and Indian War.

INTERVIEWER
That could be.

SAROYAN
I saw a football picture of you in the cellar of Horace Mann. You
were pretty fat in those days.

STELLA
Tuffy! Here Tuffy! Come on, kitty . . .

KEROUAC
Stella, let's have another bottle or two. Yeah, I'm going to murder everybody if they let me go. I did. Hot fudge sundaes! Boom! I
used to have two or three hot fudge sundaes before every game.
Lou Little . . .

INTERVIEWER
He was your coach at Columbia?

KEROUAC

Lou Little was my coach at Columbia. My father went up to him and said, "You sneaky long-nosed finagler . . ." He says, "Why don't you let my son, Ti Jean, Jack, start in the Army game so he can get back at his great enemy from Lowell?" And Lou Little says, "Because he's not ready." "Who says he's not ready?" "I say he's not ready." My father says, "Why you long nose banana nose big crook, get out of my sight!" And he comes stomping out of the office smoking a big cigar. "Come out of here Jack, let's get out of here." So we left Columbia together. And also when I was in the United States Navy during the war—1942—right in front of the admirals, he walked in and says, "Jack, you are right! The Germans should not be our enemies. They should be our allies, as it will be proven in time." And the admirals were all there with their mouths open, and my father would take no shit from nobody—my father didn't have nothing but a big belly about this big [gestures with arms out in front of him] and he would go *poom*! [Kerouac gets up and demonstrates, by puffing his belly out in front of him with explosive force and saying "poom!"] One time he was walking down the street with my mother, arm in arm, down the Lower East Side. In the old days, you know, the 1940s. And here comes a whole bunch of rabbis walking arm in arm . . . tee-dah tee-dah tee-dah . . . and they wouldn't part for this Christian man and his wife. So my father went *poom*! And he knocked a rabbi right in the gutter. Then he took my mother and walked on through.

Now, if you don't like that, Berrigan, that's the history of my family. They don't take no shit from nobody. In due time I ain't going to take no shit from nobody. You can record that. Is this my wine?

INTERVIEWER

Was *The Town and the City* written under spontaneous composition principles?

KEROUAC

Some of it, sire. I also wrote another version that's hidden under the floorboards, with Burroughs.

INTERVIEWER

Yes, I've heard rumors of that book. Everybody wants to get at that book.

KEROUAC

It's called *And the Hippos Were Boiled in Their Tanks.* The hippos. Because Burroughs and I were sitting in a bar one night and we heard a newscaster saying ". . . and so the Egyptians attacked blah blah . . . and meanwhile there was a great fire in the zoo in London and the fire raced across the fields and the hippos were boiled in their tanks! Goodnight everyone!" That's Bill, he noticed that. Because he notices them kind of things.

INTERVIEWER

You really did type up his *Naked Lunch* manuscript for him in Tangier?

KEROUAC

No . . . the first part. The first two chapters. I went to bed, and I had nightmares . . . of great long bolognas coming out of my mouth. I had nightmares typing up that manuscript . . . I said, "Bill!" He said, "Keep typing it." He said, "I bought you a goddamn kerosene stove here in North Africa, you know." Among the Arabs . . . it's hard to get a kerosene stove. I'd light up the kerosene stove, and take some bedding and a little pot, or kef as we called it there . . . or maybe sometimes hashish . . . there, by the way, it's legal . . . and I'd go toke toke toke toke and when I went to bed at night these things kept coming out of my mouth. So finally these other guys showed up like Alan Ansen and Allen Ginsberg, and they spoiled the whole manuscript because they didn't type it up the way he wrote it.

INTERVIEWER

Grove Press has been issuing his Olympia Press books with lots of changes and things added.

KEROUAC

Well, in my opinion Burroughs hasn't given us anything that would interest our breaking hearts since he wrote like he did in *Naked Lunch*. Now all he does is that "breakup" stuff . . . where you write a page of prose, you write another page of prose . . . then you fold it over and you cut it up and you put it together . . . and shit like that . . .

INTERVIEWER

What about *Junky*, though?

KEROUAC

It's a classic. It's better than Hemingway—it's just like Hemingway but even a little better, too. It says: "Danny comes into my pad one night and says, 'Hey, Bill, can I borrow your sap.'" Your sap—do you know what a sap is?

SAROYAN

A blackjack?

KEROUAC

It's a blackjack. Bill says, "I pulled out my underneath drawer, and underneath some nice shirts I pulled out my blackjack. I gave it to Danny and said, 'Now don't lose it, Danny'—Danny says, 'Don't worry I won't lose it.' He goes off and loses it."
Sap . . . blackjack . . . that's me. Sap . . . blackjack.

INTERVIEWER

That's a haiku: Sap, blackjack, that's me. You better write that down.

KEROUAC

No.

INTERVIEWER

Maybe I'll write that down. Do you mind if I use that one?

KEROUAC

Up your ass with Mobil gas!

INTERVIEWER

You don't believe in collaborations? Have you ever done any collaborations, other than with publishers?

KEROUAC

I did a couple of collaborations in bed with Bill Cannastra in lofts. With blondes.

INTERVIEWER

Was he the guy that tried to climb off the subway train at Astor Place, in Holmes's *Go*?

KEROUAC

Yes. Yeah, well he says, "Let's take all our clothes off and run around the block" . . . It was raining you know. Sixteenth Street off Seventh Avenue. I said, "Well, I'll keep my shorts on"—he says, "No, no shorts." I said, "I'm going to keep my shorts on." He said, "All right, but I'm not going to wear mine." And we trot-trot-trot-trot down the block. Sixteenth to Seventeenth . . . and we come back and run up the stairs—nobody saw us.

INTERVIEWER

What time of day?

KEROUAC

But he was absolutely naked . . . about three or four A.M. It rained. And everybody was there. He was dancing on broken glass and playing Bach. Bill was the guy who used to teeter off his roof—six flights up, you know? He'd go, "You want me to fall?" We'd say, "No, Bill, no." He was an Italian. Italians are wild, you know.

INTERVIEWER

Did he write? What did he do?

KEROUAC

He says, "Jack, come with me and look down through this peep-hole." We looked down through the peephole, we saw a lot of things . . . into his toilet.

I said, "I'm not interested in that, Bill." He said, "You're not interested in anything." Auden would come the next day, the next afternoon, for cocktails. Maybe with Chester Kallman. Tennessee Williams.

INTERVIEWER

Was Neal Cassady around in those days? Did you already know Neal Cassady when you were involved with Bill Cannastra?

KEROUAC

Oh yes, yes, ahem . . . he had a great big pack of pot. He always was a pot-happy man.

INTERVIEWER

Why do you think Neal doesn't write?

KEROUAC

He has written . . . beautifully! He has written better than I have. Neal's a very funny guy. He's a real Californian. We had more fun than five thousand Socony Gasoline Station attendants can have. In my opinion he's the most intelligent man I've ever met in my life. Neal Cassady. He's a Jesuit by the way. He used to sing in the choir. He was a choirboy in the Catholic churches of Denver. And he taught me everything that I now do believe about anything that there may be to be believed about divinity.

INTERVIEWER

About Edgar Cayce?

KEROUAC

No, before he found out about Edgar Cayce he told me all these things in the section of the life he led when he was on the road with me—he said, "We know God, don't we Jack?" I said, "Yessir boy." He said, "Don't we know that nothing's going to happen wrong?" "Yessir." "And we're going to go on and on . . . and hmmmmm ja-bmmmmmmmm . . ." He was perfect. And he's always perfect. Every time he comes to see me I can't get a word in edgewise.

INTERVIEWER

You wrote about Neal playing football in *Visions of Cody*.

KEROUAC

Yes, he was a very good football player. He picked up two beatniks that time in blue jeans in North Beach, Frisco. He said, "I got to go, bang bang, do I got to go?" He's working on the railroad . . . had his watch out . . . "Two-fifteen, boy I got to be there by two-twenty. I tell you boys drive me over down there so I be on time with my train . . . So I can get my train on down to"—what's the name of that place— San Jose? They say, "Sure kid" and Neal says, "Here's the pot." So— "We maybe look like great beatniks with great beards . . . but we are cops. And we are arresting you."

So, a guy went to the jailhouse and interviewed him from the *New York Post* and he said, "Tell that Kerouac if he still believes in me to send me a typewriter." So I sent Allen Ginsberg one hundred dollars to get a typewriter for Neal. And Neal got the typewriter. And he wrote notes on it, but they wouldn't let him take the notes out. I don't know where the typewriter is. Genet wrote all of *Our Lady of the Flowers* in the shithouse . . . the jailhouse. There's a great writer, Jean Genet. He kept writing and kept writing until he got to a point where he was going to come by writing about it . . . until he came into his bed—in the can. The French can. The French jail. Prison. And that was the end of the chapter. Every chapter is Genet coming off. Which I must admit Sartre noticed.

INTERVIEWER

You think that's a different kind of spontaneous writing?

KEROUAC

Well, I could go to jail and I could write every night a chapter about Magee, Magoo, and Molly. It's beautiful. Genet is really the most honest writer we've had since Kerouac and Burroughs. But he came before us. He's older. Well, he's the same age as Burroughs. But I don't think I've been dishonest. Man, I've had a good time! God, man, I rode around this country free as a bee. But Genet is a very tragic and beautiful writer. And I give them the crown. And the laurel wreath. I don't give the laurel wreath to Richard Wilbur! Or Robert Lowell. Give it to Jean Genet and William Seward Burroughs. And to Allen Ginsberg and to Gregory Corso, especially.

INTERVIEWER

Jack, how about Peter Orlovsky's writings. Do you like Peter's things?

KEROUAC

Peter Orlovsky is an idiot!! He's a Russian idiot. Not even Russian, he's Polish.

INTERVIEWER

He's written some fine poems.

KEROUAC

Oh yeah. My . . . what poems?

INTERVIEWER

He has a beautiful poem called "Second Poem."

KEROUAC

"My brother pisses in the bed . . . and I go in the subway and I see two people kissing . . ."

INTERVIEWER

No, the poem that says "it's more creative to paint the floor than to sweep it."

KEROUAC

That's a lot of shit! That is the kind of poetry that was written by another Polish idiot who was a Polish nut called Apollinaire. Apollinaire is not his real name, you know.

There are some fellows in San Francisco that told me that Peter was an idiot. But I like idiots, and I enjoy his poetry. Think about that, Berrigan. But for my taste, it's Gregory.

Give me one of those.

INTERVIEWER

One of these pills?

KEROUAC

Yeah. What are they? Forked clarinets?

INTERVIEWER

They're called Obetrol. Neal is the one that told me about them.

KEROUAC

Overtones?

INTERVIEWER

Overtones? No, overcoats.

SAROYAN

What was that you said . . . at the back of the Grove anthology . . . that you let the line go a little longer to fill it up with secret images that come at the end of the sentence?

KEROUAC

He's a real Armenian! Sediment. Delta. Mud. It's where you start a poem . . .

> As I was walking down the street one day
> I saw a lake where people were cutting off my rear,
> 17,000 priests singing like George Burns

and then you go on . . .

> And I'm making jokes about me
> and breaking my bones in the earth
> and here I am the great John Armenian
> coming back to earth

now you remember where you were in the beginning and you say . . .

> Ahaha! Tatatatadooda . . . Screw Turkey!

See? You remembered the line at the end . . . you lose your mind in the middle.

SAROYAN

Right.

KEROUAC

That applies to prose as well as poetry.

INTERVIEWER

But in prose you are telling a story . . .

KEROUAC

In prose you make the paragraph. Every paragraph is a poem.

INTERVIEWER

Is that how you write a paragraph?

KEROUAC

When I was running downtown there, and I was going to do this, and I was laying there, with that girl there, and a guy took out his scissors and I took him inside there, he showed me some dirty pictures. And I went out and fell downstairs with the potato bags.

INTERVIEWER

Did you ever like Gertrude Stein's work?

KEROUAC

Never interested me too much. I liked "Melanctha" a little bit.

I should really go to school and teach these kids. I could make two thousand bucks a week. You can't learn these things. You know why? Because you have to be born with tragic fathers.

INTERVIEWER

You can only do that if you are born in New England.

KEROUAC

Incidentally, my father said your father wasn't tragic.

SAROYAN

I don't think my father is tragic.

KEROUAC

My father said that Saroyan . . . William Saroyan ain't tragic at all . . . he's fulla shit. And I had a big argument with him. "The Daring Young Man on the Flying Trapeze" is pretty tragic, I would say.

SAROYAN

He was just a young man then, you know.

KEROUAC

Yeah, but he was hungry, and he was on Times Square. Flying. A young man on the flying trapeze. That was a beautiful story. It killed me when I was a kid.

INTERVIEWER

Do you remember a story by William Saroyan about the Indian who came to town and bought a car and got the little kid to drive it for him?

STELLA

A Cadillac.

KEROUAC

What town was that?

SAROYAN

Fresno. That was Fresno.

KEROUAC

Well, you remember the night I was taking a big nap and you came up outside my window on a white horse . . .

SAROYAN

"The Summer of the Beautiful White Horse."

KEROUAC

And I looked out the window and said, What is this? You said, My name is Aram. And I'm on a white horse.

SAROYAN

Mourad.

KEROUAC

My name is Mourad, excuse me. No, my name is . . . I was Aram, you were Mourad. You said, Wake up! I didn't want to wake up. I wanted to sleep. "My Name Is Aram" is the name of the book. You stole a white horse from a farmer and you woke up me, Aram, to go riding with you.

SAROYAN

Mourad was the crazy one who stole the horse.

KEROUAC

Hey, what's that you gave me there?

INTERVIEWER

Obetrol.

KEROUAC

Oh, obies.

INTERVIEWER

What about jazz and bop as influences rather than . . . Saroyan, Hemingway, and Wolfe?

KEROUAC

Yes, jazz and bop, in the sense of, say, a tenor man drawing a breath and blowing a phrase on his saxophone till he runs out of breath, and when he does, his sentence, his statement's been made . . . That's how I therefore separate my sentences, as breath separations of the mind . . . I formulated the theory of breath as measure, in prose and verse, never mind what Olson, Charles Olson says, I formulated that theory in 1953 at the request of Burroughs and Ginsberg. Then there's the raciness and freedom and humor of jazz instead of all that dreary analysis and things like, James entered the room, and lit a cigarette. He thought Jane might have thought this too vague a gesture . . . You know the stuff. As for Saroyan, yes, I loved him as a teenager, he really got me out of the nineteenth-century rut I was trying to study, not only with his funny tone but also with his neat Armenian poetic I don't know what . . . he just got me . . . Hemingway was fascinating, the pearls of words on a white page giving you an exact picture . . . but Wolfe was a torrent of American heaven and hell that opened my eyes to America as a subject in itself.

INTERVIEWER

How about the movies?

KEROUAC

Yes, we've all been influenced by movies. Malcolm Cowley incidentally mentioned this many times. He's very perceptive sometimes. He mentioned that *Doctor Sax* continually mentions urine, and quite naturally it does because I had no other place to write it but on a closed toilet seat in a little tile toilet in Mexico City, so as to get away from the guests inside the apartment. There, incidentally, is a style truly hallucinated, as I wrote it all on pot. No pun intended. Ho ho.

INTERVIEWER

How has Zen influenced your work?

KEROUAC

What's really influenced my work is the Mahayana Buddhism, the original Buddhism of Gautama Śākyamuni, the Buddha himself, of the India of old . . . Zen is what's left of his Buddhism, or Bodhi, after its passing into China and then into Japan. The part of Zen that's influenced my writing is the Zen contained in the haiku, like I said, the three-line, seventeen-syllable poems written hundreds of years ago by guys like Bashō, Issa, Shiki, and there've been recent masters. A sentence that's short and sweet with a sudden jump of thought in it is a kind of haiku, and there's a lot of freedom and fun in surprising yourself with that, let the mind willy-nilly jump from the branch to the bird. But my serious Buddhism, that of ancient India, has influenced that part in my writing that you might call religious, or fervent, or pious, almost as much as Catholicism has. Original Buddhism referred to continual conscious compassion, brotherhood, the *dana paramita* (meaning the perfection of charity), don't step on the bug, all that, humility, mendicancy, the sweet sorrowful face of the Buddha (who was of Aryan origin by the way, I mean of Persian warrior caste, and not Oriental as pictured) . . . in original Buddhism no young kid coming to a monastery was warned that "Here we bury them alive." He was simply given soft encouragement to meditate and be kind. The beginning of Zen was when Buddha, however, assembled all the monks together to announce a sermon and choose the first patriarch of the Mahayana church: instead of speaking, he simply held up a flower. Everybody was flabbergasted except Kāśyapīya, who smiled. Kāśyapīya was appointed the first patriarch. This idea appealed to the Chinese, like the sixth patriarch Hui-Neng who said, "From the beginning nothing ever was," and wanted to tear up the records of Buddha's sayings as kept in the sutras—sutras are "threads of discourse." In a way, then, Zen is a gentle but goofy form of heresy, though there must be some real kindly old monks somewhere and we've heard about the nutty ones. I haven't been to Japan. Your Maha Roshi Yoshi is simply a disciple of all this and not the founder of anything new at all, of course. On the Johnny Carson show he didn't even mention Buddha's name. Maybe his Buddha is Mia.

INTERVIEWER

How come you've never written about Jesus? You've written about Buddha. Wasn't Jesus a great guy, too?

KEROUAC

I've never written about Jesus? In other words, you're an insane phony who comes to my house . . . and . . . *all I write about* is Jesus. I am Everhard Mercurian, General of the Jesuit Army.

SAROYAN

What's the difference between Jesus and Buddha?

KEROUAC

That's a very good question. There is no difference.

SAROYAN

No difference?

KEROUAC

But there is a difference between the original Buddha of India, and the Buddha of Vietnam who just shaves his hair and puts on a yellow robe and is a communist agitating agent. The original Buddha wouldn't even walk on young grass so that he wouldn't destroy it. He was born in Gorakhpur, the son of the consul of the invading Persian hordes. And he was called Sage of the Warriors, and he had seventeen thousand broads dancing for him all night, holding out flowers, saying, You want to smell it, my lord? He says, Git outta here you whore. He laid a lot of them you know. But by the time he was thirty-one years old he got sick and tired . . . his father was protecting him from what was going on outside the town. And so he went out on a horse, against his father's orders and he saw a woman dying—a man being burnt on a ghat. And he said, What is all this death and decay? The servant said, That is the way things go on. Your father was hiding you from the way things go on.

He says, What? My father! Get my horse, saddle my horse! Ride me into the forest! They ride into the forest. He says, Now take the saddle off the horse. Put it on your horse, hang it on . . . Take my horse by the rein and ride back to the castle and tell my father I'll never see him again! And the servant, Channa, cried. He said, I'll never see you again. I don't care! Go on! Shoosh! Get away!

He spent seven years in the forest. Biting his teeth together. Nothing happened. Tormenting himself with starvation. He said, I will keep my teeth bit together until I find the cause of death. Then one day he was stumbling across the Rapti River, and he fainted in the river. And a young girl came by with a bowl of milk and said, My lord, a bowl of milk. [*Slurppp*] He said, That gives me great energy, thank you my dear. Then he went and sat under the Bo tree. *Figuerosa.* The fig tree. He said, Now . . . I will cross my legs [*demonstrates posture*] . . . and grit my teeth until I find the cause of death. Two o'clock in the morning, one hundred thousand phantoms assailed him. He didn't move. Three o'clock in the morning, the great blue ghosts! Arghhh! All *accosted* him. (You see I am really Scottish.) Four o'clock in the morning the mad maniacs of hell . . . came out of manhole covers . . . in New York City. You know Wall Street where the steam comes out? You know Wall Street, where the manhole covers . . . steam comes up? You take off them covers—yaaaaaahhh! Six o'clock, everything was peaceful—the birds started to trill, and he said, Aha! The cause of death . . . the cause of death is birth.

Simple? So he started walking down the road to Benares in India . . . with long hair, like you, see.

So, three guys. One says, Hey, here comes Buddha there who, uh, starved with us in the forest. When he sits down here on that bucket, don't wash his feet. So Buddha sits down on the bucket. The guy rushes up and washes his feet. Why dost thou wash his feet? Buddha says, Because I go to Benares to beat the drum of life. And what is that? That the cause of death is birth. What do you mean? I'll show you.

A woman comes up with a dead baby in her arms. Says, Bring my child back to life if you are the Lord. He says, Sure I'll do that anytime. Just go and find one family in Srāvastī that ain't had a death in the last five years. Get a mustard seed from them and bring it to me. And I'll bring your child back to life. She went all over town, man, two million people, Srāvastī the town was, a bigger town than Benares by the way, and she came back and said, I can't find no such family. They've all had deaths within five years. He said, Then, bury your baby.

Then, his jealous cousin, Devadatta (that's Ginsberg you see . . . I am Buddha and Ginsberg is Devadatta), gets this elephant drunk . . .

great big bull elephant drunk on whiskey. The elephant goes up—
[*trumpets like elephant going up*] with a big trunk, and Buddha comes
up in the road and gets the elephant and goes like this [*kneels*]. And the
elephant kneels down. You are buried in sorrow's mud! Quiet your
trunk! Stay there! He's an elephant trainer. Then Devadatta rolled a
big boulder over a cliff. And it almost hit Buddha's head. Just missed.
Boooom! He says, That's Devadatta again. Then Buddha went like
this [*paces back and forth*] in front of his boys, you see. Behind him
was his cousin that loved him . . . Ananda . . . which means love in
Sanskrit [*keeps pacing*]. This is what you do in jail to keep in shape.

I know a lot of stories about Buddha, but I don't know exactly what he
said every time. But I know what he said about the guy who spit at him.
He said, Since I can't use your abuse you may have it back. He was great.

[*Kerouac plays piano. Drinks are served.*]

SAROYAN

There's something there.

INTERVIEWER

My mother used to play that. I'm not sure how we can transcribe
those notes onto a page. We may have to include a record of you playing
the piano. Will you play that piece again for the record, Mr. Paderewski?
Can you play "Alouette"?

KEROUAC

No. Only Afro-Germanic music. After all, I'm a square head. I
wonder what whiskey will do to those obies.

INTERVIEWER

What about ritual and superstition? Do you have any about yourself when you get down to work?

KEROUAC

I had a ritual once of lighting a candle and writing by its light and
blowing it out when I was done for the night . . . also kneeling and

praying before starting (I got that from a French movie about George Frideric Handel) . . . but now I simply hate to write. My superstition? I'm beginning to suspect the full moon. Also I'm hung up on the number nine—though I'm told a Piscean like myself should stick to number seven—but I try to do nine touchdowns a day, that is, I stand on my head in the bathroom, on a slipper, and touch the floor nine times with my toe tips, while balanced. This is incidentally more than yoga, it's an athletic feat. I mean imagine calling me "unbalanced" after that. Frankly I do feel that my mind is going. So another "ritual" as you call it, is to pray to Jesus to preserve my sanity and my energy so I can help my family: that being my paralyzed mother, and my wife, and the everpresent kitties. Okay?

INTERVIEWER

You typed out *On the Road* in three weeks, *The Subterraneans* in three days and nights. Do you still produce at this fantastic rate? Can you say something of the genesis of a work before you sit down and begin that terrific typing—how much of it is set in your mind, for example?

KEROUAC

You think out what actually happened, you tell friends long stories about it, you mull it over in your mind, you connect it together at leisure, then when the time comes to pay the rent again you force yourself to sit at the typewriter, or at the writing notebook, and get it over with as fast as you can . . . and there's no harm in that because you've got the whole story lined up. Now how that's done depends on what kind of steel trap you've got up in that little old head. This sounds boastful but a girl once told me I had a steel-trap brain, meaning I'd catch her with a statement she'd made an hour ago even though our talk had rambled a million light-years away from that point . . . you know what I mean, like a lawyer's mind, say. All of it is in my mind, naturally, except that language that is used at the time that it is used . . . And as for *On the Road* and *The Subterraneans*, no I can't write that fast anymore . . . Writing *The Subs* in three nights was really a fantastic athletic feat as well as mental, you shoulda seen me after I was done . . . I was pale as a sheet and had lost fifteen pounds and looked strange in the mirror. What I do now is write something like an average of eight thousand words a sitting, in the middle of the night, and another about a week later, resting and sighing in between. I really hate to write. I get no fun out of it because I can't get up and say I'm working, close my door, have coffee brought to me, and sit there camping like a "man of letters" doing his eight hour day of work and thereby incidentally filling the printing world with a lot of dreary self-imposed cant and bombast, *bombast* being Scottish for pillow stuffing. Haven't you heard a politician use fifteen hundred words to say something he could have said in exactly three words? So I get it out of the way so as not to bore myself either.

SAROYAN

Do you usually try to see everything clearly and not think of any words—just to see everything as clear as possible and then write out of the feeling? With *Tristessa*, for example.

KEROUAC

You sound like a writing seminar at Indiana University.

SAROYAN

I know but . . .

KEROUAC

All I did was suffer with that poor girl and then when she fell on her head and almost killed herself . . . remember when she fell on her head? She was all busted up and everything. She was the most gorgeous little Indian chick you ever saw. I say Indian, pure Indian. Esperanza Villa-nueva. Villanueva is a Spanish name from I don't know where—Castile. But she's Indian. So she's a half Indian, half Spanish . . . beauty. Absolute beauty. She had bones, man, just bones, skin and bones. And I didn't write in the book how I finally nailed her. You know? I did.

I finally nailed her. She said, "Shhhhhhhhh! Don't let the landlord hear." She said, "Remember, I'm very weak and sick." I said, "I know, I've been writing a book about how you're weak and sick."

INTERVIEWER

How come you didn't put that part in the book?

KEROUAC

Because Claude's wife told me not to put it in. She said it would spoil the book.

But it was not a conquest. She was out like a light. On M. *M*—that's morphine. And in fact I made a big run for her from way uptown to downtown to the slum district . . . and I said, "Here's your stuff." She said, "Shhhhh!" She gave herself a shot and I said, "Ah . . . now's the time." And I got my little no-good piece. But . . . it was certainly justification of Mexico!

STELLA

Here kitty! He's gone out again.

KEROUAC

She was nice, you would have liked her. Her real name was Esperanza. You know what that means?

INTERVIEWER

No.

KEROUAC

In Spanish, "hope." *Tristessa* means, in Spanish, "sadness," but her real name was Hope. And she's now married to the police chief of Mexico City.

STELLA

Not quite.

KEROUAC

Well, you're not Esperanza—I'll tell you that.

STELLA

No, I know that, dear.

KEROUAC

She was the skinniest . . . and shy . . . as a rail.

STELLA

She's married to one of the lieutenants, you told me, not to the chief.

KEROUAC

She's all right. One of these days I'm going to go see her again.

STELLA

Over my dead body.

INTERVIEWER

Were you really writing *Tristessa* while you were there in Mexico? You didn't write it later?

KEROUAC

First part written in Mexico, second part written in . . . Mexico. That's right. Nineteen fifty-five first part, '56 second part. What's the importance about that? I'm not Charles Olson, the great artist!

INTERVIEWER

We're just getting the facts.

KEROUAC

Charles Olson gives you all the dates. You know. Everything about how he found the hound on the beach in Gloucester. Found somebody jacking off on the beach at . . . what do they call it? Vancouver Beach? Dig Dog River? . . . Dogtown. That's what they call it, "Dogtown." Well this is Shittown on the Merrimack. Lowell is called "Shittown on the Merrimack." I'm not going to write a poem called Shittown and insult my town. But if I were six foot six I could write anything, couldn't I?

INTERVIEWER

How do you get along now with other writers? Do you correspond with them?

KEROUAC

I correspond with John Clellon Holmes, but less and less each year—I'm getting lazy. I can't answer my fan mail because I haven't got a secretary to take dictation, do the typing, get the stamps, envelopes, all that . . . and I have nothing to answer. I ain't gonna spend the rest of my life smiling and shaking hands and sending and receiving platitudes, like a candidate for political office, because I'm a writer—I've got to let my mind alone, like Greta Garbo. Yet when I go out, or receive sudden guests, we all have more fun than a barrel of monkeys.

INTERVIEWER

What are the work destroyers?

KEROUAC

Work destroyers . . . work destroyers. Time killers? I'd say mainly the attentions which are tendered to a writer of "notoriety" (notice I don't say "fame") by secretly ambitious would-be writers who come around, or write, or call, for the sake of the services that are properly the services of a bloody literary agent. When I was an unknown struggling young writer, as the saying goes, I did my own footwork, I hot-footed up and down Madison Avenue for years, publisher to publisher, agent to agent, and never once in my life wrote a letter to a published famous author asking for advice, or help, or, in Heaven above, had the nerve to actually *mail* my manuscripts to some poor author who then has to hustle to mail it back before he's accused of stealing my ideas. My advice to young writers is to get themselves an agent on their own, maybe through their college professors (as I got my first publishers through my prof Mark Van Doren), and do their own footwork, or "thing" as the slang goes . . . So the work destroyers are nothing but certain *people.*

The work preservers are the solitudes of night, "when the whole wide world is fast asleep."

INTERVIEWER

What do you find the best time and place for writing?

KEROUAC

The desk in the room, near the bed, with a good light, midnight till dawn, a drink when you get tired, preferably at home, but if you have no home, make a home out of your hotel room or motel room or pad—peace. [*Picks up harmonica and plays.*] Boy, can I play!

INTERVIEWER

What about writing under the influence of drugs?

KEROUAC

Poem 230 from *Mexico City Blues* is a poem written purely on morphine. Every line in this poem was written within an hour of one another . . . high on a big dose of M. [*Finds volume and reads.*]

Love's multitudinous boneyard of decay,

An hour later:

The spilled milk of heroes,

An hour later:

Destruction of silk kerchiefs by dust storm,

An hour later:

Caress of heroes blindfolded to posts,

An hour later:

Murder victims admitted to this life,

An hour later:

Skeletons bartering fingers and joints,

An hour later:

The quivering meat of the elephants of kindness being torn apart
by vultures,

(See where Ginsberg stole that from me?) An hour later:

Conceptions of delicate kneecaps.

Say that, Saroyan.

SAROYAN
Conceptions of delicate kneecaps.

KEROUAC
Very good.

Fear of rats dripping with bacteria.

An hour later:

Golgotha Cold Hope for Gold Hope.

Say that.

SAROYAN
Golgotha Cold Hope for Cold Hope.

KEROUAC
That's pretty cold. An hour later:

Damp leaves of autumn against the wood of boats,

An hour later:

Seahorse's delicate imagery of glue.

Ever see a little seahorse in the ocean? They're built of glue . . . Did you ever sniff a sea horse? No, say that.

SAROYAN
Seahorse's delicate imagery of glue.

KEROUAC
You'll do, Saroyan.

Death by long exposure to defilement.

SAROYAN
Death by long exposure to defilement.

KEROUAC
Frightening ravishing mysterious beings concealing their sex.

SAROYAN

Frightening ravishing mysterious beings concealing their sex.

KEROUAC

Pieces of the Buddha-material frozen and sliced microscopically
in Morgues of the North.

SAROYAN

Hey, I can't say that. Pieces of the Buddha-material frozen and
sliced microscopically in Morgues of the North.

KEROUAC

Penis apples going to seed.

SAROYAN

Penis apples going to seed.

KEROUAC

The severed gullets more numerous than sands.

SAROYAN

The severed gullets more numerous than sands.

KEROUAC

Like kissing my kitten in the belly.

SAROYAN

Like kissing my kitten in the belly.

KEROUAC

The softness of our reward.

SAROYAN

The softness of our reward.

KEROUAC

Is he really William Saroyan's son? That's wonderful! Would you mind repeating that?

INTERVIEWER

We should be asking you a lot of very straight serious questions. When did you meet Allen Ginsberg?

KEROUAC

First I met Claude.* And then I met Allen and then I met Burroughs. Claude came in through the fire escape . . . There were gunshots down in the alley—Pow! Pow!—and it was raining, and my wife says, Here comes Claude. And here comes this blond guy through the fire escape, all wet. I said, What's this all about, what the hell is this? He says, They're chasing me. Next day in walks Allen Ginsberg carrying books. Sixteen years old with his ears sticking out. He says, Well, discretion is the better part of valor! I said, Aw shutup. You little twitch. Then the next day here comes Burroughs wearing a seersucker suit, followed by the other guy.

INTERVIEWER

What other guy?

KEROUAC

It was the guy who wound up in the river. This was the guy from New Orleans that Claude killed and threw in the river. Stabbed him twelve times in the heart with a Boy Scout knife. When Claude was fourteen he was the most beautiful blond boy in New Orleans. And he joined the Boy Scout troop . . . and the Boy Scout master was a big redheaded fairy who went to school at Saint Louis University, I think it was.

And he had already been in love with a guy who looked just like Claude in Paris. And this guy chased Claude all over the country; this

---

* "Claude," Kerouac's pseudonym for Lucien Carr, is also used in *Vanity of Duluoz.*

guy had him thrown out of Baldwin, Tulane, and Andover Prep . . . It's a queer tale, but Claude isn't a queer.

INTERVIEWER

What about the influence of Ginsberg and Burroughs? Did you ever have any sense then of the mark the three of you would have on American writing?

KEROUAC

I was determined to be a "great writer," in quotes, like Thomas Wolfe, see . . . Allen was always reading and writing poetry . . . Burroughs read a lot and walked around looking at things. The influence we exerted on one another has been written about over and over again . . . We were just three interested characters, in the interesting big city of New York, around campuses, libraries, cafeterias. You can find a lot of the details in *Vanity* . . . in *On the Road*, where Burroughs is Bull Lee and Ginsberg is Carlo Marx, and in *Subterraneans*, where they're Frank Carmody and Adam Moorad, respectively. In other words, though I don't want to be rude to you for this honor, I am so busy interviewing myself in my novels, and have been so busy writing down these self-interviews, that I don't see why I should draw breath in pain every year for the last ten years to repeat and repeat to everybody who interviews me (hundreds of journalists, thousands of students) what I've already explained in the books themselves. It begs sense. And it's not that important. It's our work that counts, if anything at all, and I'm not too proud of mine or theirs or anybody's since Thoreau and others like that, maybe because it's still too close to home for comfort. Notoriety and public confession in the literary form is a frazzler of the heart you were born with, believe me.

INTERVIEWER

Allen once said that he learned how to read Shakespeare, that he never did understand Shakespeare until he heard you read Shakespeare to him.

KEROUAC

Because in a previous lifetime, that's who I was.

How like a winter hath my absence been from thee?
The pleasure of the fleeting year . . . what freezings
have I felt? What dark days seen? Yet Summer with his
lord surcease hath laid a big turd in my orchard.
And one hog after another comes to eat
and break my broken mountain trap, and my mousetrap
too! And here to end the sonnet, you must make sure
to say, tara-tara-tara!

INTERVIEWER

Is that spontaneous composition?

KEROUAC

Well, the first part was Shakespeare . . . and the second part was . . .

INTERVIEWER

Have you ever written any sonnets?

KEROUAC

I'll give you a spontaneous sonnet. It has to be what, now?

INTERVIEWER

Fourteen lines.

KEROUAC

That's twelve lines with two dragging lines. That's where you
bring out your heavy artillery.

Here the fish of Scotland seen your eye
and all my nets did creak . . .

Does it have to rhyme?

INTERVIEWER

No.

KEROUAC

My poor chapped hands fall awry and seen the Pope, his devilled eye. And maniacs with wild hair hanging about my room and listening to my tomb which does not rhyme.

Seven lines?

INTERVIEWER

That was eight lines.

KEROUAC

And all the orgones of the earth will crawl like dogs across the graves of Peru and Scotland too.

That's ten.

Yet do not worry, sweet angel of mine that hast thine inheritance imbedded in mine.

INTERVIEWER

That's pretty good, Jack. How did you do that?

KEROUAC

Without studying dactyls . . . like Ginsberg . . . I met Ginsberg . . . I'd hitchhiked all the way back from Mexico City to Berkeley, and that's a long way baby, a long way. Mexico City across Durango . . . Chihuahua . . . Texas. I go back to Ginsberg, I go to his cottage, I say, Hah, we're gonna play the music. He says, You know what I'm going to do tomorrow? I'm going to throw on Mark Schorer's desk a new theory of prosody! About the dactylic arrangements of Ovid! [*laughter.*]

I said, Quit, man. Sit under a tree and forget it and drink wine with me . . . and Phil Whalen and Gary Snyder and all the bums of San Francisco. Don't you try to be a big Berkeley teacher. Just be a poet under the trees . . . and we'll wrestle and we'll break holds. And he did take my advice. He remembered that. He said, What are you going to teach . . . you have parched lips! I said, Naturally, I just came from Chihuahua. It's very hot down there, phew! You go out and little pigs rub against your legs. Phew!

So here comes Snyder with a bottle of wine . . . and here comes Whalen, and here comes what's his name, Rexroth, and everybody and we had the poetry renaissance of San Francisco.

INTERVIEWER

What about Allen getting kicked out of Columbia? Didn't you have something to do with that?

KEROUAC

Oh, no . . . he let me sleep in his room. He was not kicked out of Columbia for that. The first time he let me sleep in his room, and the guy that slept in our room with us was Lancaster who was descended from the White Roses or Red Roses of England. But a guy came in . . . the guy that ran the floor and he thought that I was trying to make Allen, and Allen had already written in the paper that I wasn't sleeping there because I was trying to make him, but he was trying to make me. But we were just actually sleeping. Then after that he got a pad . . . he got some stolen goods in there . . . and he got some thieves up there, Vicky and Huncke. And they were all busted for stolen goods, and a car turned over, and Allen's glasses broke. It's all in John Holmes's *Go*.

Allen Ginsberg asked me when he was nineteen years old, Should I change my name to Allen Renard? You change your name to Allen Renard I'll kick you right in the balls! Stick to Ginsberg. . . . And he did. That's one thing I like about Allen. Allen *Renard*!

What was it that brought all of you together in the fifties? What was it that seemed to unify the Beat Generation?

Oh, the Beat Generation was just a phrase I used in the 1951 written manuscript of *On the Road* to describe guys like Moriarty who run around the country in cars looking for odd jobs, girlfriends, kicks. It was thereafter picked up by West Coast Leftist groups and turned into a meaning like "Beat mutiny" and "Beat insurrection" and all that nonsense; they just wanted some youth movement to grab on to for their own political and social purposes. I had nothing to do with any of that. I was a football player, a scholarship college student, a merchant seaman, a railroad brakeman on road freights, a script synopsizer, a secretary . . . And Moriarty-Cassady was an actual cowboy on Dave Uhl's ranch in New Raymer, Colorado . . . What kind of beatnik is that?

Was there any sense of community among the Beat crowd?

That community feeling was largely inspired by the same characters I mentioned, like Ferlinghetti, Ginsberg—they are very socialistically minded and want everybody to live in some kind of frenetic kibbutz, solidarity and all that. I was a loner. Snyder is not like Whalen, Whalen is not like McClure, I am not like McClure, McClure is not like Ferlinghetti, Ginsberg is not like Ferlinghetti, but we all had fun over wine anyway. We knew thousands of poets and painters and jazz musicians. There's no "Beat crowd" like you say . . . What about Scott Fitzgerald and his "lost crowd," does that sound right? Or Goethe and his "Wilhelm Meister crowd"? The subject is such a bore. Pass me that glass.

INTERVIEWER

Well, why did they split in the early sixties?

KEROUAC

Ginsberg got interested in left wing politics . . . Like Joyce, I say, as Joyce said to Ezra Pound in the 1920s, Don't bother me with politics, the only thing that interests me is style. Besides I'm bored with the new avant-garde and the skyrocketing sensationalism. I'm reading Blaise Pascal and taking notes on religion. I like to hang around now with nonintellectuals, as you might call them, and not have my mind proselytized, ad infinitum. They've even started crucifying chickens in happenings, what's the next step? An actual crucifixion of a man . . . The Beat group dispersed as you say in the early sixties, all went their own way, and this is my way: home life, as in the beginning, with a little toot once in a while in local bars.

INTERVIEWER

What do you think of what they're up to now? Allen's radical political involvement? Burroughs's cut-up methods?

KEROUAC

I'm pro-American and the radical political involvements seem to tend elsewhere . . . The country gave my Canadian family a good break, more or less, and we see no reason to demean said country. As for Burroughs's cut-up method, I wish he'd get back to those awfully funny stories of his he used to write and those marvelously dry vignettes in *Naked Lunch*. Cut-up is nothing new, in fact that steel-trap brain of mine does a lot of cutting up as it goes along . . . as does everyone's brain while talking or thinking or writing . . . It's just an old Dada trick, and a kind of literary collage. He comes out with some great effects though. I like him to be elegant and logical and that's why I don't like the cut-up which is supposed to teach us that the mind is cracked. Sure the mind's cracked, as anybody can see in a hallucinated high, but how about an explanation of the crackedness that can be understood in a workaday moment?

INTERVIEWER

What do you think about the hippies and the LSD scene?

KEROUAC

They're already changing, I shouldn't be able to make a judgment. And they're not all of the same mind. The Diggers are different . . . I don't know one hippie anyhow . . . I think they think I'm a truck-driver. And I am. As for LSD, it's bad for people with incidence of heart disease in the family [*knocks microphone off footstool . . . recovers it*].

Is there any reason why you can see anything good in this here mortality?

INTERVIEWER

Excuse me, would you mind repeating that?

KEROUAC

You said you had a little white beard in your belly. Why is there a little white beard in your mortality belly?

INTERVIEWER

Let me think about it. Actually it's a little white pill.

KEROUAC

A little white pill?

INTERVIEWER

It's good.

KEROUAC

Give me.

INTERVIEWER

We should wait till the scene cools a little.

KEROUAC

Right. This little white pill is a little white beard in your mortality which advises you and advertises to you that you will be growing long fingernails in the graves of Peru.

SAROYAN

Do you feel middle-aged?

KEROUAC

No. Listen, we're coming to the end of the tape. I want to add something on. Ask me what Kerouac means.

INTERVIEWER

Jack, tell me again what Kerouac means.

KEROUAC

Now, *kairn*. K (or C) A-I-R-N. What is a cairn? It's a heap of stones. Now *Cornwall*, cairn-wall. Now, right, *kern*, also K-E-R-N, means the same thing as *cairn*. Kern. Cairn. *Ouac* means "language of." So, *Kernouac* means the language of Cornwall. *Kerr*, which is like Deborah Kerr. *Ouack* means language of water. Because *Kerr, Carr*, etcetera means water. And *cairn* means heap of stones. There is no language in a heap of stones. Kerouac. *Ker-* (water), -*ouac* (language of). And it's related to the old Irish name, Kerwick, which is a corruption. And it's a Cornish name, which in itself means cairnish. And according to Sherlock Holmes, it's all Persian. Of course you know he's not Persian. Don't you remember in Sherlock Holmes when he went down with Dr. Watson and solved the case down in old Cornwall and he solved the case and then he said, Watson, the needle! Watson, the needle . . . He said, I've solved this case here in Cornwall. Now I have the liberty to sit around here and decide and read books, which will prove to me . . . why the Cornish people, otherwise known as the Kernuaks, or Kerouacs, are of Persian origin. The enterprise which I am about to embark upon, he then said, after he got his shot, is fraught with eminent peril, and not fit for a lady of your tender years. Remember that?

MCNAUGHTON

I remember that.

KEROUAC

McNaughton remembers that. McNaughton. You think I would forget the name of a Scotsman?

Issue 43, 1968

E. B. White

The Art of the Essay

In the issue of The New Yorker *dated two weeks after E. B. White died, his stepson, Roger Angell, wrote the following in the magazine's Talk of the Town section:*

Last August, a couple of sailors paid an unexpected visit to my summer house in Maine: young sailors—a twelve-year-old girl and an eleven-year-old boy. They were a crew taking part in a state-wide small-boat-racing competition at a local yacht club, and because my wife and I had some vacant beds just then we were willingly dragooned as hosts. They were fine company—tanned and shy and burning with tactics but amenable to blueberry muffins and our exuberant fox terrier. They were also readers, it turned out. On their second night, it came out at the dinner table that E. B. White was a near neighbor of ours, and our visitors reacted to the news with incredulity. "No!" the boy said softly, his eyes traveling back and forth over the older faces at the table. "No-o-o-o!" The girl, being older, tried to keep things in place. "He's my favorite author," she said. "Or at least he was when I was younger." They were both a bit old for *Stuart Little*, *Charlotte's Web*, and *The Trumpet of the Swan*, in fact, but because they knew the books so well, and because they needed cheering up (they had done badly in the racing), arrangements were made for a visit to E. B. White's farm the next morning.

White, who had been ill, was not able to greet our small party that

(unorthodox)

Was it for the man
Was they? Who? Why?
Was Coolidge?

The question has been raised: is Russell
Wiggins the man for the job? He has been named as our
Ambassador to the United Nations. The Times, as soon as
it learned of this appointment jumped on Wiggins with both feet. "He is
not the man for this job," said the Times.

This pronouncement struck me as a snap
judgment. It~~×××××××××××××××××××××Wiggins×is×the×man~~
Who knows who is the man for a job?
~~for×the×job××~~ The Times complained that Wiggins had had
no training in diplomacy, and this isnt true. Wiggins
is not a diplomat, he is the editor of a good newspaper. I
looked up "diplomacy" in Webster's, and found a definition that
said: "Artful management in securing advantages without
arousing hostility." A newspaper editor, if he's any good,
never gives a thought to arousing hostility, he just goes
ahead and prints the facts as he sees them. Maybe the
time has come for our Ambassador to the United Nations to act
with the same kind of ~~candor~~ abandon.

Wiggins has some very unusual qualifications
for his new post. ~~He is unquestionably the only man to~~
~~represent us in the United Nations who owns a Friendship~~
~~sloop.~~ I think he bought the sloop ~~in××××for×the×××××××~~
~~for×××××××××~~ because he fell in love with the name Friendship.
~~Friends in~~ sloops are not a dime a dozen--they are a
rare breed these days. They were built in Friendship, Maine,
and were originally a work boat, mostly for hauling traps.
They are very close-winded, have a deep forefoot, and a
powerful ~~lines~~ hull. Off the wind they are ~~×××××××~~ On
the wind, they ~~can eat up into the sea~~

day, but there were other sights and creatures there to make us welcome: two scattered families of bantam hens and chicks on the lawn;
the plump, waggly incumbent dog, name of Red; and the geese who
came scuttling and hissing up the pasture lane, their wings out-
spread in wild alarm. It was a glazy, windless morning, with some
thin scraps of fog still clinging to the water in Allen Cove, beyond
the pasture; later on, I knew, the summer southwest breeze would
stir, and then Harriman Point and Blue Hill Bay and the islands
would come clear again. What wasn't there this time was Andy
White himself: emerging from the woodshed, say, with an egg basket
or a length of line in his hand; or walking away (at a mid-slow pace,
not a stroll—never a stroll—with the dog just astern) down the grassy
lane that turns and then dips to the woods and shore; or perhaps getting into his car for a trip to town, getting aboard, as he got aboard
any car, with an air of mild wariness, the way most of us start up on a
bicycle. We made do without him, as we had to. We went into the
barn and examined the vacant pens and partitions and the old cattle
tie-ups; we visited the vegetable garden and the neat stacks of freshly
cut stove wood; we saw the cutting beds, and the blackberry patch
behind the garage, and the place where the pigpen used to be—the
place where Wilbur was born, surely. The children took turns on the
old single-rope swing that hung in the barn doorway, hoisting themselves up onto the smoothed seat, made out of a single chunk of birch
firewood, and then sailing out into the sunshine and back into barn-
shadow again and again, as the crossbeam creaked above them and
swallows dipped in and out of an open barn window far overhead. It
wasn't much entertainment for them, but perhaps it was all right,
because of where they were. The girl asked which doorway might
have been the one where Charlotte had spun her web, and she mentioned Templeton, the rat, and Fern, the little girl who befriends
Wilbur. She was visiting a museum, I sensed, and she would remember things here to tell her friends about later. The boy, though, was
quieter, and for a while I thought that our visit was a disappointment
to him. Then I stole another look at him, and I understood. I think I
understood. He was taking note of the place, almost checking off

corners and shadows and smells to himself as we walked about the old farm, but he wasn't trying to remember them. He looked like someone who had been there before, and indeed he had, for he was a reader. Andy White had given him the place long before he ever set foot on it—not this farm, exactly, but the one in the book, the one now in the boy's mind. Only true writers—the rare few of them—can do this, but their deed to us is in perpetuity. The boy didn't get to meet E. B. White that day, but he already had him by heart. He had him for good.

—*George Plimpton, Frank H. Crowther, 1969*

INTERVIEWER

So many critics equate the success of a writer with an unhappy childhood. Can you say something of your own childhood in Mount Vernon?

E. B. WHITE

As a child, I was frightened but not unhappy. My parents were loving and kind. We were a large family (six children) and were a small kingdom unto ourselves. Nobody ever came to dinner. My father was formal, conservative, successful, hardworking, and worried. My mother was loving, hardworking, and retiring. We lived in a large house in a leafy suburb, where there were backyards and stables and grape arbors. I lacked for nothing except confidence. I suffered nothing except the routine terrors of childhood: fear of the dark, fear of the future, fear of the return to school after a summer on a lake in Maine, fear of making an appearance on a platform, fear of the lavatory in the school basement where the slate urinals cascaded, fear that I was unknowing about things I should know about. I was, as a child, allergic to pollens and dusts, and still am. I was allergic to platforms, and still am. It may be, as some critics suggest, that it helps to have an unhappy childhood. If so, I have no knowledge of it. Perhaps it helps to have been scared or allergic to pollens—I don't know.

INTERVIEWER

At what age did you know you were going to follow a literary profession? Was there a particular incident, or moment?

WHITE

I never knew for sure that I would follow a literary profession. I was twenty-seven or twenty-eight before anything happened that gave me any assurance that I could make a go of writing. I had done a great deal of writing, but I lacked confidence in my ability to put it to good use. I went abroad one summer and on my return to New York I found an accumulation of mail at my apartment. I took the letters, unopened, and went to a Childs restaurant on Fourteenth Street, where I ordered dinner and began opening my mail. From one envelope, two or three checks dropped out from *The New Yorker*. I suppose they totaled a little under a hundred dollars, but it looked like a fortune to me. I can still remember the feeling that this was it—I was a pro at last. It was a good feeling and I enjoyed the meal.

INTERVIEWER

What were those first pieces accepted by *The New Yorker*? Did you send them in with a covering letter, or through an agent?

WHITE

They were short sketches—what Ross called "casuals." One, I think, was a piece called "The Swell Steerage," about the then new college cabin class on transatlantic ships. I never submitted a manuscript with a covering letter or through an agent. I used to put my manuscript in the mail, along with a stamped envelope for the rejection. This was a matter of high principle with me—I believed in the doctrine of immaculate rejection. I never used an agent and did not like the looks of a manuscript after an agent got through prettying it up and putting it between covers with brass clips. (I now have an agent for such mysteries as movie rights and foreign translations.)

A large part of all early contributions to *The New Yorker* arrived uninvited and unexpected. They arrived in the mail or under the arm of people who walked in with them. O'Hara's "Afternoon Delphians" is one example out of hundreds. For a number of years, *The New Yorker* published an average of fifty new writers a year. Magazines that refuse unsolicited manuscripts strike me as lazy, incurious, self-assured, and self-important. I'm speaking of magazines of general circulation. There may be some justification for a technical journal to limit its list of contributors to persons who are known to be qualified. But if I were a publisher, I wouldn't want to put out a magazine that failed to examine everything that turned up.

INTERVIEWER

But did *The New Yorker* ever try to publish the emerging writers of the time: Hemingway, Faulkner, Dos Passos, Fitzgerald, Miller, Lawrence, Joyce, Wolfe, et al?

WHITE

The New Yorker had an interest in publishing any writer that could turn in a good piece. It read everything submitted. Hemingway, Faulkner, and the others were well established and well paid when *The New Yorker* came on the scene. The magazine would have been glad to publish them, but it didn't have the money to pay them off, and for the most part they didn't submit. They were selling to *The Saturday Evening Post* and other well-heeled publications, and in general were not inclined to contribute to the small, new, impecunious weekly. Also, some of them, I would guess, did not feel sympathetic to *The New Yorker*'s frivolity. Ross had no great urge to publish the big names—he was far more interested in turning up new and yet undiscovered talent, the Helen Hokinsons and the James Thurbers. We did publish some things by Wolfe—"Only the Dead Know Brooklyn" was one. I believe we published something by Fitzgerald. But Ross didn't waste much time trying to corral "emerged" writers. He was looking for the ones that were found by turning over a stone.

INTERVIEWER

What were the procedures in turning down a manuscript by a *New Yorker* regular? Was this done by Ross?

WHITE

The manuscript of a *New Yorker* regular was turned down in the same manner as was the manuscript of a *New Yorker* irregular. It was simply rejected, usually by the subeditor who was handling the author in question. Ross did not deal directly with writers and artists, except in the case of a few old friends from an earlier day. He wouldn't even take on Woollcott—regarded him as too difficult and fussy. Ross disliked rejecting pieces, and he disliked firing people—he ducked both tasks whenever he could.

INTERVIEWER

Did feuds threaten the magazine?

WHITE

Feuds did not threaten *The New Yorker*. The only feud I recall was the running battle between the editorial department and the advertising department. This was largely a one-sided affair, with the editorial department lobbing an occasional grenade into the enemy's lines just on general principles, to help them remember to stay out of sight. Ross was determined not to allow his magazine to be swayed, in the slightest degree, by the boys in advertising. As far as I know, he succeeded.

INTERVIEWER

When did you first move to New York, and what were some of the things you did before joining *The New Yorker*? Were you ever a part of the Algonquin group?

WHITE

After I got out of college, in 1921, I went to work in New York but did not live in New York. I lived at home, with my father and mother in Mount Vernon, and commuted to work. I held three jobs in about

seven months—first with the United Press, then with a public relations man named Wheat, then with the American Legion News Service. I disliked them all, and in the spring of 1922 I headed west in
a Model T Ford with a college mate, Howard Cushman, to seek my
fortune and as a way of getting away from what I disliked. I landed in
Seattle six months later, worked there as a reporter on the *Times* for
a year, was fired, shipped to Alaska aboard a freighter, and then returned to New York. It was on my return that I became an advertising man—Frank Seaman & Co., J. H. Newmark. In the mid-twenties,
I moved into a two-room apartment at 112 West Thirteenth Street
with three other fellows, college mates of mine at Cornell—Burke
Dowling Adams, Gustave Stubbs Lobrano, and Mitchell T. Gal-
breath. The rent was $110 a month. Split four ways it came to $27.50,
which I could afford. My friends in those days were the fellows already mentioned. Also, Peter Vischer, Russell Lord, Joel Sayre,
Frank Sullivan (he was older and more advanced but I met him and
liked him), James Thurber, and others. I was never a part of the Algonquin group. After becoming connected with *The New Yorker*,
I lunched once at the Round Table but didn't care for it and was embarrassed in the presence of the great. I never was well acquainted
with Benchley or Broun or Dorothy Parker or Woollcott. I did not
know Don Marquis or Ring Lardner, both of whom I greatly admired. I was a younger man.

INTERVIEWER

Were you a voracious reader during your youth?

WHITE

I was never a voracious reader and, in fact, have done little reading
in my life. There are too many other things I would rather do than
read. In my youth I read animal stories—William J. Long and Ernest
Seton Thompson. I have read a great many books about small boat
voyages—they fascinate me even though they usually have no merit.
In the twenties, I read the newspaper columns—F.P.A., Christopher
Morley, Don Marquis. I tried contributing and had a few things

published. (As a child, I was a member of the St. Nicholas League and from that eminence was hurled into the literary life, wearing my silver badge and my gold badge.) My reading habits have not changed over the years, only my eyesight has changed. I don't like being indoors and get out every chance I get. In order to read, one must sit down, usually indoors. I am restless and would rather sail a boat than crack a book. I've never had a very lively literary curiosity, and it has sometimes seemed to me that I am not really a literary fellow at all. Except that I write for a living.

INTERVIEWER

The affinity with nature has been very important to you. This seems a contradiction considering the urbanity of *The New Yorker* and its early contributions.

WHITE

There is no contradiction. New York is part of the natural world. I love the city, I love the country, and for the same reasons. The city is part of the country. When I had an apartment on East Forty-eighth Street, my backyard yielded more birds during the migratory season than I ever saw in Maine. I could step out on my porch, spring or fall, and there was the hermit thrush, picking around in McEvoy's yard. Or the white-throated sparrow, the brown thrasher, the jay, the kinglet. John Kieran has recorded the immense variety of flora and fauna within the limits of Greater New York.

But it is not just a question of birds and animals. The urban scene is a spectacle that fascinates me. People are animals, and the city is full of people in strange plumage, defending their territorial rights, digging for their supper.

INTERVIEWER

Although you say you are "not really a literary fellow at all," have you read any books, say in the past ten years, that deeply impressed you?

WHITE

I admire anybody who has the guts to write anything at all. As for what comes out on paper, I'm not well equipped to speak about it. When I should be reading, I am almost always doing something else. It is a matter of some embarrassment to me that I have never read Joyce and a dozen other writers who have changed the face of literature. But there you are. I picked up *Ulysses* the other evening, when my eye lit on it, and gave it a go. I stayed with it only for about twenty minutes, then was off and away. It takes more than a genius to keep me reading a book. But when I latch onto a book like *They Live by the Wind*, by Wendell P. Bradley, I am glued tight to the chair. It is because Bradley wrote about something that has always fascinated (and uplifted) me—sailing. He wrote about it very well, too.

I was deeply impressed by Rachel Carson's *Silent Spring*. It may well be the book by which the human race will stand or fall. I enjoyed *Speak, Memory* by Nabokov when I read it—a fine example of remembering.

INTERVIEWER

Do you have a special interest in the other arts?

WHITE

I have no special interest in any of the other arts. I know nothing of music or of painting or of sculpture or of dance. I would rather watch the circus or a ball game than ballet.

INTERVIEWER

Can you listen to music, or be otherwise half-distracted when you're working on something?

WHITE

I never listen to music when I'm working. I haven't that kind of attentiveness, and I wouldn't like it at all. On the other hand, I'm able to work fairly well among ordinary distractions. My house has a living room that is at the core of everything that goes on—it is a passageway to the cellar, to the kitchen, to the closet where the phone lives. There's a lot of traffic. But it's a bright, cheerful room, and I often use it as a room to write in, despite the carnival that is going on all around me. A girl pushing a carpet sweeper under my typewriter table has never annoyed me particularly, nor has it taken my mind off my work, unless the girl was unusually pretty or unusually clumsy. My wife, thank God, has never been protective of me, as I am told the wives of some writers are. In consequence, the members of my household never pay the slightest attention to my being a writing man—they make all the noise and fuss they want to. If I get sick of it, I have places I can go. A writer who waits for ideal conditions under which to work will die without putting a word on paper.

INTERVIEWER

Do you have any warm-up exercises to get going?

WHITE

Delay is natural to a writer. He is like a surfer—he bides his time, waits for the perfect wave on which to ride in. Delay is instinctive with him. He waits for the surge (of emotion? of strength? of courage?) that will carry him along. I have no warm-up exercises, other than to take an occasional drink. I am apt to let something simmer for a while in my mind before trying to put it into words. I walk around, straightening pictures on the wall, rugs on the floor—as though not until everything in the world was lined up and perfectly true could anybody reasonably expect me to set a word down on paper.

INTERVIEWER

You have wondered at Kenneth Roberts's working methods—his stamina and discipline. You said you often went to zoos rather than write. Can you say something of discipline and the writer?

WHITE

Kenneth Roberts wrote historical novels. He knew just what he wanted to do and where he was going. He rose in the morning and went to work, methodically and industriously. This has not been true of me. The things I have managed to write have been varied and spotty—a mishmash. Except for certain routine chores, I never knew in the morning how the day was going to develop. I was like a hunter, hoping to catch sight of a rabbit. There are two faces to discipline. If a man (who writes) feels like going to a zoo, he should by all means go to a zoo. He might even be lucky, as I once was when I paid a call at the Bronx Zoo and found myself attending the birth of twin fawns. It was a fine sight, and I lost no time writing a piece about it. The other face of discipline is that, zoo or no zoo, diversion or no diversion, in the end a man must sit down and get the words on paper, and against great odds. This takes stamina and resolution. Having got them on paper, he must still have the discipline to discard them if they fail to measure up—he must view them with a jaundiced eye and do the whole thing over as many times as is necessary to achieve excellence, or as close to excellence as he can get. This varies from one time to maybe twenty.

INTERVIEWER

Does the finished product need a gestation period—that is, do you put a finished work away and look at it a month hence?

WHITE

It depends on what kind of product it is. Many a poem could well use more than nine months. On the other hand, a newspaper report of a fire in a warehouse can't be expected to enjoy a gestation period. When I finished *Charlotte's Web*, I put it away, feeling that something was wrong. The story had taken me two years to write, working on and off, but I was in no particular hurry. I took another year to rewrite it, and it was a year well spent. If I write something and feel doubtful about it, I soak it away. The passage of time can be a help in evaluating it. But in general, I tend to rush into print, riding a wave of emotion.

Do you revise endlessly? How do you know when something is right? Is perhaps this critical ability the necessary equipment for the writer?

I revise a great deal. I know when something is right because bells begin ringing and lights flash. I'm not at all sure what the "necessary equipment" is for a writer—it seems to vary greatly with the individual. Some writers are equipped with extrasensory perception. Some have a good ear, like O'Hara. Some are equipped with humor—although not nearly as many as those who think they are. Some are equipped with a massive intellect, like Wilson. Some are prodigious. I do think the ability to evaluate one's own stuff with reasonable accuracy is a helpful piece of equipment. I've known good writers who've had it, and I've known good writers who've not. I've known writers who were utterly convinced that anything at all, if it came from their pen, was the work of genius and as close to being right as anything can be.

In your essay, "An Approach to Style," your first rule for the writer is to place himself in the background. But recently you are quoted as saying: "I am an egoist, inclined to inject myself into almost everything I write." Is this not contradictory?

There is no contradiction. The precept "place yourself in the background" is a useful one. It's true that I paid little attention to it. Neither have a lot of other writers. It all depends on what's going on, and it depends on the nature of the beast. An accomplished reporter usually places himself in the background. An experienced novelist usually does. But certainly nobody would want B. Cory Kilvert Jr. to place himself in the background—there would be nothing left. As for me, I'm no Kilvert, neither am I a reporter or a novelist. I live by my wits and started at an early age to inject myself into the act, as a clown does in the ring. This is all very well if you can get away with it, but a young writer will find that it is better discipline to stay in the background than to lunge forward on the assumption that his presence is necessary for the success of the occasion.

INTERVIEWER

Since your interest with Strunk on style, have there been any other such books you would recommend?

WHITE

I'm not familiar with books on style. My role in the revival of Strunk's book was a fluke—just something I took on because I was not doing anything else at the time. It cost me a year out of my life, so little did I know about grammar.

INTERVIEWER

Is style something that can be taught?

WHITE

I don't think it can be taught. Style results more from what a person is than from what he knows. But there are a few hints that can be thrown out to advantage.

INTERVIEWER

What would these few hints be?

WHITE

They would be the twenty-one hints I threw out in Chapter V of *The Elements of Style*. There was nothing new or original about them, but there they are, for all to read.

INTERVIEWER

Thurber said that if there was such a thing as a *New Yorker* style, possibly it was "playing it down." Would you agree?

WHITE

I don't agree that there is such a thing as *New Yorker* style. The magazine has published an enormous volume of stuff, written by a very long and varied roster of contributors. I see not the slightest resemblance between, say, Cheever's style and the style of the late Alva Johnston. I see no resemblance between, say, Thurber's style and the style of Muriel Spark. If sometimes there seems to be a sort of sameness of sound in *The New Yorker*, it probably can be traced to the magazine's copy desk, which is a marvelous fortress of grammatical exactitude and stylish convention. Commas in *The New Yorker* fall with the precision of knives in a circus act, outlining the victim. This may sometimes have a slight tendency to make one writer sound a bit like another. But on the whole, *New Yorker* writers are jealous of their own way of doing things and they are never chivied against their will into doing it some other way.

INTERVIEWER

Do you think media such as television and motion pictures have had any effect on contemporary literary styles?

WHITE

Television affects the style of children—that I know. I receive letters from children, and many of them begin, Dear Mr. White, My name is Donna Reynolds. This is the Walter Cronkite gambit, straight out of TV. When I was a child I never started a letter, My name is Elwyn White. I simply signed my name at the end.

INTERVIEWER

You once wrote that English usage is often "sheer luck, like getting across a street." Could one deduce from this that great writers are also lucky?

WHITE

No, I don't think so. My remark about the ingredient of luck in English usage merely referred to the bog hole that every writer occasionally steps into. He begins a sentence, gets into the middle of it, and finds there is no way out short of retracing his steps and starting again. That's all I meant about luck in usage.

INTERVIEWER

Could we ask some questions about humor? Is one of the problems that humor is so perishable?

WHITE

I find difficulty with the word *humor* and with the word *humorist* to peg a writer. I was taken aback, the other day, when I looked in *Who's Who* to discover Frank Sullivan's birthday and found him described as "humorist." It seemed a wholly inadequate summary of the man. Writing funny pieces is a legitimate form of activity, but the durable humor in literature, I suspect, is not the contrived humor of a funnyman commenting on the news but the sly and almost imperceptible ingredient that sometimes gets into writing. I think of Jane Austen, a deeply humorous woman. I think of Thoreau, a man of some humor along with his bile.

INTERVIEWER

Dorothy Parker said that S. J. Perelman was the only humorist around and that he must be pretty lonely.

WHITE

Perelman is our dean of humor, because he has set such a high standard of writing and has been at it for so long. His virtuosity is unchallenged. But he's not the only humorist around. I can't stand the word *humorist* anyway. It does not seem to cover the situation. Perelman is a satirist who writes in a funny way. If you part the bushes, I'm sure you will find somebody skulking there—probably a younger, if not a better, man. I don't know what his name is.

INTERVIEWER

Parker makes a great distinction between wit and wisecracking. She said that the satirists were the "big boys . . . those boys in the other centuries."

WHITE

I agree that satire is the thing but not that it is the property of "other centuries." We have had Wolcott Gibbs, Russell Maloney, Clarence Day, Ring Lardner, Frank Sullivan, Sid Perelman, and Don Marquis, to mention a few. Satire is a most difficult and subtle form of writing, requiring a kind of natural genius. Any reasonably well-educated person can write in a satirical vein, but try and find one that comes off.

INTERVIEWER

You were also an artist. What did Thurber and the other *New Yorker* artists think of your drawings and *New Yorker* covers?

WHITE

I'm not an artist and never did any drawings for *The New Yorker*. I did turn in a cover and it was published. I can't draw or paint, but I was sick in bed with tonsillitis or something, and I had nothing to occupy me, but I had a cover idea—of a sea horse wearing a nose bag. I borrowed my son's watercolor set, copied a sea horse from a picture in Webster's dictionary, and managed to produce a cover that was bought. It wasn't much of a thing. I even loused up the whole business finally by printing the word *oats* on the nose bag, lest somebody fail to get the point. I suppose the original of that cover would be a collector's item of a minor sort, since it is my only excursion into the world of art. But I don't know where it is. I gave it to Jed Harris. What he did with it, knows God.

INTERVIEWER

You did write the famous caption for the Carl Rose drawing of a mother saying to her youngster, "It's broccoli, dear"—with the child's reply, "I say it's spinach, and I say the hell with it." Why do you think it caused so much reaction as to become, as Thurber said, "part of the American language"?

WHITE

It's hard to say why a certain thing takes hold, as that caption did. The Carl Rose drawing turned up in the office with an entirely different caption—I can't recall what it was, but it had nothing to do with broccoli or spinach. The drawing landed on my desk for recaptioning, and I abandoned the theme of the Rose caption and went off on my own. I can't say why it got into the language. Perhaps it struck a responsive chord with parents who found it true of children, or, more likely, true of what they liked to think a child might say under such circumstances.

INTERVIEWER

Many people have said that your wife, Katharine S. White, was the "intellectual soul" of *The New Yorker* in the early days, and her enormous influence and contributions have never been recorded adequately.

WHITE

I have never seen an adequate account of Katharine's role with *The New Yorker*. Then Mrs. Ernest Angell, she was one of the first editors to be hired, and I can't imagine what would have happened to the magazine if she hadn't turned up. Ross, though something of a genius, had serious gaps. In Katharine, he found someone who filled them in. No two people were ever more different than Mr. Ross and Mrs. Angell. What he lacked, she had. What she lacked, he had. She complemented him in a way that, in retrospect, seems to me to have been indispensable to the survival of the magazine. She was a product of Miss Winsor's and Bryn Mawr. Ross was a high school dropout. She had a natural refinement of manner and speech. Ross mumbled and bellowed and swore. She quickly discovered, in this fumbling and impoverished new weekly, something that fascinated her—its quest for humor, its search for excellence, its involvement with young writers and artists. She enjoyed contact with people. Ross, with certain exceptions, despised it—especially during hours. She was patient and quiet. He was impatient and noisy. Katharine was soon sitting in on art sessions and planning sessions, editing fiction and poetry, cheering and steering authors and artists along the paths they were eager to follow, learning makeup, learning pencil editing, heading the Fiction Department, sharing the personal woes and dilemmas of innumerable contributors and staff people who were in trouble or despair, and, in short, accepting the whole unruly business of a tottering magazine with the warmth and dedication of a broody hen.

I had a bird's-eye view of all this because, in the midst of it, I became her husband. During the day, I saw her in operation at the office. At the end of the day, I watched her bring the whole mess home with her in a cheap and bulging portfolio. The light burned late, our bed was lumpy with page proofs, and our home was alive with laughter and the pervasive spirit of her dedication and her industry. In forty-four years, this dedication has not cooled. It is strong today, although she is out of the running, from age and ill health. Perhaps the nearest thing to an adequate glimpse of her role with the magazine is a collection of books in our upstairs sitting room. They are the published works of the dozens of fiction writers and poets she edited over the years, and their flyleaves are full of words of love and admiration and gratitude.

Everyone has a few lucky days in his life. I suspect one of Ross's luckiest was the day a young woman named Mrs. Angell stepped off the elevator, all ready to go to work.

INTERVIEWER

Is there any shifting of gears in writing such children's books as *Charlotte's Web* and *Stuart Little*? Do you write to a particular age group?

WHITE

Anybody who shifts gears when he writes for children is likely to wind up stripping his gears. But I don't want to evade your question. There *is* a difference between writing for children and for adults. I am lucky though, as I seldom seem to have my audience in mind when I am at work. It is as though they don't exist.

Anyone who writes down to children is simply wasting his time. You have to write up, not down. Children are demanding. They are the most attentive, curious, eager, observant, sensitive, quick, and generally congenial readers on earth. They accept, almost without question, anything you present them with, as long as it is presented honestly, fearlessly, and clearly. I handed them, against the advice of experts, a mouse-boy, and they accepted it without a quiver. In *Charlotte's Web*, I gave them a literate spider, and they took that.

Some writers for children deliberately avoid using words they think a child doesn't know. This emasculates the prose and, I suspect, bores the reader. Children are game for anything. I throw them hard words, and they backhand them over the net. They love words that give them a hard time, provided they are in a context that absorbs their attention. I'm lucky again—my own vocabulary is small, compared to most writers, and I tend to use the short words. So it's no problem for me to write for children. We have a lot in common.

INTERVIEWER

What are your views about the writer's commitment to politics, international affairs? You have written so much (*The Wild Flag*, for example,) about federal and international issues.

WHITE

A writer should concern himself with whatever absorbs his fancy, stirs his heart, and unlimbers his typewriter. I feel no obligation to deal with politics. I do feel a responsibility to society because of going into print—a writer has the duty to be good, not lousy; true, not false; lively, not dull; accurate, not full of error. He should tend to lift people up, not lower them down. Writers do not merely reflect and interpret life, they inform and shape life.

For a number of years, I was thinking almost continuously about the needless chaos and cruelty of a world that is essentially parochial, composed of more than a hundred parishes, or nations, each spying on the others, each plotting against the others, each concerned almost solely with its own bailiwick and its own stunt. I wrote some pieces about world government, or "supranational" government. I didn't do it from any sense of commitment, I did it because it was what I felt like writing. Today, although I seldom discuss the theme, I am as convinced as I ever was that our only chance of achieving an orderly world is by constructing a governed world. I regard disarmament as a myth, diplomacy as a necessary evil under present conditions, and absolute sovereignty as something to outgrow.

INTERVIEWER

Can you suggest something about the present state of letters, and, perhaps, the future of letters?

WHITE

I don't suppose a man who hasn't read *Portnoy's Complaint* should comment on the present state of letters. In general, I have no objection to permissiveness in writing. Permissiveness, however, lets down the bars for a whole army of nonwriters who rush in to say the words, take the profits, and foul up the room. Shocking writing is like murder— the questions the jury must decide are the questions of motive and intent.

INTERVIEWER

In a country such as ours, which has become increasingly enamored of and dependent upon science and technology, what role do you see for the writer?

WHITE

The writer's role is what it has always been—he is a custodian, a secretary. Science and technology have perhaps deepened his responsibility but not changed it. In "The Ring of Time," I wrote: "As a writing man, or secretary, I have always felt charged with the safekeeping of all unexpected items of worldly or unworldly enchantment, as though I might be held personally responsible if even a small one were to be lost. But it is not easy to communicate anything of this nature."

A writer must reflect and interpret his society, his world. He must also provide inspiration and guidance and challenge. Much writing today strikes me as deprecating, destructive, and angry. There are good reasons for anger, and I have nothing against anger. But I think some writers have lost their sense of proportion, their sense of humor, and their sense of appreciation. I am often mad, but I would hate to be nothing but mad. I think I would lose what little value I may have as a writer if I were to refuse, as a matter of principle, to accept the warming rays of the sun, and to report them whenever, and if ever, they happen to strike me. One role of the writer today is to sound the alarm. The environment is disintegrating, the hour is late, and not much is being done. Instead of carting rocks from the moon, we should be carting the feces out of Lake Erie.

INTERVIEWER

How extensive are the journals you have kept and do you hope to publish them? Could you tell us something of their subject matter?

WHITE

The journals date from about 1917 to about 1930, with a few entries of more recent date. They occupy two-thirds of a whiskey carton. How many words that would be I have no idea, but it would be an awful lot.

The journals are callow, sententious, moralistic, and full of rubbish. They are also hard to ignore. They were written sometimes in longhand, sometimes typed (single spaced). They contain many clippings. Extensive is the word for them. I do not hope to publish them, but I would like to get a little mileage out of them. After so many years, they tend to hold my attention even though they do not excite my admiration. I have already dipped into them on a couple of occasions, to help out on a couple of pieces.

In most respects they are disappointing. Where I would like to discover facts, I find fancy. Where I would like to learn what I did, I learn only what I was thinking. They are loaded with opinion, moral thoughts, quick evaluations, youthful hopes and cares and sorrows. Occasionally, they manage to report something in exquisite honesty and accuracy. This is why I have refrained from burning them. But usually, after reading a couple of pages, I put them aside in disgust and pick up Reverend Robert Francis Kilvert, to see what a good diarist can do.

INTERVIEWER

Faulkner has said of writers, "All of us failed to match our dreams of perfection." Would you put yourself in this category?

WHITE

Yes. My friend, John McNulty, had a title for a popular song he always intended to write and never did: "Keep your dreams within reason." We both thought this was a very funny idea for a song. I still think it is funny. My dreams have never been kept within reason. I'm glad they've not been. And Faulkner was right—all of us failed.

INTERVIEWER

Could you say what those dreams were?

WHITE

No. Here I think you are asking me to be specific, or explicit, about something that is essentially vague and inexpressible. Don Marquis said it perfectly: "My heart has followed all my days / Something I cannot name."

INTERVIEWER

What is it, do you think, when you try to write an English sentence at this date, that causes you to "fly into a thousand pieces"? Are you still encouraged (as Ross once wrote you after reading a piece of yours) "to go on"?

WHITE

It isn't just "at this date"—I've always been unstable under pressure. When I start to write, my mind is apt to race, like a clock from which the pendulum has been removed. I simply can't keep up, with pen or typewriter, and this causes me to break apart. I think there are writers whose thoughts flow in a smooth and orderly fashion, and they can transcribe them on paper without undue emotion or without getting too far behind. I envy them. When you consider that there are a thousand ways to express even the simplest idea, it is no wonder writers are under a great strain. Writers care greatly how a thing is said—it makes all the difference. So they are constantly faced with too many choices and must make too many decisions.

I am still encouraged to go on. I wouldn't know where else to go.

Issue 48, 1969

P. G. Wodehouse
The Art of Fiction

When I first went to see him, I telephoned P. G. Wodehouse and asked for directions from New York to his house on Long Island. He merely chuckled, as if I had asked him to compare Euclid with Einstein or attempt some other laughably impossible task. "Oh, I can't tell you that," he said. "I don't have a clue." I learned the route anyway, and my arrival for lunch, only ten minutes late, seemed to astonish him. "You had no trouble? Oh, that is good. That's wonderful!" His face beaming at having in his house such a certified problem solver, a junior Jeeves almost, he led me without further to-do to a telephone, which he had been dialing all morning in a futile effort to reach a number in New York. He had, of course, done everything right but dial the area code, an addition to the Bell system that had somehow escaped his attention since he had last attempted long distance. He was intensely pleased when New York answered, and I sunned myself in the warm glow of his gratitude for the rest of the day. All of which is by way of saying that Wodehouse, who lived four months past his ninety-third birthday, had discovered his own secret of long life: he simply ignored what was worrisome, bothersome, or confusing in the world around him.

His wife, Ethel, or his sister-in-law, Helen, did the worrying for him. On my three visits Ethel would hover around him at the beginning of our conversation to plump his pillow or fill his sherry glass, then discreetly disappear to tend to an ailing dog or cat. They had

A's first scene with L. C. P. stayed in London to clear up to pal when P.'s husband. They tell J.'s hardness

V. Good

Bringing In Florence's husband.

1. He might be spoken of in Gally's scene with Beach in Ch 2 No
; A: Ah Vicky mention him in the first scene with Gally? No

2. Also in Gally's first scene with Florence. (G. cd reproach her with being hard on husband. Yes

3. On p.31. Piper at lunch and Gally stay on to — more keen Enter husband (———). He cd ask Gally about how Florence is and how to get reconciliation.
   Gally cd go in to castle and tell F. husband wants reconciliation — F. throats,

4. The big scene wd be when L. C. finds Claude second, Jeff's bedroom (Let Coot reason why L. C. comes to Jeff's room). Claude says I suspect Jeff & Rett. L. C. furious, rushes up, accuses F.
   See noted for some reason why husband is there (It cd be from Gally's advance) Husband stands up for J, tells L. C. he is a bully, (but he is) urges J. to come back to him and J. says she will.

_____

& Because | Problems.
see notes | A. Who is husband? Is he old pal of Gally?
| B. How comes he to be in J's room? Of G. ought to have told him to hide and spring out and have the 3. He has given husband some method or he was; we thundering

5. It looks as if husband ought not to be rich or he wd
   Good | give V. money. Try this. Make Florence widow of ? millionaire who has married a careless near a alarming penniless man.

_____

4 cts. F's husband reconciled. They are leaving. Gally tells F. to give V. money to everyone. She refused and leaves.
∴ Then wd come the Piper — Mavration stuff.
   No. Before that L. C. must find jewel., then the P. M. stuff.
   P grateful to Gally who assigns getting Jeff the architectural job.

about a half-dozen of each, most of them strays that had come begging to the door. Wodehouse himself had not found it necessary to carry money in twenty years, and though he had spent most of his adult life in America, he still reckoned such things as book prices in pounds and shillings. His accent, like his arithmetic, remained pure English. Aside from his writing, his two passions were the New York Mets and a soap opera called *The Edge of Night*. On those extremely rare occasions when he had to leave the house for the day, Ethel was assigned to watch the program and write down exactly what had happened. "I understand that you're going to watch *The Edge of Night* with me," he said on one of my visits. "That's splendid!"

Wodehouse lived on twelve acres in Remsenburg, a pretty, quiet little town in eastern Long Island, and from his glass-enclosed study, and most of the rest of the house, all that he could see was greenery. He was as happily isolated there as if he were living in Blandings Castle itself. He enjoyed all the hoopla that surrounded him in his old age, but he also found the attention very tiring. "Everything more or less quiet here now," he wrote me a week after he had been dubbed Sir Pelham, "but it has been hell with all the interviewers." A month after that he died, as peacefully and as quietly as he had lived, according to all accounts.

—*Gerald Clarke, 1975*

INTERVIEWER

The last time I saw you was at your ninetieth birthday party in 1971.

P. G. WODEHOUSE

Oh, yes. All that ninetieth-birthday thing gave me not exactly a heart attack. But I had to have treatment, you know. I'm always taking pills and things. One good effect of the treatment, however, is that I lost about twenty pounds. I feel frightfully fit now, except my legs are a bit wobbly.

INTERVIEWER

You're ninety-one now, aren't you?

WODEHOUSE

Ninety-one and a half! Ninety-two in October.

INTERVIEWER

You don't have any trouble reading now, do you?

WODEHOUSE

Oh, no!

INTERVIEWER

How about writing?

WODEHOUSE

Oh, as far as the brain goes, I'm fine. I've just finished another novel, in fact. I've got a wonderful title for it, *Bachelors Anonymous*. Don't you think that's good? Yes, everybody likes that title. Peter Schwed, my editor at Simon and Schuster, nearly always alters my titles, but he raved over that one. I think the book is so much better than my usual stuff that I don't know how I can top it. It really is funny. It's worked out awfully well. I'm rather worried about the next one. It will be a letdown almost. I don't want to be like Bernard Shaw. He turned out some awfully bad stuff in his nineties. He said he knew the stuff was bad but he couldn't stop writing.

INTERVIEWER

What is your working schedule these days?

P. G. WODEHOUSE

I still start the day off at seven-thirty. I do my daily dozen exercises, have breakfast, and then go into my study. When I am between books, as I am now, I sit in an armchair and think and make notes. Before I start a book I've usually got four hundred pages of notes.

Most of them are almost incoherent. But there's always a moment when you feel you've got a novel started. You can more or less see how it's going to work out. After that it's just a question of detail.

INTERVIEWER

You block everything out in advance, then?

WODEHOUSE

Yes. For a humorous novel you've got to have a scenario, and you've got to test it so that you know where the comedy comes in, where the situations come in . . . splitting it up into scenes (you can make a scene of almost anything) and having as little stuff in between as possible.

INTERVIEWER

Is it really possible to know in a scenario where something funny is going to be?

WODEHOUSE

Yes, you can do that. Still, it's curious how a scenario gets lost as you go along. I don't think I've ever actually kept completely to one. If I've got a plot for a novel worked out and I can really get going on it, I work all the time. I work in the morning, and then I probably go for a walk or something, and then I have another go at the novel. I find that from four to seven is a particularly good time for working. I never work after dinner. It's the plots that I find so hard to work out. It takes such a long time to work one out. I like to think of some scene, it doesn't matter how crazy, and work backward and forward from it until eventually it becomes quite plausible and fits neatly into the story.

INTERVIEWER

How many words do you usually turn out on a good day?

WODEHOUSE

Well, I've slowed up a good deal now. I used to write about two thousand words. Now I suppose I do about one thousand.

INTERVIEWER

Do you work seven days a week?

WODEHOUSE

Oh, yes, rather. Always.

INTERVIEWER

Do you type or do you write in longhand?

WODEHOUSE

I used to work entirely on the typewriter. But this last book I did sitting in a lawn chair and writing by hand. Then I typed it out. Much slower, of course. But I think it's a pretty good method—it does pretty well.

INTERVIEWER

Do you go back and revise very much?

WODEHOUSE

Yes. And I very often find that I've got something that ought to come in another place—a scene that I originally put in chapter two, but then when I get to chapter ten, I feel it would come in much better there. I'm sort of molding the whole time.

INTERVIEWER

How long does it take you to write a novel?

WODEHOUSE

Well, in the old days I used to rely on it being about three months, but now it might take any length of time. I forget exactly how long *Bachelors Anonymous* took, but it must have been six or seven months.

INTERVIEWER

That still seems very fast to me.

WODEHOUSE

It's still good, yes.

INTERVIEWER

If you were asked to give advice to somebody who wanted to write humorous fiction, what would you tell him?

WODEHOUSE

I'd give him practical advice, and that is always get to the dialogue as soon as possible. I always feel the thing to go for is speed. Nothing puts the reader off more than a great slab of prose at the start. I think the success of every novel—if it's a novel of action—depends on the high spots. The thing to do is to say to yourself, Which are my big scenes? and then get every drop of juice out of them. The principle I always go on in writing a novel is to think of the characters in terms of actors in a play. I say to myself, if a big name were playing this part, and if he found that after a strong first act he had practically nothing to do in the second act, he would walk out. Now, then, can I twist the story so as to give him plenty to do all the way through? I believe the only way a writer can keep himself up to the mark is by examining each story quite coldly before he starts writing it and asking himself if it is all right *as a story*. I mean, once you go saying to yourself, This is a pretty weak plot as it stands, but I'm such a hell of a writer that my magic touch will make it okay—you're sunk. If they aren't in interesting situations, characters can't be major characters, not even if you have the rest of the troop talk their heads off about them.

INTERVIEWER

What do you think makes a story funny?

WODEHOUSE

I think character mostly. You know instinctively what's funny and what isn't if you're a humorous writer. I don't think a man can deliberately sit down to write a funny story unless he has got a sort of slant on life that leads to funny stories. If you take life fairly easily, then you take a humorous view of things. It's probably because you were born that way. Lord Emsworth and his pig—I *know* they're funny.

INTERVIEWER

Did you ever know anyone who was actually like Lord Emsworth?

WODEHOUSE

No. Psmith is the only one of my characters who is drawn from life. He started in a boys' story, and then I did a grown-up story about him in *The Saturday Evening Post*. People sometimes want to know why I didn't go on with Psmith. But I don't think that the things that made him funny as a very young man would be funny in an older man. He had a very boring sort of way of expressing himself. Called everybody comrade and all that sort of thing. I couldn't go on with him. I don't think he'd have worked as a maturer character. In a way my character Galahad is really Psmith grown up.

INTERVIEWER

But Galahad works very well as a character.

WODEHOUSE

Yes, Galahad is fine.

INTERVIEWER

How old is he supposed to be?

WODEHOUSE

How old all those characters are I don't know. The first short story I wrote about Lord Emsworth said that he had been to Eton in 1864, which would make him a hundred and something now!

INTERVIEWER

What period are the books set in?

WODEHOUSE

Well, between the wars, rather. I try not to date them at all, but it's rather difficult. I'm bad at remembering things, like when flying really became fashionable. The critics keep saying that the world I write about never existed. But of course it did. It was going strong between the wars. In a way it is hard to write the sort of stuff I do now because it really is so out-of-date. The character of Jeeves is practically unknown in England now, though I believe someone told me the butler was creeping back. Bertie Wooster and Oofy Proster have more or less vanished, too. I suppose a typical member of the Drones Club now is someone with a job and very earnest about it. Those rather hit-or-miss days have passed away. But thank God, that doesn't seem to matter!

INTERVIEWER

I suppose that the world has gone the way of spats. You were very fond of spats, weren't you? Tell me a little about them.

WODEHOUSE

I don't know why spats went out! The actual name was spatter-dashers, and you fastened them over your ankles, you see, to prevent the spatter from dashing you. They certainly lent tone to your appearance, and they were awfully comfortable, especially when you wore them in cold weather. I've written articles, which were rather funny, about how I used to go about London. I would borrow my brother's frock coat and my uncle's hat, but my spats were always new and impeccable. The butler would open the door and take in my old topcoat and hat and sniff as if to say, Hardly the sort of thing we are accustomed to. And then he would look down at the spats and everything would be all right. It's a shame when things like spats go out.

INTERVIEWER

Did you ever have a butler like Jeeves?

WODEHOUSE

No, never like Jeeves. My butlers were quite different, though I believe J. M. Barrie had one just like Jeeves.

INTERVIEWER

How did you create Jeeves, then?

WODEHOUSE

I only intended to use him once. His first entrance was: "Mrs. Gregson to see you, sir," in a story called "Extricating Young Gussie." He only had one other line, "Very good, sir. Which suit will you wear?" But then I was writing a story, "The Artistic Career of Corky," about two young men, Bertie Wooster and his friend Corky, getting into a lot of trouble, and neither of them had brains enough to get out of the trouble. I thought, Well, how can I get them out? And I thought, Suppose one of them had an omniscient valet? I wrote a short story about him, then another short story, then several more short stories and novels. That's how a character grows. I think I've written nine Jeeves novels now and about thirty short stories.

INTERVIEWER

I like Jeeves, but my favorite character of yours is really Lord Emsworth.

WODEHOUSE

Oh, yes. He's about my favorite character, too. Well, now, he must be entirely out-of-date. I don't suppose anybody in England is living in a castle like that anymore.

INTERVIEWER

Maybe not, but I suspect that there are still some woolly-headed English aristocrats around.

WODEHOUSE

Oh, yes?

INTERVIEWER

Will you write any more Lord Emsworth stories?

WODEHOUSE

I don't know if I shall. I've got him in such a pleasant position now. He's free of both his sisters. He's got his pig, and he's living alone and loving it. He's comfortable by himself. It seems rather unkind to disturb him. . . . I do think I'd like to have a try, though. You see, that's the problem. I'd love to do a Lord Emsworth story, but what could it be about? I mean, what could happen? The trouble is, you see, that I've so featured the pig that I couldn't leave her out. And yet, what could happen to a pig? It is difficult to find plots when you have written so much. The ideas don't seem to come to me now. I suppose it's temporary. I've always felt like this in between books. But I have used up every possible situation. If I do get a good idea, I find it is something I wrote in the thirties.

INTERVIEWER

I think the closest you have come to sex in your novels is a kiss on the cheek. Have you ever been tempted to put anything spicier into them?

WODEHOUSE

No. No, I don't think the framework of the novel would stand it. Sex, of course, can be awfully funny, but you have to know how to handle it. And I don't think I can handle it properly.

INTERVIEWER

Sex aside, have you ever thought of writing anything more serious?

WODEHOUSE

No. I don't think I'm capable of writing anything but the sort of thing I do write. I couldn't write a serious book.

INTERVIEWER

Did you always know you would be a writer?

WODEHOUSE

Yes, always. I know I was writing stories when I was five. I don't remember what I did before that. Just loafed, I suppose. I was about twenty when I sold my first story, and I've been a full-time writer since 1902. I can't think of myself as anything but a writer.

INTERVIEWER

Did you ever have another career?

WODEHOUSE

When I left school. I was first working for scholarship at Oxford when my father's finances took rather a nasty jar and I wasn't able to go up to Oxford, and instead was put in the bank, the Hong Kong and Shanghai Bank, which I hated at first but later got to like. The bank had branches all over the East. After two years in the London branch you'd get your orders to go out there, which of course appalled me because in my two years I never learned a thing about banking. The idea of going out to Bombay or somewhere and being a branch manager and being paid in rupees scared me stiff.

All this time I was writing and getting rejections. Because the trouble is when you start writing, you write awful stuff. And I was writing on banking hours, too. My second year I got into the cash department and my job was to enter the deposits on the ledger. After a while a new ledger was provided and I sat down and suddenly thought of a wonderful idea—to write in the new ledger an account of the Great Opening of the New Ledger, with the King coming and all that. And I did this and, having done it, repented and thought this was going to get me into trouble, and I got a knife and I cut the first page of the ledger out. It so happened that the chief cashier had got a long feud on with the stationers and he'd been trying to catch them out for years and when he saw this ledger with the front page missing, he thought, Ah, this is my chance, and he went and cursed them for giving us an imperfect ledger. But I didn't get the sack for it.

I left the bank after that second year, however, to go to the *Globe*. I had been doing occasional day jobs for an old master of mine who'd become a journalist and ran the comic column at the *Globe*. I'd pretend I'd sprained my back lifting a ledger or something, and I'd do my work for the *Globe*. Then when he went on summer holiday, I took his place and eventually got on the staff in 1902 when he resigned. In those days the pay was three pounds a week (about fifteen dollars) and I could live on that very well.

INTERVIEWER

From those days to now, have you continued to read criticism of your own work?

WODEHOUSE

Yes. I get a lot of reviews sent to me. They are invariably favorable. And somehow I always read them really carefully. You do get tips from them. Now, that last Jeeves book of mine, *Jeeves and the Tie That Binds*, I forget which critic it was, but he said that the book was dangerously near to self-parody. I know what he meant. I had exaggerated Jeeves and Bertie. Jeeves always reciting some poetry or something. I'll correct that in the next one. I do think one can learn from criticism. In fact, I'm a pretty good critic of my own work. I know when it isn't as good as it ought to be.

INTERVIEWER

Do you ever feel angry at critics? Do you ever feel they are unfair?

WODEHOUSE

No, I don't think so. You always feel that you can't please everybody.

INTERVIEWER

Some critics, going beyond any particular book, think that your short stories are better than your novels. What do you think?

WODEHOUSE

Yes, I think I'd sooner write short stories than novels. I feel really happy with a short story. I like the sense of completing something.

The only trouble is that if I do get a good idea, I rather want to work it into a novel. I mean, I'm rather wasting a novel if I write a short story.

INTERVIEWER

Who are your own favorite humorists?

WODEHOUSE

The ones I like most are all dead—James Thurber, Robert Benchley, Wolcott Gibbs, George S. Kaufman.

INTERVIEWER

Do you like S. J. Perelman?

WODEHOUSE

Oh, yes, yes, yes. He's quite a favorite of mine. But there are very few writers like that now, just writing funny stuff, not like in the twenties and thirties. When I first came over here all the evening papers, the evening *World* and the others, all had funny poems and columns in them. I liked F.P.A.'s column very much. But I don't think people buy funny books nowadays. I never have had a big sale over here. Where I get my money is England, Sweden, Italy, France, and Germany.

INTERVIEWER

Do you think there are more humorous writers in England than America?

WODEHOUSE

They haven't got any in England either.

INTERVIEWER

Do you like Peter De Vries?

WODEHOUSE

I'm not frightfully keen on him. I haven't read very much of his stuff. But I'll tell you who is awfully good is Jean Kerr. Ooooh, she's wonderful. *Mary, Mary* was one of the best plays I've ever read. Anthony Powell is also a good writer. It's extraordinary how interesting his stuff is, you know. And it just goes on and on, with nothing much in the way of scenes or anything. You wouldn't call it funny stuff, though, would you?

INTERVIEWER

No, I don't suppose so. What have you been reading most recently?

WODEHOUSE

I've been reading the old books, books that I've read before. The first time you read a book, you don't read it at all carefully—you just read it for the story. You have to keep rereading. Every year or so I read Shakespeare straight through. But then I go to the latest by Agatha Christie or Rex Stout. I read every book of theirs. I do like a book with an elaborate plot. But I haven't any definite plan of reading. I read almost everything, and I like anything that's good. I've just reread a book of A. A. Milne's called *Two People*, which I had read several times before. His novel is simply a novel of character. It's not the sort of thing I can write myself, but as a reader I enjoy it thoroughly.

INTERVIEWER

Do you read any contemporary novels?

WODEHOUSE

I've read some of Norman Mailer.

INTERVIEWER

Do you like his writing?

WODEHOUSE

I don't like his novels very much, but he writes very interesting nonfiction stuff. I liked *Advertisements for Myself* very much.

INTERVIEWER

How about the Beats? Someone like Jack Kerouac, for instance, who died a few years ago?

WODEHOUSE

Jack Kerouac died! Did he?

INTERVIEWER

Yes.

WODEHOUSE

Oh . . . Gosh, they do die off, don't they?

INTERVIEWER

Do you ever go back and reread your own books?

WODEHOUSE

Oh, yes.

INTERVIEWER

Are you ever surprised by them?

WODEHOUSE

I'm rather surprised that they're so good.

INTERVIEWER

Of all the books you've written, do you have any favorites?

WODEHOUSE

Oh, I'm very fond of a book called *Quick Service* and another called *Sam in the Suburbs*, a very old one. But I really like them all. There are very few exceptions.

INTERVIEWER

Have you ever been envious of another writer?

WODEHOUSE

No, never. I'm really such a voracious reader that I'm only too grateful to get some stuff I can read.

INTERVIEWER

Have any other writers ever been envious of you?

WODEHOUSE

Well, I always thought A. A. Milne was rather. We were supposed to be quite good friends, but, you know, in a sort of way I think he was a pretty jealous chap. I think he was probably jealous of all other writers. But I loved his stuff. That's one thing I'm very grateful for—I don't have to like an awful person to like his stuff. I like Somerset Maugham's stuff tremendously, for example, but I should think he was unhappy all the time, wouldn't you? He was an unpleasant man.

INTERVIEWER

Was he unpleasant to you?

WODEHOUSE

No. He was all right to me. We got along on just sort of "how do you do" terms. I remember walking back from a cricket match at Lords in London, and Maugham came along on the other side. He looked at me and I looked at him, and we were thinking the same thing—Oh my God, shall we have to stop and talk? Fortunately, we didn't.

INTERVIEWER

I don't think writers get along very well with one another.

WODEHOUSE

No, I don't think they do, really. I think they're jealous of each other. I do get along with them superficially, if everything's all right. But you feel they're resenting you, rather . . . What do you imagine the standing of a writer like Arnold Bennett is now?

INTERVIEWER

I don't think anybody reads him.

WODEHOUSE

That's what I think, too. But when he was alive, he was very much a sort of great literary man.

INTERVIEWER

Let's switch to your own life for a minute. You and Ethel were living in France when the Germans invaded in 1940. You were interned for about a year in Germany and Ethel had to live in Berlin. Why didn't you escape to England when you had a chance?

WODEHOUSE

Oh, everything happened so suddenly. Until the Germans arrived there didn't seem to be any danger at all. I suppose really the whole thing was that we had two dogs we were very fond of, and because of the English quarantine laws we couldn't take them into England. We weren't very good at organizing a thing like that.

INTERVIEWER

You later made some broadcasts from Berlin for CBS radio describing your life in the camp. Those broadcasts caused great controversy in Britain, and for a time you were rather savagely denounced there. Do you regret making them?

WODEHOUSE

Oh, yes. Oh, rather. I wish I hadn't. It never occurred to me that there was anything wrong in the broadcasts. They altered my whole life. I suppose I would have gone back to England and so on if it hadn't been for them. Yet they were so perfectly harmless, just a comic description of my adventures in camp. Of course, nobody ever published them.

INTERVIEWER

Do you resent the way you were treated by the English?

WODEHOUSE

Oh, no, no, no. Nothing of that sort. The whole thing seems to have blown over now.

INTERVIEWER

Would you ever like to go back to England?

WODEHOUSE

I'd certainly like to, but at my age it's awfully difficult to get a move on. But I'd like to go back for a visit in the spring. They all seem to want me to go back. The trouble is that I've never flown. I suppose that would solve everything.

INTERVIEWER

I imagine most people think that you live in England even now. But you are an American citizen, and you have spent most of your life here.

WODEHOUSE

Yes, that is true. I have always been awfully fond of America. It always seemed like my own country. I don't know why. I'd much sooner live here than in England, I think. I can't think of any place in England I prefer to this. I used to like London, but I don't think I'd like it now. I had always wanted to go to America, and when I got a holiday from the *Globe*, in 1904, I came over for about three weeks. Indeed, I saw more of New York then than I've ever seen since, and having been in America gave my reputation in London a tremendous boost. I was suddenly someone who counted to the editors who threw me out before. Then I came back in 1909 for another visit and lived in Greenwich Village. It was a quiet sort of place, all of us young writers trying to get on. I was going to return to England when I sold two short stories to *Cosmopolitan* and *Collier's* for a total of five hundred dollar—much more than I had ever earned before. So I resigned from the *Globe* and stayed. But the wolf was always at the door. I used to think I was being followed about by little men with black beards. If it hadn't been for Frank Crowninshield, the editor of *Vanity Fair*, taking all the articles I could do, I should have been in real trouble. When Ethel and I got married in September 1914, she had seventy-five dollars and I had fifty dollars.

The Saturday Evening Post gave me my first break. I wrote a novel called *Something New* and they bought it for three thousand five hundred dollars and serialized it. They then bought *Uneasy Money*, *Piccadilly Jim*, and *A Damsel in Distress* and gave me a raise with each one, five thousand dollars, seven thousand five hundred dollars, and ten thousand dollars.

Just about that time I started writing musical comedies—eighteen in all—with Guy Bolton and Jerry Kern. I did the lyrics to Jerry's melodies. Our terrific smash was *Oh, Boy!* It all came in a rush. Guy is one of the best fellows I ever met. He lives a mile from here—that's why we came down here. We were spending the weekend with him, and Ethel went out and came back for lunch and said, I've bought a house.

INTERVIEWER

You once told me that when you worked with Ziegfeld, he said that he envied your happy temperament.

WODEHOUSE

Yes, he always used to say that.

INTERVIEWER

To what do you attribute your good nature? Was it a happy childhood?

WODEHOUSE

I certainly had a very happy childhood. My position was the same as Rudyard Kipling's. His parents were in India and boarded him out with a family in England. My parents were in Hong Kong, and I was also boarded out in England. Yet Kipling had one hell of a time, and I got on marvelously with the people I was with and I loved them. What can you attribute a good nature to, I wonder. Do you think you're born with it? I suppose you are.

INTERVIEWER

There must have been some bad times for you, even so.

WODEHOUSE

Do you know, I don't think I've had any really bad times. I disliked the bank I had to work in when I was young very much my first month or so. But once I got used to it, I became very fond of it.

INTERVIEWER

How about the war years, particularly the year in the German internment camp? That must have been pretty bad.

WODEHOUSE

I don't know. Looking back to it, it wasn't at all unpleasant. Everybody seems to think a German internment camp must be a sort of torture chamber. It was really perfectly normal and ordinary. The camp had an extraordinarily nice commander, and we did all sorts of things, you know. We played cricket, that sort of thing. Of course, I was writing all the time. Most writers would have gotten fifty novels out of the experience—the men they met there—but I have never written a word about it, except those broadcasts.

INTERVIEWER

It sounds as if you've never had any worries at all.

WODEHOUSE

I'm rather blessed in a way. I really don't worry about anything much. I can adjust myself to things pretty well.

INTERVIEWER

Do you think it is essential for a writer to have a happy home life?

WODEHOUSE

Well, I think it's a tremendous help, yes. Ethel has always been wonderful in that way. You've got to be alone quite a bit when you're writing. She doesn't mind that at all. I've always had great luck with the things that really matter in life. I should imagine an unhappy marriage would simply kill a man.

INTERVIEWER

Do you think you would have been so happy if you had not been a writer?

WODEHOUSE

No. I think a writer's life is the ideal life. I can never understand these fellows like Evelyn Waugh who did not always have the idea of being a writer. I *always* wanted to be a writer.

INTERVIEWER

Do you always enjoy writing?

WODEHOUSE

Oh, yes. I love writing. I never feel really comfortable unless I am either actually writing or have a story going. I could not stop writing.

Issue 64, 1975

John Ashbery

The Art of Poetry

The interview was conducted at John Ashbery's apartment in the section of Manhattan known as Chelsea. When I arrived, Ashbery was away, and the doorman asked me to wait outside. Soon the poet arrived and we went up by elevator to a spacious, well-lighted apartment in which a secretary was hard at work. We sat in easy chairs in the living room, Ashbery with his back to the large windows. The predominant decor was blue and white, and books lined the whole of one wall.

We talked for more than three hours with only one short break for refreshment—soda, tea, water, nothing stronger. Ashbery's answers to my questions required little editing. He did, however, give the impression of distraction throughout the conversation, as though he wasn't quite sure just what was going on or what his role in the proceedings might be. The interviewer attempted valiantly to extract humorous material, but—as is often the case for readers of Ashbery's poetry—wasn't sure when he succeeded. Since that afternoon a few additional questions were asked and answered, and these have been incorporated into the whole.

—Peter Stitt, 1983

Forties Flick

The shadows of the venetian blinds on the *painted* opposite wall,
Shadows of the cacti, of the china animals
Focus the tragic melancholy of the bright stare
Into nowhere, a hole like the black holes in space.
In bra and panties she sidles to the window:
Zip! Up with the blind. A fragile street scene offers itself
With wafer-thin pedetstrians who know where they are going.
The blind comes down slowly, the slats are slowly tilted up.

Why must it always *cut film* come to this?
A dais with woman reading, with the eddies of her hair *to her,*
And all that is unsaid about her sucking us back with her
Into the silence that night alone doesn't explain?
Silence of the library, of the telephone with its pad
But we didn't have to reinvent these either:
They had gone away into construction of a plot,
The "art" part; as as it seemed: knowing what details to leave out
And about the development of character: things too real
To be of much concern, hence artificial, yet now all over the page
The indoors with the outside becoming part of you
As you realize you had never left off laughing at death,
The "background," dark vine at edge of porch.

Larry and Herman, Herman and Larry, lumber
Greasers, companions, rivals at the XXXXXXXX compnay
Purposely ignorant of so much that is being said
Yet conspirators too in your ambiguity:
What is it like up on the screen?
Do the faces so adroit at the end of their batons of light
Curl up once "The End" has come XXXXXXXXX XXXXXXXXXXXXX
Or do you figure that by keeping up a front
You will be saved from your own gift of gab
As it becomes time to unravel these old motions
And whatever meant something recedes into the past?

the way character is developed

INTERVIEWER

I would like to start at the very beginning. When and why did you first decide on a career as a poet?

JOHN ASHBERY

I don't think I ever decided on a career as a poet. I began by writing a few little verses, but I never thought any of them would be published or that I would go on to publish books. I was in high school at the time and hadn't read any modern poetry. Then in a contest I won a prize in which you could choose different books; the only one that seemed appealing was Untermeyer's anthology, which cost five dollars—a great deal of money. That's how I began reading modern poetry, which wasn't taught in the schools then, especially in rural schools like the one I attended. I didn't understand much of it at first. There were people like Elinor Wylie whom I found appealing—wonderful craftsmanship—but I couldn't get very far with Auden and Eliot and Stevens. Later I went back to them and started getting their books out of the library. I guess it was just a desire to emulate that started me writing poetry. I can't think of any other reason. I am often asked why I write, and I don't know really—I just want to.

INTERVIEWER

When did you get more serious about it, thinking about publishing and that sort of thing?

ASHBERY

For my last two years of high school, I went to Deerfield Academy, and the first time I saw my work in print was in the school paper there. I had tried painting earlier, but I found that poetry was easier than painting. I must have been fifteen at the time. I remember reading *Scholastic* magazine and thinking I could write better poems than the ones they had in there, but I was never able to get one accepted. Then a student at Deerfield sent in some of my poems under his name to *Poetry* magazine, and when I sent them the same poems a few months later the editors there naturally assumed that I was the plagiarist.

Very discouraging. *Poetry* was the most illustrious magazine to be published in at that time, and for a long time after they shunned my work. Then I went on to Harvard and in my second year I met Kenneth Koch. I was trying to get on *The Harvard Advocate*, and he was already one of the editors. He saw my poetry and liked it, and we started reading each other's work. He was really the first poet that I ever knew, so that was rather an important meeting. Of course I was published in the *Advocate*, and then in 1949 I had a poem published in *Furioso*. That was a major event in my life because, even though it was a relatively small magazine, it did take me beyond the confines of the college. But it was hard to follow that up with other publications, and it really wasn't until my late twenties that I could submit things with some hope of them getting accepted.

INTERVIEWER

Was there ever a time when you thought you would have to make a choice between art criticism and poetry, or have the two just always worked out well together?

ASHBERY

I was never interested in doing art criticism at all—I'm not sure that I am even now. Back in the fifties, Thomas Hess, the editor of *ARTnews*, had a lot of poets writing for the magazine. One reason was that they paid almost nothing and poets are always penurious. Trained art historians would not write reviews for five dollars, which is what they were paying when I began. I needed some bread at the time— this was in 1957 when I was thirty—and my friends who were already writing for *ARTnews* suggested that I do it too. So I wrote a review of Bradley Tomlin, an abstract expressionist painter who had a post- humous show at the Whitney. After that I reviewed on a monthly basis for a while until I returned to France. Then in 1960 it happened that I knew the woman who was writing art criticism for the *Herald Tribune*. She was going back to live in America and asked if I knew anybody who would like to take over her job. It didn't pay very much, but it enabled me to get other jobs doing art criticism, which I didn't want to do very much, but as so often when you exhibit reluctance to do something, people think you must be very good at it. If I had set out to be an art critic, I might never have succeeded.

INTERVIEWER

Are there any aspects of your childhood that you think might have contributed to making you the poet you are?

ASHBERY

I don't know what the poet that I am is, very much. I was rather an outsider as a child—I didn't have many friends. We lived out in the country on a farm. I had a younger brother whom I didn't get along with—we were always fighting the way kids do—and he died at the age of nine. I felt guilty because I had been so nasty to him, so that was a terrible shock. These are experiences that have been important to me. I don't know quite how they may have fed into my poetry. My ambition was to be a painter, so I took weekly classes at the art museum in Rochester from the age of about eleven until fifteen or sixteen. I fell deeply in love with a girl who was in the class but who wouldn't have anything to do with me. So I went to this weekly class knowing that I would see this girl, and somehow this being involved with art may have something to do with my poetry. Also, my grandfather was a professor at the University of Rochester, and I lived with him as a small child and went to kindergarten and first grade in the city. I always loved his house; there were lots of kids around, and I missed all that terribly when I went back to live with my parents. Then going back there each week for art class was a returning to things I had thought were lost, and gave me a curious combination of satisfaction and dissatisfaction.

INTERVIEWER

Those are all rather traumatic things. I think of how most critics seem to see your poetry as rather lighthearted. One critic, however, has spoken of your "rare startlements into happiness." Is happiness so rare in your work?

ASHBERY

Some people wouldn't agree that my poetry is lighthearted. Frank O'Hara once said, I don't see why Kenneth likes John's work so much because he thinks everything should be funny and John's poetry is about as funny as a wrecked train. In my life I am reasonably happy now. There are days when I think I am not, but I think there are probably more days when I think I am. I was impressed by an Ingmar Bergman movie I saw years ago—I can't remember the name of it—in which a woman tells the story of her life, which has been full of tragic experiences. She's telling the story in the dressing room of a theater where she is about to go on and perform in a ballet. At the end of it she says, "But I am happy." Then it says, "The End."

INTERVIEWER

Do you like to tease or play games with the reader?

ASHBERY

Funny you should ask—I just blew up at a critic who asked me the same question, though I shouldn't have, in a list of questions for a book she is compiling of poets' statements. I guess it depends on what you mean by "tease." It's all right if it's done affectionately, though how can this be with someone you don't know? I would like to please the reader, and I think that surprise has to be an element of this, and that may necessitate a certain amount of teasing. To shock the reader is something else again. That has to be handled with great care if you're not going to alienate and hurt him, and I'm firmly against that, just as I disapprove of people who dress with that in mind—dye their hair blue and stick safety pins through their noses and so on. The message here seems to be merely aggression—"hey, you can't be part of my strangeness" sort of thing. At the same time I try to dress in a way that is just slightly off, so the spectator, if he notices, will feel slightly bemused but not excluded, remembering his own imperfect mode of dress.

INTERVIEWER

But you would not be above inflicting a trick or a gag on your readers?

ASHBERY

A gag that's probably gone unnoticed turns up in the last sentence of the novel I wrote with James Schuyler. Actually it's my sentence. It reads: "So it was that the cliff dwellers, after bidding their cousins good night, moved off toward the parking area, while the latter bent their steps toward the partially rebuilt shopping plaza in the teeth of the freshening foehn." *Foehn* is a kind of warm wind that blows in Bavaria that produces a fog. I would doubt that many people know that. I liked the idea that people, if they bothered to, would have to open the dictionary to find out what the last word in the novel meant. They'd be closing one book and opening another.

INTERVIEWER

Were there older living poets whom you visited, learned from, or studied with as a young writer?

ASHBERY

I particularly admired Auden, who I would say was the first big in-fluence on my work, more so than Stevens. I wrote an honors thesis on his poetry and got a chance to meet him at Harvard. When I was at Harvard I also studied with Theodore Spencer, a poet who is no lon-ger very well known. He actually taught a poetry-writing workshop, which was very rare in those days—especially at Harvard, where they still are rare. It wasn't that I was particularly fond of Spencer's poetry, but he was a "genuine" poet, a real-live poet, and the feedback I got from him in class was very valuable to me. I also read Elizabeth Bishop quite early and met her once. I wrote her a letter about one of her po-ems that I had liked and she wrote back, and then after I moved to New York I met her. But I was rather shy about putting myself forward, so there weren't very many known poets then that I did have any contact with. I wish I could have visited older poets! But things were different then—young poets simply didn't send their poems to older ones with requests for advice and criticism and "suggestions for publication." At least I don't think they did—none of the ones I knew did. Everyone is bolder now. This leads to a sad situation (and I've often discussed this with poets of my generation like Kinnell and Merwin) of having a tremendous pile of unanswered correspondence about poetry—Kinnell calls it his "guilt pile"—from poets who want help and should receive it; only in this busy world of doing things to make a living and trying to find some time for oneself to write poetry, it isn't usually possible to summon the time and energy it would require to deal seriously with so many requests; at least for me it isn't. But I feel sad because I would like to help—you remember how valuable it would have been for you, and it's an honor to get these requests. People think they have gotten to know you through your poetry and can address you familiarly (I get lots of "Dear John" letters from strangers) and that in itself is a tremendous reward, a satisfaction—if only we could attend to everybody! Actually the one poet I really wanted to know when I was young was Auden. I met him briefly twice after he gave readings at Harvard, and later on in New York I saw a bit of him through Chester Kallman, who was a great friend of Jimmy Schuyler's, but it was very hard to talk to him since he already knew everything. I once said to Kenneth Koch, What are you supposed to say to Auden? And he said that about the only thing there was to say was, I'm glad you're alive.

INTERVIEWER

Why is it always Auden?

ASHBERY

It's odd to be asked today what I saw in Auden. Forty years ago when I first began to read modern poetry no one would have asked—he was *the* modern poet. Stevens was a curiosity, Pound probably a monstrosity, William Carlos Williams—who hadn't yet published his best poetry—an "imagist." Eliot and Yeats were too hallowed and anointed to count. I read him at the suggestion of Kathrine Koller, a professor of English at the University of Rochester who was a neighbor of my parents. She had been kind enough to look at my early scribblings and, probably shaking her head over them, suggested Auden as perhaps a kind of antidote. What immediately struck me was his use of colloquial speech—I didn't think you were supposed to do that in poetry. That, and his startling way of making abstractions concrete and alive—remember: "Abruptly mounting her ramshackle wheel / Fortune has pedaled furiously away; / The sobbing mess is on our hands today," which seem to crystallize the thirties into a few battered and quirky images. And again a kind of romantic tone that took abandoned mines and factory chimneys into account. There is perhaps a note of both childishness and sophistication that struck an answering chord in me. I cannot agree, though, with the current view that his late work is equal to if not better than the early stuff. Except for "The Sea and the Mirror" there is little that enchants me in the poetry he wrote after coming to America. There are felicities, of course, but on the whole it's too chatty and too self-congratulatory at not being "poetry with a capital P," as he put it. Auden was of two minds about my own work. He once said he never understood a line of it. On the other hand he published *Some Trees* in the Yale Younger Poets series. You'll remember, though, that he once said in later life that one of his early works, *The Orators*, must have been written by a madman.

INTERVIEWER

Tell me about the New York school—were there regular meetings, perhaps classes or seminars? Did you plot to take over the literary world?

ASHBERY

No. This label was foisted upon us by a man named John Bernard Myers, who ran the Tibor de Nagy Gallery and published some pamphlets of our poems. I found out recently from one of my students that Myers coined the term in 1962 in an article he wrote for a little magazine in California called *Nomad*. I think the idea was that, since everybody was talking about the New York school of painting, if he created a New York school of poets then they would automatically be considered important because of the sound of the name. But by that time I was living in France, and wasn't part of what was happening in New York. I don't think we ever were a school. There are vast differences between my poetry and Koch's and O'Hara's and Schuyler's and Guest's. We were a bunch of poets who happened to know each other; we would get together and read our poems to each other and sometimes we would write collaborations. It never occurred to us that it would be possible to take over the literary world, so that was not part of the plan. Somebody wrote an article about the New York school a few years ago in *The Times Book Review*, and a woman wrote in to find out how she could enroll.

INTERVIEWER

What was your relation to Paris at the time when you were there— you used to drink Coca-Colas . . .

ASHBERY

That question probably requires a book-length essay. I did at one point in Paris develop an addiction to Coca-Cola that I've never had before or since, but I don't know whether that was due to nostalgia for America or the fact that the French like it so much. Paris is *the* city, isn't it, and I am a lover of cities. It can be experienced much more pleasantly and conveniently than any other city I know. It's so easy to get around on the metro, and so interesting when you get there—each arrondissement is like a separate province, with its own capital and customs and even costumes. I used to pick a different section to explore and set out on a mini expedition, often with a movie theater in mind where they were showing some movie I wanted to see, often an old Laurel and Hardy film since I love them, especially when dubbed into French with comic American accents. And then there is always a principal cafe in the neighborhood where you can sample some nice wine and look at the people. You get to know a lot of life this way. Sometimes I would do a Proustian excursion, looking at buildings he or his characters had lived in. Like his childhood home in the boulevard Malesherbes or Odette's house in the rue La Pérouse.

I didn't have many friends the first years I was there—they were mainly the American writers Harry Mathews and Elliott Stein, and Pierre Martory, a French writer with whom I lived for the last nine of the ten years I spent in France, and who has remained a very close friend. He once published a novel but never anything after that, though the novel was well received and he continues to write voluminously— poems, novels, and stories that he produces constantly but never tries to publish or show to anybody, even me—the only writer of that kind I've ever met. I've translated a few of his poems but they haven't appeared in France, where they don't fit in with the cliques that prevail there. Some were published in *Locus Solus*, a small magazine Harry Mathews and I edited—the title is taken from a novel by Raymond Roussel, whom we both loved and on whom I was once going to do a dissertation. A little later I met Anne and Rodrigo Moynihan, English painters who live mostly in France, who sponsored a review called *Art and Literature*, which I helped to edit. They too have remained close friends whom I see often. I return to Pierre—most of my knowledge of France and things French comes from him. He is a sort of walking encyclopedia of French culture but at the same time views it all from a perspective that is somewhat American. He once spent six months in New York working for *Paris-Match*, for which he still works, and we sailed back to France together on the SS *France*. When he set foot on French soil at Le Havre he said, It is so wonderful to be back in France! *But I hate ze French*!

INTERVIEWER

What early reading did you do, say in high school or college, that has stayed with you?

ASHBERY

Like many young people, I was attracted by long novels. My grandfather had several sets of Victorian writers in his house. The first long novel I read was *Vanity Fair*, and I liked it so much that I decided to read *Gone with the Wind*, which I liked too. I read Dickens and George Eliot then, but not very much poetry. I didn't really get a feeling for the poetry of the past until I had discovered modern poetry. Then I began to see how nineteenth-century poetry wasn't just something lifeless in an ancient museum but must have grown out of the lives of the people who wrote it. In college I majored in English and read the usual curriculum. I guess I was particularly attracted to the Metaphysical poets and to Keats, and I had a Chaucer course, which I enjoyed very much. I also had a modern poetry course from F. O. Matthiessen, which is where I really began to read Wallace Stevens. I wrote a paper, I recall, on "Chocorua to Its Neighbor." Mostly I wasn't a very good student and just sort of got by—laziness. I read Proust for a course with Harry Levin, and that was a major shock.

INTERVIEWER

Why?

ASHBERY

I don't know. I started reading it when I was twenty (before I took Levin's course) and it took me almost a year. I read very slowly anyway, but particularly in the case of a writer whom I wanted to read every word of. It's just that I think one ends up feeling sadder and wiser in equal proportions when one is finished reading him—I can no longer look at the world in quite the same way.

INTERVIEWER

Were you attracted by the intimate, meditative voice of his work?

ASHBERY

Yes, and the way somehow everything could be included in this vast, open form that he created for himself—particularly certain almost surreal passages. There's one part where a philologist or specialist on place names goes on at great length concerning place names in Normandy. I don't know why it is so gripping, but it seizes the way life sometimes seems to have of droning on in a sort of dreamlike space. I also identified, on account of the girl in my art class, with the narrator, who had a totally impractical passion that somehow both enveloped the beloved like a cocoon and didn't have much to do with her.

INTERVIEWER

You said a minute ago that reading modern poetry enabled you to see the vitality present in older poetry. In your mind, is there a close connection between life and poetry?

ASHBERY

In my case I would say there is a very close but oblique connection. I have always been averse to talking about myself, and so I don't write about my life the way the confessional poets do. I don't want to bore people with experiences of mine that are simply versions of what everybody goes through. For me, poetry starts after that point. I write with experiences in mind, but I don't write about them, I write out of them. I know that I have exactly the opposite reputation, that I am totally self-involved, but that's not the way I see it.

INTERVIEWER

You have often been characterized as a solipsist, and I wonder if this isn't related to your reputation for obscurity. The way the details of a poem will be so clear, but the context, the surrounding situation, unclear. Perhaps this is more a matter of perspective than any desire to befuddle.

ASHBERY

This is the way that life appears to me, the way that experience happens. I can concentrate on the things in this room and our talking together, but what the context is is mysterious to me. And it's not that I want to make it more mysterious in my poems—really, I just want to make it more photographic. I often wonder if I am suffering from some mental dysfunction because of how weird and baffling my poetry seems to so many people and sometimes to me too. Let me read you a comment that appeared in a review of my most recent book, from some newspaper in Virginia. It says: "John Ashbery is emerging as a very

important poet, if not by unanimous critical consent then certainly by
the admiration and awe he inspires in younger poets. Oddly, no one
understands Ashbery." That is a simplification, but in a sense it is true,
and I wonder how things happened that way. I'm not the person who
knows. When I originally started writing, I expected that probably
very few people would read my poetry because in those days people
didn't read poetry much anyway. But I also felt that my work was not
beyond understanding. It seemed to me rather derivative of, or at least
in touch with, contemporary poetry of the time, and I was quite surprised that nobody seemed to see this. So I live with this paradox—on
the one hand, I am an important poet, read by younger writers, and on
the other hand, nobody understands me. I am often asked to account
for this state of affairs, but I can't.

INTERVIEWER

When you say that sometimes you think your poetry is weird, what
do you mean exactly?

ASHBERY

Every once in a while I will pick up a page and it has something,
but what is it? It seems so unlike what poetry "as we know it" is. But
at other moments I feel very much at home with it. It's a question of a
sudden feeling of unsureness at what I am doing, wondering why I am
writing the way I am, and also not feeling the urge to write in another
way.

INTERVIEWER

Is the issue of meaning or message something that is uppermost in
your mind when you write?

ASHBERY

Meaning yes, but message no. I think my poems mean what they say,
and whatever might be implicit within a particular passage, but there is
no message, nothing I want to tell the world particularly except what
I am thinking when I am writing. Many critics tend to want to see an

allegorical meaning in every concrete statement, and if we just choose a line at random, I think we will find this isn't the way it works . . . I can't seem to find anything that's an example of what I mean. Well, let's take this . . . no. Everything I look at does seem to mean something other than what is being said, all of a sudden. Ah, here—the beginning of "Daffy Duck in Hollywood," for instance, where all these strange objects avalanche into the poem. I meant them to be there for themselves, and not for some hidden meaning. Rumford's Baking Powder (by the way, it's actually Rumford and not Rumford's Baking Powder. I knew that, but preferred the sound of my version—I don't usually do that), a celluloid earring, Speedy Gonzales—they are just the things that I selected to be exhibited in the poem at that point. In fact, there is a line here, "The allegory comes unsnarled too soon," that might be my observation of poetry and my poetry in particular. The allegory coming unsnarled meaning that the various things that make it up are dissolving into a poetic statement, and that is something that I feel is both happening and that I don't want to happen. And, as so often, two opposing forces are working to cancel each other out. "Coming unsnarled" is probably a good thing, but "too soon" isn't.

INTERVIEWER

So for you a poem is an object in and of itself rather than a clue to some abstraction, to something other than itself?

ASHBERY

Yes, I would like it to be what Stevens calls a completely new set of objects. My intention is to present the reader with a pleasant surprise, not an unpleasant one, not a nonsurprise. I think this is the way pleasure happens when you are reading poetry. Years ago Kenneth Koch and I did an interview with each other, and something I said then, in 1965, is pertinent to what we are talking about: It's rather hard to be a good artist and also be able to explain intelligently what your art is about. In fact, the worse your art is, the easier it is to talk about, at least I would like to think so. Ambiguity seems to be the same thing as happiness or pleasant surprise. I am assuming that, from the moment life cannot be one continual orgasm, real happiness is impossible, and pleasant surprise is promoted to the front rank of the emotions. The idea of relief from pain has something to do with ambiguity. Ambiguity supposes eventual resolution of itself, whereas certitude implies further ambiguity. I guess that is why so much "depressing" modern art makes me feel cheerful.

INTERVIEWER

Could you explain the paradox concerning ambiguity and certitude?

ASHBERY

Things are in a continual state of motion and evolution, and if we come to a point where we say, with certitude, right here, this is the end of the universe, then of course we must deal with everything that goes on after that, whereas ambiguity seems to take further developments into account. We might realize that the present moment may be one of an eternal or sempiternal series of moments, all of which will resemble it because, in some ways, they are the present, and won't in other ways, because the present will be the past by that time.

INTERVIEWER

Is it bothersome that critics seem to have considerable trouble saying exactly what your poems are about?

ASHBERY

You have probably read David Bromwich's review of *As We Know* in the *Times*. He decided that the entire book deals with living in a silver age rather than a golden age. This is an idea that occurs only briefly, along with a great many other things, in "Litany." By making this arbitrary decision he was able to deal with the poetry. I intended, in "Litany," to write something so utterly discursive that it would be beyond criticism—not because I wanted to punish critics, but because this would somehow exemplify the fullness or, if you wish, the emptiness of life or, at any rate, its dimensionless quality. And I think that any true work of art does defuse criticism; if it left anything important to be said, it wouldn't be doing its job. (This is not an idea I expect critics to sympathize with, especially at a time when criticism has set itself up as a separate branch of the arts, and, perhaps by implication, the most important one.) The poem is of an immense length, and there is a lack of coherence between the parts. Given all this, I don't really see how one could deal critically with the poem, so I suppose it is necessary for the critic to draw up certain guidelines before beginning. It was a very sympathetic review, and I admire Bromwich, but it seemed to leave a great deal out of account. I guess I am pleased that my method has given every critic something to hate or like. For me, my poems have their own form, which is the one that I want, even though other people might not agree that it is there. I feel that there is always a resolution in my poems.

INTERVIEWER

Did you see the controversy that erupted in *The New York Review* about how "Litany" should be read? Whether one should read all of voice A, then all of voice B, or intermingle them in some way . . .

ASHBERY

I don't think there is any particular way. I seem to have opened up a can of worms with my instruction, which the publisher asked me to put in, that the parts should be read simultaneously. I don't think people ever read things the way they are supposed to. I myself will skip ahead several chapters, or read a little bit of this page and a little bit of that page, and I assume that is what everybody does. I just wanted the whole thing to be, as I have said, presentable. It's not a form that has a cohesive structure, so it could be read just as one pleases. I think I consider the poem as a sort of environment, and one is not obliged to take notice of every aspect of one's environment—one can't, in fact. That is why it came out the way it did.

INTERVIEWER

One's environment at a single moment?

ASHBERY

No, it is a succession of moments. I am always impressed by how difficult and yet how easy it is to get from one moment to the next of one's life—particularly while traveling, as I just was in Poland. There is a problem every few minutes—one doesn't know whether one is going to get on the plane, or will they confiscate one's luggage. Somehow I did all this and got back, but I was aware of so much difficulty, and at the same time of the pleasure, the novelty of it all. Susan Sontag was at this writers' conference also—there were just four of us—and one night in Warsaw we were provided with tickets to a ballet. I said, Do you think we should go? It doesn't sound like it will be too interesting. And she said, Sure, we should go. If it is boring that will be interesting too—which turned out to be the case.

INTERVIEWER

Given what you said about "Litany," it seems that in a way you are leaving it up to each reader to make his or her own poem out of the raw materials you have given. Do you visualize an ideal reader when you write, or do you conceive of a multitude of different apprehending sensibilities?

ASHBERY

Every writer faces the problem of the person that he is writing for, and I don't think anybody has ever been able to imagine satisfactorily who this *homme moyen sensuel* will be. I try to aim at as wide an audience as I can so that as many people as possible will read my poetry. Therefore I depersonalize it, but in the same way personalize it, so that a person who is going to be different from me—but who is also going to resemble me just because he is different from me, since we are all different from each other—can see something in it. You know—I shot an arrow into the air but I could only aim it. Often after I have given a poetry reading, people will say, I never really got anything out of your work before, but now that I have heard you read it, I can see something in it. I guess something about my voice and my projection of myself meshes with the poems. That is nice, but it is also rather saddening because I can't sit down with every potential reader and read aloud to him.

INTERVIEWER

Your poems often have a spoken quality, as though they are monologues or dialogues. Do you try to create characters who then speak in your poems, or is this all your own voice? In the dialogues perhaps it is two aspects of your own voice that are speaking.

ASHBERY

It doesn't seem to me like my voice. I have had many arguments about this with my analyst, who is actually a South American concert pianist—more interested in playing the piano than in being a therapist. He says, Yes, I know, you always think that these poems come from somewhere else. You refuse to realize that it is really you who is writing the poems and not having them dictated by some spirit somewhere. It is hard for me to realize that because I have such an imprecise impression of what kind of a person I am. I know I appear differently to other people because I behave differently on different occasions. Some people think that I am very laid-back and charming and some people think I am egotistical and disagreeable. Or as Edward Lear put it in his great poem "How Pleasant to Know Mr. Lear": "Some think him ill-tempered and queer, but a few think him pleasant enough." Any of the above, I suppose. Of course, my reason tells me that my poems are not dictated, that I am not a *voyant*. I suppose they come from a part of me that I am not in touch with very much except when I am actually writing. The rest of the time I guess I want to give this other person a rest, this other one of my selves that does the talking in my poems, so that he won't get tired and stop.

INTERVIEWER

So you have a sense of several selves?

ASHBERY

No. No more than the average person, I shouldn't think. I mean, we are all different depending on who we happen to be with and what we are doing at a particular moment, but I wouldn't say that it goes any further than that.

INTERVIEWER

Some people have thought that you set up characters who converse in several poems. One could say that in "Litany" you have character A and character B, who are very similar to one another. It is possible at times to see them as lovers on the point of separating, while at other times they look like two aspects of one personality.

ASHBERY

I think I am trying to reproduce the polyphony that goes on inside me, which I don't think is radically different from that of other people. After all, one is constantly changing one's mind and thereby becoming something slightly different. But what was I doing? Perhaps the two columns are like two people whom I am in love with simultaneously. A student of mine who likes this poem says that when you read one column you start to miss the other one, as you would miss one beloved when you spend time with the other. I once half-jokingly said that my object was to direct the reader's attention to the white space between the columns. Maybe that's part of it. Reading is a pleasure, but to finish reading, to come to the blank space at the end, is also a pleasure.

INTERVIEWER

This notion of your poems being dictated makes me wonder whether, for you, composition involves something like inspiration—the poems just springing out already finished, rather than a laborious process of writing and revision.

ASHBERY

That is the way it has happened to me in more recent times. In fact, since I don't have very much free time (poets seldom do, since they must somehow make a living), I've conditioned myself to write at almost any time. Sometimes it doesn't work, but on the whole I feel that poetry is going on all the time inside, an underground stream. One can let down one's bucket and bring the poem back up. (This is very well put in a passage that occurs early on in Heimito von Doderer's novel *The Demons*, which I haven't to hand at the moment.) It will be not dissimilar to what I have produced before because it is coming from the same source, but it will be dissimilar because of the different circumstances of the particular moment.

INTERVIEWER

Many poets have spoken of poetry coming from the subconscious mind rather than the conscious mind. Would you agree with that?

ASHBERY

I think that is where it probably starts out, but I think that in my case it passes through the conscious mind on its way out and is monitored by it. I don't believe in automatic writing as the surrealists were supposed to have practiced it, simply because it is not a reflection of the whole mind, which is partly logical and reasonable, and that part should have its say too.

INTERVIEWER

Do you compose on the typewriter or in longhand?

ASHBERY

I write on the typewriter. I didn't use to, but when I was writing "The Skaters," the lines became unmanageably long. I would forget the end of the line before I could get to it. It occurred to me that perhaps I should do this at the typewriter, because I can type faster than

I can write. So I did, and that is mostly the way I have written ever since. Occasionally I write a poem in longhand to see whether I can still do it. I don't want to be forever bound to this machine.

Do you have rituals?

Well, one of them is to use this very old, circa 1930 I would say, Royal typewriter I mentioned. I hate to think what will happen when it finally gives out, though you can still find them sometimes in those used-office-furniture stores on West Twenty-third Street, which are themselves an endangered species. And then I procrastinate like everybody else, though surely more than most. On days when I want to write I will usually waste the morning and go for an afternoon walk to Greenwich Village. (I live nearby in Chelsea, which is a pleasant place to walk from though maybe not to.) Sometimes this takes too long and my preferred late-afternoon moment will pass. I can't really work at night. Nor in the morning, very much, when I have more ideas but am less critical of them, it seems. I never can use the time I waste doing this for some other purpose like answering letters. It's no good for anything but wasting. I've never tried Schiller's rotten apples, but I do drink tea while I write, and that is about the only time I do drink tea. On the whole, I believe I have fewer hang-ups and rituals than I used to. I feel blocked much less often, though it still happens. It's important to try to write when you are in the wrong mood or when the weather is wrong. Even if you don't succeed you'll be developing a muscle that may do it later on. And I think writing does get easier as you get older. It's a question of practice and also of realizing that you don't have the oceans of time to waste that you had when you were young.

Do you revise your poems heavily?

ASHBERY

Not anymore. I used to labor over them a great deal, but because of my strong desire to avoid all unnecessary work, I have somehow trained myself not to write something that I will either have to discard or be forced to work a great deal over. In fact, just last night a friend mentioned that she has a manuscript copy of one of my early poems, "Le livre est sur la table," with a lot of corrections in it. I remember that poem as one that gave me an immense amount of difficulty— I worked over it for a week or so and never did feel really happy with it. When she mentioned that, I realized how much my way of writing has changed over the last thirty years. But, although there are poems even today that I don't find satisfactory once I have finished them, most of the corrections I make are pretty minor. I like the idea of being as close to the original thought or voice as possible and not to falsify it by editing. Here is something I just read by Max Jacob, quoted by André Blanchet in the notes to Jacob's book *La défense de Tartufe*. He talks about composing novels or stories in a notebook while taking long walks through Paris. I'll translate, "The ideas I found in this way seemed sacred to me and I didn't change a comma. I believe that prose that comes directly from meditation is a prose that has the form of the brain and which it is forbidden to touch."

INTERVIEWER

What determines a line break for you? Is there some metrical consideration, or would you say you are writing free verse?

ASHBERY

I don't know. I just know when I feel that the line should break. I used to say that my criterion for a line of poetry was that it should have at least two interesting things in it. But this is not the case in a lot of my recent poetry. In "Litany" there are lines that are a single word long. As I was writing that poem—well, actually it began with the long poem before that, the "Nut-Brown Maid"—I became almost intoxicated by the idea of the line break. It seemed as if I were writing just to get to this point, this decision. But, although the line break is very

important to me, I don't really understand how I know when it is supposed to happen. I have felt very uncomfortable with iambic pentam-
eter ever since I discovered, when I first began writing poetry, that it
was not impossible to write acceptable blank verse. It somehow seems
to falsify poetry for me. It has an order of its own that is foreign to
nature. When I was in college, I used to write a kind of four-beat line,
which seemed much more real, genuine, to me. Now I guess it is free
verse, whatever that is.

INTERVIEWER

What gets you started in writing a poem? Is it an idea, an image, a
rhythm, a situation or event, a phrase, something else?

ASHBERY

Again, all of the above. An idea might occur to me, something very
banal—for example, isn't it strange that it is possible to both talk and
think at the same time? That might be an idea for a poem. Or certain
words or phrases might have come to my attention with a meaning I
wasn't aware of before. Also, I often put in things that I have overheard
people say, on the street for instance. Suddenly something fixes itself
in the flow that is going on around one and seems to have a significance.
In fact, there is an example of that in this poem, "What Is Poetry?" In a
bookstore I overheard a boy saying to a girl this last line: "It might give
us—what?—some flowers soon?" I have no idea what the context was,
but it suddenly seemed the way to end my poem. I am a believer in fortuitous accidents. The ending of my poem "Clepsydra," the last two
lines, came from a notebook that I kept a number of years before, during my first trip to Italy. I actually wrote some poems while I was traveling, which I don't usually do, but I was very excited by my first visit
there. So years later, when I was trying to end "Clepsydra" and getting
very nervous, I happened to open that notebook and found these two
lines that I had completely forgotten about: "while morning is still and
before the body / Is changed by the faces of evening." They were just
what I needed at that time. But it doesn't really matter so much what the
individual thing is. Many times I will jot down ideas and phrases, and

then when I am ready to write I can't find them. But it doesn't make any difference, because whatever comes along at that time will have the same quality. Whatever was there is replaceable. In fact, often in revising I will remove the idea that was the original stimulus. I think I am more interested in the movement among ideas than in the ideas themselves, the way one goes from one point to another rather than the destination or the origin.

INTERVIEWER

Three Poems is largely prose, prose poetry, rather than verse. Some readers would object rather strenuously to calling it poetry. Within this kind of form, I am wondering where, for you, the poetry specifically is to be found? What is the indispensable element that makes poetry?

ASHBERY

That is one of those good but unanswerable questions. For a long time a very prosaic language, a language of ordinary speech, has been in my poetry. It seems to me that we are most ourselves when we are talking, and we talk in a very irregular and antiliterary way. In *Three Poems*, I wanted to see how poetic the most prosaic language could be. And I don't mean just the journalese, but also the inflated rhetoric that is trying very hard to sound poetic but not making it. One of my aims has been to put together as many different kinds of language and tone as possible, and to shift them abruptly, to overlap them all. There is a very naive, romantic tone at times, all kinds of clichés, as well as a more deliberate poetic voice. I also was reacting to the minimalism of some of the poems in *The Tennis Court Oath*, such as "Europe," which is sometimes just a few scattered words. I suppose I eventually thought of covering page after page with words, with not even any break for paragraphs in many cases—could I do this and still feel that I was getting the satisfaction that poetry gives me? I don't quite understand why some people are so against prose poetry, which is certainly a respectable and pedigreed form of poetry. In fact, too much so for my taste. I had written almost none before *Three Poems* because there always seemed to be a kind of rhetorical falseness in much that had been done in the past—Baudelaire's, for instance. I wanted to see if prose poetry could be written without that self-conscious drama that seems so much a part of it. So if it is poetic, it is probably because it tries to stay close to the way we talk and think without expecting what we say to be recorded or remembered. The pathos and liveliness of ordinary human communication is poetry to me.

INTERVIEWER

You were talking once about reading younger poets and being aware that you have influenced their work. You said one of the primary benefits for you in seeing this is that it alerts you to watch out for "Ashberyisms" in your own work. What do you mean by Ashberyisms?

ASHBERY

Well, there are certain stock words that I have found myself using a great deal. When I become aware of them, it is an alarm signal meaning I am falling back on something that has served in the past—it is a sign of not thinking at the present moment, not that there is anything intrinsically bad about certain words or phrases. The word *climate* occurs in my poetry a great deal, for instance. So I try to censor it, unless I feel that there is no alternative. I also seem to be very fond of words involving a kind of osmosis, like *absorb* and *leach*, as something leaching into the soil. I don't know why these particular words attract me, unless it's because they are indicative of the slow but kinetic quality of existence and experience. Also there is a typical kind of tone, the chatty quality that my poetry tends to have, the idea behind it being that there are things more important than "all this fiddle," perhaps, and sometimes I correct this.

INTERVIEWER

I suppose there are many things we might expect from a poet who has so strong an interest in painting as you do. Various critics have suggested that you are a mannerist in words, or an abstract expressionist.

Are you conscious of anything like that—or perhaps of performing a cubist experiment with words?

ASHBERY

I suppose the "Self-Portrait in a Convex Mirror" is a mannerist work in what I hope is the good sense of the word. Later on, mannerism became mannered, but at first it was a pure novelty—Parmigianino was an early mannerist, coming right on the heels of Michelangelo. I have probably been influenced, more or less unconsciously I suppose, by the modern art that I have looked at. Certainly the simultaneity of cubism is something that has rubbed off on me, as well as the abstract expressionist idea that the work is a sort of record of its own coming-into-existence—it has an "anti-referential sensuousness," but it is nothing like flinging a bucket of words on the page, as Pollock did with paint. It is more indirect than that. When I was fresh out of college, abstract expressionism was the most exciting thing in the arts. There was also experimental music and film, but poetry seemed quite conventional in comparison. I guess it still is, in a way. One can accept a Picasso woman with two noses, but an equivalent attempt in poetry baffles the same audience.

INTERVIEWER

Though it has its admirers, *The Tennis Court Oath* seems to have been a widely disliked book—for its difficulty, its obscurity, and so on. How do you feel about that volume from the perspective of today?

ASHBERY

There are a lot of poems in that book that don't interest me as much as those that came before or since. I didn't expect to have a second book published, ever. The opportunity came about very suddenly, and when it did I simply sent what I had been doing. But I never expected these poems to see the light of day. I felt at that time that I needed a change in the way I was writing, so I was kind of fooling around and trying to do something I hadn't done before. I was conscious that often what I hadn't done before was inferior to what

I had done. But I like a number of the poems in the book. I hadn't realized this until recently, but there was a period, after I had begun
living in Paris and decided that I wanted to write in a different way,
when I achieved a kind of intermediate style, say between the poems
in *Some Trees* and the poem "Europe." For instance, the poem "They
Dream Only of America" or "Our Youth" or "How Much Longer
Will I Be Able to Inhabit the Divine Sepulcher . . ." Those are the
earlier poems in *The Tennis Court Oath*. I don't know quite why I
stopped writing that way, but I feel that those are valid poems in a
new way that I might well have gone on pursuing, but didn't. In the
last two or three years, I have gone back and reread some of the poems
that I hadn't liked before and decided that they did have something
that I could work on again. I think I did this somewhat in "Litany."
There are certainly things in that poem that are as outrageous as the
poems that outraged the critics of *The Tennis Court Oath*.

INTERVIEWER

How do you feel about the general critical reception of your work?

ASHBERY

I am very pleased that my poems seem to have found readers. I
don't know quite how this came about. But it is disappointing to me
that my poetry has become a kind of shibboleth, that people feel they
have to join one side or the other. It seems to me that the poetry gets
lost in all the controversy that surrounds it. I feel often that people
on both sides are much more familiar with the myth that has grown
up about my work than they are with the work itself. I am either
an inspired seer or a charlatan who is trying to torment readers. My
work has become a sort of political football and has the quality of a
red flag for some people before they have even begun to pay any attention to it. I suppose that is the way reputations, some of them
anyway, are created, but I hate to see people intimidated—before they
even have begun to read me—by their preconceived notion of what
my poetry is. I think it has something to offer, that it was not written
not to be read.

INTERVIEWER

Have you found that your students ever taught you anything about writing?

ASHBERY

I try to avoid the well-known cliché that you learn from your students. Neither do I believe that there's something ennobling for a writer to teach, that it's narcissistic to spend time wallowing in your writing when you could be out helping in the world's work. Writers should write, and poets especially spend altogether too much time at other tasks such as teaching. However, since so many of us have to do it, there are certain things to be said for it. You are forced to bring a critical attention into play when you are reading students' work that you would not use otherwise, and that can help when you return to your own writing. And being immersed in a group of young unproven writers who are fiercely serious about what they are doing can have a chastening effect sometimes on us blasé oldsters. Besides, they may be writing great poetry, only nobody knows it because nobody has seen it yet. I sometimes think that the "greatness" my friends and I used to see in each other's poetry when we were very young had a lot to do with the fact that it was unknown. It could turn out to be anything— the possibilities were limitless, more so than when we were at last discovered and identified and pinned down in our books.

Issue 90, 1983

Philip Roth

The Art of Fiction

I met Philip Roth after I had published a short book about his work for the Methuen Contemporary Writers Series. He read the book and wrote me a generous letter. After our first meeting, he sent me the fourth draft of *The Anatomy Lesson*, which we later talked about because, in the final stages of writing a novel, Roth likes to get as much criticism and response as he can from a few interested readers. Just after he finished *The Anatomy Lesson* we began *The Paris Review* interview. We met in the early summer of 1983 at the Royal Automobile Club in Pall Mall, where Roth occasionally takes a room to work in when he's visiting England. The room had been turned into a small, meticulously organized office—IBM golf-ball typewriter, alphabetical file holders, Anglepoise lamps, dictionaries, aspirin, copyholder, felt-tip pens for correcting, a radio—with a few books on the mantelpiece, among them the recently published autobiography by Irving Howe, *A Margin of Hope*; Erik Erikson's *Young Man Luther: A Study in Psychoanalysis and History*; Leonard Woolf's autobiography; David Magarshaek's *Chekhov*; John Cheever's *Oh What a Paradise It Seems*; Fordyce's *Behavioral Methods for Chronic Pain and Illness* (useful for Zuckerman); Claire Bloom's autobiography, *Limelight and After*; and some *Paris Review* interviews. We talked in this businesslike cell for a day and a half, pausing only for meals. I was looked after with great thoughtfulness. Roth's manner, which matches his

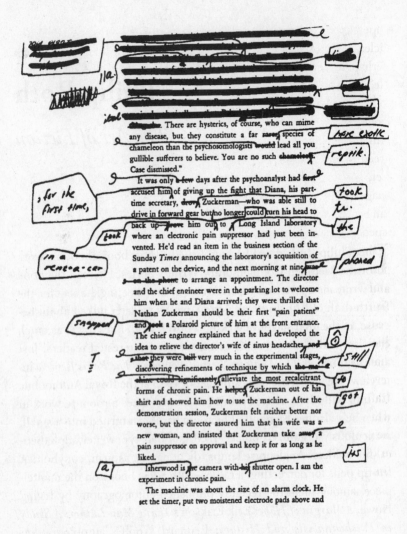

[heavily struck-through/blacked-out lines at top]

"... There are hysterics, of course, who can mime any disease, but they constitute a far ~~rarer~~ *more exotic* species of chameleon than the psychosomologists ~~would~~ lead all you gullible sufferers to believe. You are no such ~~chameleon~~ *reptile.* Case dismissed."

It was only ~~a few~~ days after the psychoanalyst had ~~first~~ *took the* accused him, *for the first time,* of giving up the fight that Diana, his part-time secretary, ~~drove~~ Zuckerman—who was able still to drive in forward gear but/no longer/could turn his head to *took* back up ~~drove him out~~ to *a* Long Island laboratory *the* where an electronic pain suppressor had just been invented. He'd read an item in the business section of the Sunday *Times* announcing the laboratory's acquisition of *phoned* a patent on the device, and the next morning at nine ~~went~~ *in a rent-a-car* ~~on the phone~~ to arrange an appointment. The director and the chief engineer were in the parking lot to welcome him when he and Diana arrived; they were thrilled that Nathan Zuckerman should be their first "pain patient" *snapped* and ~~took~~ a Polaroid picture of him at the front entrance. The chief engineer explained that he had developed the idea to relieve the director's wife of sinus headaches, ~~and~~ *T* ~~after~~ they were ~~still~~ *still* very much in the experimental stages, *to* discovering refinements of technique by which ~~the machine could significantly~~ *got* alleviate the most recalcitrant forms of chronic pain. He ~~helped~~ *got* Zuckerman out of his shirt and showed him how to use the machine. After the demonstration session, Zuckerman felt neither better nor worse, but the director assured him that his wife was a new woman, and insisted that Zuckerman take ~~away~~ a pain suppressor on approval and keep it for as long as he liked.

a Isherwood is ~~the~~ camera with ~~his~~ *its* shutter open. I am the experiment in chronic pain.

The machine was about the size of an alarm clock. He set the timer, put two moistened electrode pads above and

A galley proof of *The Anatomy Lesson* with Philip Roth's corrections.

appearance—subdued, conventional clothes, gold-rimmed spectacles, the look of a quiet professional American visitor to London, perhaps an academic or a lawyer—is courteous, mild, and responsive. He listens carefully to everything, makes lots of quick jokes, and likes to be amused. Just underneath this benign appearance there is a ferocious concentration and mental rapacity; everything is grist for his mill, no vagueness is tolerated, differences of opinion are pounced on greedily, and nothing that might be useful is let slip. Thinking on his feet, he develops his ideas through a playful use of figurative language—as much as a way of avoiding confessional answers (though he can be very direct) as of interesting himself. The transcripts from this taped conversation were long, absorbing, funny, disorganized, and repetitive. I edited them down to a manageable size and sent my version on to him. Then there was a long pause while he went back to America and *The Anatomy Lesson* was published. Early in 1984, on his next visit to England, we resumed; he revised my version and we talked about the revision until it acquired its final form. I found this process extremely interesting. The mood of the interview had changed in the six months between his finishing a novel and starting new work; it became more combative and buoyant. And the several drafts in themselves displayed Roth's methods of work—raw chunks of talk were processed into stylish, energetic, concentrated prose, and the return to past thoughts generated new ideas. The result provides an example, as well as an account, of Philip Roth's presentation of himself.

—*Hermione Lee, 1984*

INTERVIEWER

How do you get started on a new book?

PHILIP ROTH

Beginning a book is unpleasant. I'm entirely uncertain about the character and the predicament, and a character in his predicament is what I have to begin with. Worse than not knowing your subject is not knowing how to treat it, because that's finally everything. I type out beginnings and they're awful, more of an unconscious parody of my previous book than the breakaway from it that I want. I need something driving down the center of a book, a magnet to draw everything to it—that's what I look for during the first months of writing something new. I often have to write a hundred pages or more before there's a paragraph that's alive. OK, I say to myself, that's your beginning, start there; that's the first paragraph of the book. I'll go over the first six months of work and underline in red a paragraph, a sentence, sometimes no more than a phrase, that has some life in it, and then I'll type all these out on one page. Usually it doesn't come to more than one page, but if I'm lucky, that's the start of page one. I look for the liveliness to set the tone. After the awful beginning come the months of freewheeling play, and after the play come the crises, turning against your material and hating the book.

INTERVIEWER

How much of a book is in your mind before you start?

ROTH

What matters most isn't there at all. I don't mean the solutions to problems, I mean the problems themselves. You're looking, as you begin, for what's going to resist you. You're looking for trouble. Sometimes in the beginning uncertainty arises not because the writing is difficult, but because it isn't difficult enough. Fluency can be a sign that nothing is happening. Fluency can actually be my signal to stop, while being in the dark from sentence to sentence is what convinces me to go on.

INTERVIEWER

Must you have a beginning? Would you ever begin with an ending?

ROTH

For all I know I *am* beginning with the ending. My page one can wind up a year later as page two hundred, if it's still even around.

What happens to those hundred or so pages that you have left over? Do you save them up?

ROTH

I generally prefer never to see them again.

INTERVIEWER

Do you work best at any particular time of the day?

ROTH

I work all day, morning and afternoon, just about every day. If I sit there like that for two or three years, at the end I have a book.

INTERVIEWER

Do you think other writers work such long hours?

ROTH

I don't ask writers about their work habits. I really don't care. Joyce Carol Oates says somewhere that when writers ask each other what time they start working and when they finish and how much time they take for lunch, they're actually trying to find out, Is he as crazy as I am? I don't need that question answered.

INTERVIEWER

Does your reading affect what you write?

ROTH

I read all the time when I'm working, usually at night. It's a way of keeping the circuits open. It's a way of thinking about my *line* of work while getting a little rest from the work at hand. It helps inasmuch as it fuels the overall obsession.

INTERVIEWER

Do you show your work in progress to anyone?

ROTH

It's more useful for my mistakes to ripen and burst in their own good time. I give myself all the opposition I need while I'm writing, and praise is meaningless to me when I know something isn't even half finished. Nobody sees what I'm doing until I absolutely can't go any further and might even like to believe that I'm done.

INTERVIEWER

Do you have a Roth reader in mind when you write?

ROTH

No. I occasionally have an anti-Roth reader in mind. I think, How he is going to hate this! That can be just the encouragement I need.

INTERVIEWER

You spoke of the last phase of writing a novel being a "crisis" in which *you* turn against the material and hate the work. Is there always this crisis, with every book?

ROTH

Always. Months of looking at the manuscript and saying, This is wrong—but what's wrong? I ask myself, If this book were a dream, it would be a dream of what? But when I'm asking this I'm also trying to *believe* in what I've written, to forget that it's writing and to say, This *has* taken place, even if it hasn't. The idea is to perceive your invention as a reality that can be understood as a dream. The idea is to turn flesh and blood into literary characters and literary characters into flesh and blood.

INTERVIEWER

Can you say more about these crises?

ROTH

In *The Ghost Writer* the crisis—one among many—had to do with
Zuckerman, Amy Bellette, and Anne Frank. It wasn't easy to see that
Amy Bellette *as* Anne Frank was Zuckerman's own creation. Only by
working through numerous alternatives did I decide that not only
was she his creation, but that she might possibly be her own creation
too, a young woman inventing herself *within* Zuckerman's invention.
To enrich his fantasy without obfuscation or muddle, to be ambiguous *and* clear—well, that was my writing problem through one whole
summer and fall. In *Zuckerman Unbound* the crisis was a result of
failing to see that Zuckerman's father shouldn't already be dead when
the book begins. I eventually realized that the death should come at
the conclusion of the book, allegedly as a consequence of the son's
blasphemous bestseller. But starting off, I'd got the thing back to front
and then I stared at it dumbly for months, seeing nothing. I knew that
I wanted the book to veer away from Alvin Pepler—I like to be steam-
rolling along in one direction and then to spring my surprise—but I
couldn't give up the premise of my earliest drafts until I saw that the
novel's obsessive concern with assassinations, death threats, funerals,
and funeral homes was leading up to, rather than away from, the
death of Zuckerman's father. How you juxtapose the events can tie
you up in knots and rearranging the sequence can free you suddenly
to streak for the finish line. In *The Anatomy Lesson* the discovery I
made—having banged the typewriter with my head far too long—was
that Zuckerman, in the moment that he takes flight for Chicago to try
to become a doctor, should begin to impersonate a pornographer.
There had to be willed extremism at either end of the moral spec-
trum, each of his escape dreams of self-transformation subverting the
meaning and mocking the intention of the other. If he had gone off
solely to become a doctor, driven only by that high moral ardor, or if
he had just gone around impersonating a pornographer, spewing only
that anarchic and alienating rage, he wouldn't have been my man. He
has two dominant modes, his mode of self-abnegation and his fuck-
'em mode. You want a bad Jewish boy, that's what you're going to get.
He rests from one by taking up the other; though, as we see, it's not

much of a rest. The thing about Zuckerman that interests me is that everybody's split, but few so openly as this. Everybody is full of cracks and fissures, but usually we see people trying very hard to hide the places where they're split. Most people desperately want to heal their lesions and keep trying to. Hiding them is sometimes taken for healing them—or for not having them. But Zuckerman can't successfully do either, and by the end of the trilogy has proved it even to himself. What's determined his life and his work are the lines of fracture in what is by no means a clean break. I was interested in following those lines.

INTERVIEWER

What happens to Philip Roth when he turns into Nathan Zuckerman?

ROTH

Nathan Zuckerman is an act. It's all the art of impersonation, isn't it? That's the fundamental novelistic gift. Zuckerman is a writer who wants to be a doctor impersonating a pornographer. I am a writer writing a book impersonating a writer who wants to be a doctor impersonating a pornographer—who then to compound the impersonation, to barb the edge, pretends he's a well-known literary critic. Making fake biography, false history, concocting a half-imaginary existence out of the actual drama of my life *is* my life. There has to be some pleasure in this job, and that's it. To go around in disguise. To act a character. To pass oneself off as what one is not. To *pretend*. The sly and cunning masquerade. Think of the ventriloquist. He speaks so that his voice appears to proceed from someone at a distance from himself. But if he weren't in your line of vision you'd get no pleasure from his art at all. His art consists of being present *and* absent; he's most himself by simultaneously being someone else, neither of whom he "is" once the curtain is down. You don't necessarily, as a writer, have to abandon your biography completely to engage in an act of impersonation. It may be more intriguing when you don't. You distort it, caricature it, parody it, you torture and subvert it, you exploit it—

all to give the biography that dimension that will excite your verbal life. Millions of people do this all the time, of course, and not with the justification of making literature. They *mean* it. It's amazing what lies people can sustain behind the mask of their real faces. Think of the art of the adulterer, under tremendous pressure and against enormous odds, ordinary husbands and wives who would freeze with self-consciousness up on a stage—yet in the theater of the home, alone before the audience of the betrayed spouse, they act out roles of innocence and fidelity with flawless dramatic skill. Great, great performances, conceived with genius down to the smallest particulars, impeccably meticulous naturalistic acting, and all done by rank amateurs. People beautifully pretending to be "themselves." Make believe can take the subtlest forms, you know. Why should a novelist, a pretender by profession, be any less deft or more reliable than a stolid, unimaginative suburban accountant cheating on his wife? Jack Benny used to pretend to be a miser, remember? Called himself by his own good name and claimed that he was stingy and mean. It excited his comic imagination to do this. He probably wasn't all that funny as just another nice fellow writing checks to the UJA and taking his friends out to dinner. Céline pretended to be a rather indifferent, even irresponsible physician, when he seems in fact to have worked hard at his practice and to have been conscientious about his patients. But that wasn't interesting.

INTERVIEWER

But it is. Being a good doctor is interesting.

ROTH

For William Carlos Williams maybe, but not for Céline. Being a devoted husband, an intelligent father, and a dedicated family physician in Rutherford, New Jersey, might have seemed as admirable to Céline as it does to you, or to me for that matter, but *his* writing drew its vigor from the demotic voice and the dramatization of his outlaw side—which was considerable—and so he created the Céline of the great novels in somewhat the way Jack Benny, also flirting with the taboo, created himself as a miser. You have to be awfully naive not to understand that a writer is a performer who puts on the act he does best—not least when he dons the mask of the first-person singular. That may be the best mask of all for a second self. Some—many—pretend to be more lovable than they are and some pretend to be less. Beside the point. Literature isn't a moral beauty contest. Its power arises from the authority and audacity with which the impersonation is pulled off; the belief it inspires is what counts. The question to ask about the writer isn't why does he behave so badly but what does he gain by wearing this mask? I don't admire the Genet that Genet presents as himself any more than I admire the unsavory Molloy impersonated by Beckett. I admire Genet because he writes books that won't let me forget who that Genet is. When Rebecca West was writing about Augustine, she said that his *Confessions* was too subjectively true to be objectively true. I think this is so in the first-person novels of Genet and Céline, as it is in Colette, books like *The Shackle* and *The Vagabond*. Gombrowicz has a novel called *Pornographia* in which he introduces himself as a character, using his own name—the better to implicate himself in certain highly dubious proceedings and bring the moral terror to life. Konwicki, another Pole, in his last two novels, *The Polish Complex* and *A Minor Apocalypse*, works to close the gap between the reader and the narrative by introducing "Konwicki" as the central character. He strengthens the illusion that the novel is true—and not to be discounted as "fiction"—by impersonating himself. It all goes back to Jack Benny. Need I add, however, that it's hardly a disinterested undertaking? Writing for me isn't a natural thing that I just keep doing, the way fish swim and birds fly. It's something that's done under a certain kind of provocation, a particular urgency. It's the transformation, through an elaborate impersonation, of a personal emergency into a public act—in both senses of that word. It can be a very trying spiritual exercise to siphon through your being qualities that are alien to your moral makeup—as trying for the writer as for the reader. You can wind up feeling more like a sword-swallower than a ventriloquist or impersonator. You sometimes use yourself very harshly in order to reach what is, literally speaking, beyond you.

The impersonator can't afford to indulge the ordinary human instincts that direct people in what they want to present and what they want to hide.

If the novelist is an impersonator, then what about the autobiography? What is the relationship, for example, between the deaths of the parents, which are so important in the last two Zuckerman novels, and the death of your own parents?

Why not ask about the relationship between the death of my parents and the death of Gabe Wallach's mother, the germinating incident in my 1962 novel *Letting Go*? Or ask about the death and funeral of the father, which is at the heart of "The Day It Snowed," my first published story in the *Chicago Review* in 1955? Or ask about the death of Kepesh's mother, wife of the owner of a Catskills hotel, which is the turning point in *The Professor of Desire*? The terrible blow of the death of a parent is something I began writing about long before any parent of mine had died. Novelists are frequently as interested in what hasn't happened to them as in what has. What may be taken by the innocent for naked autobiography is, as I've been suggesting, more than likely mock-autobiography or hypothetical autobiography or autobiography grandiosely enlarged. We know about the people who walk into the police station and confess to crimes they haven't committed. Well, the false confession appeals to writers too. Novelists are even interested in what happens to other people and, like liars and con men everywhere, will pretend that something dramatic or awful or hair-raising or splendid that happened to someone else actually happened to them. The physical particulars and moral circumstances of Zuckerman's mother's death have practically nothing to do with the death of my own mother. The death of the mother of one of my dearest friends—whose account of her suffering stuck in my mind long after he'd told me about it—furnished the most telling details for the mother's death in *The Anatomy Lesson*. The black cleaning woman who commiserates with Zuckerman in Miami Beach about his mother's death is modeled on the housekeeper of old friends in Philadelphia, a woman I haven't seen for ten years and who never laid eyes on anybody in my family but me. I was always entranced by her tangy style of speech, and when the right moment came, I used it. But the words in her mouth I invented. Olivia, the eighty-three-year-old black Florida cleaning woman, *c'est moi*.

As you well know, the intriguing biographical issue—and critical issue, for that matter—isn't that a writer will write about some of what has happened to him, but *how* he writes about it, which, when understood properly, takes us a long way to understanding *why* he writes about it. A more intriguing question is why and how he writes about what hasn't happened—how he feeds what's hypothetical or imagined into what's inspired and controlled by recollection, and how what's recollected spawns the overall fantasy. I suggest, by the way, that the best person to ask about the autobiographical relevance of the climactic death of the father in *Zuckerman Unbound* is my own father, who lives in Elizabeth, New Jersey. I'll give you his phone number.

INTERVIEWER

Then what is the relationship between your experience of psycho-analysis and the use of psychoanalysis as a literary stratagem?

ROTH

If I hadn't been analyzed I wouldn't have written *Portnoy's Complaint* as I wrote it, or *My Life as a Man* as I wrote it, nor would *The Breast* resemble itself. Nor would I resemble myself. The experience of psychoanalysis was probably more useful to me as a writer than as a neurotic, although there may be a false distinction there. It's an experience that I shared with tens of thousands of baffled people, and anything that powerful in the private domain that joins a writer to his generation, to his class, to his moment, is tremendously important for him, providing that afterwards he can separate himself enough to examine the experience objectively, imaginatively, in the writing clinic. You have to be able to become your doctor's doctor, even if only to write about patienthood, which was, certainly in part, a subject in *My Life as a Man*. Why patienthood interested me—and as far back as *Letting Go*, written four or five years before my own analysis—was because so many enlightened contemporaries had come to accept the view of themselves as patients, and the ideas of psychic disease, cure, and recovery. You're asking me about the relationship between art and life? It's like the relationship between the eight hundred or so hours that it took to be psychoanalyzed, and the eight or so hours that it would take to read *Portnoy's Complaint* aloud. Life is long and art is shorter.

INTERVIEWER

Can you talk about your marriage?

ROTH

It took place so long ago that I no longer trust my memory of it. The problem is complicated further by *My Life as a Man*, which diverges so dramatically in so many places from its origin in my own nasty situation that I'm hard put, some twenty-five years later, to sort out the invention of 1974 from the facts of 1959. You might as well ask the author of *The Naked and the Dead* what happened to him in the Philippines. I can only tell you that that was my time as an infantryman, and that *My Life as a Man* is the war novel I wrote some years after failing to receive the Distinguished Service Cross.

INTERVIEWER

Do you have painful feelings on looking back?

ROTH

Looking back I see these as fascinating years—as people of fifty often do contemplating the youthful adventure for which they paid with a decade of their lives a comfortingly long time ago. I was more aggressive then than I am today, some people were even said to be intimidated by me, but I was an easy target all the same. We're easy targets at twenty-five, if only someone discovers the enormous bull's-eye.

And where was it?

Oh, where it can usually be found in self-confessed budding literary geniuses. My idealism. My romanticism. My passion to capitalize the *L* in Life. I wanted something difficult and dangerous to happen to me. I wanted a hard time. Well, I got it. I'd come from a small, safe, relatively happy provincial background—my Newark neighborhood in the thirties and forties was just a Jewish Terre Haute—and I'd absorbed, along with the ambition and drive, the fears and phobias of my generation of American Jewish children. In my early twenties, I wanted to prove to myself that I wasn't afraid of all those things. It wasn't a mistake to want to prove that, even though after the ball was over I was virtually unable to write for three or four years. From 1962 to 1967 is the longest I've gone, since becoming a writer, without publishing a book. Alimony and recurrent court costs had bled me of every penny I could earn by teaching and writing and, hardly into my thirties, I was thousands of dollars in debt to my friend and editor Joe Fox. The loan was to help pay for my analysis, which I needed primarily to prevent me from going out and committing murder because of the alimony and court costs incurred for having served two years in a childless marriage. The image that teased me during those years was of a train that had been shunted onto the wrong track. In my early twenties, I had been zipping right along there, you know—on schedule, express stops only, final destination clearly in mind; and then suddenly I was on the wrong track, speeding off into the wilds. I'd ask myself, How the hell do you get this thing back on the right track? Well, you can't. I've continued to be surprised, over the years, whenever I discover myself, late at night, pulling into the wrong station.

INTERVIEWER

But not getting back on the same track was a great thing for you, presumably.

ROTH

John Berryman said that for a writer any ordeal that doesn't kill him is terrific. The fact that his ordeal did finally kill him doesn't make what he was saying wrong.

INTERVIEWER

What do you feel about feminism, particularly the feminist attack on you?

ROTH

What is it?

INTERVIEWER

The force of the attack would be in part that the female characters are unsympathetically treated, for instance that Lucy Nelson in *When She Was Good* is hostilely presented.

ROTH

Don't elevate that by calling it a feminist attack. That's just stupid reading. Lucy Nelson is a furious adolescent who wants a decent life. She is presented as better than her world and conscious of being better. She is confronted and opposed by men who typify deeply irritating types to many women. She is the protector of a passive, defenseless mother whose vulnerability drives her crazy. She happens to be raging against aspects of middle-class American life that the new militant feminism was to identify as the enemy only a few years after Lucy's appearance in print—hers might even be thought of as a case of premature feminist rage. *When She Was Good* deals with Lucy's struggle to free herself from the terrible disappointment engendered in a daughter by an irresponsible father. It deals with her hatred of the father he was and her yearning for the father he couldn't be. It would be sheer idiocy, particularly if this *were* a feminist attack, to contend that such powerful feelings of loss and contempt and shame do not exist in the daughters of drunks, cowards, and criminals. There is also the helpless mama's boy Lucy marries, and her hatred of his incompetence and professional innocence. Is there no such thing in the world as marital hatred? That will come as news to all the rich divorce lawyers, not to mention to Thomas Hardy and Gustave Flaubert. By the way, is Lucy's father treated "hostilely" because he's a drunk and a petty thief who ends up in jail? Is Lucy's husband treated "hostilely" because he happens to be a big baby? Is the uncle who tries to destroy Lucy "hostilely" treated because he's a brute? This is a novel about a wounded daughter who has more than sufficient cause to be enraged with the men in her life. She is only "hostilely" presented if it's an act of hostility to recognize that young women can be wounded and young women can be enraged. I'd bet there are even some enraged and wounded women who are feminists. You know, the dirty little secret is no longer sex; the dirty little secret is hatred and rage. It's the tirade that's taboo. Odd that this should be so a hundred years after Dostoyevsky—and fifty after Freud—but nobody nice likes to be identified with the stuff. It's the way folks used to feel about fellatio in the good old days. "Me? Never heard of it. Disgusting." But is it "hostile," really, to take a look at the ferocity of the emotion they call "hostility"? *When She Was Good* is not serving the cause—that's true. The anger of this young woman isn't presented to be endorsed with a hearty "Right on!" that will move the populace to action. The nature of the anger is examined, as is the depth of the wound. So are the consequences of the anger, for Lucy as for everyone. I hate to have to be the one to say it, but the portrait isn't without its poignancy. I don't mean by poignancy what the compassionate book reviewers call "compassion." I mean you see the suffering that real rage is.

INTERVIEWER

But supposing I say to you that nearly all the women in the books are there to obstruct, or to help, or to console the male characters. There's the woman who cooks and consoles and is sane and calming, or the other kind of woman, the dangerous maniac, the obstructor. They occur as means of helping or obstructing Kepesh or Zuckerman or Tarnopol. And that could be seen as a limited view of women.

ROTH

Let's face it, some women who are sane also happen to know how to cook. So do some of the dangerous maniacs. Let's leave out the sin of cooking. A great book on the order of *Oblomov* could be written about a man allying himself with woman after woman who gorges him with marvelous meals, but I haven't written it. If your description of the "sane," "calm," and "consoling" woman applies to anyone, it's to Claire Ovington in *The Professor of Desire*, with whom Kepesh establishes a tender liaison some years after the breakup of his marriage. Now, I'd have no objection to your writing a novel about this relationship from the point of view of Claire Ovington—I'd be intrigued to see how she saw it—so why do you take a slightly critical tone about my writing the novel from the point of view of David Kepesh?

INTERVIEWER

There's nothing wrong with the novel's being written from David Kepesh's point of view. What might cause difficulties for some readers is that Claire and the other women in the novel are there to help or hinder him.

ROTH

I'm not pretending to give you anything other than his sense of his life with this young woman. My book doesn't stand or fall on the fact that Claire Ovington is calm and sane, but on whether I am able to depict what calmness and sanity are like and what it is to have a mate—and why it is one would want a mate—who possesses those and other virtues in abundance. She is also vulnerable to jealousy when Kepesh's ex-wife turns up uninvited, and she carries with her a certain sadness about her family background. She isn't there "as a means" of helping Kepesh. She *helps* him—and he helps her. *They are in love.* She is there because Kepesh has fallen in love with a sane and calm and consoling woman after having been unhappily married to a difficult and exciting woman he was unable to handle. Don't people do that? Someone more doctrinaire than you might tell me that the state of being in love, particularly of being passionately in love, is no basis for establishing permanent relationships between men and women. But, alas, people, even people of intelligence and experience, *will* do it—have done it and seem intent on going on doing it—and I am not interested in writing about what people *should* do for the good of the human race and pretending that's what they *do* do, but writing about what they do indeed do, lacking the programmatic efficiency of the infallible theorists. The irony of Kepesh's situation is that having found the calm and consoling woman he can live with, a woman of *numerous* qualities, he then finds his desire for her perversely seeping away, and realizes that unless this involuntary diminution of passion can be arrested he'll become alienated from the best thing in his life. Doesn't that happen either? From what I hear this damn seeping away of desire happens all the time and is extremely distressing to the people involved. Look, I didn't invent the loss of desire, and I didn't invent the lure of passion, and I didn't invent sane companions, and I didn't invent maniacs. I'm sorry if my men don't have the correct feelings about women, or the universal range of feelings about women, or the feelings about women that it will be OK for men to have in 1995, but I do insist that there is some morsel of truth in my depiction of what it might be like for a man to be a Kepesh or a Portnoy or a breast.

INTERVIEWER

Why have you never reused the character of Portnoy in another book, the way that you have used Kepesh and Zuckerman?

ROTH

But I did use Portnoy in another book. *Our Gang* and *The Great American Novel* are Portnoy in another book. Portnoy wasn't a character for me, he was an explosion and I wasn't finished exploding after *Portnoy's Complaint*. The first thing I wrote after *Portnoy's Complaint* was a long story that appeared in Ted Solotaroff's *American*

Review called "On the Air." John Updike was here a while ago and while we were all having dinner one night, he said, How come you've never reprinted that story? I said, It's too disgusting. John laughed. He said, It is, it's a truly disgusting story. And I said, I didn't know what I was thinking about when I wrote it. And that is true to some degree—I didn't want to know; the idea was *not* to know. But I also did know. I looked in the arsenal and found another dynamite stick, and I thought, Light the fuse and see what happens. I was trying to blow up more of myself. This phenomenon is known to students of literary survey courses as the writer changing his style. I was blowing up a lot of old loyalties and inhibitions, literary as well as personal. I think this may be why so many Jews were incensed by *Portnoy's Complaint*. It wasn't that they'd never heard about kids masturbating before or about Jewish family fighting. It was, rather, that if they couldn't even control someone like me anymore, with all my respectable affiliations and credentials, all my seriousness of purpose, something had gone wrong. After all, I wasn't Abbie Hoffman or Lenny Bruce, I was a university teacher who had published in *Commentary*. But at the time it seemed to me that the next thing to be serious about was not being so goddamn serious. As Zuckerman reminds Appel, seriousness can be as stupid as anything else.

INTERVIEWER

Weren't you also looking for a fight, writing *Portnoy's Complaint?*

ROTH

I'd found a fight without looking for it long before that. They'd never really got off my ass for publishing *Goodbye, Columbus*, which was considered in some circles to be my *Mein Kampf*. Unlike Alexander Portnoy, my education in petit-bourgeois morality didn't come at home, but after I'd left home and begun to publish my first short stories. My own household environment as a youngster was much closer to Zuckerman's than to Portnoy's. It had its constraints, but there was nothing resembling the censorious small-mindedness and shame-ridden xenophobia that I ran into from the official Jews who wanted me to shut up. The moral atmosphere of the Portnoy household, in its repressive aspects, owes a lot to the response of persistent voices within the official Jewish community to my debut. They did much to help make it seem auspicious.

INTERVIEWER

You've been talking about the opposition to *Portnoy's Complaint*. What about the recognition—how did its enormous success affect you?

ROTH

It was too big, on a larger and much crazier scale than I could begin to deal with, so I took off. A few weeks after publication, I boarded a bus at the Port Authority terminal for Saratoga Springs and holed up at Yaddo, the writers' colony, for three months. Precisely what Zuckerman should have done after *Carnovsky*—but he hung around, the fool, and look what happened to him. He would have enjoyed Yaddo more than he enjoyed Alvin Pepler. But it made *Zuckerman Unbound* funnier keeping him in Manhattan and it made my own life easier, not being there.

INTERVIEWER

Do you dislike New York?

ROTH

I lived there from 1962 until I moved to the country after *Portnoy's Complaint*, and I wouldn't trade those years for anything. New York *gave* me *Portnoy's Complaint* in a way. When I was living and teaching in Iowa City and Princeton, I didn't ever feel so free as I did in New York in the sixties to indulge myself in comic performance on paper and with friends. There were raucous evenings with my New York friends, there was uncensored shamelessness in my psychoanalytic sessions, there was the dramatic, stagy atmosphere of the city itself in the years after Kennedy's assassination—all this inspired me to try out a new voice, a fourth voice, a less page-bound voice than the voice of *Goodbye, Columbus*, or of *Letting Go*, or of *When She Was Good*. So did the opposition to the war in Vietnam. There's always something behind a book to which it has no seeming connection, something invisible to the reader that has helped to release the writer's initial impulse. I'm thinking about the rage and rebelliousness that were in the air, the vivid examples I saw around me of angry defiance and hysterical opposition. This gave me a few ideas for my act.

INTERVIEWER

Did you feel you were part of what was going on in the sixties?

ROTH

I felt the power of the life around me. I believed myself to be feeling the full consciousness of a place—this time New York—for the first time really since childhood. I was also, like others, receiving a stunning education in moral, political, and cultural possibilities from the country's eventful public life and from what was happening in Vietnam.

INTERVIEWER

But you published a famous essay in *Commentary* in 1960 called "Writing American Fiction" about the way that intellectuals or thinking people in America felt that they were living in a foreign country, a country in whose communal life they were *not* involved.

ROTH

Well, that's the difference between 1960 and 1968. Being published in *Commentary* is another difference. Alienated in America, a stranger to its pleasures and preoccupations—that was how many young people like me saw their situation in the fifties. It was a perfectly honorable stance, I think, shaped by our literary aspirations and modernist enthusiasms, the high-minded of the second postimmigrant generation coming into conflict with the first great eruption of postwar media garbage. Little did we know that some twenty years later the philistine ignorance on which we would have liked to turn our backs would infect the country like Camus's plague. Any satirist writing a futuristic novel who had imagined a President Reagan during the Eisenhower years would have been accused of perpetrating a piece of crude, contemptible, adolescent, anti-American wickedness, when in fact he would have succeeded as prophetic sentry just where Orwell failed; he would have seen that the grotesquerie to be visited upon the English-speaking world would not be an extension of the repressive Eastern totalitarian nightmare but a proliferation of the Western farce of media stupidity and cynical commercialism—American-style philistinism run amok. It wasn't Big Brother who'd be watching us from the screen, but we who'd be watching a terrifyingly powerful world leader with the soul of an amiable, soap-opera grandmother, the values of a civic-minded Beverly Hills Cadillac dealer, and the historical background and intellectual equipment of a high-school senior in a June Allyson musical.

INTERVIEWER

What happened to you later, in the seventies? Did what was happening in the country continue to mean much to someone like you?

ROTH

I have to remember what book I was writing and then I can remember what happened to me—though what was happening to me was largely the book I was writing. Nixon came and went in '73, and while Nixon was coming and going I was being driven quite crazy by *My Life as a Man*. In a way I had been writing that book on and off since 1964. I kept looking for a setting for the sordid scene in which Maureen buys a urine specimen from a poor pregnant black woman in order to get Tarnopol to think he's impregnated her. I thought of it first as a scene for *When She Was Good*, but it was all wrong for Lucy and Roy in Liberty Center. Then I thought it might go into *Portnoy's Complaint*, but it was too malevolent for that kind of comedy. Then I wrote cartons and cartons of drafts of what eventually turned out to be *My Life as a Man*—"eventually," after I finally realized that my solution lay in the very problem I couldn't overcome, my inability to find the setting appropriate to the sordid event, rather than the sordid event itself, was really at the heart of the novel. Watergate made life interesting when I wasn't writing, but from nine to five every day I didn't think too much about Nixon or about Vietnam. I was trying to solve the problem of this book. When it seemed I never would, I stopped and wrote *Our Gang*; when I tried again and still couldn't write it, I stopped and wrote the baseball book; then while finishing the baseball book, I stopped to write *The Breast*. It was as though I were blasting my way through a tunnel to reach the novel that I couldn't write. Each of one's books *is* a blast, clearing the way for what's next. It's all one book you write anyway. At night you dream six dreams. But *are* they six dreams? One dream prefigures or anticipates the next, or somehow concludes what hasn't yet even been fully dreamed. Then comes the next dream, the corrective of the dream before—the alternative dream, the antidote dream—enlarging upon it, or laughing at it, or contradicting it, or trying just to get the dream dreamed *right*. You can go on trying all night long.

INTERVIEWER

After *Portnoy* and after leaving New York you moved to the country. What about rural life? Obviously it was used as material in *The Ghost Writer*.

ROTH

I might never have become interested in writing about a reclusive writer if I hadn't first had my own small taste of E. I. Lonoff's thirty-five years of rural splendor. I need something solid under my feet to kick off my imagination. But aside from giving me a sense of the Lonoffs' lives, the country existence hasn't offered anything as yet in the way of subject. Probably it never will and I should get the hell out. Only I happen to love living there, and I can't make *every* choice conform to the needs of my work.

INTERVIEWER

What about England, where you spend part of each year? Is that a possible source of fiction?

ROTH

Ask me twenty years from now. That's about how long it took Isaac Singer to get enough of Poland out of his system—and to let enough of America in—to begin, little by little, as a writer, to see and depict his upper-Broadway cafeterias. If you don't know the fantasy life of a country, it's hard to write fiction about it that isn't just description of the decor, human and otherwise. Little things trickle through when I see the country dreaming out loud—in the theater, at an election, during the Falklands crisis, but I know nothing really about what means what to people here. It's very hard for me to understand who people are, even when they tell me, and I don't even know if that's *because* of who they are or because of me. I don't know who is impersonating what, if I'm necessarily seeing the real thing or just a fabrication, nor can I easily see where the two overlap. My perceptions are clouded by the fact that I speak the language. I believe I know what's being said, you see, even if I don't. Worst of all, I don't hate anything here. What a relief it is to have no culture grievances, not to have to hear the sound of one's voice taking positions and having opinions and recounting all that's wrong! What bliss—but for the writing that's no asset. Nothing drives me crazy here and a writer *has* to be driven crazy to help him to *see*. A writer needs his poisons. The antidote to his poisons is often a book. Now if I *had* to live here, if for some reason I were forbidden ever to return to America, if my position and my personal well-being were suddenly to become permanently bound up with England, well, what was maddening and meaningful might begin to come into focus, and yes, in about the year 2005, maybe 2010, little by little I'd stop writing about Newark and I would dare to set a story at a table in a wine bar on Kensington Park Road. A story about an elderly exiled foreign writer, in this instance reading not *The Jewish Daily Forward*, but the *Herald Tribune*.

INTERVIEWER

In these last three books, the Zuckerman novels, there has been a reiteration of the struggle with Jewishness and Jewish criticism. Why do you think these books go over the past as much as they do? Why is that happening now?

ROTH

In the early seventies, I began to be a regular visitor to Czechoslovakia. I went to Prague every spring and took a little crash course in political repression. I'd only known repression firsthand in somewhat more benign and covert forms—as psychosexual constraint or as social restriction. I knew less about anti-Semitic repression from personal experience than I did about the repressions Jews practiced upon themselves and upon one another as a consequence of the history of anti-Semitism. Portnoy, you remember, considers himself just such a practicing Jew. Anyway, I became highly attuned to the differences between the writer's life in totalitarian Prague and in freewheeling New York, and I decided, after some initial uncertainty, to focus on the unreckoned consequences of a life in art in the world that I knew best. I realized that there were already many wonderful and famous stories and novels by Henry James and Thomas Mann and James Joyce about the life of the artist, but none I knew of about the comedy that an artistic vocation can turn out to be in the USA. When Thomas Wolfe tackled the subject he was rather rhapsodic. Zuckerman's struggle with Jewishness and Jewish criticism is seen in the context of his comical career as an American writer, ousted by his family, alienated from his fans, and finally at odds with his own nerve endings. The Jewish quality of books like mine doesn't really reside in their subject matter. Talking about Jewishness hardly interests me at all. It's a kind of sensibility that makes, say, *The Anatomy Lesson* Jewish, if anything does, the nervousness, the excitability, the arguing, the dramatizing, the indignation, the obsessiveness, the touchiness, the playacting—above all the *talking*. The talking and the shouting. Jews will go on, you know. It isn't what it's talking *about* that makes a book Jewish—it's that the book won't shut up. The book won't leave you alone. Won't let up.

Gets too close. "Listen, listen—that's only the half of it!" I knew what I was doing when I broke Zuckerman's jaw. For a Jew a broken jaw is a terrible tragedy. It was to avoid this that so many of us went into teaching rather than prizefighting.

INTERVIEWER

Why is Milton Appel, the good, high-minded Jew who was a guru for Zuckerman in his early years, a punching-bag in *The Anatomy Lesson*, someone that Zuckerman wants to desanctify?

ROTH

If I were not myself, if someone else had been assigned the role of being Roth and writing his books, I might very well, in this other incarnation, have been his Milton Appel.

INTERVIEWER

Is Zuckerman's rage at Milton Appel the expression of a kind of guilt on your part?

ROTH

Guilt? Not at all. As a matter of fact, in an earlier draft of the book, Zuckerman and his young girlfriend Diana took exactly opposite positions in their argument about Appel. She, with all her feisty inexperience, said to Zuckerman, "Why do you let him push you around, why do you take this shit sitting down?" and Zuckerman, the older man, said to her, "Don't be ridiculous, dear, calm down, he doesn't matter." There was the real autobiographical scene and it had no life at all. I had to absorb the rage into the main character even if my own rage on this topic had long since subsided. By being true to life I was actually ducking the issue. So I reversed their positions, and had the twenty-year-old college girl telling Zuckerman to grow up and gave Zuckerman the tantrum. Much more fun. I wasn't going to get anywhere with a Zuckerman as eminently reasonable as myself.

INTERVIEWER

So your hero always has to be enraged or in trouble or complaining.

ROTH

My hero has to be in a state of vivid transformation or radical displacement. I am not what I am—I am, if anything, what I am not. The litany begins something like that.

INTERVIEWER

How conscious are you as you are writing of whether you are moving from a third- to a first-person narrative?

ROTH

It's not conscious or unconscious—the movement is spontaneous.

INTERVIEWER

But how does it feel, to be writing in the third person as opposed to the first person?

ROTH

How does it feel looking through a microscope, when you adjust the focus? Everything depends upon how close you want to bring the naked object to the naked eye. And vice versa. Depends on what you want to magnify, and to what power.

INTERVIEWER

But do you free yourself in certain ways by putting Zuckerman in the third person?

ROTH

I free myself to say about Zuckerman what it would be inappropriate for him to say about himself in quite the same way. The irony would be lost in the first person, or the comedy; I can introduce a note of gravity that might be jarring coming from him. The shifting within a single narrative from the one voice to the other is how a reader's moral perspective is determined. It's something like this that we all want to do in ordinary conversation when we employ the indefinite pronoun "one" in speaking of ourselves. Using "one" places your observation in a looser relationship to the self that's uttering it. Look, sometimes it's more telling to let him speak for himself, sometimes it's more telling to speak about him; sometimes it's more telling to narrate obliquely, sometimes not. *The Ghost Writer* is narrated in the first person, probably because what's being described is largely a world Zuckerman's discovered outside of himself, the book of a young explorer. The older and more scarred he gets, the more inward-looking he gets, the further out *I* have to get. The crisis of solipsism he suffers in *The Anatomy Lesson* is better seen from a bit of a distance.

INTERVIEWER

Do you direct yourself as you are writing to make distinctions between what is spoken and what is narrative?

ROTH

I don't "direct" myself. I respond to what seem the liveliest possibilities. There's no necessary balance to be achieved between what is spoken and what is narrated. You go with what's alive. Two thousand pages of narrative and six lines of dialogue may be just the ticket for one writer, and two thousand pages of dialogue and six lines of narrative the solution for another.

INTERVIEWER

Do you ever take long chunks that have been dialogue and make them into narrative, or the other way around?

ROTH

Sure. I did that with the Anne Frank section of *The Ghost Writer*. I had trouble getting that right. When I began in the third person

I was somehow *revering* the material. I was taking a high elegiac
tone in telling the story of Anne Frank surviving and coming to
America. I didn't know where I was going so I began by doing what
you're supposed to do when writing the life of a saint. It was the
tone appropriate to hagiography. Instead of Anne Frank gaining
new meaning within the context of my story, I was trying to draw
from the ready store of stock emotions that everybody is supposed
to have about her. It's what even good actors sometimes will do during the first weeks of rehearsing a play—gravitate to the conventional form of presentation, cling to the cliché while anxiously
waiting for something authentic to take hold. In retrospect, my difficulties look somewhat bizarre, because just what Zuckerman was
fighting against I was in fact succumbing to—the officially autho-
rized and most consoling legend. I tell you, no one who later complained that in *The Ghost Writer* I had abused the memory of Anne
Frank would have batted an eye had I let those banalities out into
the world. That would have been just fine; I might even have got a
citation. But I couldn't have given myself any prizes for it. The difficulties of telling a Jewish story—How should it be told? In what
tone? To whom should it be told? To what end? Should it be told at
all?—was finally to become *The Ghost Writer*'s theme. But before it
became a theme, it apparently had to be an ordeal. It often happens,
at least with me, that the struggles that generate a book's moral life
are naively enacted upon the body of the book during the early, uncertain stages of writing. That *is* the ordeal, and it ended when I
took that whole section and recast it in the first person—Anne
Frank's story told by Amy Bellette. The victim wasn't herself going
to talk about her plight in the voice of "The March of Time." She
hadn't in the *Diary*, so why should she in life? I didn't want this section to *appear* as first-person narration, but I knew that by passing it
through the first-person sieve, I stood a good chance of getting rid
of this terrible tone, which wasn't hers, but mine. I did get rid of it.
The impassioned cadences, the straining emotions, the somber,
overdramatized, archaic diction—I cleared it all out, thanks to Amy
Bellette. Rather straightforwardly, I then cast the section *back* into

the third person, and then I was able to get to work on it—to write
rather than to rhapsodize or eulogize.

INTERVIEWER

How do you think you have influenced the environment, the culture, as a writer?

ROTH

Not at all. If I had followed my early college plans to become an
attorney, I don't see where it would matter to the culture.

INTERVIEWER

Do you say that with bitterness or with glee?

ROTH

Neither. It's a fact of life. In an enormous commercial society that
demands complete freedom of expression, the culture is a maw. Recently, the first American novelist to receive a special Congressional
Gold Medal for his "contribution to the nation" was Louis L'Amour.
It was presented to him at the White House by the president. The
only other country in the world where such a writer would receive his
government's highest award is the Soviet Union. In a totalitarian
state, however, *all* culture is dictated by the regime; fortunately we in
America live in Reagan's and not Plato's Republic and, aside from
their stupid medal, culture is almost entirely ignored. And that is
preferable by far. As long as those on top keep giving the honors to
Louis L'Amour and couldn't care less about anything else, everything
will be just fine. When I was first in Czechoslovakia, it occurred to
me that I work in a society where as a writer everything goes and
nothing matters, while for the Czech writers I met in Prague, nothing
goes and everything matters. This isn't to say I wished to change
places. I didn't envy them their persecution and the way in which it
heightens their social importance. I didn't even envy them their seemingly more valuable and serious themes. The trivialization in the
West of much that's deadly serious in the East is itself a subject, one

requiring considerable imaginative ingenuity to transform into compelling fiction. To write a serious book that doesn't signal its seriousness with the rhetorical cues or thematic gravity that's traditionally associated with seriousness is a worthy undertaking too. To do justice to a spiritual predicament that is *not* blatantly shocking and monstrously horrible, which does *not* elicit universal compassion, or occur on a large historical stage, or on the grandest scale of twentieth-century suffering—well, that's the lot that has fallen to those who write where everything goes and nothing matters. I recently heard the critic George Steiner on English television, denouncing contemporary Western literature as utterly worthless and without quality and claiming that the great documents of the human soul, the masterpieces, could only arise from souls being crushed by regimes like those in Czechoslovakia. I wonder then why all the writers I know in Czechoslovakia loathe the regime and passionately wish that it would disappear from the face of the earth. Don't they understand, as Steiner does, that this is their chance to be great? Sometimes one or two writers with colossal brute strength do manage, miraculously, to survive and, taking the system as their subject, to make art of a very high order out of their persecution. But most of them who remain sealed up inside totalitarian states are, as writers, destroyed by the system. That system doesn't make masterpieces; it makes coronaries, ulcers, and asthma, it makes alcoholics, it makes depressives, it makes bitterness and desperation and insanity. The writers are intellectually disfigured, spiritually demoralized, physically sickened, and culturally bored. Frequently they are silenced completely. Nine-tenths of the best of them will never do their best work just because of the system. The writers nourished by this system are the party hacks. When such a system prevails for two or three generations, relentlessly grinding away at a community of writers for twenty, thirty, or forty years, the obsessions become fixed, the language grows stale, the readership slowly dies out from starvation, and the existence of a national literature of originality, variety, vibrancy—which is very different from the brute survival of a single powerful voice—is nearly impossible. A literature that has the misfortune of remaining isolated underground for too long will inevitably become provincial, backwards, even naive, despite the fund of dark experience that may inspire it. By contrast, our work here hasn't been deprived of authenticity because as writers we haven't been stomped on by a totalitarian government. I don't know of any Western writer, aside from George Steiner, who is so grandiosely and sentimentally deluded about human suffering—and "masterpieces"—that he's come back from behind the Iron Curtain thinking himself devalued because he hasn't had to contend with such a wretched intellectual and literary environment. If the choice is between Louis L'Amour and our literary freedom and our extensive, lively, national literature on the one hand, and Solzhenitsyn and that cultural desert and crushing suppression on the other, I'll take L'Amour.

INTERVIEWER

But don't you feel powerless as a writer in America?

ROTH

Writing novels is not the road to power. I don't believe that, in my society, novels effect serious changes in anyone other than the handful of people who are writers, whose own novels are of course seriously affected by other novelists' novels. I can't see anything like that happening to the ordinary reader, nor would I expect it to.

INTERVIEWER

What do novels do then?

ROTH

To the ordinary reader? Novels provide readers with something to read. At their best writers change the *way* readers read. That seems to me the only realistic expectation. It also seems to me quite enough. Reading novels is a deep and singular pleasure, a gripping and mysterious human activity that does not require any more moral or political justification than sex.

INTERVIEWER

But are there no other aftereffects?

ROTH

You asked if I thought my fiction had changed anything in the culture and the answer is no. Sure, there's been some scandal, but people are scandalized all the time; it's a way of life for them. It doesn't mean a thing. If you ask if I *want* my fiction to change anything in the culture, the answer is still no. What I want is to possess my readers while they are reading my book—if I can, to possess them in ways that other writers don't. Then let them return, just as they were, to a world where everybody else is working to change, persuade, tempt, and control them. The best readers come to fiction to be free of all that noise, to have set loose in them the consciousness that's otherwise conditioned and hemmed in by all that *isn't* fiction. This is something that every child, smitten by books, understands immediately, though it's not at all a childish idea about the importance of reading.

INTERVIEWER

Last question. How would you describe yourself? What do you think you are like, compared with those vividly transforming heroes of yours?

ROTH

I am like somebody who is trying vividly to transform himself out of himself and into his vividly transforming heroes. I am very much like somebody who spends all day writing.

Issue 93, 1984

Maya Angelou

The Art of Fiction

This interview was conducted on the stage of the YMHA on Manhattan's upper East Side. A large audience, predominantly women, was on hand, filling indeed every seat, with standees in the back—a testament to Maya Angelou's drawing power. Close to the stage was a small contingent of black women dressed in the white robes of the Black Muslim order. Her presence dominated the proceedings. Many of her remarks drew fervid applause, especially those which reflected her views on racial problems, the need to persevere, and "courage." She is an extraordinary performer and has a powerful stage presence. Many of the answers seemed as much directed to the audience as to the interviewer so that when Maya Angelou concluded the evening by reading aloud from her work—again to a rapt audience—it seemed a logical extension of a planned entertainment.

—*George Plimpton, 1990*

Before a long journey begins, which includes crossing

boundaries and time zones, (the prudent traveler) checks her *maps*

checks, addresses and

travel documents, passport, Visa, medical innoculations,)

, makes certain that her *that she has*

clothes ~~will~~ fit the weather, and apt currencies for the

will

destination. *If the journey include crossing regional*

national boundaries and time zones, the traveller

checks the validity of her

The less careful traveler is not so superb in her

and as a result frequently encounters delays, *disruption*

planning. *Lie* Once the journey commences she unfailingly *disappointment*

with despair

reaches ~~a~~ destination, ~~although possibly not the~~

some

one of her choice

It is *who experiences*

The desperate traveler ~~assures~~ the greatest surprises and

she holds of a breath ~~th~~ anxiously for her, since her

the most exquisite thrills, ~~and~~ her sole preparation for

~~the road~~ is the fierce determination to leave where she is,

and her only certain destination is somewhere other than

where she has been.

"I got the key to the Highway,

Booked down and I'm bound to go

INTERVIEWER

You once told me that you write lying on a made-up bed with a bottle of sherry, a dictionary, *Roget's Thesaurus*, yellow pads, an ashtray, and a Bible. What's the function of the Bible?

MAYA ANGELOU

The language of all the interpretations, the translations, of the Judaic Bible and the Christian Bible, is musical, just wonderful. I read the Bible to myself. I'll take any translation, any edition, and read it aloud, just to hear the language, hear the rhythm, and remind myself how beautiful English is. Though I do manage to mumble around in about seven or eight languages, English remains the most beautiful of languages. It will do anything.

INTERVIEWER

Do you read it to get inspired to pick up your own pen?

ANGELOU

For melody. For content also. I'm working at trying to be a Christian and that's serious business. It's like trying to be a good Jew, a good Muslim, a good Buddhist, a good Shintoist, a good Zoroastrian, a good friend, a good lover, a good mother, a good buddy—it's serious business. It's not something where you think, Oh, I've got it done. I did it all day, hotdiggety. The truth is, all day long you try to do it, try to be it, and then in the evening if you're honest and have a little courage you look at yourself and say, Hmm. I only blew it eighty-six times. Not bad. I'm trying to be a Christian and the Bible helps me to remind myself what I'm about.

INTERVIEWER

Do you transfer that melody to your own prose? Do you think your prose has that particular ring that one associates with the King James version?

ANGELOU

I want to hear how English sounds, how Edna St. Vincent Millay heard English. I want to hear it, so I read it aloud. It is not so that I can then imitate it. It is to remind me what a glorious language it is. Then I try to be particular and even original. It's a little like reading Gerard Manley Hopkins or Paul Laurence Dunbar or James Weldon Johnson.

INTERVIEWER

And is the bottle of sherry for the end of the day or to fuel the imagination?

ANGELOU

I might have it at six-fifteen A.M. just as soon as I get in, but usually it's about eleven o'clock when I'll have a glass of sherry.

INTERVIEWER

When you are refreshed by the Bible and the sherry, how do you start a day's work?

ANGELOU

I have kept a hotel room in every town I've ever lived in. I rent a hotel room for a few months, leave my home at six, and try to be at work by six-thirty. To write, I lie across the bed, so that this elbow is absolutely encrusted at the end, just so rough with callouses. I never allow the hotel people to change the bed, because I never sleep there. I stay until twelve-thirty or one-thirty in the afternoon, and then I go home and try to breathe; I look at the work around five; I have an orderly dinner—proper, quiet, lovely dinner; and then I go back to work the next morning. Sometimes in hotels I'll go into the room and there'll be a note on the floor which says, Dear Miss Angelou, let us change the sheets. We think they are moldy. But I only allow them to come in and empty wastebaskets. I insist that all things are taken off the walls. I don't want anything in there. I go into the room and I feel as if all my beliefs are suspended. Nothing holds me to anything. No milkmaids, no flowers, nothing. I just want to *feel* and then when I start to work I'll remember. I'll read something, maybe the Psalms, maybe, again, something from Mr. Dunbar, James Weldon Johnson. And I'll remember how beautiful, how pliable the language is, how it will lend itself. If you pull it, it says, OK. I remember that and I start to write. Nathaniel Hawthorne says, "Easy reading is damn hard writing." I try to pull the language into such a sharpness that it jumps off the page. It must look easy, but it takes me forever to get it to look so easy. Of course, there are those critics—New York critics as a rule—who say, Well, Maya Angelou has a new book out and of course it's good but then she's a natural writer. Those are the ones I want to grab by the throat and wrestle to the floor because it takes me forever to get it to sing. I *work* at the language. On an evening like this, looking out at the auditorium, if I had to write this evening from my point of view, I'd see the rust-red used worn velvet seats and the lightness where people's backs have rubbed against the back of the seat so that it's a light orange, then the beautiful colors of the people's faces, the white, pink-white, beige-white, light beige, and brown and tan—I would have to look at all that, at all those faces and the way they sit on top of their necks. When I would end up writing after four hours or five hours in my room, it might sound like, It was a rat that sat on a mat. That's that. Not a cat. But I would continue to play with it and pull at it and say, I love you. Come to me. I love you. It might take me two or three weeks just to describe what I'm seeing now.

INTERVIEWER

How do you know when it's what you want?

ANGELOU

I know when it's the best I can do. It may not be the best there is. Another writer may do it much better. But I know when it's the best I can do. I know that one of the great arts that the writer develops is the art of saying, No. No, I'm finished. Bye. And leaving it alone. I will not write it into the ground. I will not write the life out of it. I won't do that.

INTERVIEWER

How much revising is involved?

ANGELOU

I write in the morning and then go home about midday and take a shower, because writing, as you know, is very hard work, so you have to do a double ablution. Then I go out and shop—I'm a serious cook—and pretend to be normal. I play sane—Good morning! Fine, thank you. And you? And I go home. I prepare dinner for myself and if I have houseguests, I do the candles and the pretty music and all that. Then after all the dishes are moved away I read what I wrote that morning. And more often than not if I've done nine pages I may be able to save two and a half or three. That's the cruelest time, you know, to really admit that it doesn't work. And to blue pencil it. When I finish maybe fifty pages and read them—fifty acceptable pages—it's not too bad.

I've had the same editor since 1967. Many times he has said to me over the years or asked me, Why would you use a semicolon instead of a colon? And many times over the years I have said to him things like: I will never speak to you again. Forever. Goodbye. That is it. Thank you very much. And I leave. Then I read the piece and I think of his suggestions. I send him a telegram that says, OK, so you're right. So what? Don't ever mention this to me again. If you do, I will never speak to you again. About two years ago I was visiting him and his wife in the Hamptons. I was at the end of a dining room table with a sit-down dinner of about fourteen people. Way at the end I said to someone, I sent him telegrams over the years. From the other end of the table he said, And I've kept every one! Brute! But the editing, one's own editing, before the editor sees it, is the most important.

INTERVIEWER

The five autobiographical books follow each other in chronological order. When you started writing *I Know Why the Caged Bird Sings*

did you know that you would move on from that? It almost works line
by line into the second volume.

ANGELOU

I know, but I didn't really mean to. I thought I was going to write
Caged Bird and that would be it and I would go back to playwriting
and writing scripts for television. Autobiography is awfully seductive—
it's wonderful. Once I got into it I realized I was following a tradition
established by Frederick Douglass—the slave narrative—speaking in
the first-person singular talking about the first-person plural, always
saying *I* meaning *we*. And what a responsibility! Trying to work with
that form, the autobiographical mode, to change it, to make it bigger,
richer, finer, and more inclusive in the twentieth century has been a
great challenge for me. I've written five now and I really hope—the
works are required reading in many universities and colleges in the
United States—that people read my work. The greatest compliment I
receive is when people walk up to me on the street or in airports and
say, Miss Angelou, I *wrote* your books last year and I really—I mean I
read . . . That is it—that the person has come into the books so seriously, so completely, that he or she, black or white, male or female,
feels, That's my story. I told it. I'm making it up on the spot. That's
the great compliment. I didn't expect, originally, that I was going to
continue with the form. I thought I was going to write a little book
and it would be fine and I would go on back to poetry, write a little
music.

INTERVIEWER

What about the genesis of the first book? Who were the people
who helped you shape those sentences that leap off the page?

ANGELOU

Oh well, they started years and years before I ever wrote, when I
was very young. I loved the black American minister. I loved the
melody of the voice and the imagery, so rich and almost impossible.

The minister in my church in Arkansas, when I was very young, would use phrases such as, God stepped out, the sun over his right shoulder, the moon nestling in the palm of his hand. I mean, I just loved it, and I loved the black poets, and I loved Shakespeare, and Edgar Allan Poe, and I liked Matthew Arnold a lot—still do. Being mute for a number of years, I read and memorized, and all those people have had tremendous influence . . . in the first book and even in the most recent book.

INTERVIEWER

Mute?

ANGELOU

I was raped when I was very young. I told my brother the name of the person who had done it. Within a few days the man was killed. In my child's mind—seven and a half years old—I thought my voice had killed him. So I stopped talking for five years. Of course I've written about this in *Caged Bird*.

INTERVIEWER

When did you decide you were going to be a writer? Was there a moment when you suddenly said, This is what I wish to do for the rest of my life?

ANGELOU

Well, I had written a television series for PBS, and I was going out to California. I thought I was a poet and playwright. That was what I was going to do the rest of my life. Or become famous as a real estate broker. This sounds like name-dropping, and it really is, but James Baldwin took me over to dinner with Jules and Judy Feiffer one evening. All three of them are great talkers. They went on with their stories and I had to fight for the right to play it good. I had to insert myself to tell some stories too. Well, the next day Judy Feiffer called Bob Loomis, an editor at Random House, and suggested that if he could get me to write an autobiography, he'd have something. So he phoned me and I said, No, under no circumstances—I certainly will not do such a thing. So I went out to California to produce this series on African and black American culture. Loomis called me out there about three times. Each time I said no. Then he talked to James Baldwin. Jimmy gave him a ploy which always works with me—though I'm not proud to say that. The next time he called, he said, Well, Miss Angelou, I won't bother you again. It's just as well that you don't attempt to write this book, because to write autobiography as literature is almost impossible. I said, What are you talking about? I'll do it. I'm not proud about this button that can be pushed and I will immediately jump.

INTERVIEWER

Do you select a dominant theme for each book?

ANGELOU

I try to remember times in my life, incidents in which there was the dominating theme of cruelty, or kindness, or generosity, or envy, or happiness, glee . . . perhaps four incidents in the period I'm going to write about. Then I select the one that lends itself best to my device and that I can write as drama without falling into melodrama.

INTERVIEWER

Do you write for a particular audience?

ANGELOU

I thought early on if I could write a book for black girls it would be good because there were so few books for a black girl to read that said this is how it is to grow up. Then, I thought, I'd better, you know, enlarge that group, the market group that I'm trying to reach. I decided to write for black boys and then white girls and then white boys.

But what I try to keep in mind mostly is my craft. That's what I really try for; I try to allow myself to be impelled by my art—if that doesn't sound too pompous and weird—accept the impulse and then try my best to have a command of the craft. If I'm feeling depressed and losing my control then I think about the reader. But that is very rare—to think about the reader when the work is going on.

INTERVIEWER

So you don't keep a particular reader in mind when you sit down in that hotel room and begin to compose or write. It's yourself.

ANGELOU

It's myself . . . and my reader. I would be a liar, a hypocrite, or a fool—and I'm not any of those—to say that I don't write for the reader. I do. But for the reader who hears, who really will work at it, going behind what I seem to say. So I write for myself and that reader who will pay the dues. There's a phrase in West Africa, in Ghana— it's called "deep talk." For instance, there's a saying: The trouble for the thief is not how to steal the chief's bugle but where to blow it. Now, on the face of it, one understands that. But when you really think about it, it takes you deeper. In West Africa they call that "deep talk." I'd like to think I write "deep talk." When you read me, you should be able to say, Gosh, that's pretty. That's lovely. That's nice. Maybe there's something else? Better read it again. Years ago I read a man named Machado de Assis who wrote a book called *Dom Casmurro*. Machado de Assis is a South American writer—black fa- ther, Portuguese mother—writing in 1865, say. I thought the book was very nice. Then I went back and read the book and said, Hmm. I didn't realize all that was in that book. Then I read it again, and again, and I came to the conclusion that what Machado de Assis had done for me was almost a trick: he had beckoned me onto the beach to watch a sunset. And I had watched the sunset with pleasure. When I turned around to come back in I found that the tide had come in over my head. That's when I decided to write. I would write so that the reader says, That's so nice. Oh boy, that's pretty. Let me read that again. I think that's why *Caged Bird* is in its twenty-first printing in hardcover and its twenty-ninth in paper. All my books are still in print, in hardback as well as paper, because people go back and say, Let me read that. Did she really say that?

INTERVIEWER

The books are episodic, aren't they? Almost as if you had put together a string of short stories. I wondered if as an autobiographer you ever fiddled with the truth to make the story better.

ANGELOU

Well, sometimes. I love the phrase "fiddle with." It's so English. Sometimes I make a character from a composite of three or four people, because the essence in any one person is not sufficiently strong to be written about. Essentially though, the work is true though sometimes I fiddle with the facts. Many of the people I've written about are alive today and I have them to face. I wrote about an ex-husband—he's an African—in *The Heart of a Woman*. Before I did, I called him in Dar es Salaam and said, I'm going to write about some of our years together. He said, Now before you ask, I want you to know that I shall sign my release, because I know you will not lie. However, I am sure I shall argue with you about your interpretation of the truth.

INTERVIEWER

Did he enjoy his portrait finally or did you argue about it?

ANGELOU

Well, he didn't argue, but I was kind too.

INTERVIEWER

I would guess this would make it very easy for you to move from autobiography into novel, where you can do anything you want with your characters.

ANGELOU

Yes, but for me, fiction is not the sweetest form. I really am trying to do something with autobiography now. It has caught me. I'm using the first-person singular and trying to make that the first-person plural, so that anybody can read the work and say, Hmm, that's the truth, yes, uh-huh, and live in the work. It's a large, ambitious dream. But I love the form.

INTERVIEWER

Aren't the extraordinary events of your life very hard for the rest of us to identify with?

ANGELOU

Oh my God, I've lived a very simple life! You can say, Oh yes, at thirteen this happened to me and at fourteen . . . But those are facts. But the facts can obscure the truth, what it really felt like. Every human being has paid the earth to grow up. Most people don't grow up. It's too damn difficult. What happens is most people get older. That's the truth of it. They honor their credit cards, they find parking spaces, they marry, they have the nerve to have children, but they don't grow up. Not really. They get older. But to grow up costs the earth, the *earth*. It means you take responsibility for the time you take up, for the space you occupy. It's serious business. And you find out what it costs us to love and to lose, to dare and to fail. And maybe even more, to succeed. What it costs, in truth. Not superficial costs—anybody can have that—I mean in truth. That's what I write. What it really is like. I'm just telling a very simple story.

INTERVIEWER

Aren't you tempted to lie? Novelists lie, don't they?

ANGELOU

I don't know about lying for novelists. I look at some of the great novelists, and I think the reason they are great is that they're telling the truth. The fact is they're using made-up names, made-up people, made-up places, and made-up times, but they're telling the truth about the human being—what we are capable of, what makes us lose, laugh, weep, fall down, and gnash our teeth and wring our hands and kill each other and love each other.

INTERVIEWER

James Baldwin, along with a lot of writers in this series, said that "when you're writing you're trying to find out something you didn't know." When you write do you search for something that you didn't know about yourself or about us?

ANGELOU

Yes. When I'm writing, I am trying to find out who I am, who we are, what we're capable of, how we feel, how we lose and stand up, and go on from darkness into darkness. I'm trying for that. But I'm also trying for the language. I'm trying to see how it can really sound. I really love language. I love it for what it does for us, how it allows us to explain the pain and the glory, the nuances and the delicacies of our existence. And then it allows us to laugh, allows us to show wit. Real wit is shown in language. We need language.

INTERVIEWER

Baldwin also said that his family urged him not to become a writer. His father felt that there was a white monopoly in publishing. Did you ever have any of those feelings—that you were going up against something that was really immensely difficult for a black writer?

ANGELOU

Yes, but I didn't find it so just in writing. I've found it so in all the things I've attempted. In the shape of American society, the white male is on top, then the white female, and then the black male, and at the bottom is the black woman. So that's been always so. That is nothing new. It doesn't mean that it doesn't shock me, shake me up . . .

INTERVIEWER

I can understand that in various social stratifications, but why in art?

ANGELOU

Well, unfortunately, racism is pervasive. It doesn't stop at the university gate, or at the ballet stage. I knew great black dancers, male and female, who were told early on that they were not shaped, physically, for ballet. Today, we see very few black ballet dancers. Unfortunately, in the theater and in film, racism and sexism stand at the door. I'm the first black female director in Hollywood. In order to direct, I went to Sweden and took a course in cinematography so I would understand what the camera would do. Though I had written a screenplay, and even composed the score, I wasn't allowed to direct it. They brought in a young Swedish director who hadn't even shaken a black person's hand before. The film was *Georgia, Georgia* with Diana Sands. People either loathed it or complimented me. Both were wrong, because it was not what I wanted, not what I would have done if I had been allowed to direct it. So I thought, Well, what I guess I'd better do is be ten times as prepared. That is not new. I wish it was. In every case I know I have to be ten times more prepared than my white counterpart.

INTERVIEWER

Even as a writer where . . .

ANGELOU

Absolutely.

INTERVIEWER

Yet a manuscript is what arrives at the editor's desk, not a person, not a body.

ANGELOU

Yes. I must have such control of my tools, of words, that I can make this sentence leap off the page. I have to have my writing so polished that it doesn't look polished at all. I want a reader, especially an editor, to be a half-hour into my book before he realizes it's reading he's doing.

INTERVIEWER

But isn't that the goal of every person who sits down at a typewriter?

ANGELOU

Absolutely. Yes. It's possible to be overly sensitive, to carry a bit of paranoia along with you. But I don't think that's a bad thing. It keeps you sharp, keeps you on your toes.

INTERVIEWER

Is there a thread one can see through the five autobiographies? It seems to me that one prevailing theme is the love of your child.

ANGELOU

Yes, well, that's true. I think that that's a particular. I suppose, if I'm lucky, the particular is seen in the general. There is, I hope, a thesis in my work: we may encounter many defeats, but we must not be defeated. That sounds goody-two-shoes, I know, but I believe that a diamond is the result of extreme pressure and time. Less time is crystal. Less than that is coal. Less than that is fossilized leaves. Less than that it's just plain dirt. In all my work, in the movies I write, the lyrics, the poetry, the prose, the essays, I am saying that we may encounter many defeats—maybe it's imperative that we encounter the defeats—but we are much stronger than we appear to be and maybe much better than we allow ourselves to be. Human beings are more alike than unalike. There's no real mystique. Every human being, every Jew, Christian, backslider, Muslim, Shintoist, Zen Buddhist, atheist, agnostic, every human being wants a nice place to live, a good place for the children to go to school, healthy children, somebody to love, the courage, the unmitigated gall to accept love in return, someplace to party on Saturday or Sunday night, and someplace to perpetuate that God. There's no mystique. None. And if I'm right in my work, that's what my work says.

INTERVIEWER
Have you been back to Stamps, Arkansas?

ANGELOU

About 1970, Bill Moyers, Willie Morris, and I were at some affair. Judith Moyers as well—I think she was the instigator. We may have had two or three scotches, or seven or eight. Willie Morris was then with *Harper's* magazine. The suggestion came up: Why don't we all go back South? Willie Morris was from Yazoo, Mississippi. Bill Moyers is from Marshall, Texas, which is just a hop, skip, and a jump—about as far as you can throw a chitterling—from Stamps, my hometown. Sometime in the middle of the night there was this idea: Why don't Bill Moyers and Maya Angelou go to Yazoo, Mississippi, to visit Willie Morris? Then why don't Willie Morris and Maya Angelou go to Marshall, Texas, to visit Bill Moyers? I said, Great. I was agreeing with both. Then they said Willie Morris and Bill Moyers would go to Stamps, Arkansas, to visit Maya Angelou, and I said, No way, José. I'm not going back to that little town with two white men! I will not do it! Well, after a while Bill Moyers called me—he was doing a series on creativity—and he said, Maya, come on, let's go to Stamps. I said, No way. He continued, I want to talk about creativity. I said, You know, I don't want to know where it resides. I really don't, and I still don't. One of the problems in the West is that people are too busy putting things under microscopes and so forth. Creativity is greater than the sum of its parts. All I want to know is that creativity is there. I want to know that I can put my hand behind my back like Tom Thumb and pull out a plum. Anyway, Moyers went on and on and so did Judith and before I knew it, I found myself in Stamps, Arkansas. Stamps, Arkansas! With Bill Moyers, in front of my grandmother's door. My God! We drove out of town—me with Bill and Judith. Back of us was the crew, a New York crew, you know, very "Right, dig where I'm comin' from, like, get it on," and so forth. We got about three miles outside of Stamps and I said, Stop the car. Let the car behind us pull up. Get those people in with you and I'll take their car. I suddenly was taken back to being twelve years old in a Southern, tiny town where my grandmother told me, Sistah, never be on a country road with any white boys. I was two hundred years older than black pepper, but I said, Stop the car. I did. I got out of the car. And I knew these guys—certainly Bill. Bill Moyers is a friend and brother-friend to me. We care for each other. But dragons, fears, the grotesques of childhood always must be confronted at childhood's door. Any other place is esoteric and has nothing to do with the great fear that is laid upon one as a child. So anyway, we did Bill Moyers's show. And it seems to be a very popular program, and it's the first of the creativity programs . . .

INTERVIEWER

Did going back assuage those childhood fears?

ANGELOU

They are there like griffins hanging off the sides of old and tired European buildings.

INTERVIEWER

It hadn't changed?

ANGELOU

No, worse if anything.

INTERVIEWER

But it was forty years before you went back to the South, to North Carolina. Was that because of a fear of finding griffins everywhere, Stamps being a typical community of the South?

ANGELOU

Well, I've never felt the need to prove anything to an audience. I'm always concerned about who I am to me first—to myself and God. I really am. I didn't go south because I didn't want to pull up whatever clout I had, because that's boring, that's not real, not true—that doesn't tell me anything. If I had known I was afraid, I would have gone earlier. I just thought I'd find the South really unpleasant. I have moved south now. I live there.

INTERVIEWER

Perhaps writing the autobiographies, finding out about yourself, would have made it much easier to go back.

ANGELOU

I know many think that writing sort of "clears the air." It doesn't do that at all. If you are going to write autobiography, don't expect that it will clear anything up. It makes it more clear to you, but it doesn't alleviate anything. You simply know it better, you have names for people.

INTERVIEWER

There's a part in *Caged Bird* where you and your brother want to do a scene from *The Merchant of Venice*, and you don't dare do it because your grandmother would find out that Shakespeare was not only deceased but white.

ANGELOU

I don't think she'd have minded if she'd known he was deceased. I tried to pacify her—my mother knew Shakespeare but my grandmother was raising us. When I told her I wanted to recite—it was actually Portia's speech—Mama said to me, Now, Sistah, what are you goin' to render? The phrase was so fetching. The phrase was "Now, little mistress Marguerite will render her rendition." Mama said, Now, Sistah, what are you goin' to render? I said, Mama, I'm going to render a piece written by William Shakespeare. My grandmother asked me, Now, Sistah, who is this very William Shakespeare? I had to tell her that he was white, it was going to come out. Somebody would let it out. So I told Mama, Mama, he's white but he's dead.

Then I said, He's been dead for centuries, thinking she'd forgive him because of this little idiosyncrasy. She said, No Ma'am, little mistress you will not. No Ma'am, little mistress you will not. So I rendered James Weldon Johnson, Paul Laurence Dunbar, Countee Cullen, Langston Hughes.

INTERVIEWER

Were books allowed in the house?

ANGELOU

None of those books were in the house; they were in the school. I'd bring them home from school, and my brother gave me Edgar Allan Poe because he knew I loved him. I loved him so much I called him EAP. But as I said, I had a problem when I was young: from the time I was seven and a half to the time I was twelve and a half I was a mute. I could speak but I didn't speak for five years and I was what was called a "volunteer mute." But I read and I memorized just masses—I don't know if one is born with photographic memory but I think you can develop it. I just have that.

INTERVIEWER

What is the significance of the title *All God's Children Need Traveling Shoes*?

ANGELOU

I never agreed, even as a young person, with the Thomas Wolfe title *You Can't Go Home Again*. Instinctively I didn't. But the truth is, you can never *leave* home. You take it with you—it's under your fingernails; it's in the hair follicles; it's in the way you smile; it's in the ride of your hips, in the passage of your breasts; it's all there, no matter where you go. You can take on the affectations and the postures of other places and even learn to speak their ways. But the truth is, home is between your teeth. Everybody's always looking for it: Jews go to Israel; black Americans and Africans in the Diaspora go to Africa;

Europeans, Anglo-Saxons go to England and Ireland; people of Germanic background go to Germany. It's a very queer quest. We can kid ourselves—we can tell ourselves, Oh yes, honey, I live in Tel Aviv, actually . . . The truth is a stubborn fact. So this book is about trying to go home.

INTERVIEWER

If you had to endow a writer with the most necessary pieces of equipment, other than, of course, yellow legal pads, what would these be?

ANGELOU

Ears. Ears. To hear the language. But there's no one piece of equipment that is most necessary. Courage, first.

INTERVIEWER

Did you ever feel that you could not get your work published? Would you have continued to write if Random House had returned your manuscript?

ANGELOU

I didn't think it was going to be very easy, but I knew I was going to do something. The real reason black people exist at all today is because there's a resistance to a larger society that says you can't do it—you can't survive. And if you survive, you certainly can't thrive. And if you thrive, you can't thrive with any passion or compassion or humor or style. There's a saying, a song that says, "Don't you let nobody turn you 'round, turn you 'round. Don't you let nobody turn you 'round." Well, I've always believed that. So knowing that, knowing that nobody could turn me 'round, if I didn't publish, well, I would design this theater we're sitting in. Yes. Why not? Some human being did it. I agree with Terence. Terence said *homo sum: humani nihil a me alienum puto.* I am a human being. Nothing human can be alien to me. When you look up Terence in the encyclopedia, you see beside his name, in italics, sold to a Roman senator, freed by that senator.

He became the most popular playwright in Rome. Six of his plays and that statement have come down to us from 154 B.C. This man, not born white, not born free, without any chance of ever receiving citizenship, said, I am a human being. Nothing human can be alien to me. Well, I believe that. I ingested that, internalized that at about thirteen or twelve. I believed if I set my mind to it, maybe I wouldn't be published but I would write a great piece of music or do something about becoming a real friend. Yes, I would do something wonderful. It might be with my next-door neighbor, my gentleman friend, with my lover, but it would be wonderful as far as I could do it. So I never have been very concerned about the world telling me how successful I am. I don't need that.

INTERVIEWER

You mentioned courage . . .

ANGELOU

. . . the most important of all the virtues. Without that virtue you can't practice any other virtue with consistency.

INTERVIEWER

What do you think of white writers who have written of the black experience—Faulkner's *The Sound and the Fury* or William Styron's *Confessions of Nat Turner*?

ANGELOU

Well, sometimes I am disappointed—more often than not. That's unfair, because I'm not suggesting the writer is lying about what he or she sees. It's my disappointment, really, in that he or she doesn't see more deeply, more carefully. I enjoy seeing Peter O'Toole or Michael Caine enact the role of an upper-class person in England. There the working class has had to study the upper-class, has been obliged to do so, to lift themselves out of their positions. Well, black Americans have had to study white Americans. For centuries under slavery, the smile or the grimace on a white man's face or the flow of a hand on a white woman could inform a black person that you're about to be sold or flogged. So we have studied the white American, where the white American has not been obliged to study us. So often it is as if the writer is looking through a glass darkly. And I'm always a little—not a little—saddened by that poor vision.

INTERVIEWER

And you can pick it up in an instant if you . . .

ANGELOU

Yes, yes. There are some who delight and inform. It's so much better, you see, for me, when a writer like Edna St. Vincent Millay speaks so deeply about her concern for herself and does not offer us any altruisms. Then when I look through her eyes at how she sees a black or an Asian my heart is lightened. But many of the other writers disappoint me.

INTERVIEWER

What is the best part of writing for you?

ANGELOU

Well, I could say the end. But when the language lends itself to me, when it comes and submits, when it surrenders and says, I am yours, darling—that's the best part.

INTERVIEWER

You don't skip around when you write?

ANGELOU

No, I may skip around in revision, just to see what connections I can find.

INTERVIEWER

Is most of the effort made in putting the words down onto the paper or is it in revision?

ANGELOU

Some work flows and, you know, you can catch three days. I think the word in sailing is *scudding*—you know, three days of just scudding. Other days it's just awful—plodding and backing up, trying to take out all the *ands, ifs, tos, fors, buts, wherefores, therefores, howevers*— you know, all those.

INTERVIEWER

And then, finally, you write "The End" and there it is—you have a little bit of sherry.

ANGELOU

A lot of sherry then.

Issue 116, 1990

Stephen Sondheim

The Art of the Musical

Stephen Sondheim was born in New York in 1930. He has written the music and lyrics for twelve Broadway musicals and the lyrics for *West Side Story*, *Gypsy*, and *Do I Hear a Waltz?* as well as many other songs. He has composed film scores and has won an Academy Award for best original song for "Sooner or Later," which was sung by Madonna in *Dick Tracy*. He won the Tony Award and the Drama Critics Circle Award for best score for *Company*, *Follies*, *A Little Night Music*, *Sweeney Todd*, *Into the Woods*, and *Passion*. He received the Pulitzer Prize for *Sunday in the Park with George*. In 1983 he was elected to the American Academy of Arts and Letters. In 1990 he was appointed the first visiting professor of contemporary theater at Oxford University and, in 1993, was a recipient of the Kennedy Center Honors for Lifetime Achievement. In 1992 he refused to accept the National Endowment's Medal of Arts Award because he felt the NEA had been, in his words, "transformed into a conduit and symbol of censorship and repression rather than encouragement and support." He accepted the award in 1997.

This interview was excerpted from a craft seminar at the New School in New York City, which appeared on the Bravo network as an episode of *Inside the Actors Studio*. The seminar ended with a classroom session in which questions were invited from the audience.

—*James Lipton, 1997*

A manuscript page from the lyrics of "Barcelona" from *Company* by Stephen Sondheim.

INTERVIEWER

When you were ten and your parents divorced, your mother moved to Pennsylvania and it was there at the age of eleven that you encountered Jimmy Hammerstein and were welcomed into the family of Oscar and Dorothy Hammerstein. I understand you've said that if Hammerstein had been a geologist, you would have become a geologist.

STEPHEN SONDHEIM

Yes. He was a surrogate father and a mentor to me up until his death. When I was fifteen, I wrote a show for George School, the Friends school I went to. It was called "By George" and was about the students and the faculty. I was convinced that Rodgers and Hammerstein couldn't wait to produce it, so I gave it to Oscar and asked him to read it as if he didn't know me. I went to bed dreaming of my name in lights on Broadway, and when I was summoned to his house the next day he asked, Do you really want me to treat this as if I didn't know you? Oh yes, I said, to which he replied, In that case, it's the worst thing I've ever read. He saw me blanch and continued, I didn't say it was untalented, but let's look at it. He proceeded to discuss it as if it were a serious piece. He started right from the first stage direction; and I've often said, at the risk of hyperbole, that I probably learned more about writing songs that afternoon than I learned the rest of my life. He taught me how to structure a song, what a character was, what a scene was; he taught me how to tell a story, how not to tell a story, how to make stage directions practical.

Of course when you're fifteen you're a sponge. I soaked it all up and I still practice the principles he taught me that afternoon. From then on, until the day he died, I showed him everything I wrote, and eventually had the Oedipal thrill of being able to criticize *his* lyrics, which was a generous thing for him to let me do.

INTERVIEWER

I've read that one of the things you learned from him was the power of a single word.

SONDHEIM

Oscar dealt in very plain language. He often used simple rhymes like *day* and *May*, and a lot of identities like "Younger than springtime am I / Gayer than laughter am I." If you look at "Oh, what a beautiful mornin'! / Oh, what a beautiful day!" it doesn't seem like much on paper, but he understood what happens when music is applied to words—the words explode. They have their own rainbows, their own magic. But not on the printed page. Some lyrics read well because they're conversational lyrics. Oscar's do not read very well because they're colloquial but not conversational. Without music, they sound simplistic and *written*. Yet it's precisely the hypersimplicity of the language that gives them such force. If you listen to "What's the Use of Wond'rin'" from *Carousel*, you'll see what I mean.

INTERVIEWER

He also stressed the importance of creating character in songs.

SONDHEIM

Remember, he'd begun as a playwright before he became a songwriter. He believed that songs should be like one-act plays, that they should have a beginning, a middle, and an end. They should set up a situation, have a development, and then a conclusion . . . exactly like a classically constructed play. Arthur Pinero said about playwriting: Tell them what you're going to do, then do it, then tell them you've done it. If that's what a play is, Oscar's songs are little plays. He utilized that approach as early as *Show Boat*. That's how he revolutionized musical theater—utilizing operetta principles and pasting them onto American musical comedy.

INTERVIEWER

That afternoon, as I recall, Hammerstein also outlined for you a curriculum and told you he wanted you to write four things. It sounds like a wonderful fairy tale. What were they?

SONDHEIM

First, he said, take a play that you like, that you think is good, and musicalize it. In musicalizing it, you'll be forced to analyze it. Next, take a play that you think is good but flawed, that you think could be improved, and musicalize that, seeing if you can improve it. Then take a nonplay, a narrative someone else has written—it could be a novel, a short story—but not a play, not something that has been structured dramatically for the stage, and musicalize that. Then try an original. The first one I did was a play by George S. Kaufman and Marc Connelly, *Beggar on Horseback*, which lends itself easily to musicalization because it's essentially a long fantasy. We performed that at college when I was an undergraduate at Williams. I got permission from Kaufman to do it and we had three performances. It was a valuable experience, indeed. The second one, which I couldn't get permission for, was a play by Maxwell Anderson called *High Tor*, which I liked but thought was sort of clumsy. Then I tried to adapt *Mary Poppins*. I didn't finish that one because I couldn't figure out how to take a series of disparate short stories, even though the same characters existed throughout, and make an evening, make an arc. After that I wrote an original musical about a guy who wanted to become an actor and became a producer. He had a sort of Sammy Glick streak in him—he was something of an opportunist. So I wrote my idea of a sophisticated, cynical musical. It was called "Climb High." There was a motto on a flight of stone steps at Williams, "Climb high, climb far, your aim the sky, your goal the star." I thought, Gee, that's very Hammersteinish. I sent him the whole thing. The first act was ninety-nine pages long. Now, the entire script of *South Pacific*, which lasted almost three hours on the stage, was only ninety-two pages. Oscar sent my script back, circled the ninety-nine, and just wrote, Wow!

INTERVIEWER

That's a step up from "the worst musical I've ever read." At Williams your major was in music and your mentor there was Robert Barrow?

SONDHEIM

Yes. I was a mathematician by nature, and still am—I just knew I didn't want to be a mathematician. So I decided not to take any mathematics courses. Williams being a liberal arts college, the natural, neutral major is English. As an elective my first year, I took music, which was generally known as a gut course. Williams in those days had eleven hundred students, all male, and a tiny music department. Robert Barrow was the senior of two teachers. The students hated him because he was cold and Mary Poppinsish. He taught rigidly out of a little black book compiled over the years into which he had compressed a lot of texts. He had a completely antiromantic approach to music. I had always imagined that writing music was all about sitting in your penthouse or your studio until this lady muse twitters around your head and sits on your shoulders and goes, Da-da-da-dum, da-da-da-dum. Instead, Robert Barrow was talking about leading tones and diatonic scales, and I fell in love. He took all the mystery out of music and taught craft. Within a year I was majoring in music. He changed my life by making me aware that art is craft, not inspiration.

INTERVIEWER

When you graduated from Williams, you received the Hutchinson Prize for music, which was a fellowship for further study. With whom did you study?

SONDHEIM

Milton Babbitt, the avant-gardist's avant-gardist. When I started studying with him, he had already gone beyond twelve-tone music and was working up at Columbia on synthesized music, which in those days was a science fiction, the idea being that (his example) he could make a bassoon play a high C. He was a rigorous intellectual but also happened to be a frustrated songwriter. When I first met him, he was writing a musical for Mary Martin. I would meet with him once a week for about four hours and we'd spend the first hour analyzing his favorite songs—I can still analyze "All the Things You Are" according to Babbitt, which in fact I did for my students at Oxford. Then we'd spend the rest of the time analyzing Beethoven and Mozart.

I asked him if he would teach me atonal music. He said, There's no point until you've exhausted tonal resources for yourself. You haven't, have you? I said, No, and I suspect I'll never want to. So I never did study atonal music. He taught tonal as rigorously as Barrow did. It was a similar approach: analyze the music, look at what the music is. How do you sustain something, hold a piece together for forty-five minutes if it's a symphony, or three minutes if it's a song? How do you manage time? That's what he taught me.

INTERVIEWER

Why did you hesitate when you were offered the chance to write the lyrics of *West Side Story*?

SONDHEIM

I wanted primarily to write music. But Oscar advised me that the job would be an extraordinary opportunity to work with men of such ability, talent, and imagination as Leonard Bernstein, Jerome Robbins, and Arthur Laurents. So I took it. And he was right.

INTERVIEWER

I've heard you disparage your lyrics for *West Side Story*, but I would give a great deal to have written "oh, moon, grow bright and make this endless day endless night."

SONDHEIM

It's fine until you remember that it's sung by an adolescent in a gang.

INTERVIEWER

You've said, "I've always thought of lyric writing as a craft rather than an art, largely a matter of sweat and time. Music is more challenging, more interesting, and more rewarding." Do you still feel that way?

SONDHEIM

Sure. Because music's abstract and it's fun and it lives in you. Language is terrific, but the English language is a difficult tool to work with. Two of the hardest words in the language to rhyme are *life* and *love*. Of all words! In Italian, easy. But not in English. Making lyrics feel natural, sit on music in such a way that you don't feel the effort of the author, so that they shine and bubble and rise and fall, is very, very hard to do. Whereas you can sit at the piano and just play and feel you're making art.

INTERVIEWER

The *love* rhymes are *shove*, *above*, *dove*, *glove*, and *of*. That's all we've got.

SONDHEIM

And they're not easy to use. *Live* isn't easy, either. You have *give* and *sieve* and then you're in a lot of trouble.

INTERVIEWER

The English language has forty-two sounds in it, French a dozen, so everything rhymes with everything else. That's why Molière was able to write those alexandrines, couplet after couplet, without ever straining for a rhyme.

SONDHEIM

But lyrics are also about open vowel sounds. The Italians have it all over us and the French because everything is *ahhhh*! Try to sing *me* on a high note. And *me* is a very useful word.

INTERVIEWER

Or *him*.

SONDHEIM

Exactly. *Short* is terrible. Singers will tell you that their throats close up.

INTERVIEWER

A Funny Thing Happened on the Way to the Forum was the first Broadway show for which you wrote music and lyrics and, if memory serves, when the show was out of town, you were out on the streets giving tickets away to get people into the theater.

SONDHEIM

It was a disaster out of town. It was directed by George Abbott, who was famous as a play doctor. We would stand in the back of the auditorium in New Haven and feel the discomfort of the audience; all the while we thought that what we were seeing was terrific. Finally, one evening George said, I don't know what to do, you'd better call in George Abbott.

When we got down to Washington, we asked Jerome Robbins to come in and help. He said, It's the opening number that's killing it. It's not telling them what the show's about. You've got to write a baggy-pants number. So I wrote this song called "Comedy Tonight." Jerry insisted, though, I don't want you to tell any jokes, let me tell the jokes. Very smart of him. That's why the lyric is so bland and dull— it's background for Jerry's pyrotechnics. It may be the best opening number ever put on the stage. The audience was so satisfied at the end of it that we thought, Let's not do the rest of the show.

INTERVIEWER

You once asked Oscar Hammerstein why he never wrote a sophis- ticated musical.

SONDHEIM

He said, You mean something that takes place in penthouses? I said yes. He said, Because it doesn't interest me. Most people proba- bly think that Oscar was a hayseed and sat on a porch all the time watching cattle turn into statues, but in fact he was an urban product, a New York boy, and very—well, urbane. Sharp tongue. Pointed wit. Wonderful critic. It's just that was not what he wanted to write about.

He wanted to write about so-called simplicities. He was a morality playwright. He wrote about Everyman. And every time he tried to write something that was particularly urban or contemporary, it wasn't very good, as in *Me and Juliet* and parts of *Allegro*. He was sharp and smart, but he didn't feel it. That's why he didn't want to write about penthouses, and he was right.

INTERVIEWER

But you certainly did in *Company*, a sophisticated New York penthouse story. It has been called a revolutionary musical. Was it a plotless show?

SONDHEIM

Yes, because it didn't begin as a musical. George Furth was an actor and was in therapy. His therapist suggested that it might be good for him to do some writing. So he wrote a series of one-act plays—playlets, really. A production had been set up but had fallen through, so he sent them to me and said, I don't know what to do with these. I wrote back, Let me send them to Hal Prince because he's very shrewd about this sort of thing. Maybe he can give you some advice. Hal said, Why don't we make a musical out of them? It seemed impossible because they were such disparate plays, and that made it intriguing. So George came east, we spent two or three weeks talking, and gradually the form of the show took shape. It came from the fact that in each playlet there were two people in a relationship and a third person who often acted as a catalyst. We realized that what the show should be about is the third person. So we invented the character of Bobby, the outsider in five different marriages. We realized that there could be no plot in the conventional sense. A man comes home on his thirty-fifth birthday and realizes that all his friends are married; he's an outsider. And he has a combination breakdown and epiphany. The show really takes place in one second. His friends are there but they're not there, and they don't know each other but they do know each other. They're all fragments of his consciousness. That's what made it an unusual show: it took place in a single moment of time. It wasn't a conventional narrative nor was it a revue, because each of the playlets concerned the same characters. Also, none of the songs grew out of scenes. Each of the songs was either a comment or the entire scene itself. And all the songs, with one exception, dealt with marriage or relationships—a word I don't much like, but I did in those days. So it became this kind of twilight-zone revue. That whole area between revue and book is something I've always been interested in. It surfaced in *Follies*, then again in *Pacific Overtures* and *Assassins*. And that's what was, to use your word, revolutionary—at least in the commercial musical theater.

INTERVIEWER

There's a remarkable song in *Company* called "Barcelona" that's actually very well-written dialogue . . .

SONDHEIM

I'll tell you something funny about "Barcelona." I finished it the night before we went into rehearsal. Hal had been pushing me to get the April–Bobby song finished because it was an entire scene. So I wrote "Barcelona" and went up to his house and played it. He looked blank throughout the whole thing and said, Well, look, we can do it at the read-through tomorrow, anyway. I thought, Oh God. Then his wife Judy came in and asked if she could hear the new song. I said, I'm afraid it's not quite . . . Well, I'll play it anyway. I sang the opening line, "Where you going? / Barcelona," and she laughed. I thought, All right, maybe it's got a chance. The next day, at the read-through, we get to "Barcelona" and I play and sing it. I sing the first line and the entire cast convulses with laughter. Hal looks over at me and shrugs. He has no trouble admitting he's wrong.

INTERVIEWER

Today the concept musical is commonplace. The British seem to have inherited it from us. Some people think they invented it. *Follies* was certainly a concept musical. Could you tell us its genesis?

SONDHEIM

First of all, I would hardly call the British musicals concept musicals—they seem like traditional operettas to me. And in any event, *concept musical* is a meaningless term, useful only to critics who need to categorize and directors who want to consider themselves writers. As for *Follies*, I went to Jim Goldman, a friend and a playwright I admire, and asked him if he had any ideas for musicals. He'd always wanted to write a play about reunions, he said, and he'd recently picked up a newspaper clipping about the Ziegfeld Girls' annual reunion. We thought that might be the basis of a show.

It took four years to write *Follies*—not steadily. We wrote it first as a murder mystery—not a mystery, that's not quite right—but a murder piece. It was about four people—two couples—who had been emotionally involved with each other a long time ago and who thought their lives had been damaged because of it. The notion was that one of them was going to murder one of the others, and the suspense, so to speak, was who's going to kill whom. Every time we would do a draft, the atmosphere for the first few minutes would be fine, but then as soon as the plot came in it would start to get a little ratchety. So we decided to delay the plot, maybe for fifteen minutes. Again it started to get ratchety, so we delayed it for twenty-five. Finally, it struck us that maybe there shouldn't be any plot at all, that it should be all atmosphere. That is, in fact, what it turned out to be. There's minimal plot. It all takes place during a party. It's about people getting drunk and their old emotions surging to the surface and interconnecting . . . all in the atmosphere of the Ziegfeld Follies. What it really is about is the loss of innocence—not only among the characters but in America between the wars, which the Follies, I think, represented.

I was much influenced in those days by the movies of Alain Resnais, and I think *Follies* was probably more influenced by *Last Year at Marienbad* than anything else. It had to do with time, and Hal gave it a surreal spin in the staging—Hal and Michael Bennett. That increased the *misterioso* quality of it . . . which is the best thing about it.

INTERVIEWER

When Richard Rodgers was asked, Which comes first, the music or the lyrics? he usually replied, The check. Since you're both the composer and lyricist, what do you start with?

SONDHEIM

Two basic things—some kind of accompaniment figure and/or some sort of refrain line or central idea for a lyric. Those are the two kinds of glue for a song. The trick is to keep them going together, so you don't get boxed in.

INTERVIEWER

You've taken us all off the hook by admitting you use a rhyming dictionary. I think you and I use the same one, Clement Wood.

SONDHEIM

That's the best one, and for a very simple reason: all the words are listed vertically. If you use one that lists them horizontally, your eyes start to skip over the entries. The problem with Clement Wood is that it was published in 1938, so there are very few contemporary words in it. But I've written a lot of words into my main copy. The book was out of print for years but luckily I'd bought four copies so I had them all over the place. Happily, it's now in print again. If anybody wants to write lyrics, that's the one to use.

INTERVIEWER

The other thing that's essential is a thesaurus. Not a dictionary but a thesaurus, because you want to know what your choices are. There I also have a favorite, by Norman Lewis. It's a thesaurus in dictionary form. The way Roget arranged his thesaurus mystifies me.

SONDHEIM

But what's interesting about the Roget is that it opens your mind, because in doing the cross-referencing, when you start looking up synonyms, you have to go back and forth, you come across shadings of words you hadn't thought of, which lead to other words. The problem with the Roget is that it's been in so many editions. The one that I think offers the best balance between the number of words and the number of cross-references is the 1943 edition. That may sound fussy but, as you know, you work with the same tools over a period of time and they become important.

INTERVIEWER

I've heard you say that you don't like to work at the piano.

SONDHEIM

Well, if you work at the piano, you're limited by your own technique. I have a very good right hand, but a left hand like a ham hock. Also, muscle memory comes into it. You start playing the same chords, the same figurations. If you force yourself to write away from the piano, you come up with more inventive things. If you're too good a piano player, as some composers are, the music may become flavorless and glib. And if you're not a very good pianist, you're limited to the same patterns. I force myself to write in keys that I haven't written in for a while. I find that most composers consider sharp keys the enemy and flat keys the friends. Flat keys somehow are more welcoming. I often force myself to write in sharp keys just to get away from the pattern. I think it's very important to try to write away from the piano.

INTERVIEWER

I've always wanted to ask you this: why on earth name *A Little Night Music* after *Eine Kleine Nachtmusik*? It had nothing to do with Mozart. And you had *Smiles of a Summer Night* sitting there looking at you.

SONDHEIM

Yes, and we also had Ingmar Bergman, who wouldn't let us use the title of the film. He gave us the rights to everything else. However, when the show was subsequently done in Vienna, we realized that in German it would revert to *Eine Kleine Nachtmusik*, which would have made people think they were going to a Mozart concert. So we wrote Bergman and asked him to let us use *Smiles of a Summer Night* in German. He gave us permission that one time.

INTERVIEWER

Sweeney Todd was operatic, using leitmotifs, as opera does. Characters had themes and the themes assembled, disassembled, reassembled. You've said that you were influenced by, of all people, Bernard Herrmann.

SONDHEIM

True. When I was fifteen years old I saw a movie called *Hangover Square*, another epiphany in my life. It was a moody, romantic, gothic thriller starring Laird Cregar, about a composer in London in 1900 who was ahead of his time. And whenever he heard a high note he went crazy and ran around murdering people. It had an absolutely brilliant score by Bernard Herrmann, centered around a one-movement piano concerto. I wanted to pay homage to him with this show, because I had realized that in order to scare people, which is what *Sweeney Todd* is about, the only way you can do it, considering that the horrors out on the street are so much greater than anything you can do on the stage, is to keep music going all the time. That's the principle of suspense sequences in movies, and Bernard Herrmann was a master in that field. So *Sweeney Todd* not only has a lot of singing, it has a lot of underscoring. It's infused with music to keep the audience in a state of tension, to make them forget they're in a theater, and to prevent them from separating themselves from the action. I based a lot of the score on a specific chord that Herrmann uses in almost all his film work and spun it out from that. That and the "Dies Irae," which is one of my favorite tunes and is full of menace.

INTERVIEWER

Sunday in the Park with George marked a new collaboration. There was the long period in which Hal Prince produced and directed your musicals and now we enter the Sondheim–James Lapine period, which has given us a different sensibility. Lapine comes from photography and graphic design. He's experimental, a poet.

SONDHEIM

I admired Jim Lapine's work. I'd seen a play that he wrote and directed called *Twelve Dreams*. A mutual friend, a producer, got us together, and we were talking one night about theme and variations, because that's a kind of show I had always wanted to do. I showed him a French magazine I had that was devoted to variations on the *Mona Lisa*. And we started talking about paintings. He had used the Seurat painting *La Grande Jatte* in a piece he had done up at Yale. And he said, Did you ever notice there are over fifty people in it and nobody's looking at anybody else? We started to speculate why. Suddenly I said, It's like a stage set, you know. It's like a French farce, isn't it? You know, maybe those people aren't supposed to be seen with each other. We started to talk about how it might make a story, and then James said the crucial thing: Of course, the main character's missing. I said, Who? He said, The painter. As soon as he said that, we knew we had a show. It would be more than a stunt, it would be a play about a man and his landscape and how he controls it. And how hard it is to make art.

INTERVIEWER

Into the Woods was another groundbreaking musical. Once again you worked with Lapine.

SONDHEIM

Well, another kind of piece I'd always wanted to do was a fairy tale, so I asked James if he'd like to write one. He said, The trouble with fairy tales is that they're really only five minutes long. There's one incident, maybe two, and that's all there should be. Which is exactly the trouble with all the attempts to expand fairy tales and make them into plays and musicals. So the notion arose of mashing a number of fairy tales together. James held them together by inventing his own, the story of a baker and his wife. Some of the fairy tales got dropped on the road. We had the Three Little Pigs in there, we had Rumpelstiltskin, we had everybody—*everybody* was in the woods. But eventually we had to cut it down.

INTERVIEWER

There seems to be a philosophical war in that musical between the theories of Bruno Bettelheim and Jung.

SONDHEIM

It's interesting you say that. Everybody assumes we were influenced by Bruno Bettelheim. But if there's any outside influence, it's Jung. James is interested in Jung—*Twelve Dreams* is based on a case Jung wrote about. In fact, we spoke to a Jungian analyst about fairy tales.

INTERVIEWER

The moral of your fairy tale seems to be beware of wishes, they may come true.

SONDHEIM

It's about moral responsibility—the responsibility you have in getting your wish not to cheat and step on other people's toes, because it rebounds. The second act is about the consequences of not only the wishes themselves but of the methods by which the characters achieve their wishes, which are not always proper and moral.

AUDIENCE MEMBER

I'm wondering what your musical influences are. I hear Debussy . . .

SONDHEIM

It's Ravel more than Debussy. Ravel's responsible for virtually all popular music, anyway—all those chords really started with him. My

period is from Brahms through 1930s Stravinsky. I like music before and I like music after, but that's where I live. Britten shows up a
lot in the stuff I write. *Sunday in the Park with George* is a Britten
score, I think. I'm very fond of English music. As far as American
music goes, I was brought up on show tunes from the so-called Golden
Era, a phrase I deplore, but there it is. You know, Kern and Gershwin. Those are influences too. So it's Ravel, Rachmaninoff—another
wonderful harmonist—Britten, Stravinsky, Kern, Gershwin, Arlen.
A lot of Arlen.

AUDIENCE MEMBER

How long before the opening do you freeze a musical production?

SONDHEIM

Bear in mind that musicals are *presentational* plays. The whole
idea of a musical is out front. Numbers go out front, no matter how
intense, they go out front. Therefore the performer has to make a contact with the audience, and as a writer, out front, I have to see that
contact before I start to change things. If a scene or a number isn't
working, it may be the performer, it may be the song. And it may be
the performer not being used to the song. Or the performer still worrying about a costume change. Remember that in musicals, often
there's a lot of scenery changing, a lot of costume changing. If you're
smart, it takes a number of performances before you change anything
in a musical because during the first couple of performances, the
performers are lucky if they get away with their lives, if they don't fall
into the pit, if they don't get run over by some of the moving scenery.
At the same time, they're performing for an audience. And because
of that, freezing a show is very useful, in the sense of letting performers play the exact same thing for, let's say, three or four performances,
without our changing any of their staging, without giving them new
lines or new songs or new lyrics. Minimal changes so that they can
solidify what they're doing. Then you can look at the play and say,
Aha, OK, that scene's too long. She's doing that song wrong. Or,
That song is wrong for her. Is it my fault? Shall I rewrite or shall I tell

her to perform the song differently? As I say, it's presentational. That's what makes musicals entirely different from plays. As an actor, you can just play the scene. If you're a performer and it's a number, you have to make it land, if that's what's required. And to make it land doesn't mean just to sing loudly. It means everything—from the acting to the voice to the presentation. Also the lights. Remember, when a musical number begins, the lights go down. That doesn't often happen in a scene. So everything conspires to make the moment false. And your job is to make it true. And at the same time please the audience.

AUDIENCE MEMBER

You mentioned that playwrights today write great characters, they have great ideas, but very few write great stories. I just wondered what you think is a great story.

SONDHEIM

I didn't use the word *great*. That's not one of my favorite words because it implies a value judgment. I said that it's very hard to write narratives, very hard to write stories. I happen to like strong narratives. I also happen to be a worshipper of Chekhov. His stories are going on inside the people, and the narrative pull is perhaps not very strong. But I also like Lillian Hellman's plays where the narrative sometimes teeters over into melodrama. The Ibsen school. I'm a big melodrama fan. I'm a big farce fan. I'm a big plot fan. But I don't think it's necessary to have one. I mean, *A Streetcar Named Desire* doesn't have much of a plot. But it sure has a strong story. And by story, I mean something that takes you in a state of tension from scene to scene and moment to moment, as opposed to just inundating you with colors and moods. That's all. Something that keeps your attention going for two hours and doesn't let you off the hook. And that could be a comedy. That could be Chekhov. It could be a murder mystery. But it must have something to keep you going. Anyway, inventive narrative is very hard to do, so it isn't about "great" or even "good," it's about whether you can do it at all. I'll bet if you made a list of, say, twenty plays over the last five years, there might be two that had a real plot. You might have enjoyed some of the others, but I'll bet it was the acting, I'll bet it was a scene, a character, Wasn't that moment wonderful when . . . ? as opposed to a substantial two-hour experience.

Issue 142, 1997

V. S. Naipaul

The Art of Fiction

Sir Vidiadhar Surajprasad Naipaul was born on August 17, 1932, in Chaguanas, Trinidad, where his ancestors had emigrated from India—his maternal grandfather, at the turn of the century, had traveled from that country as an indentured servant.

Naipaul, in his essay "Prologue to an Autobiography" from *Finding the Center*, has written: "Half a writer's work . . . is the discovery of his subject. And a problem for me was that my life had been varied, full of upheavals and moves: from grandmother's Hindu house in the country, still close to the rituals and social ways of village India; to Port of Spain, the negro, and G.I. life of its streets, the other, ordered life of my colonial English school, which is called Queen's Royal College, and then Oxford, London and the freelancers' room at the BBC. Trying to make a beginning as a writer, I didn't know where to focus."

After two failed attempts at novels and three months before his twenty-third birthday, Naipaul found his start in the childhood memory of a neighbor in Port of Spain. The memory provided the first sentence for *Miguel Street*, which he wrote over six weeks in 1955 in the BBC freelancers' room at the Langham Hotel, where he was working part-time editing and presenting a literary program for the Caribbean Service. The book would not be published until 1959, after the success of *The Mystic Masseur* (1957), which received the John Llewellyn Rhys Memorial Prize, and *The Suffrage of Elvira* (1958), which was

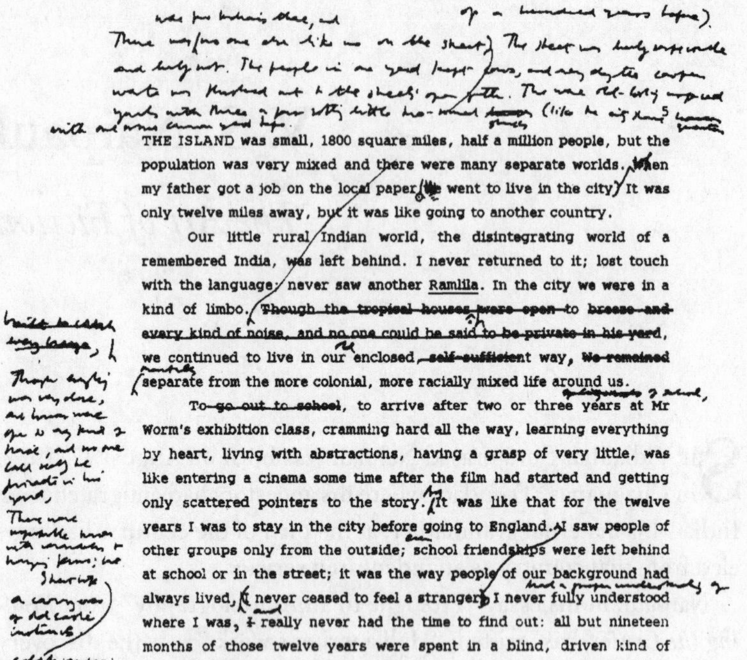

THE ISLAND was small, 1800 square miles, half a million people, but the population was very mixed and there were many separate worlds. When my father got a job on the local paper we went to live in the city. It was only twelve miles away, but it was like going to another country.

Our little rural Indian world, the disintegrating world of a remembered India, was left behind. I never returned to it; lost touch with the language; never saw another Ramlila. In the city we were in a kind of limbo. ~~Though the tropical houses were open to breeze and every kind of noise, and no one could be said to be private in his yard~~, we continued to live in our enclosed, ~~self-sufficient~~ way. ~~We remained~~ separate from the more colonial, more racially mixed life around us.

To ~~go out to school~~, to arrive after two or three years at Mr Worm's exhibition class, cramming hard all the way, learning everything by heart, living with abstractions, having a grasp of very little, was like entering a cinema some time after the film had started and getting only scattered pointers to the story. It was like that for the twelve years I was to stay in the city before going to England. I saw people of other groups only from the outside; school friendships were left behind at school or in the street; it was the way people of our background had always lived. I never ceased to feel a stranger. I never fully understood where I was, I really never had the time to find out: all but nineteen months of those twelve years were spent in a blind, driven kind of colonial studying.

~~And~~ I got to know very soon that there was a further world outside, of which our colonial world was only a shadow. This outer world — England principally, but also United States and Canada — ruled us in every way. It sent us governors and everything else we lived by: the ~~special~~ foods the island had needed since the slave days (smoked herrings, salted cod, condensed milk, New Brunswick sardines in oil); the special medicines (Dodd's Kidney Pills, Dr Sloan's Liniment, the tonic called Six Sixty-Six). It sent us the coins of England, from the halfpenny to the half-crown, to which we automatically gave values in our dollars and cents, one cent to a halfpenny. It sent us text books and ~~examination~~ question papers for the various school certificates (and even during the war students' scripts were sent back to England to be marked). It sent us films, and Life and Time. It sent ~~folded packets~~ of The Illustrated London News to Mr Worm's office. It sent us everything.

A manuscript page from "Reading and Writing," an unpublished essay by V.S. Naipaul.

awarded the Somerset Maugham Award. *A House of Mr. Biswas* was published in 1961, and in 1971 Naipaul received the Booker Prize for *In a Free State*. Four novels have appeared since then: *Guerrillas* (1975), *A Bend in the River* (1979), *The Enigma of Arrival* (1987), and *A Way in the World*. Naipaul received a knighthood in 1990 for his service to literature.

In the early 1960s, Naipaul began writing about his travels. He has written four books on India: *The Middle Passage* (1962), *An Area of Darkness* (1964), *India: A Wounded Civilization* (1977), and *India: A Million Mutinies Now* (1990). *The Return of Eva Peron* and *The Killings in Trinidad* (published in the same volume in 1980) recorded his experiences in Argentina, Trinidad, and the Congo. Indonesia, Iran, Pakistan, and Malaysia are the subject of *Among the Believers: An Islamic Journey* (1981). He returned to those countries in 1995; *Beyond Belief*, an account of those travels, was published this year.

In conversation with Naipaul, one finds that issues and ideas are always highly subtle and complex—of which he keeps reminding you, lest you see things only in monochrome—but the language steers clear of obfuscation and cant. Indeed, Naipaul can be a difficult companion. The humbleness of his beginnings, the long struggles, the sheer scale of his artistic beginnings clearly have bred in him deep neuroses—at sixty-six, the neurotic circuitry is still buzzing. Despite the edginess, and the slight air of unpredictability it brings into any interaction with him, Naipaul proved to be an interviewer's delight.

The interview is culled from a series of conversations in New York City and India. Part of the interview was conducted by Jonathan Rosen at the Carlyle Hotel on May 16, 1994. Naipaul spent several minutes rearranging the furniture in the hotel suite in an effort to locate the chair best suited to his aching back. He has the habit of removing glasses before answering a question, though that only enhances his scrutinizing expression and attitude of mental vigilance. The occasion for the interview was the publication of *A Way in the World*, but despite an initial wish to "stay with the book," Naipaul relaxed into a larger conversation that lasted several hours and touched on many aspects of his life and career.

—Tarun Tejpal, Jonathan Rosen, 1998

V.S. NAIPAUL

Let me know the range of what you are doing and how you are going to approach it. I want to know with what intensity to talk. Are we going to stay with the book?

INTERVIEWER

Would you like to?

NAIPAUL

It's a long career. There are many books. If things are to be interesting, it is better to be specific and focused. It's more stimulating to me, too.

INTERVIEWER

Was *A Way in the World* a difficult book to write?

NAIPAUL

In what way?

INTERVIEWER

There are so many different pieces to it, yet it fits together as a whole.

NAIPAUL

It was written as a whole—from page one to the end. Many writers tend to write summing-up books at the end of their lives.

INTERVIEWER

Were you conscious of trying to sum things up?

NAIPAUL

Yes. What people have done—people like Waugh in his war tril-ogy, or Anthony Powell—is create a character like themselves to whom they can attach these reinterpreted adventures. Powell has a character running through his books who is like him but not him, because he doesn't play a dominant role. I think this is one of the falsities that the form imposes on people, and for many years I've been thinking how to overcome it.

INTERVIEWER

How to overcome . . .

NAIPAUL

You didn't understand what I was saying?

INTERVIEWER

I'm guessing that you mean the space between Marcel Proust the author and Marcel the narrator of *Remembrance of Things Past*.

NAIPAUL

No, I was thinking—well, yes, put it like that. I was thinking that to write about the war, which was a big experience for him, Waugh had to invent a Waugh character. Whenever I have had to write fic-tion, I've always had to invent a character who roughly has my back-ground. I thought for many years how to deal with this problem. The answer was to face it boldly—not to create a bogus character but to create, as it were, stages in one's evolution.

INTERVIEWER

I'm struck by how much your autobiography overlaps with the vast history of the West. Do you have a sense that to write about yourself is to write about the larger world? Did you strive to achieve this rela-tionship or did you find it naturally evolving?

NAIPAUL

Naturally, it had to evolve, because that's learning, isn't it? You can't deny what you've learned; you can't deny your travels; you can't deny the nature of your life. I grew up in a small place and left it when I was quite young and entered the bigger world. You have to contain this in your writing. Do you understand what I am saying?

INTERVIEWER

I do understand, but I was wondering about something a little different.

NAIPAUL

Try it again. Rephrase it. Make it simple and concrete so we can deal with it.

INTERVIEWER

I imagine you as having begun in a place that you were eager to leave but that has turned out—the more you studied it and returned to it—actually to be at the center of issues that are of enormous importance to the West. You call Trinidad a small place, but as you've written, Columbus wanted it, Raleigh wanted it . . . When did you become conscious of Trinidad as a focus of the desires of the West, and a great subject?

NAIPAUL

I have been writing for a long time. For most of that time people were not interested in my work, so my discoveries have tended to be private ones. If it has happened, it's just a coincidence. I wasn't aware of it. Also, it is important to note, the work has not been political or polemic. Such a work written in the 1950s would be dead now. One must always try to see the truth of a situation—it makes things universal.

INTERVIEWER

You mentioned that your readers are coming to you late—do you
think that the world is now catching up with you? Is this a change in
readership or a change in the world?

NAIPAUL

It's a change in the world. When I began to write, there were
large parts of the world that were not considered worth writing
about. Do you know my book *The Loss of El Dorado*? It contains all
the research on Raleigh and Miranda. When it was published, the
literary editor of a very important paper in London told me that I
only should have written an essay because it wasn't a big enough
subject. He was a foolish man. But it gives you an idea of how the
world has changed.

INTERVIEWER

Do you think the world is more understanding now of the psychological displacement with which you deal?

NAIPAUL

It's such a widespread condition now. People still have the idea of
the single cultural unit, which has never actually existed. All cultures
have been mingled forever. Look at Rome—Etruria was there before,
and there were city-states around Rome. Or the East Indies—people
from India went out to found further India, then there was the Muslim influence . . . People come and go all the time—the world has always been in movement.

INTERVIEWER

Do you think you have become an exemplar of that mixed world?

NAIPAUL

I don't think so. I am always thinking about the book. You are
writing to write a book—to satisfy that need, to make a living, to leave
a fair record behind, to alter what you think is incomplete and make it

good. I am not a spokesman for anybody. I don't think anybody would want me to be a spokesman.

INTERVIEWER

The three explorers in *A Way in the World* are drawn back to Trinidad at their peril. I sense from your earlier writing that you fear you might make one trip too many—that there is an annihilating aspect to that place from which you came, which might this time overwhelm you.

NAIPAUL

You mustn't talk like that. It's very frightening. I think I have made my trips there and I won't go back again.

INTERVIEWER

But imaginatively Trinidad does pull you.

NAIPAUL

No. I'm finished with it imaginatively. You see, a writer tries very hard to see his childhood material as it exists. The nature of that childhood experience is very hard to understand—it has a beginning, a distant background, very dark, and then it has an end when a writer becomes a man. The reason that this early material is so important is that he needs to understand it to make it complete. It is contained, complete. After that there is trouble. You have to depend on your intelligence, on your inner strength. Yes, the later work rises out of this inner strength.

INTERVIEWER

I am struck by your title *A Way in the World*. It reminds me of the end of *Paradise Lost*—wandering out after the expulsion. Is the world what you enter when you leave home?

NAIPAUL

I suppose it depends on the nature of where you live. I don't know whether it is a fair question or if it should be answered. Put it another way.

INTERVIEWER

I guess I'm asking what you mean by *world*.

NAIPAUL

People can live very simple lives, can't they? Tucked away, without thinking. I think the world is what you enter when you think—when you become educated, when you question—because you can be in the big world and be utterly provincial.

INTERVIEWER

Did you grow up with a larger idea of the world? An idea represented by the word *world*?

NAIPAUL

I always knew that there was a world outside. I couldn't accept that with which I grew up—an agricultural, colonial society. You cannot get any more depressing or limited.

INTERVIEWER

You left Trinidad in 1950 to study at Oxford—setting out across the seas to an alien land in pursuit of ambition. What were you looking for?

NAIPAUL

I wanted to be very famous. I also wanted to be a writer—to be famous for writing. The absurdity about the ambition was that at the time I had no idea what I was going to write about. The ambition came long before the material. The filmmaker Shyam Benegal once told me that he knew he wanted to make films from the age of six. I wasn't as precocious as he—I wanted to be a writer by the age of ten.

I went to Oxford on a colonial government scholarship, which guaranteed to see you through any profession you wanted. I could have become a doctor or an engineer, but I simply wanted to do English at Oxford—not because it was English and not because it was Oxford, but only because it was away from Trinidad. I thought that I would learn about myself in the three or four years I was going to be away. I thought that I would find out my material and miraculously become a writer. Instead of learning a profession, I chose this banality of English—a worthless degree, it has no value at all.

But I wanted to escape Trinidad. I was oppressed by the pettiness of colonial life and by (this relates more particularly to my Indian Hindu family background) the intense family disputes in which people were judged and condemned on moral grounds. It was not a generous society—neither the colonial world nor the Hindu world. I had a vision that in the larger world people would be appreciated for what they were—people would be found interesting for what they were.

INTERVIEWER

Unconnected to the family from which they came?

NAIPAUL

Yes. I imagined that one would not be subject to that moralizing judgment all the time. People would find what you were saying interesting, or they would find you uninteresting. It actually did happen in England—I did find a more generous way of looking at people. I still find it more generous.

INTERVIEWER

Did you enjoy Oxford?

NAIPAUL

Actually, I hated Oxford. I hate those degrees and I hate all those ideas of universities. I was far too well prepared for it. I was far more intelligent than most of the people in my college or in my course. I am not boasting, you know well—time has proved all these things. In a way, I had prepared too much for the outer world. There was a kind of solitude and despair, really, at Oxford. I wouldn't wish anyone to go through it.

INTERVIEWER

Do you ever wonder what would have become of you if you had stayed in Trinidad?

NAIPAUL

I would have killed myself. A friend of mine did—out of stress, I think. He was a boy of mixed race. A lovely boy, and very bright. It was a great waste.

INTERVIEWER

Is he the boy that you mention in the introduction to *A House for Mr. Biswas?*

NAIPAUL

Yes, he is the boy I had in mind. We shared an admiration for each other. His death was terrible.

INTERVIEWER

Do you still feel the wounds of your early life?

NAIPAUL

I think about how lucky I was to escape. I think about how awful and oppressive it was. I see it now more clearly for what it was: the plantation—perhaps a part of the New World, but entirely autonomous. No doubt I've healed the wounds because I have thought about it so much. I think about how lucky I was not to have been destroyed utterly. There has been a life of work since then, a life of endeavor.

INTERVIEWER

Why has writing always been the central need of your life—the way out of everything?

NAIPAUL

It was given to me as an ambition. Or rather, I took my father's example; he was a writer—a journalist, but he also wrote stories. This was very important to me. My father examined our Hindu background in his stories. He found it a very cruel background, and I understood from his stories that it was a very cruel world. So I grew up with the idea that it is important to look inwards and not always define an external enemy. We must examine ourselves—our own weaknesses. I still believe that.

INTERVIEWER

You have said that you see writing as the only truly noble calling.

NAIPAUL

Yes, for me it is the only noble calling. It is noble because it deals with the truth. You have to look for ways of dealing with your experience. You have to understand it and you have to understand the world. Writing is a constant striving after a deeper understanding. That is pretty noble.

INTERVIEWER

When did you start writing?

NAIPAUL

I started work on a novel in 1949. It was a very farcical, a very interesting idea—a black man in Trinidad giving himself the name of an African king. This is the idea I tried to explore. It dragged on as a piece of writing for two years because I was too young to know much. I began it a little bit before I left home and finished it during a long vacation from Oxford. I was very glad I did finish it because at least it gave me the experience of finishing a long book. Of course nothing happened to it.

Then, after I left Oxford, really in great conditions of hardship, I began to write something intensely serious. I was trying to find my own voice, my tone—what was really me and not borrowed or acting.

This serious voice led me into great shallows of depression, which dragged on for a while until I was told to abandon it by someone to whom I had sent the manuscript. He told me it was rubbish; I wanted to kill him but deep down in my heart I knew he was absolutely right. I spent many weeks feeling wretched because it had been five years and nothing was happening. There was this great need to write, you see. I had decided it was to be my livelihood—I had committed my life to it. Then something happened: out of that gloom, I hit upon my own voice. I found the material that was my own voice. It was inspired by two literary sources—the stories of my father and a Spanish picaresque novel, the very first published, in 1554, *Lazarillo Tormes*. It is a short book about a little poor boy growing up in imperial Spain, and I loved its tone of voice. I married these two things together and found that it fitted my personality—what became genuine and original and mine really was fed by these two quite distinct sources.

INTERVIEWER

This is when you began writing *Miguel Street*?

NAIPAUL

Yes. It is immensely hard to be the first to write about anything. It is always easy afterwards to copy. So the book I wrote—that mixture of observation and folklore and newspaper cuttings and personal memory—many people can do, but at the time it was something that had to be worked out.

Imagine writing a book like *Miguel Street* in 1955. Today people are interested in writing from India or other former colonies, but at the time it was not considered writing. It was very hard to have this book with me for four years before it was published. It really upset me and it is still a great shadow over me.

INTERVIEWER

You had written two books by 1955, *The Mystic Masseur* and *Miguel Street*, but the first book was not published until 1957 and the stories not until 1959.

NAIPAUL

My life was very hard. When you are young, when you are desti-tute, when you wish to make known your presence in the world, two years is a very long time to wait. I was really made to suffer. Then *The Mystic Masseur* was finally published, and it was dismissed by my own paper (I was working at the *New Statesman* at the time) where an Oxford don, quite famous later, described it as a little savory from a colonial island. A little savory, which didn't represent labor.

It would be interesting to see the books that were considered real books by the reviewers at that time. It is useless to tell me now, All right, the books have been around for forty years, they are still printed. I was damaged. I was wounded by this neglect. People today have it much easier, which is why they complain. I never complained; I just had to go on.

INTERVIEWER

You must have been sustained largely by self-belief?

NAIPAUL

Yes. I never doubted. From the time I was a child, I had the feeling that I was marked.

INTERVIEWER

You started writing *A House for Mr. Biswas* just as your first novel was published.

NAIPAUL

Yes. I was casting around in a desperate way for a subject. It was so despairing that I actually began to write with a pencil—I didn't feel secure enough. The idea I had involved someone like my father, who at the end of his life would be looking at the objects by which he is sur-rounded and considering how they came into his life. I wrote labori-ously without inspiration for a very long time—about nine months.

INTERVIEWER
INTERVIEWER

Did you write every day?

NAIPAUL

Not strictly every day, because when you are not inspired you do things with a heavy heart. Also, I was trying at the same time to become a reviewer. Someone had recommended me to the *New Statesman*—they sent me one thing and then another, but I was trying too hard and it failed. Then they sent me some books on Jamaica, and this nice, easy voice came to me. So there was some achievement at the time—learning how to write short, interesting pieces about a book and to make the book absolutely real to the reader. Eventually, the novel caught fire and thereafter it was all right. I began to devote three weeks out of every four to this work. I think that I knew pretty soon that it was a great work. I was very pleased that, although I was so young, I was committing myself to a major piece of writing because I had begun rather small—thinking that only when one had trained oneself enough would one attempt grand work. If someone had stopped me on the street and said, I'll give you a million pounds now on one condition: you must not finish your book, I would have told him to go away. I knew I must finish my book.

INTERVIEWER

How was the book received?

NAIPAUL

It was received well from the moment it was read by the publisher. It would be nice to say that there was a rush on the book when it was published, but of course there wasn't. It would be nice to say that the world stood up and took notice, but of course the world didn't. The book just clanked along in the way of my earlier books, and it was some time before it made its way.

INTERVIEWER

A House for Mr. Biswas was a departure from your first three books, which were social comedies—you moved away from light, frothy comedy toward a more grim and serious tone.

NAIPAUL

Actually the tone is not grim. The book is full of comedy. Perhaps the comedy is less verbal, less farcical but it is in everything, I assure you. I can read you a page of my writing from any book, however dark you might think it is, and you will laugh. The jokes have become deeper. The comedy has become more profound. Without the humorous view, you couldn't go on. You can't give a dark, tragic view all the time—it must be supported by this underlying comedy.

INTERVIEWER

In *A Way in the World*, you write, "It was that idea of the absurd never far away from us that preserved us. It was the other side of that anger and the passion that made the crowd burn the black policeman . . ." It reminds me of the humor in your early books about Trinidad, and the other side of that humor—hysteria—in the books that followed.

NAIPAUL

It's very curious, isn't it—the same people who burned a policeman alive would dance and sing and tell a funny story about it.

INTERVIEWER

I was particularly struck by the word *us*—your inclusion of yourself in that situation.

NAIPAUL

Well, it was in Port of Spain. It has to be *us* because one is growing up in that atmosphere. It was our idea of the absurd, which comes out in the calypso—it's African, this idea of the absurd. It is something in late life I have come to understand—the hysteria and the sense of the absurd.

INTERVIEWER

And appreciate it more?

NAIPAUL

I'm more frightened by it. Understanding that the people who can be so absurd and write such funny songs also have a capacity for burning policemen. I fear cruelty.

INTERVIEWER

I can't help noticing that *A Way in the World* ends, like *The Enigma of Arrival*, with a funeral.

NAIPAUL

That was pure accident. I probably didn't think of it until you told me now. What I was aware of as I was writing was an emphasis on dead bodies and funerals and corpses. It begins with a man dressing a corpse and goes on to corpses in the Red House, where I worked, and there are lots of corpses in the Raleigh story.

INTERVIEWER

Is that a growing sense of mortality or is that a sense of the way of the world?

NAIPAUL

Probably it's facing it more boldly when one is older. When one is young, one has ways of dealing. Really, this is the physical thing of dying—I don't know what prompts it. It is for the reader to assess it; the writer mustn't judge himself.

INTERVIEWER

Are you conscious of reworking the elements of earlier fiction?

NAIPAUL

Yes. Getting the angle right: having acquired the material, writing about it another way and so producing new material.

INTERVIEWER

Would you agree that your later fiction takes a gentler angle? It seems to me that you now have a more accepting approach.

NAIPAUL

Be concrete. Where am I rough? Where have you found me harsh? Give me an example.

INTERVIEWER

Well, *In a Free State*.

NAIPAUL

That book was written out of great pain and very personal stress. It was written very carefully—put together like a watch or a piece of engineering. It is very well made. In 1979, for the first time, I was asked to give a reading in New York, and at the moment of the reading, I was aware of the extraordinary violence of the work—I didn't know it until then, so it wasn't conscious. I was shocked by the violence. When the jokes were made, people laughed; but what followed immediately stopped them. It was a very unsettling experience. Probably that reflects the way it was created—out of personal pain related to my own life, my own anguish.

INTERVIEWER

Can you describe the way you write?

NAIPAUL

I write slowly.

INTERVIEWER

Always?

NAIPAUL

I used to write faster when I was younger—about one thousand words a day when I was really going. I can't do that now. Now, on a good day, I write about three hundred words—very little.

INTERVIEWER

Do you ever not write?

NAIPAUL

Very often. Most days are like that.

INTERVIEWER

Hemingway called a day he had not written a day closer to death.

NAIPAUL

I'm not romantic like that. I just feel rather irritated. But I'm wise enough now and experienced enough to know that it will be all right. If it's in my head, it'll come out all right eventually. It's just finding the right way.

INTERVIEWER

Do you think language should only convey and not, as with John Updike, dance and dazzle?

NAIPAUL

Well, people have to do what they want to do. I wish my prose to be transparent—I don't want the reader to stumble over me. I want him to look through what I'm saying to what I'm describing. I don't want him ever to say, Oh goodness, how nicely written this is. That would be a failure.

INTERVIEWER

So even as the ideas are complex, the prose stays uncluttered.

NAIPAUL

Simple, yes. Also, I mustn't use jargon. You are surrounded by jargon—in the newspapers, in friends' conversations—and as a writer, you can become very lazy. You can start using words lazily. I don't want that to happen. Words are valuable. I like to use them in a valuable way.

INTERVIEWER

Do you despair for English literature?

NAIPAUL

No, I don't despair for it. It doesn't exist now, partly because it is very hard to do again what has been done before. It is in a bad, bad way in England. It has ceased to exist—but so much has existed in the past, perhaps there is no cause for grief.

INTERVIEWER

What about writers emerging from India? Do you feel the same about them?

NAIPAUL

I haven't examined that, but I think India will have a lot of writing. For many centuries India has had no intellectual life at all. It was a ritualized society, which didn't require writing. But when such societies emerge from a purely ritualistic life and begin to expand industrially, economically, and in education, then people begin to need to understand what is happening. People turn to writers, who are there to guide them, to provoke them, to stimulate them. I think there will be a lot of writing in India now. The situation will draw it out.

INTERVIEWER

To return to the question of violence, I'd like to read a passage from *A Way in the World*: "I had grown up thinking of cruelty as something always in the background. There was an ancient, or not-

so-ancient, cruelty in the language of the streets: casual threats, man
to man and parents to children, of punishments and degradation that
took you back to plantation times."

NAIPAUL

Yes. You always heard people saying things in calm language that
were what the driver would have said to the slave: I'll beat you till you
pee; I'll take the skin off your back. These were awful things to hear,
don't you think?

INTERVIEWER

Yet you have always resisted simplifying the anger—blaming it on
colonialism or on the white masters of black slaves. There is no easy
villain for you.

NAIPAUL

Of course there is no easy villain. These are safe things to say.
They're not helpful in any way, they're not additions to any argument
or discussion. They are just chants. Blaming colonialism is a very safe
chant. These people would have been very quiet in colonial days; they
would have been prepared for a life of subordination. Now that there is
no colonialism, they speak very fearlessly. But other people were fearless long before.

INTERVIEWER

You have been criticized for running into the arms of the oppressor.

NAIPAUL

Who's criticized me?

INTERVIEWER

Derek Walcott, for one.

NAIPAUL

I don't know. I don't read these things. You mustn't ask me; you must ask him. You must judge these things yourself. I can't deal with all these things. It's been a long career.

INTERVIEWER

I'd like to ask . . .

NAIPAUL

You shouldn't have asked me that question about running to the British and the masters . . . Does it show in my work?

INTERVIEWER

I wouldn't say so.

NAIPAUL

Then why did you ask it?

INTERVIEWER

Because you always have resisted the simplifications, but you have been surrounded by critics who have not resisted them.

NAIPAUL

Well, that's their problem. Have you read my book *The Middle Passage*? That book tells black people they can't be white people, which caused immense offense. In 1962, black people thought that because independence was coming, they had become closer to white people.

INTERVIEWER

The Middle Passage was your first attempt at nonfiction.

NAIPAUL

It is wrong to think of anyone as a producer of fiction because there is a limited amount of material you can work on. Yet to be a writer is to be observing, to be feeling and to be sensitive all the time. To be a serious writer is not to do what you have done before, to move on. I felt the need to move on. I felt I couldn't do again what I had done before—I shouldn't just stay at home and pretend to be writing novels. I should move and travel and explore my world—and let the form take its own natural course. Then a happy thing: a racial government, thinking they should give an appearance of being nonracial, invited me to come back and travel around the region. That's how I began to travel, and how I wrote *The Middle Passage*.

INTERVIEWER

You travel to India often. You first visited thirty-five years ago and keep coming back, both to write and to holiday. What is the source of your continuing fascination with India?

NAIPAUL

It is my ancestry, really, because I was born with a knowledge of the past that ended with my grandparents. I couldn't go beyond them, the rest was just absolute blankness. It's really to explore what I call the area of darkness.

INTERVIEWER

Do you think it is crucial to your function and material as a writer to know where you came from and what made you what you are?

NAIPAUL

When you're like me—born in a place where you don't know the history, and no one tells you the history, and the history, in fact, doesn't exist, or in fact exists only in documents—when you are born like that, you have to learn about where you came from. It takes a lot of time. You can't simply write about the world as though it is all there, all granted to you. If you are a French or an English writer, you are born to a great knowledge of your origins and your culture. When you are born like me, in an agricultural colony far away, you have to learn everything. The writing has been a process of inquiry and learning for me.

INTERVIEWER

You have written three books on India over the last thirty-five years: *An Area of Darkness*, *A Wounded Civilization*, and *A Million Mutinies Now*. Your response to the country has varied with each book.

NAIPAUL

Actually, the three books stand. Please understand that I do not want any one to supercede another. All three books stand because I think that they all remain true. The books are written in different modes: one is autobiographical, one is analytical, and the last is an account of the people's experience in that country. They were written at different times, and of course, like India, people exist in different times. So you could say that *An Area of Darkness* is still there—the analysis of the invasions and defeat, the psychological wound, is still there. With the *Mutinies* book, in which people are discovering some little voice with which to express their personality and speak of their needs—that remains true. The books have to be taken as a whole—as still existing, still relevant, still important.

In all of this, you must remember that I am a writer—a man writing a paragraph, a chapter, a section, a book. It is a craft. I am not just a man making statements. So the books represent the different stages of my craft. *An Area of Darkness* is an extraordinary piece of craft—an extraordinary mix of travel and memory and reading. *A Million Mutinies Now* represents the discovery that the people in the country are important. It's a very taxing form, in the way that a lot happens during the actual traveling—a lot happens when you meet people. If you don't know how to talk to them, if you don't know how to get them to talk to you, there is no book. You use your judgment and your flair. I look at this and then that person, what he says about himself . . . His experiences lead you to consider something else and then something else and so on. The book happens during the actual traveling, although the writing takes time, as always. So the books are different bits of craft—always remember that I am a craftsman, changing the craft. I am trying to do new things all the time.

INTERVIEWER

Do you use a tape recorder when you interview people for your nonfiction?

NAIPAUL

I never use a recorder. It shortens the labor and makes the whole thing more precise—it puts me in control. Also, people find it hard to believe, but an hour and a half with anyone is as much as any text of mine can take.

INTERVIEWER

Do you begin an interview as soon as you meet a person?

NAIPAUL

First I'd meet you and talk to you; then I'd ask to come and see you. In ninety minutes, I can get two or three thousand words. You'll see me writing by hand and you'll speak slowly and instinctively. Yet it will be spoken and have the element of speech.

INTERVIEWER

An Area of Darkness suggests a lot of anger, as does much of your journalism about India. Do you think anger works better than understanding for a writer?

NAIPAUL

I don't like to think of it as journalism—journalism is news, an event that is important today. My kind of writing tries to find a spring, the motives of societies and cultures, especially in India. This is not journalism. Let me correct that—it is not something that anybody can do. It's a more profound gift. I'm not competing with journalists.

INTERVIEWER

But does anger work better than understanding?

NAIPAUL

I think it isn't strictly anger alone. It is deep emotion. Without that deep emotion there is almost no writing—then you do journalism. When you are deeply churned up, you know that you cannot express this naked raw emotion; you have to come to some resolution about it. It is this refinement of emotion, what you call understanding, that really makes the writing. These two things are not opposed to one another—understanding derives from what you call anger. I would call it emotion, deep emotion. Emotion is necessary to writing.

INTERVIEWER

I want to ask a question that comes from reading *An Area of Darkness*. You write about the Hindu idea that the world is illusion, which seems enormously attractive and, at the same time, terrifying to you. I'm wondering if I read that right?

NAIPAUL

I think you put your finger on it. It is both frightening and alluring. People can use it as an excuse for inactivity—when things are really bad and you are in a mess, it can be comforting to possess and enter that little chamber of thought where the world is an illusion. I find it very easy to enter that mode of thinking. It was with me for some weeks before writing *A Bend in the River*. I had the distinct sense of the world as an illusion—I saw it spinning in space as though I really had imagined it all.

INTERVIEWER

You have been to so many places—India, Iran, West Africa, the American Deep South. Are you still drawn to travel?

NAIPAUL

It gets harder, you know. The trouble is that I can't go places without writing about them. I feel I've missed the experience. I once went to Brazil for ten days and didn't write anything. Well, I wrote something about Argentina and the Falklands, but I didn't possess the experience—I didn't work at it. It just flowed through me. It was a waste of my life. I'm not a holiday-taker.

INTERVIEWER

Didn't Valéry say that the world exists to be put in a book? Do you agree?

NAIPAUL

Or to be thought about, to be contemplated. Then you enjoy it, then it means something. Otherwise you live like a puppy: *woof woof*, I need my food now, *woof woof*.

INTERVIEWER

Your new book, *Beyond Belief*, returns to the subject of Islam, which you also examined in *Among the Believers*. Do you anticipate any trouble from the prickliness of Islam's defenders with the book's publication?

NAIPAUL

People might criticize me, but I am very careful never to criticize a faith or articles of a faith. I am just talking now about the historical and social effects. Of course, all one's books are criticized, which is how it should be. But remember this is not a book of opinion. This goes back to my earlier point about all one's work standing together: in the books of exploration that I have been writing, I've been working toward a form where, instead of the traveler being more important than the people he travels among, the people are important. I write about the people I meet—I write about their experiences and I define the civilization by their experiences. This is a book of personal experiences, so it will be very difficult to find fault in the way you said because you can't say that it is maligning anything. I looked at personal experiences and made a pattern. In one way, you might simply say that it is a book of stories. It is a book of tales.

INTERVIEWER

Much in the way of *A Turn in the South* and *A Million Mutinies Now*?

NAIPAUL

Absolutely, yes. This book was a different challenge because I am very particular about not repeating a form, and here there were thirty narratives, which I tried to do differently—each one differently so that the reader would not understand the violation that was being done him. I didn't want the stories to read alike.

INTERVIEWER

Are you drained when you finish a book?

NAIPAUL

Yes, one is drained. These careers are so slow—I write a book, and at the end of it I am so tired. Something is wrong with my eyes; I feel I'm going blind. My fingers are so sore that I wrap them in tape. There are all these physical manifestations of a great labor. Then there is a process of just being nothing—utterly vacant. For the past nine months, really, I've been vacant.

INTERVIEWER

Does something begin to agitate you to get back to writing?

NAIPAUL

I actually find myself being agitated now. I want to get back to my work.

INTERVIEWER

Do you have a new project in mind?

NAIPAUL

I'm unusual in that I have had a long career. Most people from limited backgrounds write one book. I'm a prose writer. A prose book contains many thousands of sentiments, observations, thoughts—it is a lot of work. The pattern for most people is to do a little thing about their own lives. My career has been other. I found more and more to write. If I had the strength, I probably would do more; there is always more to write about. I just don't have the energy, the physical capacity. You know, one can spend so many days now being physically wretched. I'm aging badly. I've given so much to this career for so long. I spend so much time trying to feel well. One becomes worn out by living, by writing, by thinking.

Have you got enough now?

INTERVIEWER

Yes.

NAIPAUL

Do you think I've wasted a bit of myself talking to you?

INTERVIEWER

Not, of course, how I'd put it.

NAIPAUL

You'll cherish it?

INTERVIEWER

You don't like interviews.

NAIPAUL

I don't like them because I think that thoughts are so precious you can talk them away. You can lose them.

Issue 148, 1998

Paul Auster

The Art of Fiction

Paul Auster is best known as a novelist today, but he began his writing life as a poet, translator, and essayist. In the 1970s he published half a dozen poetry collections, contributed articles to the *New York Review of Books*, *Harper's*, *Parnassus*, and other periodicals, and began work on the anthology *The Random House Book of Twentieth-Century French Poetry*, which was published in 1982, the same year in which his first book-length prose work appeared, *The Invention of Solitude*.

Auster has written about his early years in *Hand to Mouth: A Chronicle of Early Failure* (1997). He studied at Columbia University in the late sixties, then worked for several months on an oil tanker before moving to France, where for the next three and a half years he eked out his living as a translator, tutor, ghost writer, nighttime switchboard operator for the *New York Times*, and farmhouse caretaker before returning to New York in 1974.

Between 1981 and 1984, Auster wrote the novels of The New York Trilogy, *City of Glass* (1985), *Ghosts* (1986), and *The Locked Room* (1986), which were rejected by seventeen publishers before being accepted by Sun and Moon Press in Los Angeles. With their publication, Auster was established as one of the major novelists of our time. Eight more novels have followed, including *Moon Palace* (1989), *Leviathan* (1992), *The Book of Illusions* (2002), and *Oracle Night*, which will be published later this year.

A manuscript page from *Oracle Night* by Paul Auster.

Other recent books include the anthology *I Thought My Father Was God and Other True Tales from NPR's National Story Project* (2001) and *The Red Notebook: True Stories* (2002). He has also written three screenplays: *Smoke* (1995), for which he received an Independent Spirit Award, *Blue in the Face* (1995), which he codirected with Wayne Wang, and *Lulu on the Bridge* (1998), which he directed solo. Auster was made a chevalier of the Order of Arts and Letters by the French government in 1991 (he was elevated to an officer in 1997).

The following conversation started last fall with a live interview at the Unterberg Poetry Center of the 92nd Street Y in New York City. The interview was completed one afternoon this summer at Auster's house in Brooklyn, where he lives with his wife, the writer Siri Hustvedt. The living room is decorated with paintings by his friends Sam Messer, David Reed, Jean-Paul Riopelle, and Norman Bluhm. In their front hall, there is a collection of family photographs. Bookshelves line the walls of his office on the ground floor. And, of course, on his desk the famous typewriter.

—*Michael Wood, 2003*

INTERVIEWER

Let's start by talking about the way you work. About how you write.

PAUL AUSTER

I've always written by hand. Mostly with a fountain pen, but sometimes with a pencil—especially for corrections. If I could write directly on a typewriter or a computer, I would do it. But keyboards have always intimidated me. I've never been able to think clearly with my fingers in that position. A pen is a much more primitive instrument. You feel that the words are coming out of your body and then you dig the words into the page. Writing has always had that tactile quality for me. It's a physical experience.

And you write in notebooks. Not legal pads or loose sheets of paper.

Yes, always in notebooks. And I have a particular fetish for notebooks with quadrille lines—the little squares. I think of the notebook as a house for words, as a secret place for thought and self-examination. I'm not just interested in the results of writing, but in the process, the act of putting words on a page. Don't ask me why. It might have something to do with an early confusion on my part, an ignorance about the nature of fiction. As a young person, I would always ask myself, Where are the words coming from? Who's saying this? The third-person narrative voice in the traditional novel is a strange device. We're used to it now, we accept it, we don't question it anymore. But when you stop and think about it, there's an eerie, disembodied quality to that voice. It seems to come from nowhere and I found that disturbing. I was always drawn to books that doubled back on themselves, that brought you into the world of the book, even as the book was taking you into the world. The manuscript as hero, so to speak. *Wuthering Heights* is that kind of novel. *The Scarlet Letter* is another. The frames are fictitious, of course, but they give a groundedness and credibility to the stories that other novels didn't have for me. They posit the work as an illusion—which more traditional forms of narrative don't—and once you accept the "unreality" of the enterprise, it paradoxically enhances the truth of the story. The words aren't written in stone by an invisible author-god. They represent the efforts of a flesh-and-blood human being and this is very compelling. The reader becomes a participant in the unfolding of the story—not just a detached observer.

But what about the famous Olympia typewriter? We know quite a bit about that machine—last year you published a wonderful book with the painter Sam Messer, *The Story of My Typewriter*.

AUSTER

I've owned that typewriter since 1974—more than half my life now. I bought it secondhand from a college friend and at this point it must be about forty years old. It's a relic from another age, but it's still in good condition. It's never broken down. All I have to do is change ribbons every once in a while. But I'm living in fear that a day will come when there won't be any ribbons left to buy and I'll have to go digital and join the twenty-first century.

INTERVIEWER

A great Paul Auster story. The day when you go out to buy that last ribbon.

AUSTER

I've made some preparations. I've stocked up. I think I have about sixty or seventy ribbons in my room. I'll probably stick with that typewriter till the end, although I've been sorely tempted to give it up at times. It's cumbersome and inconvenient, but it also protects me against laziness.

INTERVIEWER

How so?

AUSTER

Because the typewriter forces me to start all over again once I'm finished. With a computer, you make your changes on the screen and then you print out a clean copy. With a typewriter, you can't get a clean manuscript unless you start again from scratch. It's an incredibly tedious process. You've finished your book, and now you have to spend several weeks engaged in the purely mechanical job of transcribing what you've already written. It's bad for your neck, bad for your back, and even if you can type twenty or thirty pages a day, the finished pages pile up with excruciating slowness. That's the moment when I always wish I'd switched to a computer, and yet every time I push myself through this final stage of a book, I wind up discovering how essential it is. Typing allows me to experience the book in a new way, to plunge into the flow of the narrative and feel how it functions as a whole. I call it "reading with my fingers," and it's amazing how many errors your fingers will find that your eyes never noticed. Repetitions, awkward constructions, choppy rhythms. It never fails. I think I'm finished with the book and then I begin to type it up and I realize there's more work to be done.

INTERVIEWER

When did you first realize you wanted to be a writer?

AUSTER

About a year after I understood that I wasn't going to be a major-league baseball player. Until I was about sixteen, baseball was probably the most important thing in my life.

INTERVIEWER

How good were you?

AUSTER

It's hard to say. If I'd stuck with it, I might have made it to the low minor leagues. I could hit well, with occasional bursts of power, but I wasn't a very fast runner. At third base, which was the position, I usually played, I had quick reflexes and a strong arm—but my throws were often wild.

In some mysterious way, baseball provided me with an opening onto the world, a chance to find out who I was. As a small child, I wasn't very well. I had all kinds of physical ailments, and I spent more time sitting in doctors' offices with my mother than running around outdoors with my friends. It wasn't until I was four or five that I was strong enough to participate in sports. And when I was, I threw myself into it with a passion—as if making up for lost time. Playing baseball taught me how to live with other people, to understand that I might actually to be able to accomplish something if I put my mind to it. But beyond my own little personal experiences, there's the beauty of the game itself. It's an unending source of pleasure.

Baseball to writing is an unusual transition—in part because writing is such a solitary enterprise.

I played baseball in the spring and summer, but I read books all year long. It was an early obsession and it only intensified as I got older. I can't imagine anyone becoming a writer who wasn't a voracious reader as an adolescent. A true reader understands that books are a world unto themselves—and that that world is richer and more interesting than any one we've traveled in before. I think that's what turns young men and women into writers—the happiness you discover living in books. You haven't been around long enough to have much to write about yet, but a moment comes when you realize that's what you were born to do.

What about early influences? Who were the writers you were reading in high school?

Americans, mostly . . . the usual suspects. Fitzgerald, Hemingway, Faulkner, Dos Passos, Salinger. By my junior year, though, I began discovering the Europeans—mostly the Russians and the French. Tolstoy, Dostoyevsky, Turgenev. Camus and Gide. But also Joyce and Mann. Especially Joyce. When I was eighteen, he towered over everyone else for me.

Did he have the biggest impact on you?

AUSTER

For a while, yes. But at one time or another, I tried to write like each one of the novelists I was reading. Everything influences you when you're young and you keep changing your ideas every few months. It's a bit like trying on new hats. You don't have a style of your own yet, so you unconsciously imitate the writers you admire.

Dozens of writers are inside me, but I don't think my work sounds or feels like anyone else's. I'm not writing their books. I'm writing my own.

INTERVIEWER

You also have a longstanding interest in Hawthorne, don't you?

AUSTER

Of all writers from the past, he's the one I feel closest to, the one who talks most deeply to me. There's something about his imagination that seems to resonate with mine, and I'm continually going back to him, continually learning from him. He's a writer who isn't afraid of ideas, and yet he's also a master psychologist, a profound reader of the human soul. His fiction was utterly revolutionary, and nothing like it had been seen in America before. I know that Hemingway said that all American literature came out of *Huck Finn*, but I don't agree. It began with *The Scarlet Letter*.

But there's more to Hawthorne than just his stories and novels. I'm equally attached to his notebooks, which contain some of his strongest, most brilliant prose. The diary he kept about taking care of his five-year-old son for three weeks in 1851 is a self-contained work. It can stand on its own, and it's so charming, so funny in its deadpan way, that it gives us an entirely new picture of Hawthorne. He wasn't the gloomy, tormented figure most people think he was. Or not only that. He was a loving father and husband, a man who liked a good cigar and a glass or two of whiskey, and he was playful, generous, and warmhearted. Exceedingly shy, yes, but someone who enjoyed the simple pleasures of the world.

INTERVIEWER

You've worked in a number of different genres. Not only poetry and fiction, but also screenplays, autobiography, criticism, and translation. Do they feel like very different activities to you, or are they all somehow connected?

AUSTER

More connected than not, but with important differences as well. And also—this needs to be taken into account, too, I think—there's the question of time, my so-called inner evolution. I haven't done any translating or critical writing in many years. Those were preoccupations that absorbed me when I was young, roughly from my late teens to my late twenties. Both were about discovering other writers, about learning how to become a writer myself. My literary apprenticeship, if you will. I've taken a few stabs at translation and criticism since then, but nothing much to speak of. And the last poem I wrote was in 1979.

INTERVIEWER

What happened? Why did you give it up?

AUSTER

I ran into a wall. For ten years, I concentrated the bulk of my energies on poetry and then I realized that I'd written myself out, that I was stuck. It was a dark moment for me. I thought I was finished as a writer.

INTERVIEWER

You died as a poet, but eventually you were reborn as a novelist. How do you think this transformation came about?

AUSTER

I think it happened at the moment when I understood that I didn't care anymore, when I stopped caring about making "Literature." I know it sounds strange, but from that point on writing became a different kind of experience for me and when I finally got going again after wallowing in the doldrums for about a year, the words came out as prose. The only thing that mattered was saying the thing that needed to be said. Without regard to preestablished conventions, without worrying about what it sounded like. That was the late seventies and I've continued working in that spirit ever since.

INTERVIEWER

Your first prose book was a work of nonfiction, *The Invention of Solitude*. After that, you wrote the three novels of The New York Trilogy. Can you pinpoint the difference between writing in the two forms?

AUSTER

The effort is the same. The need to get the sentences right is the same. But a work of the imagination allows you a lot more freedom and maneuverability than a work of nonfiction does. On the other hand, that freedom can often be quite scary. What comes next? How do I know the next sentence I write isn't going to lead me off the edge of a cliff? With an autobiographical work, you know the story in advance, and your primary obligation is to tell the truth. But that doesn't make the job any easier. For the epigraph of the first part of *The Invention of Solitude*, I used a sentence from Heraclitus—in Guy Davenport's unorthodox but elegant translation: "In searching out the truth be ready for the unexpected, for it is difficult to find and puzzling when you find it." In the end, writing is writing. *The Invention of Solitude* might not be a novel, but I think it explores many of the same questions I've tackled in my fiction. In some sense, it's the foundation of all my work.

INTERVIEWER

And what about your screenplays—*Smoke*, *Blue in the Face*, and *Lulu on the Bridge*? How does screenwriting differ from writing novels?

AUSTER

In every way—except for one crucial similarity: You're trying to tell a story. But the means at your disposal are utterly dissimilar. Novels are pure narration; screenplays resemble theater, and as with all dramatic writing, the only words that count are in the dialogue. As it happens, my novels generally don't have much dialogue, and so in order to work in film, I had to learn a completely new way of writing, to teach myself how to think in images and how to put words in the mouths of living human beings.

Screenwriting is a more restricted form than novel-writing. It has its strengths and weaknesses, the things it can do and the things it can't do. The question of time, for example, works differently in books and films. In a novel, you can collapse a long stretch of time into a single sentence: Every morning for twenty years, I walked down to the corner newsstand and bought a copy of *The Daily Bugle*. It's impossible to do that in a film. You can show a man walking down the street to buy a newspaper on one particular day, but not every day for twenty years. Films take place in the present. Even when you use flashbacks, the past is always rendered as another incarnation of the present.

INTERVIEWER

There's a phrase in *The Invention of Solitude* I've always liked: "The anecdote as a form of knowledge." That strikes me as the guiding spirit behind the pieces in *The Red Notebook*.

AUSTER

I would agree. I look at those stories as a kind of *ars poetica*—but without theory, without any philosophical baggage. So many strange things have happened to me in my life, so many unexpected and improbable events, I'm no longer certain that I know what reality is anymore. All I can do is talk about the mechanics of reality, to gather evidence about what goes on in the world and try to record it as faithfully as I can. I've used that approach in my novels. It's not a method so much as an act of faith: to present things as they really happen, not as they're supposed to happen or as we'd like them to happen. Novels are fictions, of course, and therefore they tell lies (in the strictest sense of the term), but through those lies every novelist attempts to tell the truth about the world. Taken together, the little stories in *The Red Notebook* present a kind of position paper on how I see the world. The bare-bones truth about the unpredictability of experience. There's not a shred of the imaginary in them. There can't be. You make a pact with yourself to tell the truth and you'd rather cut off your right arm than break that promise. Interestingly enough, the literary model I had in mind when I wrote those pieces was the joke. The joke is the purest, most essential form of storytelling. Every word has to count.

INTERVIEWER

There's a story in *The Red Notebook* about something that happened when you were fourteen years old. You and a group of boys went out on a hike in the woods, and you were caught in a terrible electric storm. The boy next to you was struck by lightning and killed.

AUSTER

That incident changed my life, there's no question about it. One moment the boy was alive and the next moment he was dead. I was only inches away from him. It was my first experience with random death, with the bewildering instability of things. You think you're standing on solid ground and an instant later the ground opens under your feet and you vanish.

INTERVIEWER

Tell me about the National Story Project you did with NPR. As I understand it, they liked your voice and wanted to find a way to have you on the air.

AUSTER

It must have something to do with all the cigars I've smoked over the years. That rasping rumble in the throat, the clogged-up bronchia, the diminished lung power. I've heard the results on tape. I sound like a piece of sandpaper scraping over a dry roof shingle.

INTERVIEWER

Your wife, Siri Hustvedt, suggested that the listeners send in their own stories, which you would select and read on the air.

AUSTER

I thought it was a brilliant idea. NPR has millions of listeners around the country. If enough contributions came in, I felt we would be able to form a little museum of American reality. People were free to write about anything they wanted. Big things and little things, comic things and tragic things. The only rules were that the pieces had to be short—no more than two or three pages—and they had to be true.

INTERVIEWER

But why would you want to take on such an enormous job? In the space of one year, you wound up reading over four thousand stories.

AUSTER

I think I had several motives. The most important one was curiosity. I wanted to find out if other people had lived through the same sorts of experiences that I had. Was I some kind of freak or was reality truly as strange and incomprehensible as I thought it was? With such a large reservoir of possibilities to draw from, the project could take on the dimensions of a genuine philosophical experiment.

INTERVIEWER

And what were the results?

AUSTER

I'm happy to report that I'm not alone. It's a madhouse out there.

INTERVIEWER

Did anything else draw you to this project in particular?

AUSTER

I've spent most of my adult life sitting alone in a room, writing books. I'm perfectly happy there, but when I got involved in film work in the mid-nineties, I rediscovered the pleasures of working with other people. It probably goes back to having played on so many sports teams as a kid. I liked being part of a small group, a group with a purpose, in which each person contributes to a common goal. Winning a basketball game or making a film—there's really very little difference. That was probably the best part of working in the movies for me. The sense of solidarity, the jokes we told each other, the friendships I made. By 1999, however, my movie adventures had pretty much come to an end. I was back in my hole again writing novels, not seeing anyone for weeks at a stretch. I think that's why Siri made her suggestion. Not just because it was a good idea, but because she thought I'd enjoy working on something that involved other people. She was right. I did enjoy it.

INTERVIEWER

Didn't it take up a lot of time?

AUSTER

Not enough to interfere with my other work. The stories came in slowly and steadily and as long as I kept up with the submissions, it wasn't so bad. Preparing the broadcasts usually took a day or two, but that was only once a month.

INTERVIEWER

Did you feel you were performing a public service?

AUSTER

To some degree, I suppose I did. It was an opportunity to engage in guerilla warfare against the monster.

INTERVIEWER

The monster?

AUSTER

The "entertainment-industrial complex," as the art critic Robert Hughes once put it. The media presents us with little else but celebrities, gossip, and scandal, and the way we depict ourselves on television and in the movies has become so distorted, so debased, that real life has been forgotten. What we're given are violent shocks and dimwitted escapist fantasies, and the driving force behind it all is money. People are treated like morons. They're not human beings anymore, they're consumers, suckers to be manipulated into wanting things they don't need. Call it capitalism triumphant. Call it the free-market economy. Whatever it is, there's very little room in it for representations of actual American life.

INTERVIEWER

And you thought the National Story Project could change all that?

AUSTER

No, of course not. But at least I tried to make a little dent in the system. By giving so-called ordinary people a chance to share their stories with an audience, I wanted to prove that there's no such thing as an ordinary person. We all have intense inner lives, we all burn with ferocious passions, we've all lived through memorable experiences of one kind or another.

INTERVIEWER

In *City of Glass*, you use yourself as a character in the story. Do you often draw on autobiographical material for your novels?

AUSTER

To some extent, but far less than you might think. After *City of Glass*, there was *Ghosts*. Other than announcing that the story begins on February 3, 1947—the day I was born—there are no personal references in it. In *The Locked Room*, however, several incidents come directly from my own life. Ivan Wyschnegradsky, the old Russian composer who befriends Fanshawe in Paris, was a real person. I met

him when he was eighty and saw quite a lot of him when I lived in
Paris in the early seventies. The business about giving Ivan the refrig-
erator actually happened to me—in the same way it happens to Fanshawe. The same holds for the slapstick scene in which he delivers
the captain breakfast on the oil tanker—inching along the bridge in a
seventy-mile-an-hour gale and struggling to hold onto the tray. It was
the one time in my life I truly felt I was in a Buster Keaton movie. And
then there's the crazy story the narrator tells about working for the
U.S. Census Bureau in Harlem in 1970. Word for word, that episode
is an exact account of my own experience.

INTERVIEWER

You really invented fictitious people and filed their names with the
federal government?

AUSTER

I confess. I hope the statute of limitations has run out by now or I
might wind up in jail for doing this interview. In my own defense, I
have to add that the supervisor encouraged this practice—for the
same reason he gives in the novel. "Just because a door doesn't open
when you knock on it doesn't mean that nobody's there. You've got to
use your imagination, my friend. After all, we don't want the government to be unhappy, do we?"

INTERVIEWER

What about the novels after the Trilogy? Are there any other autobiographical secrets you're willing to share with us?

AUSTER

I'm thinking . . . There's nothing that jumps to mind from *The
Music of Chance* . . . or *In the Country of Last Things* . . . or *Mr.
Vertigo*. A couple of small elements in *Leviathan*, however, and one
amusing bit in *Timbuktu*—the story about the typing dog. I projected
myself into the book as Willy's former college roommate—Anster or
Omster (Mr. Bones can't quite remember the name)—and the fact is

that I did go to Italy when I was seventeen to visit my aunt, my mother's sister. She had been living there for more than a decade and one of her friends happened to be Thomas Mann's daughter Elisabeth Mann Borgese, who was a scientist involved in the study of animals. One day we were invited to her house for lunch and I was introduced to her dog Ollie, a large English setter who had been taught how to type out his name with his snout on a specially designed typewriter. I saw it with my own eyes. It was one of the most preposterous and extraordinary things I've ever witnessed.

INTERVIEWER

In *Leviathan*, the narrator has your initials—Peter Aaron. And he's married to a woman named Iris, which is your wife's name spelled backwards.

AUSTER

Yes, but Peter isn't married to Siri. He's married to the heroine of her first novel, *The Blindfold*.

INTERVIEWER

A transfictional romance.

AUSTER

Exactly.

INTERVIEWER

You haven't mentioned *Moon Palace*, which reads more like an autobiography than any of your other novels. Fogg is exactly your age and he goes to Columbia exactly when you did.

AUSTER

Yes, I know the book sounds very personal, but almost nothing in it comes from my own life. I can think of only two significant details. The first has to do with my father and I look on it as a kind of posthumous revenge, a way of settling an old score on his behalf. Tesla is a minor character in the novel and I devote a couple of pages to the AC-DC controversy that flared up between Edison and Tesla in the 1890s. Effing, the old man who tells Fogg the story, heaps quite a lot of abuse on Edison. Well, it turns out that when my father graduated from high school in 1929, he was hired by Edison to work as an assistant in the lab at Menlo Park. My father was very gifted in electronics. Two weeks into the job, Edison found out that he was Jewish and fired him. Not only did the man invent the electric chair, but he was a notorious anti-Semite. I wanted to get back at him for my father's sake, to square the account.

INTERVIEWER

And what's the other detail?

AUSTER

The night when Effing hands out money to strangers in the street. That scene comes straight out of something that happened to me in 1969—my meeting with H. L. Humes, better known as Doc Humes, who was one of the founders of *The Paris Review*. It was such a wild business, I don't think I could have invented it myself.

INTERVIEWER

You wrote some memorable pages about Doc Humes in *Hand to Mouth*, which is about your struggles as a young man to keep yourself afloat. What prompted you to take on that subject?

AUSTER

I'd always wanted to write something about money. Not finance or business, but the experience of not having enough money, of being poor. I'd been thinking about the project for many years and my working title had always been "Essay on Want." Very Lockean, very eighteenth century, very dry. I was planning to write a serious, philosophical work, but when I finally sat down to begin, everything changed. The book turned into the story of my own problematic dealings with money and in spite of the rather dismal subject matter, the spirit of the writing was largely comic.

Still, the book wasn't only about myself. I saw it as an opportunity to write about some of the colorful characters I'd met when I was young, to give these people their due. I'd never had any interest in working in an office or holding down a steady, white-collar job. I found the idea extremely distasteful. I gravitated toward more humble kinds of work, and that gave me a chance to spend time with people who weren't like me. People who hadn't gone to college; people who hadn't read a lot of books. In this country, we tend to underestimate the intelligence of working-class people. Based on my own experience, I found most of them to be just as smart as the people who run the world. They simply aren't as ambitious—that's all. But their talk is a lot funnier. Everywhere I went, I had to struggle to keep up with them. I'd spent too much time with my nose buried in books and most of my coworkers could talk circles around me.

INTERVIEWER

Who is the source for Hector Mann, the silent comedian in *The Book of Illusions*?

AUSTER

He appeared in my head one day about ten or twelve years ago, and I walked around with him for a long time before starting the book. But Hector himself was fully formed right from the beginning. Not only his name, and not only the fact that he was born in Argentina, but the white suit and the black mustache and the handsome face— they were all there, too.

Physically, Hector Mann bears a strong resemblance to Marcello Mastroianni in *Divorce, Italian Style*, a film from the early sixties. The mustache and the white suit could have come from that movie, although I'm not certain. Hector also shares certain characteristics with Max Linder, the earliest of the great silent comedians. And perhaps there's a touch of Raymond Griffith in him as well. Most of

Griffith's films have been lost, so he's become a rather obscure figure. But he played a dapper man of the world—just as Hector does—and he also had a mustache. But Hector's movements are crisper and more artfully choreographed than Griffith's.

The descriptions of the films are extraordinary acts of visualization in words. How did you go about writing those passages?

It was a question of striking the right balance. All the visual information had to be there—the physical details of the action—so the reader could "see" what was happening, but at the same time, the prose had to move along at a quick pace, in order to mimic the experience of watching a film, which is rushing past you at twenty-four frames per second. Too many details, and you would get bogged down. Not enough, and you wouldn't see anything. I had to go over those pages many times before I felt I had them right.

The Book of Illusions tells a very complex story, but at its heart, I would say it's an exploration of grief. Do you think you could have written that book when you were younger?

I doubt it. I'm well into my fifties now and things change for you as you get older. Time begins slipping away, and simple arithmetic tells you there are more years behind you than ahead of you—many more. Your body starts breaking down, you have aches and pains that weren't there before, and little by little the people you love begin to die. By the age of fifty, most of us are haunted by ghosts. They live inside us and we spend as much time talking to the dead as to the living. It's hard for a young person to understand this. It's not that a twenty year old doesn't know he's going to die, but it's the loss of others that so profoundly affects an older person—and you can't know what that accumulation of losses is going to do to you until you experience it yourself. Life is so short, so fragile, so mystifying. After all, how many people do we actually love in the course of a lifetime? Just a few, a tiny few. When most of them are gone, the map of your inner world changes. As my friend George Oppen once said to me about getting old: what a strange thing to happen to a little boy.

INTERVIEWER

You quote that line in *The Invention of Solitude.*

AUSTER

It's the best comment about old age I've ever heard.

INTERVIEWER

In *Leviathan*, your narrator Peter Aaron writes: "No one can say where a book comes from, least of all the person who writes it. Books are born out of ignorance, and if they go on living after they are written, it's only to the degree that they cannot be understood." How close is that to your own belief?

AUSTER

I rarely speak directly through my characters. They might resemble me at times, or borrow aspects of my life, but I tend to think of them as autonomous beings with their own opinions and their own ways of expressing themselves. But in this case Aaron's opinion matches my own.

INTERVIEWER

Do you work from a plan when you start writing a novel? Have you figured out the plot in advance?

AUSTER

Each book I've written has started off with what I'd call a buzz in the head. A certain kind of music or rhythm, a tone. Most of the effort involved in writing a novel for me is trying to remain faithful to that buzz, that rhythm. It's a highly intuitive business. You can't justify it or defend it rationally, but you know when you've struck a wrong note, and you're usually pretty certain when you've hit the right one.

INTERVIEWER

Do you jump around in the story as you write?

AUSTER

No. Every book begins with the first sentence and then I push on until I've reached the last. Always in sequence, a paragraph at a time. I have a sense of the trajectory of the story—and often have the last sentence as well as the first before I begin—but everything keeps changing as I go along. No book I've published has ever turned out as I thought it would. Characters and episodes disappear; other characters and episodes develop as I go along. You find the book in the process of doing it. That's the adventure of the job. If it were all mapped out in advance, it wouldn't be very interesting.

INTERVIEWER

And yet your books always seem to be so lightly constructed. It's one of the things you're most admired for.

AUSTER

The Book of Illusions went through a number of radical shifts along the way and I was rethinking my ideas about the story right up to the last pages. *Timbuktu* was originally conceived as a much longer book. Willy and Mr. Bones were supposed to have no more than minor, fleeting roles in it, but once I started writing the first chapter, I fell in love with them and decided to scrap my plan. The project turned into a short lyrical book about the two of them with scarcely any plot. With *Mr. Vertigo*, I thought I was writing a short story of thirty or forty pages, but the thing took off and seemed to acquire a life of its own. Writing has always been like that for me. Slowly blundering my way toward consciousness.

INTERVIEWER

Can we go back to the phrase "a paragraph at a time"?

AUSTER

The paragraph seems to be my natural unit of composition. The line is the unit of a poem, the paragraph serves the same function in prose—at least for me. I keep working on a paragraph until I feel reasonably satisfied with it, writing and rewriting until it has the right shape, the right balance, the right music—until it seems transparent and effortless, no longer "written." That paragraph can take a day to complete or half a day, or an hour, or three days. Once it seems finished, I type it up to have a better look. So each book has a running manuscript and a typescript beside it. Later on, of course, I'll attack the typed page and make more revisions.

INTERVIEWER

And little by little, the pages mount up.

AUSTER

Yes, very slowly.

INTERVIEWER

Do you show your work to anyone before it's finished?

AUSTER

Siri. She's my first reader and I have total faith in her judgments. Each time I write a novel, I read to her from it every month or so— whenever I have a new stack of twenty or thirty pages. Reading aloud helps to objectify the book for me, to hear where I've gone wrong or failed to express what I was trying to say. Then Siri makes her comments. She's been doing this for twenty-two years now, and what she says is always remarkably astute. I can't think of a single instance when I haven't followed her advice.

INTERVIEWER

And do you read her work?

AUSTER

Yes. What she does for me, I try to do for her. Every writer needs a trusted reader—someone who has sympathy for what you're doing and wants the work to be as good as it can possibly be. But you have to be honest. That's the fundamental requirement. No lies, no false pats on the back, no praise for something you don't believe deserves it.

INTERVIEWER

What contemporary novelists do you read?

AUSTER

Quite a few—probably more than I'm able to count. Don DeLillo, Peter Carey, Russell Banks, Philip Roth, E. L. Doctorow, Charles Baxter, J. M. Coetzee, David Grossman, Orhan Pamuk, Salman Rushdie, Michael Ondaatje, Siri Hustvedt . . . Those are the names that jump out at me right now, but if you asked me the same question tomorrow, I'm sure I would give you a different list. Contrary to what many people want to believe, the novel is in good shape these days, as healthy and vigorous as it's ever been. It's an inexhaustible form, and no matter what the pessimists say, it's never going to die.

INTERVIEWER

How can you be so sure?

AUSTER

Because a novel is the only place in the world where two strangers can meet on terms of absolute intimacy. The reader and the writer make the book together. No other art can do that. No other art can capture the essential inwardness of human life.

INTERVIEWER

Your new novel, *Oracle Night*, will be out at the end of the year. That's just fifteen months after the publication of *The Book of Illusions*. You've always been prolific, but this seems to be some kind of record.

AUSTER

Actually, I started writing *Oracle Night* before *The Book of Illusions*. I had the first twenty pages or so, but then I stopped. I realized that I didn't quite understand what I was doing. *The Book of Illusions* took me roughly three years to write, and all during that time I continued thinking about *Oracle Night*. When I finally returned to it, it came out with remarkable speed. I felt as if I was writing in a trance.

INTERVIEWER

Was it smooth sailing all the way through—or did you run into difficulties along the way?

AUSTER

Not until the end, the last twenty pages or so. I had a different conclusion in mind when I started the book, but when I wrote it out as originally planned, I wasn't happy with it. It was too brutal, too sensational, and undermined the tone of the book. I was stuck for several weeks after that and for a while I thought I would have to leave the book unfinished. Just like Sidney's story in the novel. It was as if I had fallen under the spell of my own project and was living through the same struggles as my hero. Mercifully, something finally came to me and I was able to write the last twenty pages.

INTERVIEWER

It's an intensely intimate novel.

AUSTER

I think of it as a kind of chamber piece. There are very few characters and all the action takes place in just two weeks. It's very compact, tightly coiled in on itself—a strange little organism of interlocking parts.

INTERVIEWER

There are a number of elements you've never used before. Footnotes, for example.

AUSTER

Hardly an original idea, of course, but for this particular story, I felt they were necessary. The main body of the text confines itself to the present, to the events that take place during those two weeks, and I didn't want to interrupt the flow of the narrative. The footnotes are used to talk about things that happened in the past.

INTERVIEWER

In *Oracle Night* there are two photographs—of a 1937–1938 Warsaw telephone book. How did you come to have that telephone book and what made you decide to include those pictures?

AUSTER

I went to Warsaw for the first time in 1998 and my Polish publisher gave it to me as a gift. There's an Auster in that book, no doubt someone murdered by the Nazis just a few years later. In the same way, Sidney, the narrator of *Oracle Night*, finds the name of someone who could possibly have been a relative of his. I needed the photos to prove that the book really exists—that I wasn't just making it up. The entire novel is saturated with references to twentieth-century history. World War II and the Holocaust, World War I, the Chinese Cultural Revolution, the Kennedy assassination. It's a book about time, after all, and fleeting as those references might be, they're an essential part of the story.

INTERVIEWER

Oracle Night is your eleventh novel. Has writing fiction become easier for you over the years?

AUSTER

No, I don't think so. Each book is a new book. I've never written it before and I have to teach myself how to write it as I go along. The fact that I've written books in the past seems to play no part in it. I always feel like a beginner and I'm continually running into the same difficulties, the same blocks, the same despairs. You make so many mistakes as a writer, cross out so many bad sentences and ideas, discard so many worthless pages, that finally what you learn is how stupid you are. It's a humbling occupation.

INTERVIEWER

Do you think you've had a strange career: all that hard work and patience, but finally also all that success?

AUSTER

I try not to think about it. It's difficult for me to look at myself from the outside. I simply don't have the mental equipment to do it, at least where my work is concerned. It's for other people to make judgments about what I've done, and I wouldn't want to presume to have an answer to that question. I wish I could, but I still haven't mastered the trick of being in two places at the same time.

Issue 167, 2003

Haruki Murakami

The Art of Fiction

Haruki Murakami is not only arguably the most experimental Japanese novelist to have been translated into English, he is also the most popular, with sales in the millions worldwide. His greatest novels inhabit the liminal zone between realism and fable, whodunit and science fiction: *Hard-Boiled Wonderland and the End of the World*, for example, features a protagonist who is literally of two minds, and *The Wind-Up Bird Chronicle*, perhaps his best-known work outside of Japan, begins prosaically—as a man's search for his missing wife—then quietly mutates into the strangest hybrid narrative since Laurence Sterne's *Tristram Shandy*. Murakami's world is an allegorical one, constructed of familiar symbols—an empty well, an underground city—but the meaning of those symbols remains hermetic to the last. His debt to popular culture (and American pop culture, in particular) notwithstanding, it could be argued that no author's body of work has ever been more private.

Murakami was born in 1949 in Kyoto, Japan's ancient capital, to a middle-class family with a vested interest in the national culture: his father was a teacher of Japanese literature, his grandfather a Buddhist monk. When he was two, his family moved to Kobe, and it was this bustling port city, with its steady stream of foreigners (especially American sailors), that most clearly shaped his sensibility. Rejecting Japanese literature, art, and music at an early age, Murakami came to identify more and more closely with the world outside Japan, a world he knew only through jazz records, Hollywood movies, and dime-store paperbacks.

As a student in Tokyo in the late sixties, Murakami developed a taste for postmodern fiction while looking on, quietly but sympatheti-cally, as the protest movement reached its high-water mark. He mar-ried at twenty-three and spent the next several years of his life running a jazz club in Tokyo, Peter Cat, before the publication of his first novel made it possible for him to pay his way by writing. The novel, *Hear the Wind Sing*, translated into English but not available outside Japan at the author's request, won him the coveted Gunzo Literature Prize and the beginnings of a readership. With each book that followed, his acclaim and popularity grew, until the publication in 1987 of his first realistic novel, *Norwegian Wood*, transformed him into a literary megastar and the de facto "voice of his generation"—eighties' Japan's version of J. D. Salinger. The book has sold more than two million copies in Japan alone, the equivalent of one for every household in Tokyo.

Since then Murakami has been an unwilling celebrity in his na-tive country, living abroad for years at a time to secure a measure of distance from his public image. He has lived both in Europe and the U.S.; *The Wind-Up Bird Chronicle*, for example, was written while teaching at Princeton and Tufts. Though he has never re-turned to the straightforward lyricism of *Norwegian Wood*, his novels continue to find an ever wider audience—his new novel *Kafka on the Shore* has already sold three thousand copies in Japan and is due out in English later this year. Internationally, Murakami is now the most widely read Japanese novelist of his generation; he has won virtually every prize Japan has to offer, including its greatest, the Yomiuri Literary Prize. He is also an extremely active transla-tor, having brought writers as diverse as Raymond Carver, Tim O'Brien, and F. Scott Fitzgerald to Japanese readers, many of them for the first time.

Murakami's office sits just off the main drag in boutique-choked Aoyama, Tokyo's equivalent of New York City's SoHo. The build-ing itself is squat and dated-looking, as though the change in the neighborhood had happened without its permission. Murakami rents a moderate-sized suite on the building's sixth floor, and his rooms give much the same impression: plain wooden cabinets, swivel chairs, Mylar-covered desks—office furniture, in short. The decor seems both deeply incongruous with the notion of a writer's studio and at the same time somehow fitting: his characters are often in just such an every-day environment when the dream world first beckons to them. As it turns out, although he writes there on occasion, the office's main func-tion is as the nerve center for the business end of Murakami's career. The air hums with polite industry. No fewer than two assistants glide capably about in dainty stockinged feet.

Throughout the following interview, which took place over two consecutive afternoons, he showed a readiness to laugh that was pleasantly out of keeping with the quiet of the office. He's clearly a busy man and by his own admission a reluctant talker, but once se-rious conversation began I found him focused and forthcoming. He spoke fluently, but with extended pauses between statements, tak-ing great care to give the most accurate answer possible. When the talk turned to jazz or to running marathons, two of his great pas-sions, he could easily have been mistaken for a man twenty years younger, or even for a fifteen-year-old boy.

—*John Wray, 2004*

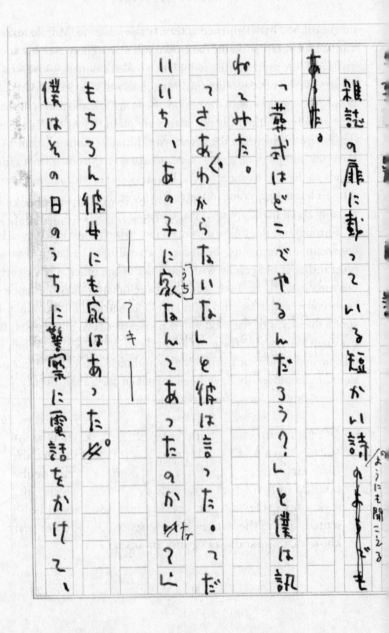

Two manuscript pages from *Wild Sheep Chase* by Haruki Murakami.

小曜の午後のピクニック

新聞で偶然彼女の死を知った友人 # # が 「電話で僕にそれを教えてくれた。彼は電話口で朝刊の一段記事をれ、く4/と読み上げた。ぜ コードで きたす平凡な記事だ。数学を出たばか りの駆けだしの記者が、練習のために書かれた ような文章だった。

何月何日、どこかの街角で、誰かの運転す

INTERVIEWER

I've just read *After the Quake*, your newest story collection and I found it interesting how freely you mixed stories that were realistic, in the style of your novel *Norwegian Wood*, let's say, with others that had more in common with *The Wind-Up Bird Chronicle* or *Hard-Boiled Wonderland and the End of the World*. Do you see a fundamental difference between those two forms?

HARUKI MURAKAMI

My style, what I think of as my style, is very close to *Hard-Boiled Wonderland*. I don't like the realistic style, myself. I prefer a more surrealistic style. But with *Norwegian Wood*, I made up my mind to write a hundred percent realistic novel. I needed that experience.

INTERVIEWER

Did you think of that book as an exercise in style or did you have a specific story to tell that was best told realistically?

MURAKAMI

I could have been a cult writer if I'd kept writing surrealistic novels. But I wanted to break into the mainstream, so I had to prove that I could write a realistic book. That's why I wrote that book. It was a bestseller in Japan and I expected that result.

INTERVIEWER

So it was actually a strategic choice.

MURAKAMI

That's right. *Norwegian Wood* is very easy to read and easy to understand. Many people liked that book. They might then be interested in my other work; so it helps a lot.

INTERVIEWER

So Japanese readers are like American readers? They want an easy story.

MURAKAMI

My latest book, *Kafka on the Shore*, sold three hundred thousand sets—it's in two volumes here, you know. I was surprised that it sold that many; that's no ordinary thing. The story is very complicated and very hard to follow. But my style, my prose, is very easy to read. It contains a sense of humor, it's dramatic, and it's a page-turner. There's a sort of magic balance between those two factors; perhaps that's another reason for my success. Still, it's incredible. I write a novel every three or four years, and people are waiting for it. I once interviewed John Irving, and he told me that reading a good book is a mainline. Once they are addicted, they're always waiting.

INTERVIEWER

You want to turn your readers into junkies.

MURAKAMI

That's what John Irving said.

INTERVIEWER

Those two factors—a straightforward, easy-to-follow narrative voice paired with an often bewildering plot—is that a conscious choice?

MURAKAMI

No, it's not. When I start to write, I don't have any plan at all. I just wait for the story to come. I don't choose what kind of story it is or what's going to happen. I just wait. *Norwegian Wood* is a different thing, because I decided to write in a realistic style. But basically, I cannot choose.

INTERVIEWER

But do you choose the voice that it's told in, that deadpan, easy-to-follow voice? Do you choose that?

MURAKAMI

I get some images and I connect one piece to another. That's the story line. Then I explain the story line to the reader. You should be very kind when you explain something. If you think, It's okay; *I* know that—it's a very arrogant thing. Easy words and good metaphors, good allegory. So that's what I do. I explain very carefully and clearly.

INTERVIEWER

Does that come naturally for you?

MURAKAMI

I'm not intelligent. I'm not arrogant. I'm just like the people who read my books. I used to have a jazz club, and I made the cocktails and I made the sandwiches. I didn't want to become a writer—it just happened. It's a kind of gift, you know, from the heavens. So I think I should be very humble.

INTERVIEWER

At what age did you become a writer? Was it a surprise to you?

MURAKAMI

When I was twenty-nine years old. Oh yes, it was a surprise. But I got used to it instantly.

INTERVIEWER

Instantly? From the first day of writing you felt comfortable?

MURAKAMI

I started writing at the kitchen table after midnight. It took ten months to finish that first book; I sent it to a publisher and I got some kind of prize, so it was like a dream—I was surprised to find it happening. But after a moment, I thought, Yes, it's happened and I'm a writer. Why not? It's that simple.

INTERVIEWER

How did your wife feel about your decision to start writing?

MURAKAMI

She didn't say anything at all; and when I said, I'm a writer, she was surprised and kind of embarrassed.

INTERVIEWER

Why was she embarrassed? Did she think you wouldn't make it?

MURAKAMI

To become a writer is kind of flashy.

INTERVIEWER

Who were your models? What Japanese writers influenced you?

MURAKAMI

I didn't read many Japanese writers when I was a child or even in my teens. I wanted to escape from this culture; I felt it was boring. Too sticky.

INTERVIEWER

Wasn't your father a teacher of Japanese literature?

MURAKAMI

Right. So it was the father-son relationship too. I just went toward Western culture: jazz music and Dostoyevsky and Kafka and Raymond Chandler. That was my own world, my fantasyland. I could go to St. Petersburg or West Hollywood if I wanted. That's the power of the novel—you can go anywhere. Now it's easy to go to the States— everyone can go anywhere in the world—but in the 1960s it was almost impossible. So I just read and listened to the music and I could go there. It was a kind of state of mind, like a dream.

INTERVIEWER

And that led at some point to writing.

MURAKAMI

Right. When I was twenty-nine, I just started to write a novel out of the blue. I wanted to write something, but I didn't know how. I didn't know how to write in Japanese—I'd read almost nothing of the works of Japanese writers—so I borrowed the style, structure, everything, from the books I had read—American books or Western books. As a result, I made my own original style. So it was a beginning.

INTERVIEWER

Your first book was published, you won a prize, and were more or less on your way. Did you begin to meet other writers?

MURAKAMI

No, not at all.

INTERVIEWER

You had no friends who were writers at that time?

MURAKAMI

None.

INTERVIEWER

And over time did you meet anyone who became a friend or a colleague?

MURAKAMI

No, not at all.

INTERVIEWER

To this day, you have no friends who are writers?

MURAKAMI

No. I don't think so.

INTERVIEWER

Is there no one you show your work to when it's in progress?

MURAKAMI

Never.

INTERVIEWER

How about your wife?

MURAKAMI

Well, I showed the first manuscript of my first novel but she claims she never read it! So she got no impression at all, I guess.

INTERVIEWER

She wasn't impressed.

MURAKAMI

No. But that was the first draft and it was terrible. I rewrote and rewrote.

INTERVIEWER

Now, when you're working on a book, is she ever curious what you're writing?

MURAKAMI

She's my first reader every time I write a book. I rely on her. She's a kind of partner to me. It's like Scott Fitzgerald—for him, Zelda was the first reader.

INTERVIEWER

So you've never felt at any point in your career that you were part of any community of writers?

MURAKAMI

I'm a loner. I don't like groups, schools, literary circles. At Princeton, there was a luncheonette, or something like that, and I was invited to eat there. Joyce Carol Oates was there and Toni Morrison was there and I was so afraid, I couldn't eat anything at all! Mary Morris was there and she's a very nice person, almost the same age as I am, and we became friends, I would say. But in Japan I don't have any writer friends because I just want to have . . . distance.

INTERVIEWER

You wrote a significant portion of *The Wind-Up Bird Chronicle* in the U.S. Did living there have any clear effect on your writing process or on the text itself?

MURAKAMI

During the four years of writing *The Wind-Up Bird Chronicle*, I was living in the U.S. as a stranger. That strangeness was always following me like a shadow and it did the same to the protagonist of the novel. Come to think of it, if I wrote it in Japan, it might have become a very different book.

My strangeness while living in the U.S. differed from the strangeness I feel while in Japan. It was more obvious and direct in the U.S. and that gave me a much clearer recognition of myself. The process of writing this novel was a process similar to making myself naked, in a way.

INTERVIEWER

Are there people currently writing in Japan whose books you read and enjoy?

MURAKAMI

Yes, some of them. Ryu Murakami. Banana Yoshimoto—some of her books I like. But I don't do any reviews or critiques; I don't want to be involved in that.

INTERVIEWER

Why not?

MURAKAMI

I think that my job is to observe people and the world, and not to judge them. I always hope to position myself away from so-called conclusions. I would like to leave everything wide open to all the possibilities in the world.

I prefer translating to criticism, because you are hardly required to judge anything when you translate. Line by line, I just let my favorite work pass through my body and my mind. We need critiques in this world, for sure, but it's just not my job.

INTERVIEWER

Getting back to your own books: hard-boiled American detective fiction has clearly been a valuable resource. When were you exposed to the genre and who turned you on to it?

MURAKAMI

As a high-school student, I fell in love with crime novels. I was living in Kobe, which is a port city where many foreigners and sailors used to come and sell their paperbacks to the secondhand bookshops. I was poor, but I could buy paperbacks cheaply. I learned to read English from those books and that was so exciting.

INTERVIEWER

What was the first book you read in English?

MURAKAMI

The Name Is Archer by Ross MacDonald. I learned a lot of things from those books. Once I started, I couldn't stop. At the same time I also loved to read Tolstoy and Dostoyevsky. Those books are also page-turners; they're very long, but I couldn't stop reading. So for me it's the same thing, Dostoyevsky and Raymond Chandler. Even now, my ideal for writing fiction is to put Dostoyevsky and Chandler together in one book. That's my goal.

INTERVIEWER

At what age did you first read Kafka?

MURAKAMI

When I was fifteen. I read *The Castle*—that was a great book. And *The Trial*.

INTERVIEWER

That's interesting. Both those novels were left unfinished, which of course means that they never resolve. Your novels too—particularly your more recent books, like *The Wind-Up Bird Chronicle*—often seem to resist a resolution of the kind that the reader is perhaps expecting. Could that in any way be due to Kafka's influence?

MURAKAMI

Not solely. You've read Raymond Chandler, of course. His books don't really offer conclusions. He might say, He is the killer, but it doesn't matter to me who did it. There was a very interesting episode when Howard Hawks made a picture of *The Big Sleep*. Hawks couldn't understand who killed the chauffeur, so he called Chandler and asked, and Chandler answered, I don't care! Same for me. The conclusion means nothing at all. I don't care who the killer is in *The Brothers Karamazov*.

INTERVIEWER

And yet the desire to find out who killed the chauffeur is part of what makes *The Big Sleep* a page-turner.

MURAKAMI

I myself, as I'm writing, don't know who did it. The readers and I are on the same ground. When I start to write a story, I don't know the conclusion at all and I don't know what's going to happen next. If there is a murder case as the first thing, I don't know who the killer is.

I write the book because I would like to find out. If I know who the killer is, there's no purpose to writing the story.

INTERVIEWER

Is there also a sense of not wanting to explain your books, in the way a dream loses its power when it comes under analysis?

MURAKAMI

The good thing about writing books is that you can dream while you are awake. If it's a real dream, you cannot control it. When writing the book, you are awake; you can choose the time, the length, everything. I write for four or five hours in the morning and when the time comes, I stop. I can continue the next day. If it's a real dream, you can't do that.

INTERVIEWER

You say that you don't know who the killer is as you're writing, but a possible exception occurs to me: the character of Gotanda in *Dance Dance Dance*. There's a certain deliberate buildup in that novel toward the moment at which Gotanda makes his confession—in classic crime-novel style, he's presented to us as the last person to suspect. Did you not perhaps know that Gotanda was guilty in advance?

MURAKAMI

In the first draft I didn't know it was Gotanda. Closer to the end— two-thirds in or so—I knew. When I wrote the second draft I rewrote the Gotanda scenes, knowing it was him.

INTERVIEWER

Is that one of the main purposes of revision, then—to take what you've learned from the end of the first draft and rework the earlier sections to give a certain feeling of inevitability?

MURAKAMI

That's right. The first draft is messy; I have to revise and revise.

INTERVIEWER

How many drafts do you generally go through?

MURAKAMI

Four or five. I spend six months writing the first draft and then spend seven or eight months rewriting.

INTERVIEWER

That's pretty fast.

MURAKAMI

I'm a hard worker. I concentrate on my work very hard. So, you know, it's easy. And I don't do anything but write my fiction when I write.

INTERVIEWER

How is your typical workday structured?

MURAKAMI

When I'm in writing mode for a novel, I get up at four A.M. and work for five to six hours. In the afternoon, I run for ten kilometers or swim for fifteen hundred meters (or do both), then I read a bit, and listen to some music. I go to bed at nine P.M. I keep to this routine every day without variation. The repetition itself becomes the important thing; it's a form of mesmerism. I mesmerize myself to reach a deeper state of mind. But to hold to such repetition for so long—six months to a year— requires a good amount of mental and physical strength. In that sense, writing a long novel is like survival training. Physical strength is as necessary as artistic sensitivity.

INTERVIEWER

I wanted to ask about your characters. How real do they become to you as you work? Is it important to you that they have a life independent of the narrative?

MURAKAMI

When I make up the characters in my books, I like to observe the real people in my life. I don't like to talk much; I like to listen to other people's stories. I don't decide what kind of people they are—I just try to think about what they feel, where they are going. I gather some factors from him, some factors from her. I don't know if this is realistic or unrealistic, but for me, my characters are more real than real people. In those six or seven months that I'm writing, those people are inside me. It's a kind of cosmos.

INTERVIEWER

Your protagonists often seem to serve as projections of your own point of view into the fantastic world of your narratives—the dreamer in the dream.

MURAKAMI

Please think about it this way: I have a twin brother. And when I was two years old, one of us—the other one—was kidnapped. He was brought to a faraway place and we haven't seen each other since. I think my protagonist is him. A part of myself, but not me, and we haven't seen each other for a long time. It's a kind of alternative form of myself. In terms of DNA we are the same, but our environment has been different, so our way of thinking would be different. Every time I write a book I put my feet in different shoes. Because sometimes I am tired of being myself. This way I can escape. It's a fantasy. If you can't have a fantasy, what's the point of writing a book?

INTERVIEWER

Another question about *Hard-Boiled Wonderland*. It has a certain symmetry to it, a certain formal quality, and also a sense of resolution that sets it apart from later books such as *The Wind-Up Bird Chronicle*, for example. Did your ideas on the function and importance of structure in the novel change at some point?

MURAKAMI

Yes. My first two books have not been published outside of Japan; I didn't want them to be. They're immature works, I think—very small books. They were flimsy, if that's the right word.

INTERVIEWER

What were their shortcomings?

MURAKAMI

What I was trying to do in my first two books was to deconstruct the traditional Japanese novel. By *deconstruct*, I mean remove everything inside, leaving only the framework. Then I had to fill the framework in with something fresh and original. I discovered how to do it successfully only after my third book, *A Wild Sheep Chase*, in 1982. The first two novels were helpful in the learning process—no more than that. I consider *A Wild Sheep Chase* to be the true beginning of my style.

Since then, my books have gotten bigger and bigger; their structures are more complicated. Every time I write a new book, I like to destroy the former structure, to make up a new thing. And I always put a new theme, or a new restriction, or a new vision into the new book. I'm always conscious of the structure. If I change the structure, I have to change the style of my prose and I have to change the characters accordingly. If I did the same thing each time, I would be tired. I'd get bored.

INTERVIEWER

And yet as much as some elements of your writing have changed, others have endured. Your novels are always told in the first person. In each of them, a man cycles between a variety of sexually charged relationships with women, and he is generally passive vis-à-vis these women, who seem to function as manifestations of his fears and fantasies.

MURAKAMI

In my books and stories, women are mediums, in a sense; the function of the medium is to make something happen through herself. It's a kind of system to be experienced. The protagonist is always led somewhere by the medium and the visions that he sees are shown to him by her.

INTERVIEWER

Mediums in the Victorian sense? Psychic mediums?

MURAKAMI

I think sex is an act of . . . a kind of soul-commitment. If the sex is good, your injury will be healed, your imagination will be invigorated. It's a kind of passage to the upper area, to the better place. In that sense, in my stories, women are mediums—harbingers of the coming world. That's why they always come to my protagonist; he doesn't go to them.

INTERVIEWER

There seem to be two distinct types of women in your novels: those with whom the protagonist has a fundamentally serious relationship— often this is the woman who disappears and whose memory haunts him—and the other kind of woman, who comes later and helps him in his search, or to do the opposite—to forget. This second type of woman tends to be outspoken, eccentric, and sexually frank, and the protagonist interacts with her in a much warmer and more humorous way than he had with the missing woman, with whom he never quite connected. What purpose do these two archetypes serve?

MURAKAMI

My protagonist is almost always caught between the spiritual world and the real world. In the spiritual world, the women—or men—are quiet, intelligent, modest. Wise. In the realistic world, as you say, the women are very active, comic, positive. They have a sense of humor. The protagonist's mind is split between these totally different worlds and he cannot choose which to take. I think that's one of the main motifs in my work. It's very apparent in *Hard-Boiled Wonderland*, in which his mind is actually, physically split. In *Norwegian Wood*, as well, there are two girls and he cannot decide between them, from the beginning to the end.

INTERVIEWER

My sympathies always seem to tend toward the girl with the sense of humor. It's easier to allow the reader into a relationship in which humor is the primary currency; it's harder to charm the reader with an earnest description of a love affair. In *Norwegian Wood* I was rooting for Midori all the way.

MURAKAMI

I think most readers would say the same. Most would choose Midori. And the protagonist, of course, chooses her in the end. But some part of him is always in the other world and he cannot abandon it. It's a part of him, an essential part. All human beings have a sickness in their minds. That space is a part of them. We have a sane part of our minds and an insane part. We negotiate between those two parts; that is my belief. I can see the insane part of my mind especially well when I'm writing—*insane* is not the right word. Unordinary, unreal. I have to go back to the real world, of course, and pick up the sane part. But if I didn't have the insane part, the sick part, I wouldn't be here. In other words, the protagonist is supported by two women; without either of them, he could not go on. In that sense, *Norwegian Wood* is a very straightforward example of what I'm doing.

INTERVIEWER

The character of Reiko in *Norwegian Wood* is interesting in that light. I wouldn't quite know where to put her; she seems to have a foot in both worlds.

MURAKAMI

She has a half-sane, half-insane mind. It's a Greek mask: if you see her from this side, she's a tragic character; if you see her from the other side, she's comic. In that sense, she's very symbolic. I like that character very much. I was happy when I wrote her, Reiko-San.

INTERVIEWER

Do you yourself feel more affection for your comic characters—for your Midoris and May Kasaharas—than you do for your Naokos?

MURAKAMI

I like to write comic dialogue; it's fun. But if my characters were all comic it would be boring. Those comic characters are a kind of stabilizer to my mind; a sense of humor is a very stable thing. You have to be cool to be humorous. When you're serious, you could be unstable; that's the problem with seriousness. But when you're humorous, you're stable. But you can't fight the war smiling.

INTERVIEWER

Few novelists have written and rewritten their obsessions so compulsively, I think, as you have. *Hard-Boiled Wonderland*, *Dance Dance Dance*, *The Wind-Up Bird Chronicle*, and *Sputnik Sweetheart* almost demand to be read as variations on a theme: a man has been abandoned by, or has otherwise lost, the object of his desire, and is drawn by his inability to forget her into a parallel world that seems to offer the possibility of regaining what he has lost, a possibility that life as he (and the reader) knows it can never offer. Would you agree with this characterization?

MURAKAMI

Yes.

INTERVIEWER

How central is this obsession to your fiction?

MURAKAMI

I don't know why I keep writing those things. I find that in John Irving's work, every book of his, there's some person with a body part that's missing. I don't know why he keeps writing about those missing parts; probably he doesn't know himself. For me it's the same thing. My protagonist is always missing something, and he's searching for that missing thing. It's like the Holy Grail, or Philip Marlowe.

INTERVIEWER

You can't have a detective unless something's missing.

MURAKAMI

Right. When my protagonist misses something, he has to search for it. He's like Odysseus. He experiences so many strange things in the course of his search . . .

INTERVIEWER

In the course of trying to come home.

MURAKAMI

He has to survive those experiences, and in the end he finds what he was searching for. But he is not sure it's the same thing. I think that's the motif of my books. Where do those things come from? I don't know. It fits me. It's the driving power of my stories: missing and searching and finding. And disappointment, a kind of new awareness of the world.

INTERVIEWER

Disappointment as a rite of passage?

MURAKAMI

That's right. Experience itself is meaning. The protagonist has changed in the course of his experiences—that's the main thing. Not what he found, but how he changed.

INTERVIEWER

I wanted to ask about the process of translation with regard to your own books. As a translator yourself, you must be aware of the hazards involved. How did you come to choose your translators?

MURAKAMI

I have three—Alfred Birnbaum, Philip Gabriel, Jay Rubin—and the rule is first come, first get. We're friends, so they are very honest. They read my books and one of them thinks, That's great! I'd like to do that. So he takes it. As a translator myself, I know that to be enthusiastic is the main part of a good translation. If someone is a good translator but doesn't like a book so much, that's the end of the story. Translation is very hard work, and it takes time.

INTERVIEWER

The translators never fight among themselves?

MURAKAMI

Not really. They have their own preferences; they are different people, with different characters. Regarding *Kafka on the Shore*, Phil liked it and took it. Jay wasn't so enthusiastic. Phil is a very modest, gentle person, and Jay is a very meticulous, precise translator. He's kind of a strong character. Alfred is a kind of bohemian; I don't know where he is right now. He's married to a woman from Myanmar, and she's an activist. Sometimes they get captured by the government. He's that kind of person. He's kind of free as a translator; he changes the prose sometimes. That's his style.

INTERVIEWER

How do you collaborate with your translators? How does the process work, exactly?

MURAKAMI

They ask me many things when they are translating, and when the first draft is completed, I read it. Sometimes I'll give them some suggestions. The English version of my books is very important; small countries, such as Croatia or Slovenia, translate from the English, not the Japanese. So it must be very precise. But in most countries, they translate from the original Japanese text.

INTERVIEWER

You yourself seem to prefer to translate realists—Carver, Fitzgerald, Irving. Does that reflect your tastes as a reader, or is it helpful to your writing in some way to immerse yourself in something very different?

MURAKAMI

The people I've translated have all written books from which I could learn something. That's the main thing. I learn a lot from the realistic writers. Their work requires a very close reading to translate, and I can see their secrets. If I were to translate postmodern writers like Don DeLillo, John Barth, or Thomas Pynchon, there would be a crash—my insanity against their insanity. I admire their work, of course, but when I translate I choose realists.

INTERVIEWER

Your writing is often talked about as being the most accessible Japanese literature for American readers, to the point that you yourself are described as the most Western of contemporary Japanese authors. I was wondering how you see your relationship to Japanese culture.

MURAKAMI

I don't want to write about foreigners in foreign countries; I want to write about us. I want to write about Japan, about our life here. That's important to me. Many people say that my style is accessible to Westerners; it might be true, but my stories are my own, and they are not Westernized.

INTERVIEWER

And many of the references that seem so Western to Americans—the Beatles, for example—are an integral part of the Japanese cultural landscape as well.

MURAKAMI

When I write about people eating a McDonald's hamburger, Americans wonder, Why is this character eating a hamburger instead of tofu? But eating a hamburger is very natural to us, an everyday thing.

INTERVIEWER

Would you say that your novels portray contemporary urban Japanese life accurately?

MURAKAMI

The way people act, the way people talk, the way people react, the way people think, is very Japanese. No Japanese readers—almost no Japanese readers—complain that my stories are different from our life. I'm trying to write about the Japanese. I want to write about what we are, where we are going, why we are here. That's my theme, I guess.

INTERVIEWER

You've said elsewhere, referring to *The Wind-Up Bird Chronicle*, that you were interested in your father, in what happened to him, and to his entire generation; but there are no father figures in the novel, or indeed almost anywhere in your fiction. Where in the book itself is this interest apparent?

MURAKAMI

Almost all my novels have been written in the first person. The main task of my protagonist is to observe the things happening around him. He sees what he must see, or he is supposed to see, in actual time. If I may say so, he resembles Nick Carraway in *The Great Gatsby*. He is neutral, and in order to maintain his neutrality, he must be free from any kinship, any connection to a vertical family system.

This might be considered my reply to the fact that "family" has played an overly significant role in traditional Japanese literature. I wanted to depict my main character as an independent, absolute individual. His status as an urban dweller has something to do with it too. He is a type of man who chooses freedom and solitude over intimacy and personal bonds.

INTERVIEWER

When I was reading "Super-Frog Saves Tokyo" in your latest collection of stories, in which an enormous subterranean worm living deep under Tokyo threatens it with destruction, I couldn't help thinking of manga, or the old-style Japanese monster movie. Then there's also the traditional myth of the giant catfish sleeping in Tokyo Bay that, according to legend, wakes up once every fifty years and causes an earthquake. Do any of these associations make sense to you? How about manga, for example? Do you see a connection to your work?

MURAKAMI

No, I don't think so. I'm not a great fan of manga comics. I was not influenced by those things.

INTERVIEWER

What about Japanese folklore?

MURAKAMI

When I was a child, I was told many Japanese folktales and old stories. Those stories are critical when you are growing up. That Super-Frog figure, for example, might come from that reservoir of stories. You have your reservoir of American folklore, Germans have theirs, Russians have theirs. But there is also a mutual reservoir we can draw from: *The Little Prince*, McDonald's, or the Beatles.

INTERVIEWER

The global pop-culture reservoir.

MURAKAMI

Narratives are very important nowadays in writing books. I don't care about theories. I don't care about vocabulary. What is important is whether the narrative is good or not. We have a new kind of folklore, as a result of this Internet world. It's a kind of metaphor. I've seen that movie, *The Matrix*—it's a folktale of the contemporary mind. But everybody here said it was boring.

INTERVIEWER

Have you seen Hayao Miyazaki's anime film *Spirited Away*? It seems to me there are certain similarities to your books, in that he also manipulates folk material in contemporary ways. Do you enjoy his movies?

MURAKAMI

No. I don't like animated movies. I saw just a little part of that movie, but that is not my style. I'm not interested in that kind of thing. When I write my books, I get an image, and that image is so strong.

INTERVIEWER

Do you go to the movies often?

MURAKAMI

Oh, yes. All the time. My favorite director is from Finland—Aki Kaurismäki. Every one of his movies I liked. He's way out of the ordinary.

INTERVIEWER

And funny.

MURAKAMI

Very funny.

INTERVIEWER

You said earlier that humor is stabilizing. Is it useful in other ways?

MURAKAMI

I want my readers to laugh sometimes. Many readers in Japan read my books on the train while commuting. The average salaryman spends two hours a day commuting and he spends those hours reading. That's why my big books are printed in two volumes: They would be too heavy in one. Some people write me letters, complaining that they laugh when they read my books on the train! It's very embarrassing for them. Those are the letters I like most. I know they are laughing, reading my books—that's good. I like to make people laugh every ten pages.

INTERVIEWER

Is that your secret formula?

MURAKAMI

I don't calculate. But if I could manage that, it would be good. I liked to read Kurt Vonnegut and Richard Brautigan while I was a college student. They had a sense of humor, and at the same time what they were writing about was serious. I like those kind of books. The first time I read Vonnegut and Brautigan I was shocked to find that there were such books! It was like discovering the New World.

INTERVIEWER

But you've never been tempted to write something in that vein?

MURAKAMI

I think this world itself is a kind of comedy, this urban life. TVs with fifty channels, those stupid people in the government—it's a comedy. So I try to be serious, but the harder I try, the more comical I get. We were dead serious when I was nineteen years old, in 1968 and 1969. It was a serious time, and people were very idealistic.

INTERVIEWER

It's interesting that *Norwegian Wood*, which is set in that time, is perhaps the least comic of your books.

MURAKAMI

In that sense, our generation is a serious generation. But looking back on those days, it was so comical! It was an ambiguous time. So we—my generation—are used to it, I guess.

INTERVIEWER

One of the cardinal rules of magic realism is not to call attention to the fantastic elements of the story. You, however, disregard this rule: your characters often comment on the strangeness of the story line, even call the reader's attention to it. What purpose does this serve? Why?

MURAKAMI

That's a very interesting question. I'd like to think about it . . . Well, I think it's my honest observation of how strange the world is. My protagonists are experiencing what I experience as I write, which is also what the readers experience as they read. Kafka or García Márquez, what they are writing is more literature, in the classical sense. My stories are more actual, more contemporary, more the post-modern experience. Think of it like a movie set, where everything—all the props, the books on the wall, the shelves—is fake. The walls are made of paper. In the classical kind of magic realism, the walls and the books are real. If something is fake in my fiction, I like to say it's fake. I don't want to act as if it's real.

INTERVIEWER

To continue the metaphor of the movie set, might the pulling back of the camera intend to show the workings of the studio?

MURAKAMI

I don't want to persuade the reader that it's a real thing; I want to show it as it is. In a sense, I'm telling those readers that it's just a story—it's fake. But when you experience the fake as real, it can be real. It's not easy to explain.

In the nineteenth and early twentieth centuries, writers offered the real thing; that was their task. In *War and Peace* Tolstoy describes the battleground so closely that the readers believe it's the real thing. But I don't. I'm not pretending it's the real thing. We are living in a fake world; we are watching fake evening news. We are fighting a fake war. Our government is fake. But we find reality in this fake world. So our stories are the same; we are walking through fake scenes, but ourselves, as we walk through these scenes, are real. The situation is real, in the sense that it's a commitment, it's a true relationship. That's what I want to write about.

INTERVIEWER

In your writing, you return to mundane details time and time again.

MURAKAMI

I like details very much. Tolstoy wanted to write the total description; my description is focused on a very small area. When you describe the details of small things, your focus gets closer and closer, and the opposite of Tolstoy happens—it gets more unrealistic. That's what I want to do.

INTERVIEWER

To take the focus so close that you pass through the zone of realism, and the everyday and the banal becomes strange again?

MURAKAMI

The closer it gets, the less real it gets. That's my style.

INTERVIEWER

Earlier you mentioned García Márquez and Kafka as writers of literature, in contrast to your own work; do you not think of yourself as a writer of literature?

MURAKAMI

I'm a writer of contemporary literature, which is very different. At the time that Kafka was writing, you had only music, books, and theater; now we have the Internet, movies, rental videos, and so much else. We have so much competition now. The main problem is time: in the nineteenth century, people—I'm talking about the leisure class—had so much time to spend, so they read big books. They went to the opera and sat for three or four hours. But now everyone is so busy, and there is no real leisure class. It's good to read *Moby-Dick* or Dostoyevsky, but people are too busy for that now. So fiction itself has changed drastically—we have to grab people by the neck and pull them in. Contemporary fiction writers are using the techniques of other fields—jazz, video games, everything. I think video games are closer to fiction than anything else these days.

INTERVIEWER

Video games?

MURAKAMI

Yes. I don't like playing video games myself, but I feel the similarity. Sometimes while I'm writing I feel I'm the designer of a video game, and at the same time, a player. I made up the program, and now I'm in the middle of it; the left hand doesn't know what the right hand is doing. It's a kind of detachment. A feeling of a split.

INTERVIEWER

Is that a way of saying that although you have no idea what is going to happen next as you write, another part of you knows exactly what's coming?

MURAKAMI

Unconsciously, I guess. When I'm absorbed in writing, I know what the author is feeling and I know what the reader is feeling. That's good—it gives my writing speed. Because I want to know what happens next as much as the reader does. But also you have to stop the current sometimes. If it gets too fast, people get tired and bored. You have to make them stop at a certain point.

INTERVIEWER

And how do you do that?

MURAKAMI

I just feel it. I know it's time to stop.

INTERVIEWER

What about jazz and music in general? How is it useful to you in your work?

MURAKAMI

I've been listening to jazz since I was thirteen or fourteen years old. Music is a very strong influence: the chords, the melodies, the rhythm, the feeling of the blues are helpful when I write. I wanted to be a musician, but I couldn't play the instruments very well, so I became a writer. Writing a book is just like playing music: first I play the theme, then I improvise, then there is a conclusion, of a kind.

INTERVIEWER

In a traditional jazz piece the initial theme would be returned to toward the end. Do you return to yours?

MURAKAMI

Sometimes. Jazz is a journey for me, a mental journey. No different than writing.

INTERVIEWER

Who are your favorite jazz musicians?

MURAKAMI

There are too many! I like Stan Getz and Gerry Mulligan. When I was a teenager, they were the coolest musicians ever. I also like Miles Davis and Charlie Parker, of course. If you ask me who I actually put on the turntable most, then the answer would be Miles from the fifties through the sixties. Miles was always an innovator, a man who kept up with his own revolutions—I admire him greatly.

INTERVIEWER

Do you like Coltrane?

MURAKAMI

Ah, so-so. Sometimes he does too much. Too insistent.

INTERVIEWER

What about other types of music?

MURAKAMI

I like classical music as well, particularly baroque music. And in my new book, *Kafka on the Shore*, the protagonist, the boy, listens to Radiohead and Prince. I was so surprised: some member of Radiohead likes my books!

INTERVIEWER

I'm not surprised.

MURAKAMI

I read the Japanese liner notes for *Kid A* the other day, and he said that he likes my books, and I was so proud.

INTERVIEWER

Can you tell me a little about *Kafka on the Shore*?

MURAKAMI

It's the most complicated book I have ever written, more complicated even than *The Wind-Up Bird Chronicle*. It's almost impossible to explain.

There are two stories that run parallel. My protagonist is a fifteen-year-old boy. His name, his first name, is Kafka. In the other story line, the protagonist is a sixty-year-old man. He's illiterate; he cannot write or read. He's kind of a simpleton, but he can talk to cats. The boy, Kafka, was cursed by his father, an Oedipal kind of curse: you will kill me, your father, and make love with your mother. He escapes from his father, to escape from his curse, and he goes to a faraway place, but he experiences a very strange world, very unrealistic, dreamlike things.

INTERVIEWER

In terms of structure, is it similar to *Hard-Boiled Wonderland and the End of the World*, in that it goes back and forth, chapter by chapter, from one story line to the other?

MURAKAMI

Right. At first, I was trying to write the sequel to *Hard-Boiled Wonderland*, but I decided to write a totally different story. But the style is very similar. The soul is very similar. The theme is this world and the other world; how you can come and go between them.

INTERVIEWER

I'm very excited to hear that, because *Hard-Boiled Wonderland* is my favorite book of yours.

MURAKAMI

Mine too. It's a very ambitious book, the new one, because the protagonists in my books are always in their twenties or their thirties. This time it's a fifteen year old.

INTERVIEWER

More like Holden Caulfield?

MURAKAMI

That's right. It was kind of exciting to write that story. When I wrote about the boy, I could remember how it was when I was fifteen years old. I think memory is the most important asset of human beings. It's a kind of fuel; it burns and it warms you. My memory is like a chest: There are so many drawers in that chest, and when I want to be a fifteen-year-old boy, I open up a certain drawer and I find the scenery I saw when I was a boy in Kobe. I can smell the air, and I can touch the ground, and I can see the green of the trees. That's why I want to write a book.

INTERVIEWER

To get back to those fifteen-year-old perceptions?

MURAKAMI

For instance. Yes.

INTERVIEWER

How important was growing up in Kobe and not elsewhere in Japan to the style that you developed? Kobe has a reputation as a worldly town, and possibly a bit eccentric.

MURAKAMI

People in Kyoto are stranger than in Kobe! They are surrounded by mountains, so their mentality is different.

INTERVIEWER

But you were born in Kyoto. Is that right?

MURAKAMI

Yes, but when I was two we moved to Kobe. So that is where I'm from. Kobe is by the sea and next to the mountains, on a kind of strip. I don't like Tokyo—it's so flat, so wide, so vast. I don't like it here.

INTERVIEWER

But you live here! I'm sure you could live anywhere you liked.

MURAKAMI

That's because I can be anonymous here. It's the same as in New York. Nobody recognizes me—I could go anywhere. I can take the train and nobody bothers me. I have a house in a small town in the suburbs of Tokyo, and everybody knows me there. Every time I take a walk, I get recognized. And sometimes it's annoying.

INTERVIEWER

You mentioned Ryu Murakami earlier. He seems to have a very different agenda as a writer.

MURAKAMI

My style is kind of postmodern; his is more mainstream. But when I read *Coin Locker Babies* for the first time, I was shocked; I decided I would like to write that kind of powerful novel. Then I started to write *A Wild Sheep Chase*. So it's a kind of rivalry.

INTERVIEWER

Are you friends?

MURAKAMI

We've had a good relationship. We are not enemies, at least. He has a very natural, powerful talent. It's as if he has an oil well just beneath the surface. But in my case, my oil was so deep that I had to dig and dig and dig. It was real toil. And it took time to get there. But once I got there, I was strong and confident. My life was systematized. It was good to be digging all the way.

Orhan Pamuk

The Art of Fiction

O rhan Pamuk was born in 1952 in Istanbul, where he continues
to live. His family had made a fortune in railroad construction
during the early days of the Turkish Republic and Pamuk attended Robert College, where the children of the city's privileged elite received a
secular, Western-style education. Early in life he developed a passion for
the visual arts, but after enrolling in college to study architecture he decided he wanted to write. He is now Turkey's most widely read author.

His first novel, *Cevdet Bey and His Sons*, was published in 1982
and was followed by *The Silent House* (1983), *The White Castle*
(1985/1991 in English translation), *The Black Book* (1990/1994), and
The New Life (1994/1997). In 2003 Pamuk received the International IMPAC Dublin Literary Award for *My Name Is Red* (1998/2001),
a murder mystery set in sixteenth-century Istanbul and narrated by
multiple voices. The novel explores themes central to his fiction: the
intricacies of identity in a country that straddles East and West, sib-
ling rivalry, the existence of doubles, the value of beauty and originality, and the anxiety of cultural influence. *Snow* (2002/2004), which
focuses on religious and political radicalism, was the first of his
novels to confront political extremism in contemporary Turkey and
it confirmed his standing abroad even as it divided opinion at home.
Pamuk's most recent book is *Istanbul: Memories and the City*
(2003/2005), a double portrait of himself—in childhood and youth—
and of the place he comes from.

This interview with Orhan Pamuk was conducted in two sustained sessions in London and by correspondence. The first conversation occurred in May of 2004 at the time of the British publication of *Snow*. A special room had been booked for the meeting—a fluorescent-lit, noisily air-conditioned corporate space in the hotel basement. Pamuk arrived, wearing a black corduroy jacket over a light-blue shirt and dark slacks, and observed, "We could die here and nobody would ever find us." We retreated to a plush, quiet corner of the hotel lobby where we spoke for three hours, pausing only for coffee and a chicken sandwich.

In April of 2005 Pamuk returned to London for the publication of *Istanbul* and we settled into the same corner of the hotel lobby to speak for two hours. At first he seemed quite strained, and with reason. Two months earlier, in an interview with the Swiss newspaper *Der Tages-Anzeiger*, he had said of Turkey, "thirty thousand Kurds and a million Armenians were killed in these lands and nobody but me dares to talk about it." This remark set off a relentless campaign against Pamuk in the Turkish nationalist press. After all, the Turkish government persists in denying the 1915 genocidal slaughter of Armenians in Turkey and has imposed laws severely restricting discussion of the ongoing Kurdish conflict. Pamuk declined to discuss the controversy for the public record in the hope that it would soon fade. In August, however, Pamuk's remarks in the Swiss paper resulted in his being charged under Article 301/1 of the Turkish Penal Code with "public denigration" of Turkish identity—a crime punishable by up to three years in prison. Despite outraged international press coverage of his case, as well as vigorous protest to the Turkish government by members of the European Parliament and by International PEN, when this magazine went to press in mid-November Pamuk was still slated to stand trial on December 16, 2005.

—*Ángel Gurría-Quintana*, 2005

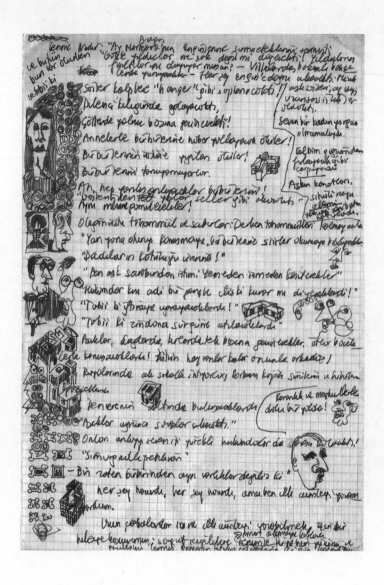

Two pages from Orhan Pamuk's notebooks for *The Black Book*.

Mhat · Orhan · Mhat Pamuk · Mhat Pamuk

Rüya'nın sorularından sanki haberdar mış gibi, bir akşam.

... bir gene aynı koltuklara oturduktan sonra Celal, "Bu akşam dedi bize "size hikâye anlatmak içeren bir hikâye anlatacağım." "Ne dersiniz?" Ama bizim cevabımızı görmek için sormadı bu soruyu.

"Bütün ... 'gibi, 'ben 'bilkisi öteki' ... bir 'öteki' kelimesiyle ve ... ta çünkü aslında ... kullanan bütün yazarlar gibi ... en ... mişiz marmış ama bir biliyorduk: Bir zamanlar, aşağı yukarı on yedi on ... yıl önce Celal ... et ... anlattığı gibi ... kartaca'nın kendi adıyla kişi yazarı yazmak isteyip de ... günlerde Celal'in ... aynı geçe şeyde tokma bir adle bir gene bir romanı tefekkür et ... biti yordu. ... "Batmakta olan ... el değiştirme ... kalabalık toplanın bir sağır ... pencerele kaçtılar. Yeni ve geçe patan, bir hamle yaya ... artmak istiyordu ama ... kemme Neder Esat Mahmut gibi o romanı ... gene bu romancılara ... parası bile ... Belkim ... yeni fusatla tonun için gene gazetecileri korkutup ... da çok ilk bir yazı ... konu yine ... ... Bir ... ... yazarlığı ... helep bulmam. Tokma, ad bulla ... kalabalık ... beyi ufuca me ... söyleyim gene bu yazılarından ... olmadığını söyledim, ... çalıştığını da söyledim. Nerde ... tür Celal ... hikâye yenin yazılarını bulmak ... Mahaurek bütün manım deşmiydi? Bunu yazacağım.

Orhan Pamuk

Zaman Zaman — Arya romanı ...
Kürmenin terhinde

INTERVIEWER

How do you feel about giving interviews?

ORHAN PAMUK

I sometimes feel nervous because I give stupid answers to certain pointless questions. It happens in Turkish as much as in English. I speak bad Turkish and utter stupid sentences. I have been attacked in Turkey more for my interviews than for my books. Political polemicists and columnists do not read novels there.

INTERVIEWER

You've generally received a positive response to your books in Europe and the United States. What is your critical reception in Turkey?

PAMUK

The good years are over now. When I was publishing my first books the previous generation of authors was fading away, so I was welcomed because I was a new author.

INTERVIEWER

When you say the previous generation, whom do you have in mind?

PAMUK

The authors who felt a social responsibility, authors who felt that literature serves morality and politics. They were flat realists, not experimental. Like authors in so many poor countries, they wasted their talent on trying to serve their nation. I did not want to be like them, because even in my youth I had enjoyed Faulkner, Virginia Woolf, Proust—I had never aspired to the social-realist model of Steinbeck and Gorky. The literature produced in the sixties and seventies was becoming outmoded, so I was welcomed as an author of the new generation.

After the mid-nineties, when my books began to sell in amounts that no one in Turkey had ever dreamed of, my honeymoon years with the Turkish press and intellectuals were over. From then on, critical reception was mostly a reaction to the publicity and sales, rather than the content of my books. Now, unfortunately, I am notorious for my political comments—most of which are picked up from international interviews and shamelessly manipulated by some Turkish nationalist journalists to make me look more radical and politically foolish than I really am.

So there is a hostile reaction to your popularity?

My strong opinion is that it's a sort of punishment for my sales figures and political comments. But I don't want to continue saying this, because I sound defensive. I may be misrepresenting the whole picture.

Where do you write?

I have always thought that the place where you sleep or the place you share with your partner should be separate from the place where you write. The domestic rituals and details somehow kill the imagination. They kill the demon in me. The domestic, tame daily routine makes the longing for the other world, which the imagination needs to operate, fade away. So for years I always had an office or a little place outside the house to work in. I always had different flats.

But once I spent half a semester in the U.S. while my ex-wife was taking her Ph.D. at Columbia University. We were living in an apartment for married students and didn't have any space, so I had to sleep and write in the same place. Reminders of family life were all around. This upset me. In the mornings I used to say good-bye to my wife like someone going to work. I'd leave the house, walk around a few blocks, and come back like a person arriving at the office.

Ten years ago I found a flat overlooking the Bosporus with a view of the old city. It has, perhaps, one of the best views of Istanbul. It is a twenty-five-minute walk from where I live. It is full of books and my desk looks out onto the view. Every day I spend, on average, some ten hours there.

INTERVIEWER

Ten hours a day?

PAMUK

Yes, I'm a hard worker. I enjoy it. People say I'm ambitious, and maybe there's truth in that too. But I'm in love with what I do. I enjoy sitting at my desk like a child playing with his toys. It's work, essentially, but it's fun and games also.

INTERVIEWER

Orhan, your namesake and the narrator of *Snow*, describes himself as a clerk who sits down at the same time every day. Do you have the same discipline for writing?

PAMUK

I was underlining the clerical nature of the novelist as opposed to that of the poet, who has an immensely prestigious tradition in Turkey. To be a poet is a popular and respected thing. Most of the Ottoman sultans and statesmen were poets. But not in the way we understand poets now. For hundreds of years it was a way of establishing yourself as an intellectual. Most of these people used to collect their poems in manuscripts called divans. In fact, Ottoman court poetry is called divan poetry. Half of the Ottoman statesmen produced divans. It was a sophisticated and educated way of writing things, with many rules and rituals. Very conventional and very repetitive. After Western ideas came to Turkey, this legacy was combined with the romantic and modern idea of the poet as a person who burns for truth. It added extra weight to the prestige of the poet. On the other hand, a novelist is essentially a person who covers distance through his patience, slowly, like an ant. A novelist impresses us not by his demonic and romantic vision, but by his patience.

INTERVIEWER

Have you ever written poetry?

PAMUK

I am often asked that. I did when I was eighteen and I published some poems in Turkey, but then I quit. My explanation is that I realized that a poet is someone through whom God is speaking. You have to be possessed by poetry. I tried my hand at poetry, but I realized after some time that God was not speaking to me. I was sorry about this and then I tried to imagine—if God were speaking through me, what would he be saying? I began to write very meticulously, slowly, trying to figure this out. That is prose writing, fiction writing. So I worked like a clerk. Some other writers consider this expression to be a bit of an insult. But I accept it; I work like a clerk.

INTERVIEWER

Would you say that writing prose has become easier for you over time?

PAMUK

Unfortunately not. Sometimes I feel my character should enter a room and I still don't know how to make him enter. I may have more self-confidence, which sometimes can be unhelpful because then you're not experimenting, you just write what comes to the tip of your pen. I've been writing fiction for the last thirty years, so I should think that I've improved a bit. And yet I still sometimes come to a dead end where I thought there never would be one. A character cannot enter a room, and I don't know what to do. Still! After thirty years.

The division of a book into chapters is very important for my way of thinking. When writing a novel, if I know the whole story line in advance—and most of the time I do—I divide it into chapters and think up the details of what I'd like to happen in each. I don't necessarily start with the first chapter and write all the others in order. When I'm blocked, which is not a grave thing for me, I continue with whatever takes my fancy. I may write from the first to the fifth chapter, then if I'm not enjoying it I skip to number fifteen and continue from there.

INTERVIEWER

Do you mean that you map out the entire book in advance?

PAMUK

Everything. *My Name Is Red*, for instance, has many characters, and to each character I assigned a certain number of chapters. When I was writing, sometimes I wanted to continue "being" one of the characters. So when I finished writing one of Shekure's chapters, perhaps chapter seven, I skipped to chapter eleven, which is her again. I liked being Shekure. Skipping from one character or persona to another can be depressing.

But the final chapter I always write at the end. That is definite. I like to tease myself, ask myself what the ending should be. I can only execute the ending once. Towards the end, before finishing, I stop and rewrite most of the early chapters.

INTERVIEWER

Do you ever have a reader while you are working?

PAMUK

I always read my work to the person I share my life with. I'm always grateful if that person says, Show me more, or, Show me what you have done today. Not only does that provide a bit of necessary pressure, but it's like having a mother or father pat you on the back and say, Well done. Occasionally, the person will say, Sorry, I don't buy this. Which is good. I like that ritual.

I'm always reminded of Thomas Mann, one of my role models. He used to bring the whole family together, his six children and his wife. He used to read to all his gathered family. I like that. Daddy telling a story.

INTERVIEWER

When you were young you wanted to be a painter. When did your love of painting give way to your love of writing?

PAMUK

At the age of twenty-two. Since I was seven I had wanted to be a painter, and my family had accepted this. They all thought that I would be a famous painter. But then something happened in my head—I realized that a screw was loose—and I stopped painting and immediately began writing my first novel.

INTERVIEWER

A screw was loose?

PAMUK

I can't say what my reasons were for doing this. I recently published a book called *Istanbul*. Half of it is my autobiography until that moment and the other half is an essay about Istanbul, or more precisely, a child's vision of Istanbul. It's a combination of thinking about images and landscapes and the chemistry of a city, and a child's perception of that city, and that child's autobiography. The last sentence of the book reads, " 'I don't want to be an artist,' I said. 'I'm going to be a writer.' " And it's not explained. Although reading the whole book may explain something.

INTERVIEWER

Was your family happy about this decision?

PAMUK

My mother was upset. My father was somewhat more understanding because in his youth he wanted to be a poet and translated Valéry into Turkish, but gave up when he was mocked by the upper-class circle to which he belonged.

Your family accepted you being a painter, but not a novelist?

Yes, because they didn't think I would be a full-time painter. The family tradition was in civil engineering. My grandfather was a civil engineer who made lots of money building railroads. My uncles and my father lost the money, but they all went to the same engineering school, Istanbul Technical University. I was expected to go there and I said, All right, I will go there. But since I was the artist in the family, the notion was that I should become an architect. It seemed to be a satisfying solution for everyone. So I went to that university, but in the middle of architectural school I suddenly quit painting and began writing novels.

Did you already have your first novel in mind when you decided to quit? Is that why you did it?

As far as I remember, I wanted to be a novelist before I knew what to write. In fact, when I did start writing I had two or three false starts. I still have the notebooks. But after about six months I started a major novel project that ultimately got published as *Cevdet Bey and His Sons*.

That hasn't been translated into English.

It is essentially a family saga, like the *Forsyte Saga* or Thomas Mann's *Buddenbrooks*. Not long after I finished it I began to regret having written something so outmoded, a very nineteenth-century novel. I regretted writing it because, around the age of twenty-five or twenty-six, I began to impose on myself the idea that I should be a modern author. By the time the novel was finally published, when I was thirty, my writing had become much more experimental.

INTERVIEWER

When you say you wanted to be more modern, experimental, did you have a model in mind?

PAMUK

At that time, the great writers for me were no longer Tolstoy, Dostoyevsky, Stendhal, or Thomas Mann. My heroes were Virginia Woolf and Faulkner. Now I would add Proust and Nabokov to that list.

INTERVIEWER

The opening line of *The New Life* is, "I read a book one day and my whole life was changed." Has any book had that effect on you?

PAMUK

The Sound and the Fury was very important to me when I was twenty-one or twenty-two. I bought a copy of the Penguin edition. It was hard to understand, especially with my poor English. But there was a wonderful translation of the book into Turkish, so I would put the Turkish and the English together on the table and read half a paragraph from one and then go back to the other. That book left a mark on me. The residue was the voice that I developed. I soon began to write in the first person singular. Most of the time I feel better when I'm impersonating someone else rather than writing in the third person.

INTERVIEWER

You say it took years to get your first novel published?

PAMUK

In my twenties I did not have any literary friendships; I didn't belong to any literary group in Istanbul. The only way to get my first book published was to submit it to a literary competition for unpublished manuscripts in Turkey. I did that and won the prize, which was to be published by a big, good publisher. At the time, Turkey's economy was in a bad state. They said, Yes, we'll give you a contract, but they delayed the novel's publication.

INTERVIEWER

Did your second novel go more easily—more quickly?

PAMUK

The second book was a political book. Not propaganda. I was already writing it while I waited for the first book to appear. I had given that book some two and a half years. Suddenly, one night there was a military coup. This was in 1980. The next day the would-be publisher of the first book, the *Cevdet Bey* book, said he wasn't going to publish it, even though we had a contract. I realized that even if I finished my second book—the political book—that day, I would not be able to publish it for five or six years because the military would not allow it. So my thoughts ran as follows: At the age of twenty-two I said I was going to be a novelist and wrote for seven years hoping to get something published in Turkey . . . and nothing. Now I'm almost thirty and there's no possibility of publishing anything. I still have the two-hundred-and-fifty pages of that unfinished political novel in one of my drawers.

Immediately after the military coup, because I didn't want to get depressed, I started a third book—the book to which you referred, *The Silent House.* That's what I was working on in 1982 when the first book was finally published. *Cevdet* was well received, which meant that I could publish the book I was then writing. So the third book I wrote was the second to be published.

INTERVIEWER

What made your novel unpublishable under the military regime?

PAMUK

The characters were young upper-class Marxists. Their fathers and mothers would go to summer resorts, and they had big spacious rich houses and enjoyed being Marxists. They would fight and be jealous of each other and plot to blow up the prime minister.

INTERVIEWER

Gilded revolutionary circles?

PAMUK

Upper-class youngsters with rich people's habits, pretending to be ultra-radical. But I was not making a moral judgment about that. Rather, I was romanticizing my youth, in a way. The idea of throwing a bomb at the prime minister would have been enough to get the book banned.

So I didn't finish it. And you change as you write books. You cannot assume the same persona again. You cannot continue as before. Each book an author writes represents a period in his development. One's novels can be seen as the milestones in the development of one's spirit. So you cannot go back. Once the elasticity of fiction is dead, you cannot move it again.

INTERVIEWER

When you're experimenting with ideas, how do you choose the form of your novels? Do you start with an image, with a first sentence?

PAMUK

There is no constant formula. But I make it my business not to write two novels in the same mode. I try to change everything. This is why so many of my readers tell me, I liked this novel of yours, it's a shame you didn't write other novels like that, or, I never enjoyed one of your novels until you wrote that one—I've heard that especially about *The Black Book*. In fact I hate to hear this. It's fun, and a challenge, to experiment with form and style, and language and mood and persona, and to think about each book differently.

The subject matter of a book may come to me from various sources. With *My Name Is Red*, I wanted to write about my ambition to become a painter. I had a false start; I began to write a monographic book focused on one painter. Then I turned the painter into various painters working together in an atelier. The point of view changed, because now there were other painters talking. At first I was thinking of writing about a contemporary painter, but then I thought this Turkish painter might be too derivative, too influenced by the West, so I went back in time to write about miniaturists. That was how I found my subject.

Some subjects also necessitate certain formal innovations or storytelling strategies. Sometimes, for example, you've just seen something, or read something, or been to a movie, or read a newspaper article, and then you think, I'll make a potato speak, or a dog, or a tree. Once you get the idea you start thinking about symmetry and continuity in the novel. And you feel, Wonderful, no one's done this before.

Finally, I think of things for years. I may have ideas and then I tell them to my close friends. I keep lots of notebooks for possible novels I may write. Sometimes I don't write them, but if I open a notebook and begin taking notes for it, it is likely that I will write that novel. So when I'm finishing one novel my heart may be set on one of these projects; and two months after finishing one I start writing the other.

INTERVIEWER

Many novelists will never discuss a work in progress. Do you also keep that a secret?

PAMUK

I never discuss the story. On formal occasions, when people ask what I'm writing, I have a one-sentence stock reply: A novel that takes place in contemporary Turkey. I open up to very few people and only when I know they won't hurt me. What I do is talk about the gimmicks— I'm going to make a cloud speak, for instance. I like to see how people react to them. It is a childish thing. I did this a lot when writing *Istanbul*. My mind is like that of a little playful child, trying to show his daddy how clever he is.

INTERVIEWER

The word *gimmick* has a negative connotation.

PAMUK

You begin with a gimmick, but if you believe in its literary and moral seriousness, in the end it turns into serious literary invention. It becomes a literary statement.

INTERVIEWER

Critics often characterize your novels as postmodern. It seems to me, however, that you draw your narrative tricks primarily from traditional sources. You quote, for instance, from *The Thousand and One Nights* and other classic texts in the Eastern tradition.

PAMUK

That began with *The Black Book*, though I had read Borges and Calvino earlier. I went with my wife to the United States in 1985, and there I first encountered the prominence and the immense richness of American culture. As a Turk coming from the Middle East, trying to establish himself as an author, I felt intimidated. So I regressed, went back to my "roots." I realized that my generation had to invent a modern national literature.

Borges and Calvino liberated me. The connotation of traditional Islamic literature was so reactionary, so political, and used by conservatives in such old-fashioned and foolish ways, that I never thought I could do anything with that material. But once I was in the United States, I realized I could go back to that material with a Calvinoesque or Borgesian mind frame. I had to begin by making a strong distinction between the religious and literary connotations of Islamic literature, so that I could easily appropriate its wealth of games, gimmicks, and parables. Turkey had a sophisticated tradition of highly refined ornamental literature. But then the socially committed writers emptied our literature of its innovative content.

There are lots of allegories that repeat themselves in the various oral storytelling traditions—of China, India, Persia. I decided to use them and set them in contemporary Istanbul. It's an experiment—put everything together, like a Dadaist collage; *The Black Book* has this quality. Sometimes all these sources are fused together and something new emerges. So I set all these rewritten stories in Istanbul, added a detective plot, and out came *The Black Book*. But at its source was the full strength of American culture and my desire to be a serious experimental writer. I could not write a social commentary about Turkey's problems—I was intimidated by them. So I had to try something else.

INTERVIEWER

Were you ever interested in doing social commentary through literature?

PAMUK

No. I was reacting to the older generation of novelists, especially in the eighties. I say this with all due respect, but their subject matter was very narrow and parochial.

INTERVIEWER

Let's go back to before *The Black Book*. What inspired you to write *The White Castle*? It's the first book where you employ a theme that recurs throughout the rest of your novels—impersonation. Why do you think this idea of becoming somebody else crops up so often in your fiction?

PAMUK

It's a very personal thing. I have a very competitive brother who is only eighteen months older than me. In a way, he was my father—my Freudian father, so to speak. It was he who became my alter ego, the representation of authority. On the other hand, we also had a competitive and brotherly comradeship. A very complicated relationship. I wrote extensively about this in *Istanbul*. I was a typical Turkish boy, good at soccer and enthusiastic about all sorts of games and competitions. He was very successful in school, better than me. I felt jealousy towards him, and he was jealous of me too. He was the reasonable and responsible person, the one our superiors addressed. While I was paying attention to games, he paid attention to rules. We were competing all the time. And I fancied being him, that kind of thing. It set a model. Envy, jealousy—these are heartfelt themes for me. I always worry about how much my brother's strength or his success might have influenced me. This is an essential part of my spirit. I am aware of that, so I put some distance between me and those feelings. I know they are bad, so I have a civilized person's determination to fight them. I'm not saying I'm a victim of jealousy. But this is the galaxy of nerve points that I try to deal with all the time. And of course, in the end, it becomes the subject matter of all my stories. In *The White Castle*, for instance, the almost sadomasochistic relationship between the two main characters is based on my relationship with my brother.

On the other hand, this theme of impersonation is reflected in the fragility Turkey feels when faced with Western culture. After writing *The White Castle*, I realized that this jealousy—the anxiety about being influenced by someone else—resembles Turkey's position when it looks west. You know, aspiring to become Westernized and then being accused of not being authentic enough. Trying to grab the spirit of Europe and then feeling guilty about the imitative drive. The ups and downs of this mood are reminiscent of the relationship between competitive brothers.

INTERVIEWER

Do you believe the constant confrontation between Turkey's Eastern and Western impulses will ever be peacefully resolved?

PAMUK

I'm an optimist. Turkey should not worry about having two spirits, belonging to two different cultures, having two souls. Schizophrenia makes you intelligent. You may lose your relation with reality—I'm a fiction writer, so I don't think that's such a bad thing—but you shouldn't worry about your schizophrenia. If you worry too much about one part of you killing the other, you'll be left with a single spirit. That is worse than having the sickness. This is my theory. I try to propagate it in Turkish politics, among Turkish politicians who demand that the country should have one consistent soul—that it should belong to either the East or the West or be nationalistic. I'm critical of that monistic outlook.

INTERVIEWER

How does that go down in Turkey?

PAMUK

The more the idea of a democratic, liberal Turkey is established, the more my thinking is accepted. Turkey can join the European Union only with this vision. It's a way of fighting against nationalism, of fighting the rhetoric of Us against Them.

INTERVIEWER

And yet in *Istanbul*, in the way you romanticize the city, you seem to mourn the loss of the Ottoman Empire.

PAMUK

I'm not mourning the Ottoman Empire. I'm a Westernizer. I'm pleased that the Westernization process took place. I'm just criticizing the limited way in which the ruling elite—meaning both the bureaucracy and the new rich—had conceived of Westernization. They lacked the confidence necessary to create a national culture rich in its own symbols and rituals. They did not strive to create an Istanbul culture that would be an organic combination of East and West; they just put Western and Eastern things together. There was, of course, a strong local Ottoman culture, but that was fading away little by little. What they had to do, and could not possibly do enough, was invent a strong local culture, which would be a combination—not an imitation—of the

Eastern past and the Western present. I try to do the same kind of thing in my books. Probably new generations will do it, and entering the European Union will not destroy Turkish identity but make it flourish and give us more freedom and self-confidence to invent a new Turkish culture. Slavishly imitating the West or slavishly imitating the old dead Ottoman culture is not the solution. You have to do something with these things and shouldn't have anxiety about belonging to one of them too much.

INTERVIEWER

In *Istanbul*, however, you do seem to identify with the foreign, Western gaze over your own city.

PAMUK

But I also explain why a Westernized Turkish intellectual can identify with the Western gaze—the making of Istanbul is a process of identification with the West. There is always this dichotomy, and you can easily identify with the Eastern anger too. Everyone is sometimes a Westerner and sometimes an Easterner—in fact a constant combination of the two. I like Edward Said's idea of Orientalism, but since Turkey was never a colony, the romanticizing of Turkey was never a problem for Turks. Western man did not humiliate the Turk in the same way he humiliated the Arab or Indian. Istanbul was invaded only for two years and the enemy boats left as they came, so this did not leave a deep scar in the spirit of the nation. What left a deep scar was the loss of the Ottoman Empire, so I don't have that anxiety, that feeling that Westerners look down on me. Though after the founding of the Republic, there was a sort of intimidation because Turks wanted to Westernize but couldn't go far enough, which left a feeling of cultural inferiority that we have to address and that I occasionally may have.

On the other hand, the scars are not as deep as other nations that were occupied for two hundred years, colonized. Turks were never suppressed by Western powers. The suppression that Turks suffered was self-inflicted; we erased our own history because it was practical.

In that suppression there is a sense of fragility. But that self-imposed Westernization also brought isolation. Indians saw their oppressors face-to-face. Turks were strangely isolated from the Western world they emulated. In the 1950s and even 1960s, when a foreigner came to stay at the Istanbul Hilton it would be noted in all the newspapers.

INTERVIEWER

Do you believe that there is a canon or that one should even exist? We have heard of a Western canon, but what about a non-Western canon?

PAMUK

Yes, there is another canon. It should be explored, developed, shared, criticized, and then accepted. Right now the so-called Eastern canon is in ruins. The glorious texts are all around but there is no will to put them together. From the Persian classics, through to all the Indian, Chinese, and Japanese texts, these things should be assessed critically. As it is now, the canon is in the hands of Western scholars. That is the center of distribution and communication.

INTERVIEWER

The novel is a very Western cultural form. Does it have any place in the Eastern tradition?

PAMUK

The modern novel, dissociated from the epic form, is essentially a non-Oriental thing. Because the novelist is a person who does not belong to a community, who does not share the basic instincts of community, and who is thinking and judging with a different culture than the one he is experiencing. Once his consciousness is different from that of the community he belongs to, he is an outsider, a loner. And the richness of his text comes from that outsider's voyeuristic vision.

Once you develop the habit of looking at the world like that and writing about it in this fashion, you have the desire to disassociate from the community. This is the model I was thinking about in *Snow*.

INTERVIEWER

Snow is your most political book yet published. How did you conceive of it?

PAMUK

When I started becoming famous in Turkey in the mid-1990s, at a time when the war against Kurdish guerillas was strong, the old leftist authors and the new modern liberals wanted me to help them, to sign petitions—they began to ask me to do political things unrelated to my books.

Soon the establishment counterattacked with a campaign of character assassination. They began calling me names. I was very angry. After a while I wondered, What if I wrote a political novel in which I explored my own spiritual dilemmas—coming from an upper-middle-class family and feeling responsible for those who had no political representation? I believed in the art of the novel. It is a strange thing how that makes you an outsider. I told myself then, I will write a political novel. I started to write it as soon as I finished *My Name Is Red*.

INTERVIEWER

Why did you set it in the small town of Kars?

PAMUK

It is notoriously one of the coldest towns in Turkey. And one of the poorest. In the early eighties, the whole front page of one of the major newspapers was about the poverty of Kars. Someone had calculated that you could buy the entire town for around a million dollars. The political climate was difficult when I wanted to go there. The vicinity of the town is mostly populated by Kurds, but the center is a combination of Kurds, people from Azerbaijan, Turks, and all other sorts. There used to be Russians and Germans too. There are religious differences as well, Shia and Sunni. The war the Turkish government was waging against the Kurdish guerillas was so fierce that it was impossible to go as a tourist. I knew I could not simply go there as a novelist, so I asked a newspaper editor with whom I'd been in touch for a press pass to visit the area. He is influential and he personally called the mayor and the police chief to let them know I was coming.

As soon as I had arrived I visited the mayor and shook hands with the police chief so that they wouldn't pick me up on the street. Actually, some of the police who didn't know I was there did pick me up and carried me off, probably with the intention of torturing me. Immediately I gave names—I know the mayor, I know the chief . . . I was a suspicious character. Because even though Turkey is theoretically a free country, any foreigner used to be suspect until about 1999. Hopefully things are much easier today.

Most of the people and places in the book are based on a real counterpart. For instance, the local newspaper that sells two hundred and fifty-two copies is real. I went to Kars with a camera and a video recorder. I was filming everything and then going back to Istanbul and showing it to my friends. Everyone thought I was a bit crazy. There were other things that actually occurred. Like the conversation I describe with the editor of the little newspaper who tells Ka what he did the previous day, and Ka asks how he knew, and he reveals he's been listening to the police's walkie-talkies and the police were following Ka all the time. That is real. And they were following me too.

The local anchorman put me on TV and said, Our famous author is writing an article for the national newspaper—that was a very important thing. Municipal elections were coming up so the people of Kars opened their doors to me. They all wanted to say something to the national newspaper, to let the government know how poor they were. They did not know I was going to put them in a novel. They thought I was going to put them in an article. I must confess, this was cynical and cruel of me. Though I was actually thinking of writing an article about it too.

Four years passed. I went back and forth. There was a little coffee shop where I occasionally used to write and take notes. A photographer friend of mine, whom I had invited to come along because Kars is a beautiful place when it snows, overheard a conversation in the little coffee shop. People were talking among themselves while I wrote some notes, saying, What kind of an article is he writing? It's been three years, enough time to write a novel. They'd caught on to me.

INTERVIEWER

What was the reaction to the book?

PAMUK

In Turkey, both conservatives—or political Islamists—and secularists were upset. Not to the point of banning the book or hurting me. But they were upset and wrote about it in the daily national newspapers. The secularists were upset because I wrote that the cost of being a secular radical in Turkey is that you forget that you also have to be a democrat. The power of the secularists in Turkey comes from the army. This destroys Turkey's democracy and culture of tolerance. Once you have so much army involvement in political culture, people lose their self-confidence and rely on the army to solve all their problems. People usually say, The country and the economy are a mess, let's call in the army to clean it up. But just as they cleaned, so did they destroy the culture of tolerance. Lots of suspects were tortured; a hundred thousand people were jailed. This paves the way for new military coups. There was a new one about every ten years. So I was critical of the secularists for this. They also didn't like that I portrayed Islamists as human beings.

The political Islamists were upset because I wrote about an Islamist who had enjoyed sex before marriage. It was that kind of simplistic thing. Islamists are always suspicious of me because I don't come from their culture, and because I have the language, attitude, and even gestures of a more Westernized and privileged person. They have their own problems of representation and ask, How can he write about us anyway? He doesn't understand. This I also included in parts of the novel.

But I don't want to exaggerate. I survived. They all read the book. They may have become angry, but it is a sign of growing liberal attitudes that they accepted me and my book as they are. The reaction of the people of Kars was also divided. Some said, Yes, that is how it is.

Others, usually Turkish nationalists, were nervous about my mentions of Armenians. That TV anchorman, for instance, put my book in a symbolic black bag and mailed it to me and said in a press conference that I was doing Armenian propaganda—which is, of course, preposterous. We have such a parochial, nationalistic culture.

INTERVIEWER

Did the book ever become a cause célèbre in the Rushdie sense?

PAMUK

No, not at all.

INTERVIEWER

It's a terribly bleak, pessimistic book. The only person in the whole novel who is able to listen to all sides—Ka—is, in the end, despised by everyone.

PAMUK

I may have been dramatizing my position as a novelist in Turkey. Although he knows he is despised, he enjoys being able to maintain a dialogue with everyone. He also has a very strong survival instinct. Ka is despised because they see him as a Western spy, which is something that has been said about me many times.

About the bleakness, I agree. But humor is a way out. When people say it's bleak, I ask them, Isn't it funny? I think there is a lot of humor in it. At least that was my intention.

INTERVIEWER

Your commitment to fiction has gotten you into trouble. It is likely to get you into further trouble. It has meant severing of emotional links. It's a high price to pay.

PAMUK

Yes, but it's a wonderful thing. When I'm traveling, and not alone at my desk, after a while I get depressed. I'm happy when I'm alone in a room and inventing. More than a commitment to the art or to the craft, which I am devoted to, it is a commitment to being alone in a room. I continue to have this ritual, believing that what I am doing now will one day be published, legitimizing my daydreams. I need solitary hours at a desk with good paper and a fountain pen like some people need a pill for their health. I am committed to these rituals.

INTERVIEWER

For whom, then, are you writing?

PAMUK

As life gets shorter, you ask yourself that question more often. I've written seven novels. I would love to write another seven novels before I die. But then, life is short. What about enjoying it more? Sometimes I have to really force myself. Why am I doing it? What is the meaning of all of it? First, as I said, it's an instinct to be alone in a room. Second, there's an almost boyish competitive side in me that wants to attempt to write a nice book again. I believe less and less in eternity for authors. We are reading very few of the books written two hundred years ago. Things are changing so fast that today's books will probably be forgotten in a hundred years. Very few will be read. In two hundred years, perhaps five books written today will be alive. Am I sure I'm writing one of those five? But is that the meaning of writing? Why should I be worrying about being read two hundred years later? Shouldn't I be worried about living more? Do I need the consolation that I will be read in the future? I think of all these things and I continue to write. I don't know why. But I never give up. This belief that your books will have an effect in the future is the only consolation you have to get pleasure in this life.

INTERVIEWER

You are a best-selling author in Turkey, but the books you sell at home are outnumbered by your sales abroad. You have been translated into forty languages. Do you now think about a wider global readership when writing? Are you now writing for a different audience?

INTERVIEWER

PAMUK

I am aware that my audience is no longer an exclusively national audience. But even when I began writing, I may have been reaching for a wider group of readers. My father used to say behind the backs of some of his Turkish author friends that they were "only addressing the national audience."

There is a problem of being aware of one's readership, whether it is national or international. I cannot avoid this problem now. My last two books averaged more than half a million readers all over the world. I cannot deny that I am aware of their existence. On the other hand, I never feel that I do things to satisfy them. I also believe that my readers would sense it if I did. I've made it my business, from the very beginning, that whenever I sense a reader's expectations I run away. Even the composition of my sentences—I prepare the reader for something and then I surprise him. Perhaps that's why I love long sentences.

INTERVIEWER

To most non-Turkish readers, the originality of your writing has much to do with its Turkish setting. But how would you distinguish your work in a Turkish context?

PAMUK

There is the problem of what Harold Bloom called "the anxiety of influence." Like all authors I had it when I was young. In my early thirties I kept thinking that I might have been too much influenced by Tolstoy or Thomas Mann—I aimed for that kind of gentle, aristocratic prose in my first novel. But it ultimately occurred to me that although I may have been derivative in my techniques, the fact that I was operating in this part of the world, so far away from Europe—or at least it seemed so at the time—and trying to attract such a different audience in such a different cultural and historical climate, it would grant me originality, even if it was cheaply earned. But it is also a tough job, since such techniques do not translate or travel so easily.

The formula for originality is very simple—put together two things that were not together before. Look at *Istanbul*, an essay about the city and about how certain foreign authors—Flaubert, Nerval, Gautier—viewed the city, and how their views influenced a certain group of Turkish writers. Combined with this essay on the invention of Istanbul's romantic landscape is an autobiography. No one had done this before. Take risks and you will come up with something new. I tried with *Istanbul* to make an original book. I don't know if it succeeds. *The Black Book* was like that too—combine a nostalgic Proustian world with Islamic allegories, stories, and tricks, then set them all in Istanbul and see what happens.

INTERVIEWER

Istanbul conveys the sense that you have always been a very lonely figure. You are certainly alone as a writer in modern Turkey today. You grew up and continue to live in a world from which you are detached.

PAMUK

Although I was raised in a crowded family and taught to cherish the community, I later acquired an impulse to break away. There is a self-destructive side to me, and in bouts of fury and moments of anger I do things that cut me off from the pleasant company of the community. Early in life I realized that the community kills my imagination. I need the pain of loneliness to make my imagination work. And then I'm happy. But being a Turk, after a while I need the consoling tenderness of the community, which I may have destroyed. *Istanbul* destroyed my relationship with my mother—we don't see each other anymore. And of course I hardly ever see my brother. My relationship with the Turkish public, because of my recent comments, is also difficult.

INTERVIEWER

How Turkish do you feel yourself to be, then?

PAMUK

First, I'm a born Turk. I'm happy with that. Internationally, I am perceived to be more Turkish than I actually see myself. I am known as a Turkish author. When Proust writes about love, he is seen as someone talking about universal love. Especially at the beginning, when I wrote about love, people would say that I was writing about Turkish love. When my work began to be translated, Turks were proud of it. They claimed me as their own. I was more of a Turk for them. Once you get to be internationally known, your Turkishness is underlined internationally, then your Turkishness is underlined by Turks themselves, who reclaim you. Your sense of national identity becomes something that others manipulate. It is imposed by other people. Now they are more worried about the international representation of Turkey than about my art. This causes more and more problems in my country. Through what they read in the popular press, a lot of people who don't know my books are beginning to worry about what I say to the outside world about Turkey. Literature is made of good and bad, demons and angels, and more and more they are only worried about my demons.

Issue 175, 2005

David Grossman

The Art of Fiction

In 1987, to mark the twentieth year of Israel's occupation of the West Bank and the Gaza Strip, the editors of the Israeli newsweekly *Koteret Rashit* dispatched the young novelist David Grossman to the West Bank for seven weeks. Grossman, a fluent speaker of Arabic, visited Palestinians in refugee camps and cities, kindergartens and universities, as well as Israeli settlers in their fortified enclaves and army officers patrolling the Palestinian territories. The resulting article filled an entire issue of the magazine and created an uproar in Israel. Grossman had made clear that the Palestinians, who had been suffering the daily brutalities of the occupation for a generation, would be docile no more. "It was a real shock," Tom Segev, one of his editors, told me. "We did not know, then, how much they hated us."

By the following year, when Grossman's report was published in English as *The Yellow Wind*, the Palestinian intifada was fully underway. Grossman's dispatches had become prophetic, launching their author—whose earlier novels had been acclaimed in Israel but not yet translated—to international prominence.

Grossman was born in Jerusalem in 1954. His mother was born in Palestine; his father came from the Polish province of Galicia. As a child he began working as an actor and reporter at Kol Israel, the state radio station, where he was employed for more than twenty years, returning after a four-year stint in the army to serve as a journalist and

הפלנלית. כשהרחרה בה לראשונה נסלד ועיווה את פניו. אבל אחר כך קרב
שוב את חוטמו ושאף בריכוז ויראת כבוד משונה.
אבא סובב את אצבעו בתור ניקבת התאנג, עד שמחא וקינח את כל המוגלה מן
הצצע. תולעת לבנה תפוחה, פרכסה בעוורון על גב ידו, והוא התבונן בה
בעיון. שריקה קלה ובשם, החלה מתגנבת בפיו כשהיה צעיר מאוד היה
אבא קומוניסט ניסתר בעיר פשטשאל שבפוליין. אחר כך התגלגל לפריס
וללייאז' שבבלגיה, ולבסוף הלך אחרי חלקת לשונו של אחד, זיגמה
סרוואז'ניקער, והפליג לרוסיה, כדי לשות שם בצבא האדום. מיד הצ'צה
אמא בחלון ובנשה בין העלים אחרי אבא. השריקה שלו העלתה בפיה רוק
חמוץ. היטב ידעה לאן נשאות אותו מחשבותיו כשהוא שורק כך. רק פעם
אחת סיפר לה את קורות נעוריו בפוליניה, ואת סיפור נדודיו והרפתקאותיו
בצרפת ובבלגיה. החרדית אותה ילדותו, ילדות של ילד ביבים, ממזר פראי
_____ וכאשר שמעה מפיו את סיפור בדנונות על בריחתו מן התאייגה, ואת
מעשה האיכרה הכלואה בביקתה הקטנה, אסה עליו לשוב ולהזכיר זאת,
וכמובן שלא לספר על כך ליניב ולאהרון, והוא הבטיח לה בהנהון הסבלני.
האיטי שלו, בקבעה הקהה החייכנית שנטעה על פניו לכבודה אבל היא קראה
את שריקותיו בבור חבטה במטעל שביד על אדן החלון, ותעלתה ענן אבק.
כרגע חדשה השריקה. אמא שבה ונבלעה בבית. אחר כך, ורעש חרש הס הס,
שבה והתמסלה השריקה.
שלוש שנים שירת אבא באוקראינה, ושמר שם על מחסנים של אבקת שריפה,
ובימים שהשתחרר באו לחדרו שני גברים מן האג.ג.ב. ובשער ממנו שילרוה
אליכם לשיחה בת חמש דקות, שמונה ימים נשער יחד ברכבת, ושני הגברים
לא דברו איתו מטוב ועד רע, עד שהגיער למוסקבה, ושם הוליכוהו לחקירות
ולעינויים בכלא לוביאנקה, וממשם כתבי כלא אחרים. לאחר שנודה בכל מה
שביקשו ממנו להודות, נשלח לעבוייה דרך למזלת ברזל, למקום שממנו קומי, לברוא מה
יצרות אשוח ואורן, כדי לסלול דרך למסילת ברזל. האנשים בטאייגה היו
תמיד קפואים למחצה, חלושים מרעב ומחוסר וטאמינים, ורבים מהם הי-ד
_____ כבר בשם, קראנוצגה להניגם, אף המתים לא היו עזובים כל ימות
החורף, וכשלג ברא היה לבכע את האדמה. מי שנחצב בעבירה על חוקי
המקום היה נכלא בחוסן, וגל גג ו יוצא מדעתו למשעע
עצמת המתים המתפרקות לאיטו בקנוד. אבא נשאר בכה על גב ידו. התולעת
הלבנה נשרה למטה, ליד רגלו. הוא מחצ אותה בעקבו היחף, וחש את נתנ
הריר המטמי.
הוא עבד כך, ביסודיות ובריגינות, שעתיים תמימות. מדי פעם הפסיק, כדי
לשוחח עם אחד השכנים שששאל לפשור מעשהו על העץ, או לענות לקריאותיה של
הינדה, שדיברה אליו מן המרפסת. בשם רוצי נשמע האות של יומן הערב מן
הדירות, ואבא שבת מכל מלאכתו והקשיב בדאגה, אבל לא הודיעו לו פיחות.
והוא שב לעמלו. אהרון רבק על אובניו והתעטכב ממנו. מדי פעם היה מסב
ראשו בסתר לאחוריו, ושורקק ממושכת ל'גומ'י שרדף אחרי אופניו.
כל אותו זמן לא מש צחי מתחת לעץ, ואסף בשקידה את פיסות הבד המטוגצות
חשב אבריו. לא טוב לעזוב ילד כזה קטן ולכסוב לאפריקה בשביל כסף,
חשב אבריו. אחר כך הרהר במלכת סמיטנקה, וששולחת את הילד שלה
לרחבות כדי שתגדל להתפסק עם הרוא, מה אישה כמה מוצאת בכלל בפלגמאטו
כזה, הוא בטח פקיד, או אולי זה, אדורוקאט, התעיקר שיש לו פריינבו, חשב
אביו של אהרון וגאנה על הבזבוז. הוא קרא לצחי מלמעלה, והורה לו ללכת
להיגדה ולהביא ממנה חוקן ישן, עשירי גומ'י, וכשהלך הילד הרהר אבא
בנקודת החן הנגנית במשחיה של מלכה סמיטנקה, ובשאלות התמולתלות,
המחרצפות, תחת בית השחי שלה. "הבאתי!" קרא אלייך צחי מתחת לעץ, נשא
אליו את בבהו, ובצ'א של אהרון שנבהל, נהם עליו בגערה,
ושלח אותו שוב, לומר לה-יגנה שערד מעט הוא חוזר הביתה.
עד שישוב, נשעו אבא אל העגנ ת הרהב ודקלים סיגריה, ויגט אותה בתאוור.
ממקרות עומדו לא נראה השיקון האפרפר כלל. לא נראה הרהב הצר, המהומר.
אפשר היה לדמות שנטוע נטוע בצמות מקומות אחרים, רחבים, פתוחים. אם זז אבא
מעט יכול היה לראות חלון אחד וכנף וילון שלפעמים נדמה היה שאיא
מרטטת. או הוא לא זז. זה היה חודש יוני ועפצי בגות קשים החלו מתעבים

A manuscript page from *The Book of Intimate Grammar* by David Grossman.

news anchor. He began to write fiction in his early twenties, and published a book of stories and two novels while working full time at the station.

Grossman's first novel, *The Smile of the Lamb* (1983), was the first Israeli novel to be set on the West Bank. It is the story of a young soldier, Uri—the eponymous lamb—who befriends and is then held hostage by Khilmi, a half-blind, elderly Palestinian tale-teller. Khilmi's yarns are spun in a languid, fevered prose, a hybrid of stream-of-consciousness and the musical phrasing of Arabic folklore. Grossman's second novel, *See Under: Love* (1986), remains his masterpiece, a wildly inventive work of historical reimagination in four parts that Edmund White compared to *The Sound and the Fury*, *The Tin Drum*, and *One Hundred Years of Solitude*; George Steiner called it simply "one of the great feats in modern fiction." It begins with Momik, an Israeli child growing up in the shadow of the Holocaust, ends with a fantastical set of encyclopedia entries detailing the adventures of aged children's book heroes raising a child in the Warsaw zoo, and in between rescues the Polish writer Bruno Schulz from death by turning him into a salmon.

Grossman followed *The Yellow Wind* with an account of the lives of Palestinian citizens in Israel, *Sleeping on a Wire*, and a book of essays on the conflict, *Death as a Way of Life*. He has published six novels in all, including two "lighter books," as he calls them, *The Zigzag Kid* and *Someone to Run With*; a play; several books for children; and an exegesis of the biblical tale of Samson, *Lion's Honey*. Today he is widely recognized as one of Israel's greatest writers, the foremost novelist among the generation that followed that of Amos Oz and A. B. Yehoshua.

Our interview took place over four days in July, at Mishkenot Sha'ananim, a cultural center within sight of the walls of Jerusalem's Old City, and on the veranda of Grossman's home in the hills of Mevasseret Zion, just outside Jerusalem, where he has lived for twenty-five years with his wife, Michal, and their three children. In the basement Grossman has a modest office, with a computer perched in one corner and, along the far wall, vines growing up to the ceiling; there is a poster on the wall from the popular film adaptation of *Someone to Run With*. Across the hall is a sparse room with two armchairs, where Michal, a clinical psychologist, sees her patients.

July marked the first anniversary of the start of the Lebanon War, and the end of a tragic year for Grossman and his family. In August 2006, Grossman's younger son, Uri, a tank commander in the Israel Defense Forces, was killed in the final days of the war against Hezbollah in southern Lebanon. Two days earlier, Grossman, along with Oz and Yehoshua, had made a public statement demanding a cease-fire. Grossman delivered a eulogy at Uri's funeral on Mount Herzl, in Israel's national cemetery: "I won't say now anything about the war you were killed in. We, our family, have already lost in this war. The state of Israel will now take stock of itself. We, the family, will withdraw into our pain, surrounded by our good friends, enveloped in the powerful love that we feel today from so many people, most of whom we do not know. I thank them for their support, which is unbounded. May we be able to give this love and solidarity to each other at other times as well."

Grossman has always worn his worry on his youthful face, but the events of the last year have left the lines heavier. His gentle demeanor— open, inquisitive, welcoming—conceals the intensity and, more recently, the anguish, of his inner life. In conversation he is contemplative and searching; he speaks quietly but decisively about his own writing, contemporary Israel, and the aims of literature. At the beginning of our first meeting I told Grossman we should delay talk of politics to concentrate on his fiction. A playful smile came to his face, and he said, "Where have you been all my life?"

—*Jonathan Shainin, 2007*

INTERVIEWER

What was the first book that meant something to you?

DAVID GROSSMAN

When I was eight, my father brought me a story by Sholem Aleichem, who wrote about the lives of the Jews in the shtetls, the little towns and villages in Galicia, in Russia, and in Poland. I was the only child in my neighborhood who read Sholem Aleichem. This was a source of embarrassment—it was not cool to dive into the diaspora past. Israel was then a new country, a strong military power surrounded by enemies. It had to be like a clenched fist. Memories about weakness, about humiliation, were not very popular. But the stories enabled me to create for myself an enclave of the Jewish shtetl amid the reality of Jerusalem.

My parents were surprised by my immersion in these stories, but they were also proud. I'll always remember the smile that my father had when he gave me the book. It was the smile of a child, something I don't remember having seen on his face before, insecure and exposed and transparent. He was reluctant to share memories with me, but the stories formed a kind of tunnel to his youth, since he was a child like the children that Sholem Aleichem describes, from a little village named Dynów, in Galicia. When my father realized how much I was affected by Aleichem, he started to tell me stories about his childhood and about himself.

As a father myself, I can tell you that when my children read my books, I know that they are discovering parts of me that they are not usually exposed to. There's a mixture of embarrassment, worry, and pride that they are making this effort, that they want to get closer to me.

INTERVIEWER

What was your father's background?

GROSSMAN

He came to Israel in 1936, when he was nine years old. His father had died two years before, which left his mother and her two children— my father and my aunt—without any protection. One day she was harassed in the street by a Polish policeman, who insulted her. We don't really know what happened there. But she came home and said, We're moving to Eretz Yisrael. She was small, like a toe, all wrinkled—a clever, ironic woman. She took my father and my aunt to Israel, on a long journey by train and ship. This woman who had never traveled even on a bus!

As an adult my father worked as a bus driver. He had to quit driving because of eye problems when he was forty-five, and he became the librarian of Jerusalem's transportation organization. He created a small library, just two rooms, but it held something like three thousand books. I always think that if life had been less cruel he would have been a university professor.

You started working at the state radio station at an early age. How did that come about?

GROSSMAN

In Israel we didn't have television until '68. So radio was everything. One day the radio station announced that it would be holding a knowledge competition about the stories of Sholem Aleichem. This quiz show was very popular in Israel at that time, in the early sixties. They had quizzes on writers, on cinema, on music. There was a lot of speculation about who was going to win, and it was an important part of life. I told my parents that I wanted to be a contestant. I was about nine years old. They said, No, you cannot go, you are only a child. Part of my family's code was not to be conspicuous, not to make yourself a target. Use your intelligence to remain in the second row—which is an efficient way to survive. But I wanted to take part in this competition, so I wrote a postcard to the show.

I had never sent a postcard before—to whom would I send a postcard? Jerusalem was provincial, and very small. I never even met a non-Jew until I was, I think, ten years old. There were no Arabs in our neighborhood then, I had only heard about them on the news. They were the enemy, they had wars with us, they were spies. They wanted to throw us into the sea. I asked my parents for swimming lessons for that reason.

So unbeknownst to my parents, I sent this postcard. I was terrified. A week later, I received a governmental envelope containing a letter inviting me to an audition. Well, when my parents saw the letter from the director of the radio station—it was as if the king or even David Ben-Gurion himself had ordered me to come. They wouldn't dare refuse.

With a mixture of pride and worry, my father accompanied me to the radio building, which would become my workplace for the next twenty-five years. Of course, everybody thought I was accompanying my father. When he explained that I was their candidate, the radio officials were amused. They quizzed me, and I knew all the answers. I had a good memory, the fresh memory of a child, and I was deeply attached, emotionally, to the stories of Sholem Aleichem. They felt relevant to my life, so I just inhaled them. I think I knew them by heart.

INTERVIEWER

What kind of things did they ask you in the audition?

GROSSMAN

Questions about details. What did Tevye in *Tevye the Dairyman* say to his daughter after she married a non-Jew? In what words did Shimek reveal his love to Buzie? I passed that exam, then another one, and finally I encountered a problem that was emblematic of Israel in that period. The general director of the radio station decided that it wouldn't be instructive for a child to win such enormous prize money. The prize money was equivalent to something like fifty dollars today, but this was a major dilemma for them.

INTERVIEWER

Did they think it would be contrary to Israel's socialist ethos?

GROSSMAN

Yes, the ascetic ethos. So they started doing something quite nasty, which I only understood was unusual years later, when I became friends with these people. They said that because of my young age, they had to perform many additional tests. So I would come home after school, and the phone would ring—which is something that happened only about once a week in our home—and when I picked up, a man from the radio would say, David, I'm going to ask you three questions, but beware: if you don't know the answer to any one of them, you will be dropped out of the competition. At some point I got an answer wrong, and he immediately said, We are sorry, we cannot allow you to be a contestant, but we do want you to attend the public recording of this program. If any one of the competitors does not know an answer, we will turn to you. So I would sit there in the audience, and when one of the show's contestants got something wrong, the host would turn to me for the correct answer.

INTERVIEWER

Were the adults embarrassed that they were being upstaged by a ten year old?

GROSSMAN

I'm sure they wanted to kill me.

INTERVIEWER

What did your parents think? Did they change their mind about your staying in the "second row"?

GROSSMAN

I think they became quite proud of me. Suddenly they were willing to accept this strange child who sits and reads those esoteric stories about the *galut*—the diaspora. After the quiz show ended, someone from the station asked if I would like to be a radio actor. I didn't know what he meant, but he had me audition, and I passed. By the time I was eleven years old, I was being flooded with radio work. And I earned, I'm sorry to say, more than my father. It was a full-time job. I'd finish school at two o'clock, go home for lunch, and go to the radio station, where I'd work until ten or eleven at night.

I had two jobs at the station. The first was conducting interviews. I traveled throughout Israel, meeting notable people—the president, football players, theater actors, even the most famous poet at the time,

Avraham Shlonsky. The other thing I did was perform in radio plays, which were often literary texts adapted for the radio. Back then, in the early sixties, most children's roles were played by women. No men could do it, and there were no child actors, except for one, Arieh Eldad. Arieh and I were friends as children because we worked together. He is now a leader of one of the most extreme right parties in Israel.

INTERVIEWER

Was the radio your first experience of creating fiction, of story-telling?

GROSSMAN

Like most children, I lived half of my life daydreaming. When you listen to the radio, you have to imagine what you hear—it's a whole reality expressed only through language. As soon as I started working at the station, I learned how much you can do with the human voice.

INTERVIEWER

What sort of plays did you perform on the radio?

GROSSMAN

All the literary classics. This was the first time I became acquainted with Chekhov, for instance, and Thomas Mann. I was too young to read their books, but I was not too young to participate in these radio plays. Another thing was that I was exposed to the bohemian milieu of radio actors. It was quite the opposite of my home atmosphere, and I liked to move between the two.

INTERVIEWER

What were you like as a teenager?

GROSSMAN

I became a more friendly child in those years, more active socially, yet I remained introverted. In *The Book of Intimate Grammar* there is

Aron, a secluded, lonely child, and his best friend Gideon, the all-Israeli boy, who goes out with girls, is in the Scouts, and wants to be a pilot. I modeled Gideon on a friend I had when I was sixteen—I even interviewed him. When the book came out, I sent a copy to him and anxiously awaited his reaction. He called me after some time and said, I liked it and, of course, I found myself. I am Aron. That was amazing to me. If I had heard him say that when I was sixteen, my entire life would have been different. My sense of solitude, of hopelessness, of being totally excommunicated—all this would have been different.

INTERVIEWER

How long did you stay at the radio station?

GROSSMAN

All through high school, and I came back after the army as well—for another thirteen years as a journalist and the host of the morning news program.

INTERVIEWER

What did you do in the army?

GROSSMAN

I was in intelligence. I served four years there, '71 to '75. I was not in the front during the 1973 war. Though in 1982, I returned to serve on the eastern front in Lebanon as a reservist.

INTERVIEWER

Did you learn Arabic in the army?

GROSSMAN

No, I learned Arabic in high school, actually. I loved Arabic. I belonged to the first group of young pupils here in Israel who studied Arabic in an intensive program from the age of fifteen.

INTERVIEWER

Why was this done?

GROSSMAN

It was intended, in some part, to produce soldiers for intelligence, and we were aware of that. Our first Arabic dictionary bore the intelligence symbol, and we felt proud and secretive. It was after the Six-Day War and people had begun to realize how important it was to make an effort to be integrated in the culture around us.

My mother was shocked when I told her that I wanted to take Arabic, and not French, as a second foreign language. She said, French is a culture. It's theater, Paris, and so on. I brought over our big atlas, and I showed her where Paris is and where we are. I said, We encounter Arabs all the time now, we go to the territories, and they come to us—so I want to study the language.

It is a beautiful language, Arabic. In a strange way, I think studying it allowed me to improve my Hebrew. The two are sister languages, they echo and mirror each other in interesting ways. We had a charismatic young teacher who conveyed to us the beauty of this language, and our little class was thrilled to discover this unknown world. We studied the Koran, the history of the Muslims, and the political situations in the Arab countries. But my Arabic did improve significantly when I went into the army.

INTERVIEWER

What was your army experience like?

GROSSMAN

The army was for me a way to mature. I was given actual responsibility, even though I was just nineteen years old. Living together with many intelligent young men and women, alone in the desert, forms a strong community. Yet I had to create a bubble for myself, because I wanted to write. I need, physically need, several hours every day to be alone and write.

INTERVIEWER

What were you writing in the army?

GROSSMAN

Stories, little things. The more serious fiction came later, after I left the army, but I liked the act of writing. Three friends and I kept special notebooks where, alongside the reports we had to fill out, we'd write personal remarks and letters to each other. Everybody knew where we kept the books, and whenever someone went on shift he'd read them. It developed into a kind of institution. Even the head of intelligence, on his official visits, used to read them.

INTERVIEWER

What exactly did you write in these notebooks?

GROSSMAN

Sometimes nasty things, sometimes poetic. Descriptions of the life of the camp, adolescent confessions, declarations of love for the women around us, dirty songs—but in the most beautiful Hebrew. I'd probably be embarrassed if I read these books today, but I have no idea where they are.

INTERVIEWER

Was this a formative experience for you, writing for an audience?

GROSSMAN

I guess so, because we received a large response. I think it was a relief from being in the base, which was a horrible place, a city of cement on one of the highest mountains in Sinai. It was one of the first places to be bombed by the Egyptians in the Yom Kippur War. Being there, besieged, surrounded by this vastness of nothingness, just sand on sand, I needed to create for myself a more imaginative atmosphere. Writing created a kind of oasis in the desert.

INTERVIEWER

When did you write your first story?

GROSSMAN

I started writing stories as soon as I came out of the army in 1975, but I never showed them to anyone. The first one was called "Donkeys." It is about an American soldier who deserts during the Vietnam War and finds shelter in Austria, of all places. His only friends are a bunch of donkeys near a *Gasthof* somewhere. Once a month he comes with a car full of bread and he feeds them and gets some warmth from them.

INTERVIEWER

This was a leap, wasn't it? You weren't a writer—you had been on the radio, and you wrote in that officers' notebook. What made you decide to write fiction?

GROSSMAN

I know how it started. I was living with Michal, though we weren't married then, and we had a usual couple's quarrel. She did what women used to do back then in such situations: she packed all her belongings in a small bag—we didn't have a lot of stuff—and she left for her parents' place in Haifa. I was left in our little room in Jerusalem, and I was devastated. I felt that my life was over and I had no one to live for. Then I went to a table and I started to write "Donkeys." A moment before I did it I had no idea what I was going to write. Why I wrote this story of all stories, I have no idea. But in the first minutes that I did it, I knew I had found myself.

I always compare it to discovering sex. The moment before you do it, you have only a vague notion of what it will be like. It's threatening, it's attractive, it's everything. The moment after, you don't understand how you lived all your life without it. You immediately become an addict. You know that this is what you want to do.

INTERVIEWER

Do your story ideas usually come about in this kind of way—
seemingly out of nowhere?

GROSSMAN

I often feel that my subjects find me. When I start writing about a
character, a young lady, for instance, I don't understand why she is so
important to me. She is totally alien and comes from another milieu.
Yet gradually I see how choosing her was inevitable, and how she
evokes in me things that without her, I never would have been able to
explore. Then sometimes I'll have a character and not know what to
do with him. Take the novella "Frenzy," which I was writing, on and
off, for eleven years, between books. I began with the character of this
obsessive, jealous husband, but I couldn't find him a partner for his
voyage through the night. I tried putting him with his brother, with
his friend, there were three or four other attempts, and each time I felt
I could not write it, because I didn't have someone capable of balanc-
ing all his craziness. And then one day a character named Esti just
jumped to the page. I wasn't sure if I liked her. She was foreign to me,
but she forced her way in, and suddenly the book was completed. I
was so relieved. Having Esti allowed me to explore this rut of feelings, this monster, jealousy.

INTERVIEWER

Do you always begin with a character?

GROSSMAN

It varies from book to book. It can be an image or a vague story
idea. When I began *See Under: Love*, for the first half year I wrote a
story that took place at an institute for lepers in Jerusalem. I had this
idea of people who work somewhere—and they have to jump against
waterfalls in order to escape. I felt it wasn't the book that I wanted to
write, but I didn't know what the real book was.

Then I read about the salmon, which jumps against the falls. I remember walking with a friend, talking with amazement about the

salmon, and I did this movement in my head of going against the falls, and when I did it, I had this pang in my brain. I thought there was something very Jewish about the salmon's life cycle. It is born in a certain place, it swims out into the world, and then suddenly it gets a pulse in its brain and returns back to the place it was hatched. It struck me that this was what I was writing about without being aware of it. As soon as I realized this, everything fell into place.

Miracles can happen in the writing process. More often than in life, unfortunately. Sometimes I start a novel and I think it's the beginning, but it's the middle of the book. One thing is clear—I never write the conclusion of a book until I am very close to the end.

INTERVIEWER

Why?

GROSSMAN

If I know the end, the book will not surprise me, and more than that, it won't betray me. This is important: the book should betray me, in the sense that it should take me to places I am afraid to go. Take, for example, *The Book of Intimate Grammar*. I started with a totally different story from what is now in the book. It began like *Be My Knife*, with a thirty-five-year-old man falling in love with a woman he saw for just a few moments. But nine months into writing this, I felt that, in order to understand the main character, I needed to know something about his childhood. It was as if I was swept over by a wave. I started to write the story of this child, later to be called Aron, and for one year, the second year of writing, I wrote, in parallel, two different novels. They diverged more and more, and I suffered all the agonies and pleasures of bigamy. In the morning I would write one, and put all my soul in it, and then in the afternoon I would shamelessly steal good ideas from it to put into the other half.

INTERVIEWER

Do you have any strategies you employ when you get stuck?

GROSSMAN

Sometimes I write a letter to my protagonist, as if he were a real human being. I ask, What's the difficulty? Why can't you make it? What is preventing me from understanding you? It's always helped.

INTERVIEWER

You have said, "When writing fiction, it is of the utmost importance to be meticulous with facts." To what extent do you conduct research for your novels?

GROSSMAN

If I am going to write about a man joining a shoal of salmon, as in *See Under: Love*, I have to start by making the reality of the salmon very concrete and credible. So I joined divers, I became a salmon. I was unable to eat salmon for years—really. I felt like a cannibal when I ate salmon. When I wrote *The Zigzag Kid*, I joined the detective squad of the Jerusalem police for six months, spending almost every night with them. This is why I loved writing *The Yellow Wind*. It wasn't just that I read about the situation and interviewed certain people. I wanted to be there in the camps and in the prisons and at the West Bank universities and on the bridges of the Jordan. Research is a way to get out of myself and be in the world. In my new novel, I'm writing about a five-hundred-kilometer journey through Israel. People walk in a zigzagging path from the very north of the country to Jerusalem. So I went to the very north, to Galilee, and walked down here to my home. It took forty-five days.

INTERVIEWER

How do you know when you have come to the end of a novel?

GROSSMAN

When you get to the point where the novel is a world of its own, you can just humbly step back and allow your protagonists to work alone. This is the point when you should stop writing—you start to be tempted by the wealth of options that are open to you, so you have to be strict with yourself not to overdo it. The book has become its own complete world. You don't have to invent it, you just document it.

INTERVIEWER

Do you ever make significant changes to a manuscript after you turn it in?

GROSSMAN

When I turned in *Be My Knife*, it was written in the form of an epistolary novel—there were alternating letters from Yair to Miriam and from Miriam to Yair, and they had an equal presence. There was this mechanical pingpong between them. And then one night I had this idea just to take out all her letters, which was something like two hundred pages of the book.

INTERVIEWER

It's funny you should say this, because the reader tries to detect Miriam's answers, to see her reflection in the letters of Yair. But they actually exist?

GROSSMAN

Of course they exist. I wrote them all. But after I made the decision to cut them, I had to sit and write for another year, because I couldn't just uproot her letters. I had to find exactly the places in which Miriam would emerge from the cracks in the letters of Yair. It was complicated because she is the engine behind the whole plot. She creates him in a way, so it deeply upset me to take her out. I loved her, and I knew her so well, but I suddenly understood that removing her was an improvement over the traditional epistolary novel because, in such a book, if you have the letters of the two protagonists, it is as if you have two keys to the same safe. If you have both keys, you have the entire treasure. If you have only one key, however, then the reader has to produce his own key.

INTERVIEWER

In *The Smile of the Lamb*, Uri says, "Where is home anyway? Abner would say that home is the empty space between the tip of his pen and the paper." Is that how you feel?

GROSSMAN

Home is where the people I love are. The more I age, the more this world becomes alien to me, even hostile. The story that I'm writing is another home, though sometimes it takes two or three years before it becomes a home. I'm never alone when I have my story, where I know the tonus of every character and of the language.

INTERVIEWER

The tonus?

GROSSMAN

The tonus, the tension of the muscles. I immediately feel connected to the emotional vibrations of people in Israel, which I don't feel when I'm abroad.

INTERVIEWER

Yet you seem to have been greatly influenced by writers of the Jewish Diaspora.

GROSSMAN

When you're starting out as a writer, everyone tells you to whom you are similar and from whom you stole. When I was young I was very obedient, and I'd agree with whatever they told me. One guy who worked in Israeli television, a newcomer from Poland, called to tell me that *The Smile of the Lamb* was obviously influenced by Bruno Schulz. I said, Well, maybe. I had never heard of Bruno Schulz, but I didn't want to admit my ignorance.

As soon as I started reading Schulz I was electrified. Every paragraph is an explosion of different realities—of dreams and nightmares, imagination and fantasy. Reading him made me want to live more.

Then I read the stories about his death. He was being protected by a German officer, who had killed the Jewish dentist of another German officer. So the second German officer went after Schulz and shot him dead in the street. You killed my Jew—I killed yours, said the officer.

When I read this, I felt a powerful physical sensation of devastation. I didn't want to live in such a world where something like that could happen, where people can be seen as replaceable, disposable. I felt that I must redeem his needless, brutal death. So I wrote *See Under: Love*. I can tell you that in almost every language that my book was published—about thirteen languages—within a year or so there was a new edition of the stories of Bruno Schulz. It is such a sweet feeling for me to know that my book did something like that for him after what he did for me.

INTERVIEWER

Who, besides Schulz, influenced you?

GROSSMAN

Kafka, though it's hard to find a writer who's not influenced by Kafka, even if he does not write in a similar style. Kafka is a literary stage you have to go through. I always imagine Kafka as standing with his hands on the window, looking inside into life. It is as if he was looking out from death, even when he was alive. I don't find this in any other writer.

INTERVIEWER

Do you relate to the political situation he lived in?

GROSSMAN

It helps, but I'm not sure that political context is responsible for forming a writer. I think Kafka would be Kafka even if he were born in America, or England, or Australia. There is something unique about the angle with which he touches life.

When I started to write, people told me I was influenced by Joyce.

I'm ashamed to say it, but I had never read Joyce before, either. But of course I was influenced by him, even without having read him. You're influenced by oxygen, by carbon, by Joyce, and by Schulz and by Kafka. Siegfried Lenz was important too, and Heinrich Böll. When I read *Billiards at Half-Past Nine*, I suddenly understood how a story should be written. I was also influenced by the early stories of A. B. Yehoshua and Amos Oz. I read Yehoshua's "Facing the Forests" when I was an adolescent, and it was a revelation.

In recent years, I feel I'm less and less influenced by writers. I do not see this as a good sign, by the way. I want to be influenced by writers. I think it is a sign of being open. One wonderful writer whom I discovered recently is Clarice Lispector, a Jewish Brazilian writer who died thirty years ago. I felt as I did the first time I read Kafka.

INTERVIEWER

Where do you write?

GROSSMAN

When I was young, I wrote in the bedroom of our small apartment in Jerusalem. I couldn't imagine any other options, so it felt natural. It was a little uncomfortable, since my wife was working there as well. When I'm writing a book, I only read books about that topic. So when I was writing *See Under: Love*, my desk, the bed, the bedside table, and the floor were covered in dozens of books about the Shoah and the Second World War, and most of them had the swastika on their covers. It was like a monument to Nazism. That's when we decided I needed to have a room of my own. We couldn't let these atrocities infest our bedroom. Soon after that, we moved to a bigger house.

INTERVIEWER

So how do you do it now?

GROSSMAN

I start every morning around six by walking for an hour in the hills of Jerusalem—of Mevasseret—where we live. Then I go to work in a one-room apartment I rented in a village close to my home. When I was looking at the place, the landlady said, Unfortunately, there is no phone line here. I said, Wonderful! I'll take it. I go there every morning, no matter what, for six hours of total isolation.

Then you're done for the day?

No, then I go back and write at home. But I do different work in the afternoon or evening. I mostly revise what I wrote in the morning. I erase. It's less creative because life is around—family and friends.

Do you write on a computer?

I start in longhand. I fill dozens of notebooks, until the quantities of written pages are uncontrollable, and then I move to a computer. I write many versions. It's not a very economical way of writing.

When you spend four or five years on a novel, is it difficult to maintain the same tone and energy throughout the entire writing period?

When I'm writing a book that takes years to complete, I emerge from the last page totally different from who I was on page one. I learn constantly from my books. This is why it takes me so many years to write a novel, because I do not really understand what I write and why I write it. Only later do I understand what it wants to tell me. I'm not trying to mystify it—in a practical way, I think it is only through writing that I allow myself to experience things I would not be courageous enough for in real life.

INTERVIEWER

Among your novels there are a few books that have a more popular sensibility, while others can be quite difficult for the reader. When you start a project, do you know whether it will be a difficult book?

GROSSMAN

The more I write, the more I find that the most personal work will be understood the least. People do not expose themselves easily to intimacy. It's much easier for people to respond to lighter books, like *The Zigzag Kid* or *Someone to Run With*.

Yet for me, the books that really matter, the books that I cannot imagine my life without having written, are the more demanding ones, like *The Book of Intimate Grammar, Be My Knife, See Under: Love*, and the book I'm writing now. I may occasionally like to write an entertaining book, but I take literature seriously. You're dealing with explosives. You can change a reader's life, and you can change—you should change, I think—your own life.

Usually a lighter book will serve as a kind of recovery for me. I devastate myself when I write a certain kind of book—there is a process of dismantling my personality. All my defense mechanisms, everything settled and functioning, all the things concealed in life break into pieces, because I need to go to the place within me that is cracked, that is fragile, that is not taken for granted. I come out of these books devastated. I don't complain, of course. This is how books should be written. But my way to recover from this sense of total solitude is to write books that will bring me into close contact with other people. I wrote *The Zigzag Kid* because I had to recover from *The Book of Intimate Grammar* and *Sleeping on a Wire*.

INTERVIEWER

Sleeping on a Wire was a continuation of your project in *The Yellow Wind*. What drew you back to this material?

GROSSMAN

That book was a deep shock to me, because I realized that *The Yellow Wind* had addressed only half of the Israeli–Palestinian question. The other half, which I already thought might be the bigger half, was the question of the Palestinians within Israel.

INTERVIEWER

The more difficult half?

GROSSMAN

More internal, and complicated. We share the same definition—as Israelis—but what do they feel toward Israel as a state? As a Jewish state? They are citizens of a state that has declared it does not belong to them.

INTERVIEWER

In *Sleeping on a Wire* you say that Israelis and West Bank Palestinians share a mutual goal: both want to be separate from one another. But this book suggests that, try as they might, the two sides cannot be so easily separated.

GROSSMAN

We have to be together. I do not see that as a curse, as most Israelis on both sides do. I don't want to have a monolithic country. I want to have a diverse country. Jews and Arabs don't feel this diversity because we are so hostile to each other. If we could live in some security, then we would be able to explore both cultures in a free way. But we're a long ways away.

When I finished writing the book, I was shocked because I realized the depth of the danger. It's one thing to have a conflict with Palestinians on the other side of the border, and it's another thing to have it within our own state. The potential for destruction is much greater here.

INTERVIEWER

But you don't consider the Palestinians in Israel to be a fifth column.

GROSSMAN

Not at all. I see them as a challenge. It didn't start as a marriage of love. The common existence was imposed on both of us. But why not make the best of it? There is one-fifth of the population here that feels no benefit from the state, culturally, economically, humanly. They feel excommunicated, humiliated. It's almost suicide to give up on one-fifth of your population. Most Israelis know almost nothing about Arabs and regard them only as a security threat. A few of them are. I met some Arabs who want to have another state within Israel—not only the Palestinian state next to our borders, but another state within Israel, so we shall have three states, in Gaza, in the West Bank, and in Galilee. For me, this is too much. The idea of a binational state has very rarely worked elsewhere, especially not in places where both sides are so traumatized. I also think that right now we need a border between us and the Palestinians in the West Bank and in Gaza. This is important for me. Not a wall, but a border that is mutually agreed upon by the two parties.

It takes a lot of political maturity to achieve this idea. It's a lofty idea, but I can think of a loftier one: no borders at all, between all countries. This is my natural tendency. But it is not reality, especially not in our region.

INTERVIEWER

Do you consider yourself a post-Zionist?

GROSSMAN

No, not at all. Post-Zionists think that Israel should be a binational state. When I talk with my Palestinian Israeli friends, they tell me that if they were a majority here, they wouldn't envy us Jews. They do not trust their own ability to protect us or to allow us freedom. I'm sorry, but I don't want to take part in such an experiment. We've been through too many experiments as a people. I want the burden of proof to be on my people, not on them. I want us to be the ones who will be able to practice generosity and political maturity. For me, a major challenge for a Jewish state is for *all* its citizens to feel at home here.

You know, it's so easy to criticize the Jewish people. But the basic inspiration for Zionism was a noble idea, in my eyes: to allow the Jewish people to recover, to experience political and social and cultural normality in its own land, defended by its own army—this is something we have been deprived of for years. I do not sanctify war, but in our crazy, violent world, especially in the Middle East, having an army is an important, necessary thing.

INTERVIEWER

Does it seem strange to you—as a writer, a liberal—to say that?

GROSSMAN

It's only strange for people who don't live here. Whenever an Italian journalist interviews me, he describes me as a *pacifista*, because I struggle for peace. I try to explain to him that I am not a pacifist. A pacifist is someone who will not carry a gun, even if his mother is killed in front of him. I was a soldier for four years, I served in the reserves for another thirty years. My two sons were tank commanders. We have to defend ourselves. Having said all that, the way for us to redeem ourselves from this situation is not to adhere to the way of power, but to be more open, generous, and courageous. We've failed to do this. We've become addicted to our powers and our fears.

The Israelis and the Jews were always regarded as the people of the book, but also the people of the story. We are often treated not as people, but as a metaphor for something else. As if there is a lesson to be learned from our experience. This is what made us such an easy target for stereotypes, for prejudices. There's also something addictive in experiencing big events for hundreds of years, again and again, and living permanently in this extremity of experience.

This is something that I think peace will cure in us. If we shall have peace—if we shall have normality, if we shall feel that we have a future here, if we shall have fixed borders—then we might lose the sense that we are living a story distinct from other stories of the world. This is important, because if you live a larger-than-life story, you do not really experience the qualities of normal life—all the petty, small, routine domestic problems.

INTERVIEWER

Sleeping on a Wire seems to make the point that the Jewish experience and the Palestinian experience are shockingly similar.

GROSSMAN

You feel it immediately. When Israelis and Palestinians are together in free circumstances, especially outside of Israel, you can see how much warmth there is between the two peoples. I deeply believe that if we are given the chance—the privilege—to live in peace together, we will be good neighbors, because we understand each other on the individual level. We hate and suspect each other so much right now that every step made by one side is regarded as a trick or manipulation by the other side. In that sense, we are trapped.

There is, however, a big difference between the two peoples, which is the experience of the Shoah. Non-Jews will talk about the Shoah as they would any past event. What happened *then?* they will ask. Jews, in every language they speak, will talk about "what happened *there.*" To ask what happened then means it was and it is over. For Jews, in a tragic way, it's never over. It exists somewhere parallel to our life, it's an alternative option. I do not say this in any judgmental way. It is just our situation. It affects our social behavior, our personal behavior, our belief in the possibility of a future, the way we raise our children, and the way we run our politics. It's everywhere.

At my own wedding, my aunt—who had a number tattooed on her arm because she came from Auschwitz—was wearing a small Band-Aid over the number. I looked at it, and I looked in her eyes, and I realized that she had put it on to avoid casting gloom on the event. I was so sad. I thought, You can't hide it with a Band-Aid!

INTERVIEWER

Yet in *Death as a Way of Life* you say, "I don't belong to those who believe that the Holocaust was a specifically Jewish event."

GROSSMAN

I don't think one can separate the Jewishness from the Shoah, but it is an event that's relevant for all humanity. Every human being should ask himself several questions regarding the Shoah. One of them is, In the face of such total arbitrariness, how can I maintain my uniqueness as a human being? What in me cannot be eradicated?

In *Be My Knife*, I call this idea the *luz*, the kernel. *Luz* is a word from the Talmud. It's the smallest bone in your backbone, which cannot be eradicated. All your essence is preserved in it, and from that you will be recreated in resurrection. Sometimes I do a little exercise: I ask people to close their eyes and for one minute to think what would be their *luz*. The pupil of the eye of their personality. I get interesting answers.

INTERVIEWER

What is your *luz*?

GROSSMAN

I guess it has to do with the urge to create.

INTERVIEWER

You write, in *Sleeping on a Wire*, of the need to "open myself to the complexity" of Palestinians in Israel, to "make room for them within us." This process seems to transpire in many of your books, of one person opening himself or herself to the existence of another. Is this a case where the political situation shapes your fiction?

GROSSMAN

I'd like to believe that I would have written about these things had I lived in the United States or anywhere else. But living in a place with such destructive potential, it's tempting to lock oneself away from the outside world.

We're sitting here on this veranda, and it's very green and birds are singing, but the tension is everywhere. It's tiring, being an Israeli. There are almost no neutral places in the landscape, in the people you encounter, in the language, in the stories people tell you. Everything here is saturated, and sometimes poisoned, with meaning. In my last two books, I wrote stories detached, in a way, from the immediate reality—I wanted to create a bubble of intimacy, of everydayness, that is unaffected by politics. Because sometimes we forget that there are some places where we are just human beings, thank God, and not Israelis.

INTERVIEWER

Is it a curse to have all your work interpreted through the lens of the Israeli–Palestinian conflict?

GROSSMAN

It feels like being abused. When *Her Body Knows* was published in Italy, an interviewer asked me, Is the broken leg of Shaul a metaphor for the shattered Israeli Zionist dream? Can you imagine? I almost walked out of the room. This tendency to interpret everything that comes from Israel politically, to pigeonhole it as a political metaphor, is infuriating. It's really a sign of misunderstanding—not of Israel, but of literature. Literature has many layers, and only one is political. Just because we're Israelis, it doesn't mean we aren't jealous of our wives, we don't fall in love, raise children, and act primal. We are human before we are Israelis. For normal people it can be quite tough to live here, but for a writer it's paradise. It's a passionate place, and I regard it as a privilege.

INTERVIEWER

What are the limitations and advantages of writing in Hebrew?

GROSSMAN

One can play with all the different layers of Hebrew, from the biblical to the Rabbinic to all the other periods, up to the most recent

Israeli slang. But bear in mind that for eighteen hundred years people did not speak Hebrew, they only used it in writing and in prayer. It was not spoken by children, or soldiers, or during sex—so it lacked the domestic layer of everydayness. Israeli slang is prolific and tight now—it's a language of its own. A lot of it is generated in the army, and you can use it to express almost everything. Since Israel is an immigrant-absorbing country, the slang also serves as a common denominator for people who come from, say, Russia and Ethiopia.

INTERVIEWER

Do you know the slang?

GROSSMAN

I have children, so I am exposed to it constantly. It gives vitality to the language, but it's dangerous in that it contributes to the constant process of Hebrew's deterioration. Fewer and fewer children are able to read the Bible, and the Talmud is out of the question. I had to translate chapters from the Bible for my children because their teachers couldn't make sense of its language, or at least its linguistic connotations and associations. Obviously, it is less significant for them than it was for those of us who grew up in the fifties and sixties, when acquiring the high Hebrew was crucial to our becoming Israelis.

Sometimes when I write a word and realize that it won't be widely understood, I ask myself whether I should use it. It worries me, because if the language we use is dull and flat, then our reality will become flat.

INTERVIEWER

In *See Under: Love*, you talk about the word *frustration*, which did not appear in the Hebrew vocabulary till the mid-seventies. You write that "people who spoke only Hebrew were never *frustrated*. They may have been *angry* or *disappointed*, or they may have experienced a sense of turmoil in certain situations, but the acute feeling of frustration itself was unknown to them until the word for it was translated from the English language."

GROSSMAN

And how happily we all became frustrated when we got the word! I remember the sense of revelation when we had suddenly found a name for this feeling. Before we had the word, *tiskul*, we just had this vague and upsetting feeling of a sense that is not accurate or not sharp. Then again, maybe there are a hundred kinds of *tiskul* that we are unaware of because we put it all in one word, and maybe later we will find other, more nuanced versions of *tiskul*.

INTERVIEWER

Does this present an open canvas to the writer—new opportunities to shape contemporary Hebrew as you're writing it?

GROSSMAN

Hebrew is a flexible language and it surrenders enthusiastically to all kinds of wordplay. You can talk in slang about the Bible and you can speak biblically about everyday life. You can invent words that people can easily understand, because almost every word has a root, and people know the derivation or can usually figure it out. It is a very sexy language. It is gigantic, heroic, and glorious, but at the same time it has large gaps that yearn to be filled by writers.

INTERVIEWER

So is this, then, the writer's duty?

GROSSMAN

Yes, the writer should never take anything for granted, not formulations or words or reality. This is one of the reasons I'm so fascinated by children—they never take anything for granted. Everything is surprising, new, a constant revelation. I remember coming back from summer vacation and finding my best friend one head taller than me. Or how, one day, the house started suddenly to fill with people, and grandma is crying and grandpa is somewhere and doesn't come back, and no one tells you where he is. Or people are whispering secrets—it seemed that whenever I entered a room as a child, somebody shut his mouth, as if something horrible had just been discussed.

One night when my son was three years old, as I was putting him to bed, I explained that it was the twenty-first of December—the longest night of the year. I tucked him in and kissed him good night. The next morning, at first light, he burst into our room, all sweaty and excited and relieved, and he shouted, Daddy, Mommy, it's over, this night is over! Can you imagine what landscapes he had wandered through all night? Because he did not take it for granted that the sun would ever rise again.

When I write, I try to bring myself to this point. I want to be betrayed, to be taken to a dangerous place that jars the basic presumptions I have about myself, my family, my country.

INTERVIEWER

Do you show your writing to anyone while you're working?

GROSSMAN

Yes, but with the book I am writing now, for example, it was only after four years of work that I was able to show it to my wife and a couple of friends.

INTERVIEWER

Is your wife your first reader?

GROSSMAN

Always. Even before she reads the text, we talk about it all the time. The novel I'm working on is something like another life within our life. We also discuss her work—she's a clinical psychologist.

INTERVIEWER

A. B. Yehoshua's wife is also a psychologist.

GROSSMAN

It's a good combination because the two professions are so close to each other. Michal affects me by her profession and I affect her by my profession. But more than her job, I have been deeply changed by our marriage, and by her family. I became a leftist because of her. I remember the first time Michal and I fought about politics. We had met in the army, as young soldiers, and one night we went to see a cabaret by Hanoch Levin, a leftist playwright, a genius. He said the most outrageous things about the occupation and about the way we treated Palestinians. I was eighteen and had never been exposed to this sentiment. I was shocked. Meanwhile her grandfather was a communist, and their family was very much against the occupation, which I learned the first time I came to their home. It was eye-opening for me.

INTERVIEWER

You are often grouped together with Yehoshua and Amos Oz. Do you feel a sense of competition with them?

GROSSMAN

I think we are good partners. In other countries there would probably be a lot of jealousy and competition. I cannot say there is no jealousy among writers in Israel—it's something that's natural. There's even a Hebrew proverb about it: *Kin'at sofrim tarbeh hochmah.* Jealousy of writers will produce more wisdom.

INTERVIEWER

What does that mean?

GROSSMAN

It means that competition is good, it forces you to be more creative.

INTERVIEWER

Your characters are often preoccupied with language and words. In *See Under: Love*, Momik plays a game where he counts out the number of letters in a word on his fingers. Aron, in *Intimate Grammar*, chooses certain special words he can't speak for seven days until they are "purified." And Shaul, in "Frenzy," becomes convinced that his wife is having an affair because she is using new words and learning Portuguese. In *Be My Knife*, Yair writes, "I once thought of teaching my son a private language. Isolating him from the speaking world on purpose, lying to him from the moment of his birth, so he would believe only the language I gave him." What does this mean to you, this private language?

GROSSMAN

I think this is probably the first motivation that makes somebody a writer: the need to name things by your own private names. It's also a way to make the outside world less alien. By using a personal language— achieved by certain tempo combinations, particular uses of specific words—readers can feel the fingerprint of your inner world, and I think they respond to it.

INTERVIEWER

At the same time, in your books there is a persistent suspicion of the potential for dishonesty and manipulation through language.

GROSSMAN

Living in Israel for so many years, I've seen how easy it is to manipulate language. People are almost eager to be manipulated, because they do not want to know about the reality in which they live—it is too harsh to bear. They use a false language that provides a buffer between them and reality, which is the opposite of what language is supposed to do. This includes, for example, the denial of the enemy by demonization, stereotypes, emphasizing only the negative elements.

At the same time, we cannot really aspire to have the total truth, we just have to point out the ambiguity of language. This is very important, because I don't know what is absolutely right or wrong, but when I use the terms my government uses to describe the situation, I should also infuse another point of view.

I am involved with an organization called Keshev, which means *attention*. It's an organization that runs a project created by Israelis and Palestinians to monitor the language that is being used in both the Israeli and the Arab press. It's fascinating to see how easy it is to manipulate public opinion through the space you give to news reports in the papers, or through a headline, which sometimes contradicts the article's contents. Lies are reported until they filter into the mind of the people. Take, for example, the idea, so deeply rooted in Israel, that we don't have a partner among the Palestinians at all. In Keshev, we systematically investigate how this opinion is created through television and radio reports.

INTERVIEWER
Not so long ago, you weren't supposed to say *Palestinian*.

GROSSMAN
People were infuriated with me, in fact, because I used the term in *Sleeping on a Wire*. They said, Why do you give them ideas? The other Arabs are Egyptians, Syrians, Jordanians—only the Israeli Palestinians are just called Arabs, because we are afraid of the term *Palestinian*.

When I was a radio anchorman, I had a specific dictionary of words and terms that I was forbidden to use. I couldn't refer to the "occupied territories." Every day I had to report about a Palestinian killed by Israeli soldiers, and the phrase I had to use was, "During disturbances in the territories, a local youngster was killed." Every word in this phrase is a lie. "During disturbances," as if there was a specific order that has been violated; "in the territories," to avoid saying the occupied territories or the occupation; "a local," to avoid saying "Palestinian"—God forbid them finding out they are Palestinians, they might rebel against us; "youngster," he could have been two or three years old. And we always used the passive construction, "was killed," so we didn't have to mention who actually took a gun and shot the child dead.

We never even used victims' names, until some of us protested that we must mention the names of the people whom the army killed. Even if people support the occupation, they should bear some responsibility for the fact that our soldiers, in the name of this policy, killed a certain person.

Are there books of yours that you feel have been misunderstood, even in Israel?

My political books have been attacked fiercely by the right-wingers. *The Yellow Wind*, for example, created a wave of hatred, and not only with letters and phone calls. They sabotaged our car. They blocked the radiator, so after driving three kilometers the car started smoking. We were with the two boys in the car. I was also scolded publicly by Prime Minister Yitzhak Shamir and I was eventually fired from the radio.

What did Shamir say?

I was an anchorman of the morning news magazine so I had to interview him on the occasion of the twentieth anniversary of the Six-Day War, a national holiday. He wanted to have a big military parade, and I asked whether that was really necessary when the country was in such a horrible economic situation. Couldn't we use the money for other purposes? I also asked him about the Palestinians, suggesting that they might stage a rebellion.

He got red in the face, and then suddenly took his microphone and threw it away. He said, You can invent everything in your fiction, writer, in your imagination. The Arabs and the Palestinians have never been in a better situation than they are under our government. They will never do what you say. He left the room and refused to continue the interview.

Then there was a lot of negotiation. I was stuck there in his cabinet room, alone with one of his assistants and a technician. What do you do in such a situation? He finally came back to finish the interview, but for the next year and a half he refused to give interviews to me. I was one of the two chief anchormen, and I couldn't interview the prime minister. Can you imagine? The irony was that half a year after that, the intifada broke out. The things that I wrote about in *The Yellow Wind* became true. His policy turned out to be a total disaster.

Despite your public persona, you are a very private person. Yet the private catastrophe of your son's death has become the grief of the country. How do you cope with that?

GROSSMAN

It has been difficult and very strange, because grief has such a private nature. Yet I feel that so many people, inside and outside of Israel, had reactions of deep empathy and shock. I got many responses from Palestinians, from Egyptians, Lebanese, Jordanians, Iraqis, and Iranians, who wrote to me or who told me on various occasions that it was the first time that they felt sorrow for an Israeli soldier. Now, for me, he is not an Israeli soldier, he is my son. But there is something that touched my heart when I was told that.

I am unable to talk about Uri publicly. I spoke in the eulogy because that is the place where a father can mourn his son, but I cannot talk about him publicly in any other way. Not even a year has passed since it happened. I need him to be private. I'm sorry.

INTERVIEWER

Has your personal tragedy affected your writing in any way?

GROSSMAN

When I'm not writing, I'm in a different place with my grief. Four years ago, when Uri joined the army, I started writing a novel that became very relevant in my life. The novel met with reality in an unexpected way. The word *glad* seems inappropriate here, but I am glad that I was writing this novel and not any other novel of mine, because the place I created in the three years and two months before he fell is now the only place where I can be with this fact of what has happened to me, to us. I can be there totally, as I want to be in any circumstances that I'm writing about—unprotected and totally exposed, to lament it and at the same time to feel the extreme vitality of what was lost. So the difficulty of diving into a novel these days is not only because I live in Israel, in this crazy, violent reality, but because I live a certain life now. It's very hard for me to talk about it.

INTERVIEWER

Do you feel life is not so good anymore?

GROSSMAN

It's a painful life now. It's like hell in slow motion, all the time. I don't try to escape grief, I face grief in an intense way in my writing, but not only in my writing. If I have to suffer, I want to understand my situation thoroughly. It's not an easy place to be, but so be it. If I'm doomed to it I want—it's a human predicament and I want to experience it.

One thing I know for sure is that if I did not write these characters, these stories, I would be much less happy and probably much less normal. Writing allows me to explore situations that are impossible for me to explore in my life. And yet they are very active parts in me. Emotionally I am an extreme person, and writing makes it possible for me to go on.

INTERVIEWER

What do you mean by *extreme*?

GROSSMAN

Intense, not afraid of extremity in other people, intrigued by the interior lives of other people, especially in the suppressed places. I'm always questioning what I observe. All the time I see the cracks, wherever I look—even before what happened to me. It's a way of seeing, and I cannot say I chose it, but I surrendered to it quite happily because I think it's an accurate view of the fragility of life. Anything that is calm and safe seems to me like an illusion.

Issue 182, 2007

Marilynne Robinson

The Art of Fiction

When Marilynne Robinson published her first novel, *House-keeping*, in 1980, she was unknown in the literary world. But an early review in *The New York Times* ensured that the book would be noticed. "It's as if, in writing it, she broke through the ordinary human condition with all its dissatisfactions, and achieved a kind of transfiguration," wrote Anatole Broyard, with an enthusiasm and awe that was shared by many critics and readers. The book became a classic, and Robinson was hailed as one of the defining American writers of our time. Yet it would be more than twenty years before she wrote another novel.

In the interval, Robinson devoted herself to writing nonfiction. Her essays and book reviews appeared in *Harper's* and *The New York Times Book Review*, and in 1989 she published *Mother Country: Britain, the Welfare State, and Nuclear Pollution*, a scathing examination of the environmental and public health dangers posed by the Sellafield nuclear reprocessing plant in England—and the political and moral corruption that sustained it. In 1998, Robinson published a collection of her critical and theological writings, *The Death of Adam: Essays on Modern Thought*, which featured reassessments of such figures as Charles Darwin, John Calvin, and Friedrich Nietzsche. Aside from a single short story—"Connie Bronson," published in *The Paris Review* in 1986—it wasn't until 2004 that she returned to fiction with the novel *Gilead*, which won the National the rope and sort. It took him the whole day, but he did it. He's a clever, good-hearted young fellow, and he's been a great comfort to his father and mother. It appears he won't choose the ministry

The thump in my chest —

— of a thorn in my heart, more particularly. It goes on and on like some old cow chewing her cud, that same dull endlessness and contentment, so it seems to me. I wake up at night, and I hear it. Once more, it says. Once more, once more, once more.

"Preservation is a creation, and more, it is a continued creation, and a creation every moment." If any heart has ever said "once more," and the moment is gone before just as the word is said the moment is gone, so there is not even any sort of promise about it. Well, if B. Roberts is right, this old body is as new a creation as you are yourself. There's a mystery in the thought of the recreation of an old man as an old man, with all the defects and injuries of what is called his life faithfully preserved in him, and all their claims and all their tendencies honored, too, as in the steady progress of arthritis in my left knee.

I have thought sometimes that the Lord must hold the whole of our lives in memory, so to speak. Of course he does. And "memory" is the wrong word, no doubt. But the finger I broke sliding into second base when I was twenty-two years old is as crookeder ever, and I can interpret that fact as a very intimate attention

A manuscript page from *Gilead* by Marilynne Robinson.

Book Critics Circle Award and the Pulitzer Prize. Her third novel, *Home*, came out this fall.

In person, even when clad in her favorite writing attire—a pair of loose pants and a sweatshirt—Robinson carries herself with a regal elegance. While she is humble about her accomplishments and the acclaim they have brought her, the force of her intellect is apparent. In her nonfiction books, as well as in her recent novels, she passionately engages public policy as well as philosophical and theological scholarship. Her experience in academia—she wrote a Ph.D. dissertation on Shakespeare's *Henry VI, Part II* at the University of Washington—made her a devout reader of primary texts, which remain the touchstones of her thought and conversation. Such intellectual pursuits clearly delight her. Her extemporizing on, say, Karl Marx's *Capital* is often punctuated with laughter and blithe phrases such as "Oh, goody!" When a question gave her pause during our interview, she'd often shrug and say, "Calvin again," and then look away as if the sixteenth-century Frenchman were standing in the room waiting to give her advice.

Robinson is a Christian whose faith is not easily reduced to generalities. Calvin's thought has had a strong influence on her, and she depicts him in her essays as a misunderstood humanist, likening his "secularizing tendencies" to the "celebrations of the human one finds in Emerson and Whitman."

Her novels could also be described as celebrations of the human— the characters that inhabit them are indelible creations. *Housekeeping* is the story of Ruth and her sister Lucille, who are cared for by their eccentric Aunt Sylvie after their mother commits suicide. Robinson dwells on how each of the three is changed by their new life together. *Gilead* is an even more intimate exploration of personality: the book is given over to John Ames, a seventy-seven-year-old pastor who is writing an account of his life and his family history to leave to his young son after he dies. *Home* borrows characters from *Gilead* but centers on Ames's friend Reverend Robert Boughton and his troubled son Jack. Robinson returned to the same territory as *Gilead* because, she said, "after I write a novel or a story, I miss the characters—I feel sort of bereaved."

Gilead and *Home* are both set in Iowa, where Robinson has lived for nearly twenty years, teaching at the Writers' Workshop at the University of Iowa. For this interview, we met on six occasions over a five-month period. During that time, Iowa City seemed to experience every extreme of weather: two blizzards, frigid temperatures, hail, fog, spring rains, and severe thunderstorms. Shortly after our final meeting, the Iowa River reached record-setting flood levels.

Robinson leads a relatively solitary life. She is divorced, and her two sons are grown with families of their own. Her intellectual and creative ambitions leave little time for socializing. "I have this sense of urgency about what I want to get done and I discipline myself by keeping to myself," she said. But she also has both a cell phone and a BlackBerry and during our conversations the world would occasionally intrude to interrupt her stream of thought. At one point her BlackBerry beeped to tell her she had an e-mail, and she said it was from a former student. "Blurbs," she said. "I owe the world blurbs."

—*Sarah Fay, 2008*

INTERVIEWER

Are there any unpublished Marilynne Robinson novels lying around that we don't know about?

MARILYNNE ROBINSON

In college, I was in a novel-writing class and I started a novel, which I loathed and detested the minute I graduated. It was as if worms had popped out of it or something. It was set in the Middle West, where I had never been—a little midwestern town with a river running through it. Isn't that odd?

INTERVIEWER

What eventually drew you to Iowa City?

ROBINSON

The Workshop. I didn't have any realistic conception of Iowa at all. I never expected to live in the Middle West because I had the same prejudices that other people have about the region. But when they invited me to teach here I thought it would be an interesting thing to do. So I came.

INTERVIEWER

Were you told that it would compromise your creative energies to teach creative writing?

ROBINSON

Yes, of course. But everything compromises your creative energies. Years ago I accepted a grant from the American Academy that was supposed to support me for five years without teaching. I lasted about a year and a half before I nearly went crazy. Teaching is a distraction and a burden, but it's also an incredible stimulus. And a reprieve, in a way. When you're trying to work on something and it's not going anywhere, you can go to school and there's a two-and-a-half-hour block of time in which you can accomplish something.

INTERVIEWER

When you were little, what did you think you'd be when you grew up?

ROBINSON

Oh, a hermit? My brother told me I was going to be a poet. I had a good brother. He did a lot of good brotherly work. There we were in this tiny town in Idaho, and he was like Alexander dividing up the world: I'll be the painter, you'll be the poet.

INTERVIEWER

Is it true that *Housekeeping* started as a series of metaphors you wrote while you were getting your Ph.D. in English literature?

ROBINSON

When I went to college, I majored in American literature, which was unusual then. But it meant that I was broadly exposed to nineteenth-century American literature. I became interested in the way that American writers used metaphoric language, starting with Emerson. When I entered the Ph.D. program, I started writing these metaphors down just to get the feeling of writing in that voice. After I finished my dissertation, I read through the stack of metaphors and they cohered in a way that I hadn't expected. I could see that I had created something that implied much more. So I started writing *Housekeeping*, and the characters became important for me. I told a friend of mine, a writer named John Clayton, that I had been working on this thing, and he asked to see it. The next thing I knew, I got a letter from his agent saying that she would be happy to represent it.

INTERVIEWER

Were you surprised?

ROBINSON

I was, but these things always came with little caveats. She said, I'll be happy to represent it but it could be difficult to place. She gave it to an editor at Farrar, Straus and Giroux, who wrote to me and said, We'd be very happy to publish it but it probably won't be reviewed.

INTERVIEWER

But then it was.

ROBINSON

Anatole Broyard—God love him—reviewed it early because he thought no one would review it and he wanted to make sure it got attention.

INTERVIEWER

How did you approach creating the characters of Ruthie and Sylvie in *Housekeeping*?

ROBINSON

In the development of every character there's a kind of emotional entanglement that occurs. The characters that interest me are the ones that seem to pose questions in my own thinking. The minute that you start thinking about someone in the whole circumstance of his life to the extent that you can, he becomes mysterious, immediately.

INTERVIEWER

Was your family religious?

ROBINSON

My family was pious and Presbyterian mainly because my grandfather was pious and Presbyterian, but that was more of an inherited intuition than an actual fact. We would talk more politics than anything else at the dinner table. And they were very Republican politics, I need hardly say. Or perhaps I do need to say.

INTERVIEWER

What did your father do for a living?

ROBINSON

He worked his way up in the lumber industry the old-fashioned way. The lumber industry was dominant in that part of Idaho. When you fly over the Rocky Mountains now, you see terrible clear-cutting, but back then there wasn't the level of exploitation that there is now.

INTERVIEWER

How did your family come to settle in the West?

ROBINSON

We have a family legend about homesteading relatives in the nineteenth century—coming in covered wagons—dark forests, wolves, American Indians coming to ask for pie. My great grandmother was one of the first white people in a certain part of eastern Washington, and supposedly she would see an Indian standing outside the door, and she would go out, and he would say, Pie. That's just a story, but the women in my family always bake pies. And they're vain about it.

INTERVIEWER

Do you bake pies?

ROBINSON

I used to bake pies, when I had people to eat them. But I don't any more.

INTERVIEWER

What was your best pie?

ROBINSON

Lemon meringue, which is a family tradition.

INTERVIEWER

You've published only one short story, "Connie Bronson," which appeared a few years after *Housekeeping*. Have you written others since then?

ROBINSON

I wrote that story in college. I had a sort of fondness for it because it seemed to me to anticipate *Housekeeping*, though I had written it more than a decade earlier. So when *The Paris Review* asked me for something, I sent it off. I am actually interested by the fact that I never feel any impulse to write a short story. It is such an attractive form.

"Connie Bronson" has for me now the interest and charm of anyone's juvenilia—that is, almost none at all.

INTERVIEWER

In your second novel, *Gilead*, the protagonist is a pastor, John Ames. Do you think of yourself as a religious writer?

ROBINSON

I don't like categories like religious and not religious. As soon as religion draws a line around itself it becomes falsified. It seems to me that anything that is written compassionately and perceptively probably satisfies every definition of religious whether a writer intends it to be religious or not.

INTERVIEWER

You said that Ames came to you as a voice. How did you know that it was your next novel?

ROBINSON

I was at the Fine Arts Work Center in Provincetown at Christmas time. Some students had asked me to come to do a reading. I reserved several rooms at an inn in the sunniest part of Provincetown, so that my sons, neither of whom was married at the time, could spend Christmas there with me. But they got delayed, so I had several days there by myself in an otherwise empty hotel, in a little room with Emily Dickinson light pouring in through the windows and the ocean roaring beyond. I had a spiral notebook, and I started thinking about this situation and the voice. And I started writing. Frankly, I was happy for the company.

I ended up writing that book like a serial novel. I would write thirty pages or so and then send it to the editor, and then write thirty more pages and send it to the editor.

INTERVIEWER

Do you write longhand normally, or on a computer, or both?

ROBINSON

On *Gilead* I went back and forth. *Housekeeping* I wrote longhand. I didn't have a computer, and I've always been distracted by the sound of a typewriter.

INTERVIEWER

How long did it take you to write *Gilead*?

ROBINSON

I wrote it in about eighteen months. I write novels quickly, which is not my reputation.

INTERVIEWER

Ames says that in our everyday world there is "more beauty than our eyes can bear." He's living in America in the late 1950s. Would he say that today?

ROBINSON

You have to have a certain detachment in order to see beauty for yourself rather than something that has been put in quotation marks to be understood as "beauty." Think about Dutch painting, where sunlight is falling on a basin of water and a woman is standing there in the clothes that she would wear when she wakes up in the morning—that beauty is a casual glimpse of something very ordinary. Or a painting like Rembrandt's *Carcass of Beef*, where a simple piece of meat caught his eye because there was something mysterious about it. You also get that in Edward Hopper: Look at the sunlight! or Look at the human being! These are instances of genius. Cultures cherish artists because they are people who can say, Look at that. And it's not Versailles. It's a brick wall with a ray of sunlight falling on it.

At the same time, there has always been a basic human tendency toward a dubious notion of beauty. Think about cultures that rarify themselves into courts in which people paint themselves with lead paint and get dumber by the day, or women have ribs removed to have their waists cinched tighter. There's no question that we have our versions of that now. The most destructive thing we can do is act as though this is some sign of cultural, spiritual decay rather than humans just acting human, which is what we're doing most of the time.

INTERVIEWER

Ames believes that one of the benefits of religion is "it helps you concentrate. It gives you a good basic sense of what is being asked of you and also what you might as well ignore." Is this something that your faith and religious practice has done for you?

ROBINSON

Religion is a framing mechanism. It is a language of orientation that presents itself as a series of questions. It talks about the arc of life and the quality of experience in ways that I've found fruitful to think about. Religion has been profoundly effective in enlarging human imagination and expression. It's only very recently that you couldn't see how the high arts are intimately connected to religion.

INTERVIEWER

Is this frame of religion something we've lost?

ROBINSON

There was a time when people felt as if structure in most forms were a constraint and they attacked it, which in a culture is like an autoimmune problem: the organism is not allowing itself the conditions of its own existence. We're cultural creatures and meaning doesn't simply generate itself out of thin air; it's sustained by a cultural framework. It's like deciding how much more interesting it would be if you had no skeleton: you could just slide under the door.

INTERVIEWER

How does science fit into this framework?

ROBINSON

I read as much as I can of contemporary cosmology because reality itself is profoundly mysterious. Quantum theory and classical physics, for instance, are both lovely within their own limits and yet at present they cannot be reconciled with each other. If different systems don't merge in a comprehensible way, that's a flaw in our comprehension and not a flaw in one system or the other.

INTERVIEWER

Are religion and science simply two systems that don't merge?

ROBINSON

The debate seems to be between a naive understanding of religion and a naive understanding of science. When people try to debunk religion, it seems to me they are referring to an eighteenth-century notion of what science is. I'm talking about Richard Dawkins here, who has a status that I can't quite understand. He acts as if the physical world that is manifest to us describes reality exhaustively. On the other side, many of the people who articulate and form religious expression have not acted in good faith. The us-versus-them mentality is a terrible corruption of the whole culture.

INTERVIEWER

You've written critically about Dawkins and the other New Atheists. Is it their disdain for religion and championing of pure science that troubles you?

ROBINSON

No, I read as much pure science as I can take in. It's a fact that their thinking does not feel scientific. The whole excitement of science is that it's always pushing toward the discovery of something that it cannot account for or did not anticipate. The New Atheist types, like Dawkins, act as if science had revealed the world as a closed system. That simply is not what contemporary science is about. A lot of scientists are atheists, but they don't talk about reality in the same way that Dawkins does. And they would not assume that there is a simple-as-that kind of response to everything in question. Certainly not on the grounds of anything that science has discovered in the last hundred years.

The science that I prefer tends toward cosmology, theories of quantum reality, things that are finer-textured than classical physics in terms of their powers of description. Science is amazing. On a mote of celestial dust, we have figured out how to look to the edge of our universe. I feel instructed by everything I have read. Science has a lot of the satisfactions for me that good theology has.

INTERVIEWER

But doesn't science address an objective notion of reality while religion addresses how we conceive of ourselves?

ROBINSON

As an achievement, science is itself a spectacular argument for the singularity of human beings among all things that exist. It has a prestige that comes with unambiguous changes in people's experience—space travel, immunizations. It has an authority that's based on its demonstrable power. But in discussions of human beings it tends to compare downwards: we're intelligent because hyenas are intelligent and we just took a few more leaps.

The first obligation of religion is to maintain the sense of the value of human beings. If you had to summarize the Old Testament, the summary would be: stop doing this to yourselves. But it is not in our nature to stop harming ourselves. We don't behave consistently with our own dignity or with the dignity of other people. The Bible reiterates this endlessly.

INTERVIEWER

Did you ever have a religious awakening?

ROBINSON

No, a mystical experience would be wasted on me. Ordinary things have always seemed numinous to me. One Calvinist notion deeply implanted in me is that there are two sides to your encounter with the world. You don't simply perceive something that is statically present, but in fact there is a visionary quality to all experience. It means something because it is addressed to *you*. This is the individualism that you find in Walt Whitman and Emily Dickinson. You can draw from perception the same way a mystic would draw from a vision.

INTERVIEWER

How would one learn to see ordinary things this way?

ROBINSON

It's not an acquired skill. It's a skill that we're born with that we lose. We learn not to do it.

INTERVIEWER

On occasion you give sermons at your church. How did that come about?

ROBINSON

If we need someone to give a sermon because the pastor is ill or out of town then typically they ask someone from the congregation to give the sermon. Since I write about these things, often they ask me.

INTERVIEWER

Do you ever get nervous being the sub?

ROBINSON

Yes, I do. You're talking within a congregation. They know the genre. There are many things that the sermon has to resonate with besides the specific text that is the subject of the sermon. In my tradition, there's a certain posture of graciousness you have to answer to no matter what the main subject matter of the sermon is.

INTERVIEWER

Graciousness?

ROBINSON

The idea that you draw a line and say, The righteous people are on this side and the bad people are on the other side—this is not gracious.

INTERVIEWER

Your new novel *Home* is set in the same time and place as *Gilead* and incorporates many of the same characters. Why did you decide to return to their story?

ROBINSON

After I write a novel or a story, I miss the characters—I feel sort of bereaved. So I was braced for the experience after *Gilead*. Then I thought, If these characters are so strongly in my mind, why not write them? With Jack and old Boughton especially, and with Glory also, I felt like there were whole characters that had not been fully realized in Ames's story. I couldn't really see the point in abandoning them.

Then I had to make sure that the chronology clicked and certain phrases that occur in the first book occur in the second. For example, the dinner party—Ames is there but doesn't say a word about it in *Gilead*. It's completely consistent with Ames as a character that he would not choose to report a situation that he found painful or that he thought would reinforce unfortunate memories. But I wanted *Home* to be a freestanding book. I didn't want it to be a sequel. I wanted it to be true that you could pick up either book first.

INTERVIEWER

Whereas *Gilead* reads almost like a meditation—John Ames is writing it to his son—*Home* has a different personality.

ROBINSON

So much of the novel is dialogue. I was really surprised. I kept thinking, I've got to stop doing this—it's just one dialogue scene after another.

INTERVIEWER

Do you plot your novels?

ROBINSON

I really don't. There was a frame, of course, for *Home*, because it had to be symbiotic with *Gilead*. Aside from that, no. I feel strongly that action is generated out of character. And I don't give anything a higher priority than character. The one consistent thing among my novels is that there's a character who stays in my mind. It's a character with complexity that I want to know better.

INTERVIEWER

The focus of the novel is Jack, but it's told from Glory's point of view. Did you ever consider putting it in his point of view?

ROBINSON

Jack is thinking all the time—thinking too much—but I would lose Jack if I tried to get too close to him as a narrator. He's alienated in a complicated way. Other people don't find him comprehensible and he doesn't find them comprehensible.

INTERVIEWER

Is it hard to write a "bad" character?

ROBINSON

Calvin says that God takes an aesthetic pleasure in people. There's no reason to imagine that God would choose to surround himself into infinite time with people whose only distinction is that they fail to transgress. King David, for example, was up to a lot of no good. To think that only faultless people are worthwhile seems like an incredible exclusion of almost everything of deep value in the human saga. Sometimes I can't believe the narrowness that has been attributed to God in terms of what he would approve and disapprove.

INTERVIEWER

How do you write historical figures in your novels?

ROBINSON

My unvarying approach to anything is to read the most primary and proximate material that I can find. I try to be discreet in my use of historical figures. My John Brown is only a voice heard in the darkness.

INTERVIEWER

Does your faith ever conflict with your "regular life"?

ROBINSON

When I'm teaching, sometimes issues come up. I might read a scene in a student's story that seems—by my standards—pornographic. I don't believe in exploiting or treating with disrespect even an imagined person. But at the same time, I realize that I can't universalize my standards. In instances like that, I feel I have to hold my religious reaction at bay. It is important to let people live out their experience of the world without censorious interference, except in very extreme cases.

INTERVIEWER

What is the most important thing you try to teach your students?

ROBINSON

I try to make writers actually see what they have written, where the strength is. Usually in fiction there's something that leaps out—an image or a moment that is strong enough to center the story. If they can see it, they can exploit it, enhance it, and build a fiction that is subtle and new. I don't try to teach technique, because frankly most technical problems go away when a writer realizes where the life of a story lies. I don't see any reason in fine-tuning something that's essentially not going anywhere anyway. What they have to do first is interact in a serious way with what they're putting on a page. When people are fully engaged with what they're writing, a striking change occurs, a discipline of language and imagination.

INTERVIEWER
Do you read contemporary fiction?

ROBINSON

I'm not indifferent to contemporary literature; I just don't have any time for it. It's much easier for my contemporaries to keep up with me than it is for me to keep up with them. They've all written fifteen books.

INTERVIEWER
What is your opinion of literary criticism?

ROBINSON

I know this is less true than it has been, but the main interest of criticism seems to be criticism. It has less to do with what people actually write. In journalistic criticism, the posture is too often that writers are making a consumer product they hope to be able to clean up on. I don't think that living writers should be treated with the awe that is sometimes reserved for dead writers, but if a well-known writer whose work tends to garner respect takes ten years to write a novel and it's not the greatest novel in the world, dismissiveness is not an appropriate response. An unsuccessful work might not seem unsuccessful in another generation. It may be part of the writer's pilgrimage.

INTERVIEWER
Do you have any writing rituals, habits, or peculiarities?

ROBINSON

I dress like a bum. John Cheever would wear a suit and a hat and go down from his apartment to the basement of his building with an attaché case. But that's not me. I like to be as forgetful of my own physical being as I can be.

INTERVIEWER

Do you write in your study or do you occupy every room of the house?

ROBINSON

I do a lot in the study, but the couch also, and so on. It's nice to be able to move around and not be completely bound to one place or another, the way some people are. Although I do stay inside my own house. That's crucial.

INTERVIEWER

Why is that crucial?

ROBINSON

Because I can forget my surroundings. And I don't get distracted by thinking, Who chose that painting? I know who chose that painting.

INTERVIEWER

Does writing come easily to you?

ROBINSON

The difficulty of it cannot be overstated. But at its best, it involves a state of concentration that is a satisfying experience, no matter how difficult or frustrating. The sense of being focused like that is a marvelous feeling. It's one of the reasons I'm so willing to seclude myself and am a little bit grouchy when I have to deal with the reasonable expectations of the world.

INTERVIEWER

Do you keep to a schedule?

ROBINSON

I really am incapable of discipline. I write when something makes a strong claim on me. When I don't feel like writing, I absolutely don't feel like writing. I tried that work ethic thing a couple of times—I can't say I exhausted its possibilities—but if there's not something on my mind that I really want to write about, I tend to write something that I hate. And that depresses me. I don't want to look at it. I don't want to live through the time it takes for it to go up the chimney. Maybe it's a question of discipline, maybe temperament, who knows? I wish I could have made myself do more. I wouldn't mind having written fifteen books.

INTERVIEWER

Even if many of them were mediocre?

ROBINSON

Well, no.

INTERVIEWER

Do you keep a journal or diary?

ROBINSON

At various times in my life I've bought a little finely ornamented volume with a clasp, and written a couple of days' worth of reflections. And then I come back to it and I think, What an idiot.

INTERVIEWER

What about revision? Is it an intensive process or do you let the first draft stand?

ROBINSON

If I write something and don't like it, I basically toss it. And I try to write it again or I write something else that has the same movement. But as far as going back and working over something that I've already written—I really don't do that. I know there's a sentence that I need, and I just run it through my mind until it sounds right. Most of my revision occurs before I put words down on the paper.

Does that happen when you're sitting at your desk or on the couch or do you write in your head all day long?

ROBINSON

If I'm writing, I write in my head all the time. But as far as inventing, I try to do that only when I'm physically writing. If I get an idea while I'm walking home on the bridge, I think, Close that down, because if I think through a scene, I'll wreck it by the time I get a pen in my hand.

INTERVIEWER

Most people know you as a novelist, but you spend a lot of your time writing nonfiction. What led you to start writing essays?

ROBINSON

To change my own mind. I try to create a new vocabulary or terrain for myself, so that I open out—I always think of the Dutch claiming land from the sea—or open up something that would have been closed to me before. That's the point and the pleasure of it. I continuously scrutinize my own thinking. I write something and think, How do I know that that's true? If I wrote what I thought I knew from the outset, then I wouldn't be learning anything new.

In this culture, essays are often written for the sake of writing the essay. Someone finds a quibble of potential interest and quibbles about it. This doesn't mean the writer isn't capable of doing something of greater interest, but we generate a lot of prose that's not vital. The best essays come from the moment in which people really need to work something out.

INTERVIEWER

How do you decide on a topic for your essays?

ROBINSON

It almost always comes as a surprise. I got to Marguerite de Navarre because I was reading a translation of Dante's *Inferno* and I started looking into the context in which it was written. The Albigensian Crusades, which killed an enormous number of people, occurred just before Dante wrote *Inferno*. Whether Dante was influenced by Albigensianism or not I don't know, but it was the *Inferno* that made me remember Albigensianism and made me start reading about the culture of southern France and discover Marguerite de Navarre, who was an older contemporary of Calvin.

INTERVIEWER

Have you gotten to a point where you welcome that kind of indirectness?

ROBINSON

I've learned to trust it. I worry about participating in the consensuses of opinion because frankly they don't bear out very well. When I notice something that seems like an anomaly to me, I try to sort it out. It's an impulse. I think, Gee, this might lead me to refurnish my mind in a certain way. I find the alternative undignified: you have your little life and live through it and trip along and fall into your grave.

INTERVIEWER

In your essay "Facing Reality," from *The Death of Adam*, you point out that many Americans have a poor sense of American history—or history in general.

ROBINSON

We archaize Abraham Lincoln—he's somehow premodern—at the same time that we use Marx to epitomize modernity. Yet the two of them were engaged in the same conversation. The slave economy and the industrial economy were interlocked. Marx is considered modern because he describes an ongoing phenomenon, industrialism, which once again is starting to resemble slavery—child labor and so on. You take a course as a sophomore in college called Modern Western Civilization and you get Marx and Nietzsche, but you don't get

Lincoln. The fact that they were all wearing frock coats and stovepipe hats doesn't register.

You've also written that Americans tend to avoid contemplating larger issues. What is it that we're afraid of?

People are frightened of themselves. It's like Freud saying that the best thing is to have no sensation at all, as if we're supposed to live painlessly and unconsciously in the world. I have a much different view. The ancients are right: the dear old human experience is a singular, difficult, shadowed, brilliant experience that does not resolve into being comfortable in the world. The valley of the shadow is part of that, and you are depriving yourself if you do not experience what humankind has experienced, including doubt and sorrow. We experience pain and difficulty as failure instead of saying, I will pass through this, everyone I have ever admired has passed through this, music has come out of this, literature has come out of it. We should think of our humanity as a privilege.

Do you suffer from anxiety?

I probably experience less anxiety than is normal. People who are literate and prosperous by world standards nevertheless choose anxiety. I consider that kind of anxiety to be unspent energy, energy that goes sour because it is not spent. Calvinism is supposed to induce emotional stoicism. One thing that comes with the tradition is the idea that you're always being posed a question: what does God want from this situation? It creates a kind of detachment, but it's a detachment that brings perception rather than the absence of perception. And at this point, my children are adults, established in life. They seem to know how to make themselves happy. When they were young

I felt anxiety for them. It was a kind of animal alertness: what do I need to head off at the pass?

INTERVIEWER

In your essay "Puritans and Prigs," you reevaluate the idea that a good diet enhances our quality of life. You point out that although fish is purported to be healthier, overfishing is destroying the equilibrium of the ocean: "The sea has been raided and ransacked to oblige our new scruple."

ROBINSON

Europeans are one of the largest importers of fish and predatory fishing fleets are destroying the fish stock off of the west coast of Africa. As a result, the destruction of fishing villages has created a wave of migration from Africa into Europe. People say, Why do they go to France if they're not happy there? Well, it's better than starving.

INTERVIEWER

Do you eat fish?

ROBINSON

I'm generally a vegetarian of the ovo-lacto type, minus the ovo, yet I'm keenly aware of the fact that Hitler was a vegetarian. When he visited Mussolini in Italy he rejected the state dinner. He didn't drink or smoke. I hold him up as an example of how an aversion virtue can be a negative sign.

INTERVIEWER

How did you decide to write about Sellafield nuclear plant in *Mother Country*?

ROBINSON

I didn't really expect to write *Mother Country*—heaven knows. I was living in England, and it was all over the newspaper and all over television. I was surprised of course because it's a terrible thing.

Sellafield extracts plutonium-239 and other salable isotopes of trans-uranic elements, very sloppily, and sends vast quantities of radioactive waste from the process into the sea. It's a real disaster. They've been doing this since 1956. It's amazing that people could have been up to this particular kind of mischief for fifty-two years, but they have.

When I came home from England, I didn't even unpack my bags, I just sat down and wrote the article and sent it to my agent. And I said, You don't have to deal with this if you don't want to. But she sent it to *Harper's* and they published it almost immediately. Then another publisher called and asked if I would write a book about it.

INTERVIEWER

Mother Country was published in 1989. How do you view the book today?

ROBINSON

If I could only have written one book, that would have been the book. It was a real education for me. It did as much as anything to undermine the education I brought with me when I started the project. It was as if I was writing a dissertation over again in my mind, trying to establish what would be the relevant thing to know and where to look next. Also, if I had not written that book, I would not have been able to live with myself. I would have felt that I was doing what we are all doing, which dooms the world.

INTERVIEWER

Which is what?

ROBINSON

Pretend we don't know what we're really up to. We know that plastic bags are killing animals in Africa at a terrific rate, but everybody still uses these things as if they just float away. We know that these new lightbulbs cut down on electricity, but where do they come from? China? Hungary? They have to be dealt with as toxic waste because they have mercury in them. So who's being exposed to these chemicals when they're manufactured and what are the environmental consequences in China or Hungary? What is the trade-off in terms of shipping them long distances to save a little bit of electricity?

I'm also partial to the Sellafield book because I think it exposes the ways in which we're racist. We assume that Europeans are white and therefore more rational than other populations and to find something weird and unaccountable and inhumane we must go to a darker continent.

INTERVIEWER

Did you ever worry about it coming across as a polemic?

ROBINSON

Eh! Not among my worries. I was angry when I wrote that book. Nothing has happened to make me feel otherwise about the issues I raised in it. Sellafield is only larger now.

INTERVIEWER

Mother Country appeared during the more than twenty-year gap between *Housekeeping* and *Gilead.* Why did it take you so long to return to writing fiction?

ROBINSON

It was largely as a consequence of the experience of writing *Mother Country* that I began what amounted to an effort to reeducate myself. After all those years of school, I felt there was little I knew that I could trust, and I did not want my books to be one more tributary to the sea of nonsense that really is what most conventional wisdom amounts to. I am not so naive as to imagine that I have escaped that fate except in isolated cases and small particulars. But the research and criticism I have done have helped me to be of my own mind in some degree, and that was a feeling I had to achieve before I could enjoy writing fiction.

INTERVIEWER

You once said that you "proceed from the assumption that the distinctions available to us in this world are not arrayed between good and bad but between bad and worse." Do you ever worry that you're too pessimistic?

ROBINSON

I worry that I'm not pessimistic enough. My own life is full of profound satisfactions, and I'm distracted from the fact that the world is not in good shape. I cherish time, for instance, and for the most part I have control over my time, which is a marker of a very high standard of living as far as I'm concerned. At some point I created an artificial tropic for myself, where I could do exactly what I wanted to do and be rewarded for it. There's a puritanical hedonism in my existence.

INTERVIEWER

Puritanical hedonism?

ROBINSON

I read books like *The Idea of the Holy: An Inquiry into the Non Rational Factor in the Idea of the Divine*. Oh, terrific. I've almost never done anything that I didn't want to do. My life has been laid out to satisfy any aspiration of mine to the power of ten or a hundred. I can only make sense of my unaccountable good fortune by assuming that it means I am under special obligation to make good use of it.

INTERVIEWER

As opposed to always wanting more or something else?

ROBINSON

I don't think I could want something else. For instance, I'm kind of a solitary. This would not satisfy everyone's hopes, but for me it's a lovely thing. I recognize the satisfactions of a more socially enmeshed

existence than I cultivate, but I go days without hearing another human voice and never notice it. I never fear it. The only thing I fear is
the intensity of my attachment to it. It's a predisposition in my family.
My brother is a solitary. My mother is a solitary. I grew up with the
confidence that the greatest privilege was to be alone and have all the
time you wanted. That was the cream of existence. I owe everything
that I have done to the fact that I am very much at ease being alone.
It's a good predisposition in a writer. And books are good company.
Nothing is more human than a book.

INTERVIEWER

You were close with Frank Conroy before he passed away. Are you
close with other writers?

ROBINSON

The social life of the Iowa Workshop seems to have changed to a
certain extent. It's the quietest among us who are left now. It's a wonderful faculty, a wonderful working environment, and I like the way
that the students who come to me have been prepared by the people
around me, but I have a sense of urgency about what I want to get
done and I discipline myself by keeping to myself. It's a nice opportunity to be able to know these people, but I have to do other things,
which take hours, days, weeks.

INTERVIEWER

Have you always felt that urgency or is this something new?

ROBINSON

It's a little new. Years ago, I was younger than I am now.

INTERVIEWER

You've said that reading a footnote in Jonathan Edwards's "The
Great Christian Doctrine of Original Sin Defended" changed your
consciousness. What was the footnote?

ROBINSON

It's not an attractive title for an essay, but in it he talks about the arbitrariness of "being" itself. He uses the metaphor of the reflected light of the moon, which we see as continuous light. Yet it is not intrinsic; it is continuously renewed as light. No physicist can tell you why things persist as they are, why one moment follows another. The reality we inhabit and treat like an old shoe is amazingly arbitrary.

INTERVIEWER

Does that arbitrariness include the supernatural?

ROBINSON

I'm not terribly persuaded by the word *supernatural*. I don't like the idea of the world as an encapsulated reality with intrusions made upon it selectively. The reality that we experience is part of the whole fabric of reality. To pretend that the universe is somewhere else doing something is really not true. We're right in the middle of it. Utterly dependent on it, utterly defined by it. If you read somebody like Wallace Stevens, he's basically saying the same thing.

INTERVIEWER

Do you believe in an afterlife?

ROBINSON

I assume immortality, but religion doesn't teach me to assume immortality. I assume immortality and this reinforces religion. But there's a qualitative difference between actually confronting death and thinking about death in the abstract. By the grace of God, it has been an abstract concept to me up to this point.

INTERVIEWER

It doesn't keep you up at night?

ROBINSON

No, I have benevolent insomnia. I wake up, and my mind is preter-
naturally clear. The world is quiet. I can read or write. It seems like
stolen time. It seems like I have a twenty-eight-hour day. When I do
think about death, the idea that life will be going on without me makes
me melancholy. There's so much to miss: history and architecture! But
it won't miss me.

INTERVIEWER

Is religion a way to feel comforted in the face of death?

ROBINSON

Faith always sounds like an act of will. Frankly, I don't know what
faith in God means. For me, the experience is much more a sense of
God. Nothing could be more miraculous than the fact that we have a
consciousness that makes the world intelligible to us and are moved
by what is beautiful.

INTERVIEWER

Someone once said that there has to be a problem with Christianity
because four hundred denominations later they still can't get it right.

ROBINSON

People in the churches worry about that, but would we be richer for
the loss of Catholicism? Would we be richer for the loss of the Quak-
ers? Isn't it true that every one of these traditions expresses Christianity in a way that the other traditions could not? It's prismatic.

Religion, however, has presented itself in some extremely unat-
tractive forms. It has recruited people into excitements that don't look
attractive to their neighbors. People seem to be profoundly disposed
toward religion, yet they're not terribly good at it.

INTERVIEWER

Do you ever censor yourself in order to try to live up to a religious
standard?

ROBINSON

It's not so much that I censor myself—I have to prod myself more often than not. I just get engulfed in whatever I'm thinking about, and I tend to forget that other people exist. I just don't do right by people in every circumstance. It's not that my religion inhibits me, it's that my religion is not always sufficient to overcome certain failings of mine, which tend toward solipsism.

INTERVIEWER

Do you feel like there's something you've missed out on in life?

ROBINSON

There's always something that I feel I've missed. I should travel more, for instance. I went to Paris last fall, which was a great departure for me. I flew Air India, which in itself was quite remarkable. I had a lovely time in France and I thought, I should do this more often. But then I come home and I think, I have all of this work to do. Look at all of these books I haven't read. Frankly, you get to a certain point in your life where you can do unusual things with your mind. So then, I think, do them.

Issue 186, 2008

Contributors

Maya Angelou was born Marguerite Johnson in St. Louis, Missouri, in 1928. She was raised largely by her maternal grandmother in Stamps, Arkansas, an experience that formed the basis of her breakthrough memoir *I Know Why The Caged Bird Sings* (1970). That book, written with the encouragement of her friend James Baldwin, was the first of six acclaimed works of autobiography. Her subsequent memoirs, *Gather Together in My Name* (1974), *Singin' and Swingin' and Gettin' Merry Like Christmas* (1976), *The Heart of a Woman* (1981), *All God's Children Need Traveling Shoes* (1986), and *A Song Flung Up To Heaven* (2002), explored her experience growing up in the segregated and impoverished South, and the tumult of her early adult life. Her first book of poetry, *Just Give Me a Cool Drink of Water 'Fore I Diiie* (1971), was nominated for the Pulitzer Prize, and she has published seven collections since, including *And Still I Rise* (1978). In 1993 she became the first poet since Robert Frost to recite a poem at a presidential inauguration, reading "On the Pulse of Morning" at the request of Bill Clinton. She was awarded the National Medal of Arts in 2000. **George Plimpton** was the editor of *The Paris Review* from its inaugural issue in 1953 until his death in 2003. He was the author of numerous books, including the best-selling works of participatory journalism *Paper Lion* (1966) and *Open Net* (1985).

John Ashbery was born in Rochester, New York, in 1927. He was educated at Harvard College, where he studied alongside Robert Bly, Robert Creeley, Kenneth Koch, and Frank O'Hara. While still in high school, Ashbery was published in *Poetry* magazine, though his poems appeared under the name of a classmate who had submitted them as his own. *Some*

Trees, his second collection, was chosen by W. H. Auden for the Yale Series of Younger Poets in 1955. In the years that followed Ashbery became
known as a leading figure of the New York School. In 1955 he went to
Paris on a Fulbright fellowship, where he wrote the poems collected in
The Tennis Court Oath (1962) and *Rivers and Mountains* (1966). *Self-
Portrait in a Convex Mirror*, published in 1975, won the Pulitzer Prize,
the National Book Award, and the National Book Critics Circle Award,
and *A Wave* (1984) won the Bollingen Prize and the Lenore Marshall
Poetry Prize. He has taught at Brooklyn College and Bard College and
has served as chancellor of the Academy of American Poets. His most recent collections are *A Worldly Country* and *Notes from Air*, both published in 2007. **Peter Stitt** is the editor of the *Gettysburg Review*.

Paul Auster was born in Newark, New Jersey, in 1947. He is the author of
fifteen novels, four screenplays, four works of nonfiction, and several
collections of poetry. After graduating from Columbia University in 1969,
he moved to Paris, where he earned a living translating French literature.
He moved back to New York City in 1974 and continued to work on
translations, poetry, and book reviews throughout the seventies. His
memoir *The Invention of Solitude* was published in 1982, and a trio of
loosely connected novels followed: *City of Glass* (1985), *Ghosts* (1986),
and *The Locked Room* (1986), collectively known as The New York Trilogy. He grew increasingly prolific over the next two decades, publishing
such novels as *In The Country of Last Things* (1987), *The Music of Chance*
(1990), *Leviathan* (1992), *Timbuktu* (1999), *The Book of Illusions* (2002),
Oracle Night (2004), *The Brooklyn Follies* (2005), *Invisible* (2009), and
another memoir, *Hand to Mouth* (1997). He was made a member of the
American Academy of Arts and Letters in 2006. **Michael Wood** is the
Charles Barnwell Straut Class of 1923 Professor of English and Compara-
tive Literature at Princeton University and a frequent contributor to the
New York Review of Books. His most recent book is *Literature and the
Taste of Knowledge* (2005).

David Grossman was born in Jerusalem in 1954. After graduating from
Hebrew University, Grossman worked as an actor and journalist at the
state radio station Kol Israel. He is the author of seven novels. His first,
The Smile of the Lamb, was published in 1983. Subsequent novels include
See Under: Love (1986), *The Zigzag Kid* (1997), *Be My Knife* (2003), *Someone to Run With* (2004), and *Lion's Honey: The Myth of Samson* (2006).
He has also published short stories, novellas, children's books, and nonfiction, including two works of immersive reportage on Israeli-Palestinian
relations, *The Yellow Wind* (1988) and *Sleeping on a Wire: Conversations*

with Palestinians in Israel (1993). Grossman was awarded the EMET Prize in 2007 and the Geschwister Scholl Prize in 2008. His work has been translated into more than twenty languages. **Jonathan Shainin** is the arts editor of *The National*, published in Abu Dhabi, and the editor, with Roane Carey, of *The Other Israel: Voices of Refusal and Dissent*. His writing has appeared in *The Nation*, *Bookforum*, and *Salon*.

Jack Kerouac (1922–1969) was born Jean Louis Kerouac in Lowell, Massachusetts, to a French-Canadian family. He did not begin to speak English until the age of six. Kerouac attended Columbia University but left before graduating, serving in the navy before returning to New York, where he became friends with a number of writers who came to be known as the Beat Generation. His first novel, *The Town and the City*, was published in 1950. Kerouac spent most of the 1950s writing and traveling, experiences that ended up in the novel *On the Road* (1957) and other books. He moved to San Francisco, where he immersed himself in the study of Zen Buddhism, which led to *The Dharma Bums* (1958). His last work, *Vanity of Duluoz* (1968), was an autobiographical novel set in his childhood hometown. **Ted Berrigan** (1934–1983) was a New York School poet, the author of many volumes of poetry, as well as a collection of interviews, essays on art, and a novel. *The Collected Poems of Ted Berrigan* was recently published by the University of California Press, and a *Selected Poems* is forthcoming.

Marianne Moore (1887–1972) was born in Kirkwood, Missouri. She graduated from Bryn Mawr College and spent several years teaching at the U.S. Industrial Indian School in Carlisle, Pennsylvania. In 1915 Moore's first poems appeared in the *Egoist*. She moved to New York in 1918; her first collection, *Poems*, was published in 1921. With the publication of two more collected works of poetry, *Marriage* (1923) and *Observations* (1924), Moore was recognized as an important voice in the modernist movement. As acting editor at *The Dial*, an American journal of literature and arts, she championed other modernist poets such as T. S. Eliot and Ezra Pound. In 1929, she moved to Brooklyn and took on work as a book reviewer, translator, and essayist. Her *Collected Poems* (1951) won the Bollingen Prize, the National Book Award, and the Pulitzer Prize. **Donald Hall** is a poet who lives in New Hampshire. He was the first poetry editor of *The Paris Review*, from 1953 to 1961, and was named U.S. Poet Laureate in 2006.

Haruki Murakami was born in Kyoto, Japan, in 1949, the son of two high-school literature teachers. He attended Waseda University in Tokyo, where he earned a degree in theater arts. He married fellow student Yoko

Takahashi, and they opened a jazz bar, Peter Cat, in 1974. Murakami worked full time at the bar while completing his first novel, *Hear the Wind Sing* (1979), which won the Gunzo New Writer Award. All of his novels have been translated into English, including *Hard-Boiled Wonderland and the End of the World* (1985), which won the Tanizaki Prize; *Norwegian Wood* (1989), which sold over four million copies in Japan; *The Wind-Up Bird Chronicle* (1994), which won the Yomiuri Literary Prize; and *Kafka on the Shore* (2005), which won the Franz Kafka Prize. Starting in 1991, he spent several years teaching in the United States, first at Princeton University and then at Tufts. He has published three story collections in English, most recently *Blind Willow, Sleeping Woman* (2006), and two books of nonfiction: *Underground* (2000), a book about the 1995 sarin gas attack on the Tokyo subway, and the memoir *What I Talk About When I Talk About Running* (2008). **John Wray** is the author of the novels *The Right Hand of Sleep* (2001) and *Canaan's Tongue* (2005). His most recent novel, *Lowboy*, was published by Farrar, Straus and Giroux in 2009.

V. S. Naipaul, born in 1932 in Trinidad as Vidiadhar Surajprasad Naipaul, was awarded the Nobel Prize in Literature in 2001. A descendent of Indian immigrants, Naipaul left Trinidad to attend Oxford University in 1950 and subsequently settled in England. Naipaul's earliest books, beginning with *The Mystic Masseur* in 1957, offer a satirical take on life in the Caribbean. His fourth novel, *A House for Mr. Biswas* (1961), was his breakthrough, earning him widespread acclaim. *In A Free State*, a collection of stories set in various postcolonial contexts, won the Booker Prize in 1971. Naipaul's travel writings include three books on India and a cross-continental exploration of the Islamic faith, *Beyond Belief* (1998). Subsequent works have included the essay collections *The Writer and the World* (2002) and *Literary Occasions* (2003) and the novels *Half a Life* (2001) and *Magic Seeds* (2004). He was knighted in 1990. **Tarun Tejpal** is a journalist, publisher, and novelist. He is the founder and editor of the Indian newsweekly *Tehelka*. His debut novel, *The Alchemy of Desire* (2005), won the Prix Millepages. **Jonathan Rosen** is the editorial director of *Nextbook* and the author of *The Talmud and the Internet* (2000) and the novels *Eve's Apple* (1997) and *Joy Comes in the Morning* (2004).

Orhan Pamuk was born in 1952 in Istanbul and was the first Turkish citizen to be awarded the Nobel Prize in Literature in 2006. Pamuk attended Istanbul Technical University, where he studied architecture, and graduated from the University of Istanbul with a degree in journalism. After spending his twenties writing, Pamuk published his first novel, *Cevdet Bey ve ogullari*, in 1982. Although he won critical acclaim for his early work, including *The White Castle* in 1985, Pamuk did not attain international fame until *The Black Book* (1990), which was widely translated. Other major novels include *My Name Is Red* (1998) and *Snow* (2002), in which an exiled Turkish poet explores the tensions between East and West in his homeland. He has also published a fictionalized memoir, *Istanbul: Memories and the City* (2003). His most recent novel is *Masumivet Müzesi* (2008). **Ángel Gurría-Quintana** is a historian, literary translator, and journalist. His work has appeared in *The Observer, The Economist, Prospect*, and *Brick*. He writes regularly about books for London's *Financial Times*.

Ezra Pound (1885–1972) was born in Hailey, Idaho Territory, but his family moved to Philadelphia when he was still a child. He received an M.A. in Romance philology from the University of Pennsylvania in 1906, and briefly taught at Wabash College. In 1908 he moved to London; he would spend most of his life in Europe. He was the foreign correspondent for *Poetry* magazine from 1912 to 1919, and he was the founder and editor of the little magazine *The Exile*. He also edited many of T. S. Eliot's major poems, including *The Waste Land*. His criticism was collected in *Literary Essays of Ezra Pound* (1954). Early collections of his poems include *Hugh Selwyn Mauberley* (1920) and *Homage to Sextus Propertius* (1934), but his life work was *The Cantos*, a series of poems published throughout his life and collected in *The Cantos of Ezra Pound* (1948; revised edition 1954). In 1945 he was arrested for treason for his wartime radio broadcasts in support of Mussolini. He was committed to St. Elizabeths Hospital in Washington for twelve years before being released; he spent his final years at his home in Italy.

Marilynne Robinson was born in Sandpoint, Idaho, in 1943. While working on her Ph.D. dissertation on Shakespeare's histories at the University of Washington, she began writing her novel *Housekeeping* (1980), for which she was nominated for a Pulitzer Prize in 1982. She spent much of the next decades producing nonfiction. In 1989, she published *Mother Country: Britain, the Welfare State, and Nuclear Pollution*, followed by *The Death of Adam: Essays on Modern Thought* (1998) and *Puritans and Prigs* (1999). It wasn't until twenty-three years after her first novel appeared that *Gilead* (2004), her second, was published. *Gilead* won both the National Book Critics Circle Award and the Pulitzer Prize. *Home*, which returned to the town of Gilead and the events depicted in her previous novel, was published in 2008. Robinson has taught at the Iowa Writers' Workshop since 1989. **Sarah Fay** is an advisory editor of *The Paris Review*. Her writing has appeared in *The New York Times Book Review, Bookforum*, and *The American Scholar*.

474

CONTRIBUTORS

Philip Roth was born in 1933 in Newark, New Jersey. He graduated from Bucknell University and the University of Chicago and served briefly in the army before publishing his first book, *Goodbye, Columbus*, a collection of short stories and a novella, which won the 1960 National Book Award. Roth published his first novel, *Letting Go*, in 1962, but it was not until *Portnoy's Complaint*, in 1969, that Roth recaptured the commercial and critical success of his debut. *The Ghost Writer* (1979) introduced an aspiring young writer named Nathan Zuckerman, a protagonist who would go on to appear in several other novels, including *Zuckerman Unbound* (1981), *The Anatomy Lesson* (1983), *American Pastoral* (1997), for which Roth was awarded the Pulitzer Prize, and *Exit Ghost* (2007). *Everyman* (2006) made Roth the first three-time winner of the PEN/Faulkner Award for Fiction, an award he had previously received for *Operation Shylock* (1993) and the Zuckerman novel *The Human Stain* (2000). Roth's most recent work is *Indignation* (2008). **Hermione Lee** is a professor of English at Oxford University and President of Wolfson College, Oxford. She is the author of biographies of Virginia Woolf and Edith Wharton; books on Philip Roth, Willa Cather, and Elizabeth Bowen; and a collection of essays on life-writing, *Body Parts*. She is a fellow of the British Academy and of the Royal Society of Literature, and was made a CBE in 2003.

Stephen Sondheim was born in 1930 in New York City, and grew up in Pennsylvania. He studied music at Williams College and composition under Milton Babbitt before a brief stint writing for television in Hollywood. In 1957 he made his Broadway debut, writing lyrics to Leonard Bernstein's score for *West Side Story*, and in 1959 he collaborated with Jule Styne on *Gypsy*. The first musical for which he wrote both music and lyrics, *A Funny Thing Happened on the Way to the Forum* (1962), won multiple Tony Awards, but none for Sondheim's score. His next musical, *Anyone Can Whistle* (1964), closed after only nine performances, but over the decade that followed Sondheim found his stride as a successful and innovative Broadway composer, with the musicals *Company* (1970), *Follies* (1971), *A Little Night Music* (1973), and *Sweeney Todd* (1979), each of which would win Tony Awards for best score. Sondheim won the Pulitzer Prize in Drama for his score for *Sunday in the Park with George* (1981), an Academy Award for his song "Sooner or Later (I Always Get My Man)" from the film *Dick Tracy*, and two more best-score Tonys for *Into the Woods* (1987) and *Passion* (1994). He was given a Kennedy Center Honor for Lifetime Achievement in 1993. **James Lipton** is executive producer, host, and writer of *Inside the Actors Studio* and dean emeritus of The Actors Studio Drama School of Pace University.

William Styron (1925–2006) was born in Newport News, Virginia, where his father worked as a shipyard engineer. *Lie Down in Darkness*, Styron's debut novel, appeared when he was twenty-six years old. The novel won him the Rome Prize and in 1953 Styron moved to Europe, where he met George Plimpton and Peter Matthiessen and helped in the founding of *The Paris Review*. *The Confessions of Nat Turner* (1967), a fictionalized account of a violent slave uprising in 1831, was awarded the Pulitzer Prize. His 1979 novel *Sophie's Choice*, the story of a Polish Catholic woman grappling with her imprisonment in Auschwitz, won the National Book Award and was adapted into a film by Alan J. Pakula. His two final books, *Darkness Visible: A Memoir of Madness* (1990) and *A Tidewater Morning: Three Tales from Youth* (1993), deal with Styron's ongoing battles with alcoholism and depression. In 1993 he was awarded the National Medal of Arts by President Bill Clinton. **Peter Matthiessen** is the author of more than twenty-five works of fiction and nonfiction, including National Book Award winners *The Snow Leopard* (1979) and *Shadow Country* (2008). Matthiessen was one of the founders of *The Paris Review* in 1953 and served as its first fiction editor.

E. B. White (1899–1985) was born in Mount Vernon, New York. After graduating from Cornell, he began his career as a reporter with two New York–based news services before getting hired as a writer and editor at *The New Yorker* in 1927. He began writing for the magazine's Talk of the Town section, eventually contributing poems, sketches, short stories, and, especially, essays over the course of five decades there. He married Katharine Angell, an editor at *The New Yorker*, in 1929; the two divided their time between New York and their home in Maine. In 1945 he published his first children's book, *Stuart Little*, followed by *Charlotte's Web* in 1952, which was a Newbery Honor Book. A third children's book, *The Trumpet of the Swan* (1970), was nominated for a National Book Award. In 1959 he published an expanded second edition of William Strunk Jr.'s *The Elements of Style*, which has gone on to sell over ten million copies. His essays were collected in 1977 in *Essays of E. B. White*. **Frank H. Crowther** (1932–1976) was an assistant at the National Endowment for the Arts and a former associate editor of *The Paris Review*.

P. G. Wodehouse (1881–1975) was born in Guildford, outside of London. He was the author of nearly a hundred novels, three hundred short stories, sixteen plays, and five hundred essays and articles. As a teenager, Wodehouse attended Dulwich College, where he was editor of the school's magazine, *Alleynian*. He intended to continue his education at Oxford University, but due to his family's depleting finances he was forced to take a job as a bank clerk, and for two years was limited to writing only in the evenings and on weekends. He was offered a job writing for *The Globe* in 1902, where he later became an editor. During the 1910s he started publishing stories regularly in *The Saturday Evening Post*, where he became known for his light, comical depictions of Edwardian lifestyles. His most famous characters were the wealthy but dimwitted Bertie Wooster and his competent butler, Jeeves; Wodehouse wrote thirty-one short stories about the duo before he gave them their own novel, *My Man Jeeves*, in 1919, the first of nine devoted to the pair. He was made a Knight Commander of the Order of the British Empire in 1974. **Gerald Clarke** is a journalist and biographer who has written for *Time*, *The Atlantic*, *The New Republic*, and *Esquire*. He is the author of *Capote* (1988), which was made into a feature film; *Get Happy* (2000), which is also being made into a film; and the editor of *Too Brief a Treat* (2004), a collection of Truman Capote's letters. He currently writes for *Architectural Digest* and is working on a novel.